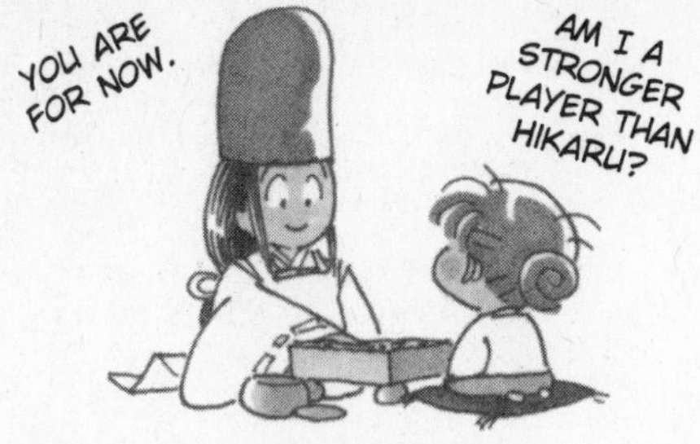
AM I A STRONGER PLAYER THAN HIKARU?
YOU ARE FOR NOW.

Yumi Hotta

Oftentimes I have trouble with storyboards. When that happens, I just keep telling myself, "It's okay, Obata Sensei will think of something!"
—Yumi Hotta

It all began when Yumi Hotta played a pick-up game of Go with her father-in-law. As she was learning how to play, Ms. Hotta thought it might be fun to create a story around the traditional board game. More confident in her storytelling abilities than her drawing skills, she submitted the beginnings of **Hikaru no Go** to **Weekly Shonen Jump**'s Story King Award. The Story King Award is an award that picks the best story, manga, character design and youth (under 15) manga submissions every year in Japan. As fate would have it, Ms. Hotta's story (originally named, "***Kokonotsu no Hoshi***"), was a runner-up in the "Story" category of the Story King Award. Many years earlier, Takeshi Obata was a runner-up for the Tezuka Award, another Japanese manga contest sponsored by **Weekly Shonen Jump** and **Monthly Shonen Jump**. An editor assigned to Mr. Obata's artwork came upon Ms. Hotta's story and paired the two for a full-fledged manga about Go. The rest is modern Go history.

HIKARU NO GO VOL. 1
The SHONEN JUMP Graphic Novel Edition

This graphic novel contains material that was originally published in English from
SHONEN JUMP #13 to #16.

STORY BY YUMI HOTTA
ART BY TAKESHI OBATA
Supervised by YUKARI UMEZAWA (5 Dan)

Translation & English Adaptation/Andy Nakatani
Touch-Up Art & Lettering/Adam Symons
Lettering Assistants/Josh Simpson, Walden Wong
Cover & Graphics Design/Sean Lee
Editor/Livia Ching

Editor in Chief, Books/Alvin Lu
Editor in Chief, Magazines/Marc Weidenbaum
VP of Publishing Licensing/Rika Inouye
VP of Sales/Gonzalo Ferreyra
Sr. VP of Marketing/Liza Coppola
Publisher/Hyoe Narita

Published by VIZ Media, LLC
P.O. Box 77010 • San Francisco, CA 94107

SHONEN JUMP Graphic Novel Edition
10 9 8 7 6 5
First printing, May 2004
Fifth printing, September 2007

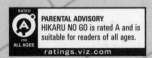

PARENTAL ADVISORY
HIKARU NO GO is rated A and is
suitable for readers of all ages.
ratings.viz.com

THE WORLD'S
MOST POPULAR MANGA

www.viz.com

www.shonenjump.com

①

DESCENT OF THE GO MASTER

STORY BY **YUMI HOTTA**
ART BY **TAKESHI OBATA**
Supervised by **YUKARI UMEZAWA (5 Dan)**

CONTENTS

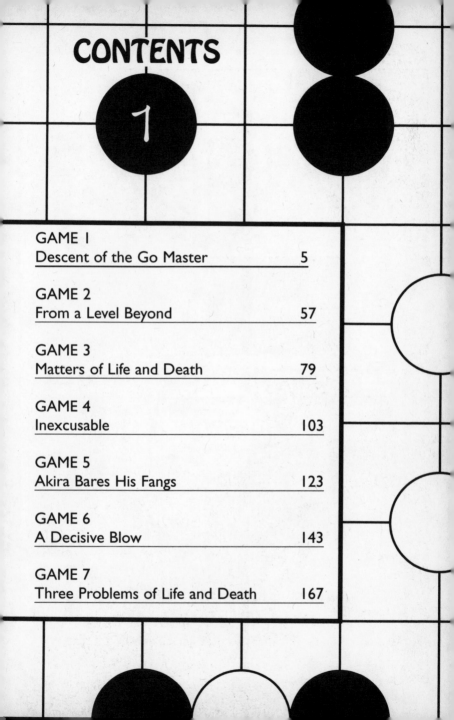

READ THIS WAY

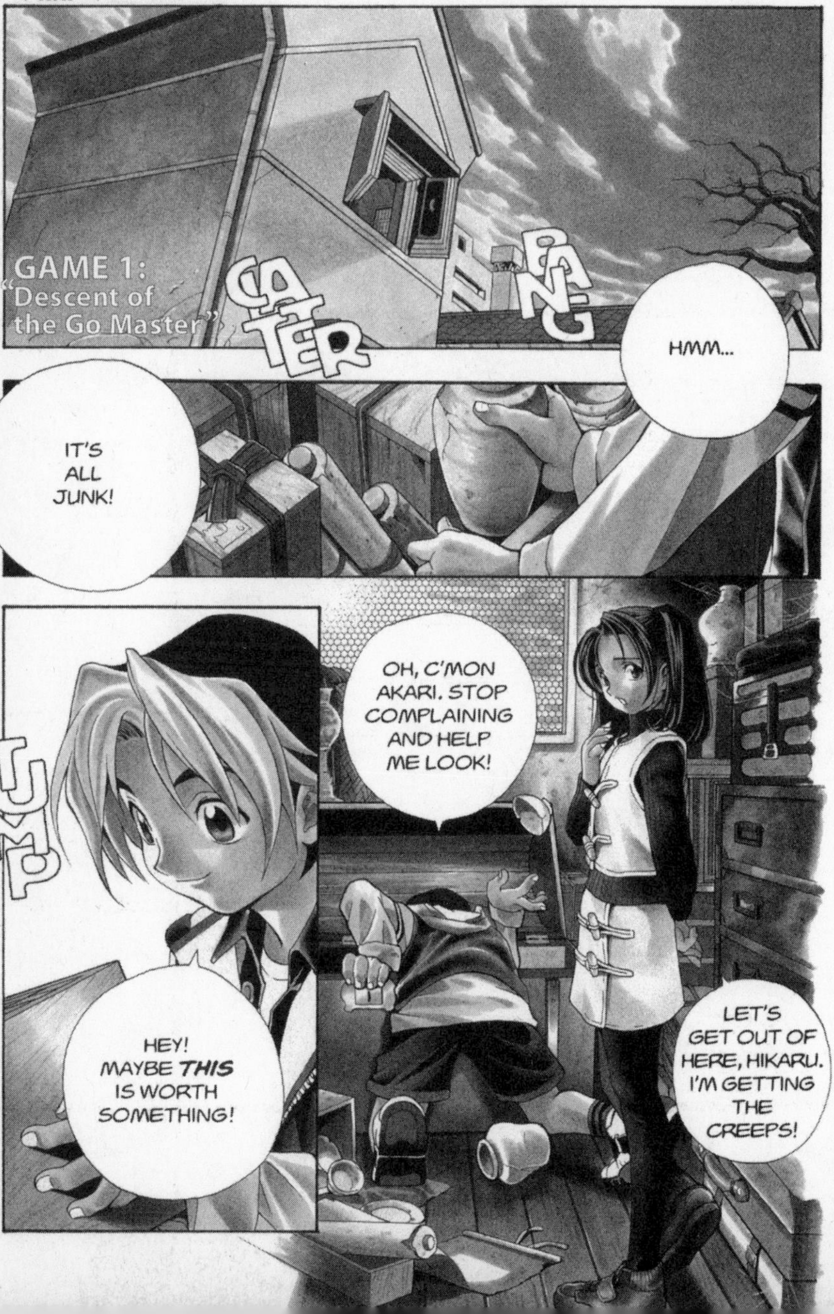

GAME 1: "Descent of the Go Master"
CLATTER
BANG
HMM...
IT'S ALL JUNK!
OH, C'MON AKARI. STOP COMPLAINING AND HELP ME LOOK!
LET'S GET OUT OF HERE, HIKARU. I'M GETTING THE CREEPS!
TUMP
HEY! MAYBE ***THIS*** IS WORTH SOMETHING!

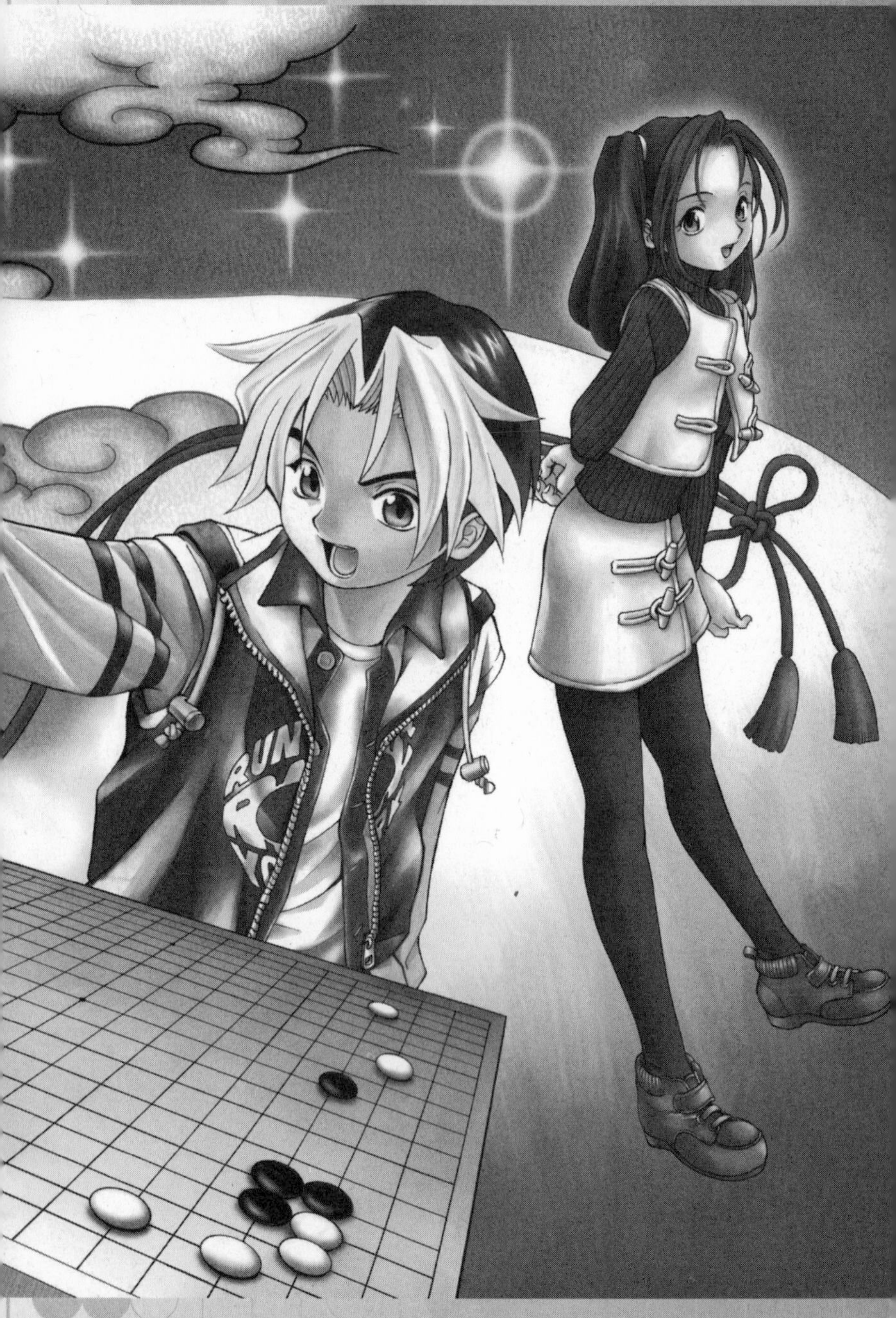
RUN

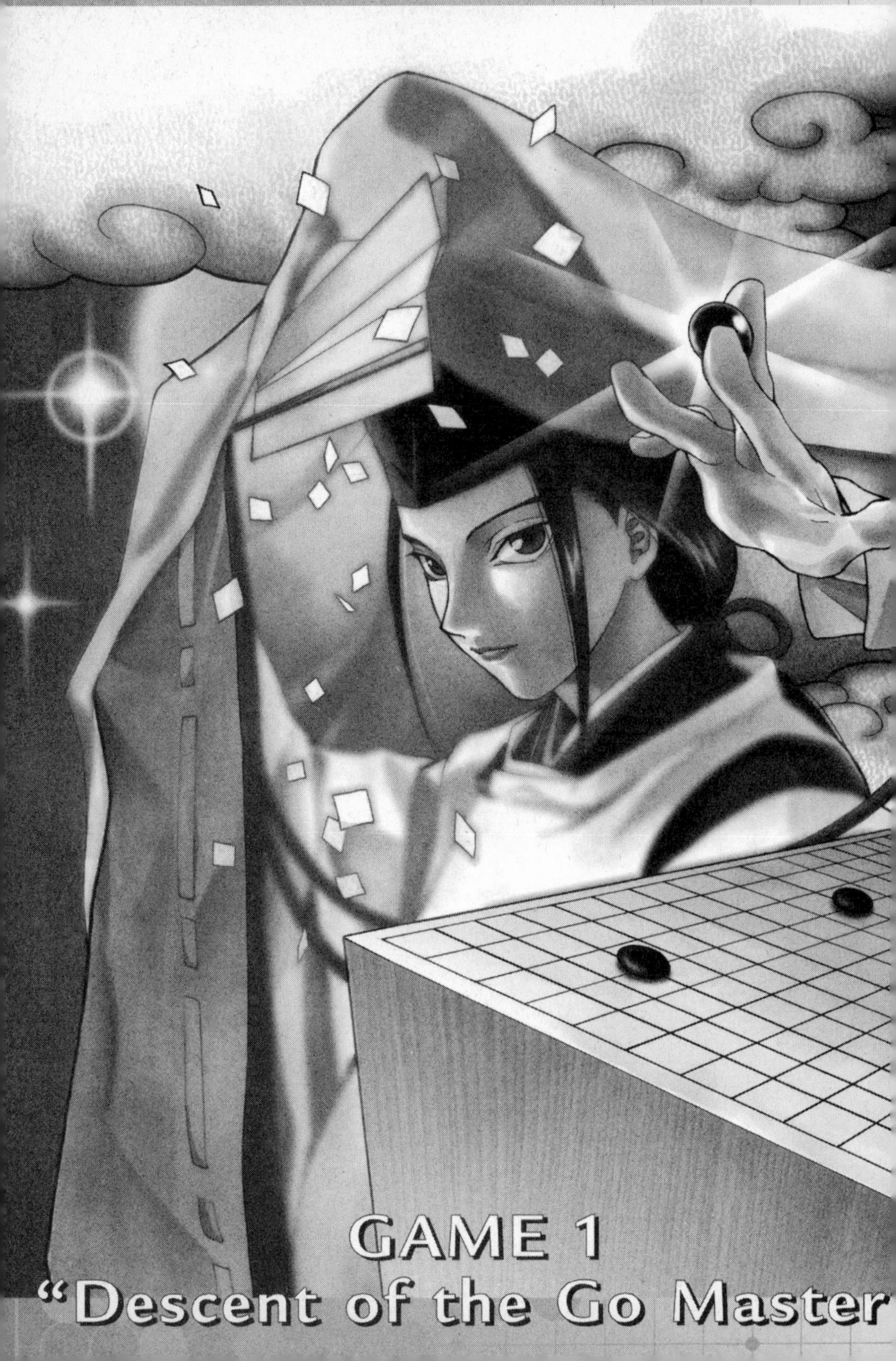
GAME 1
"Descent of the Go Master

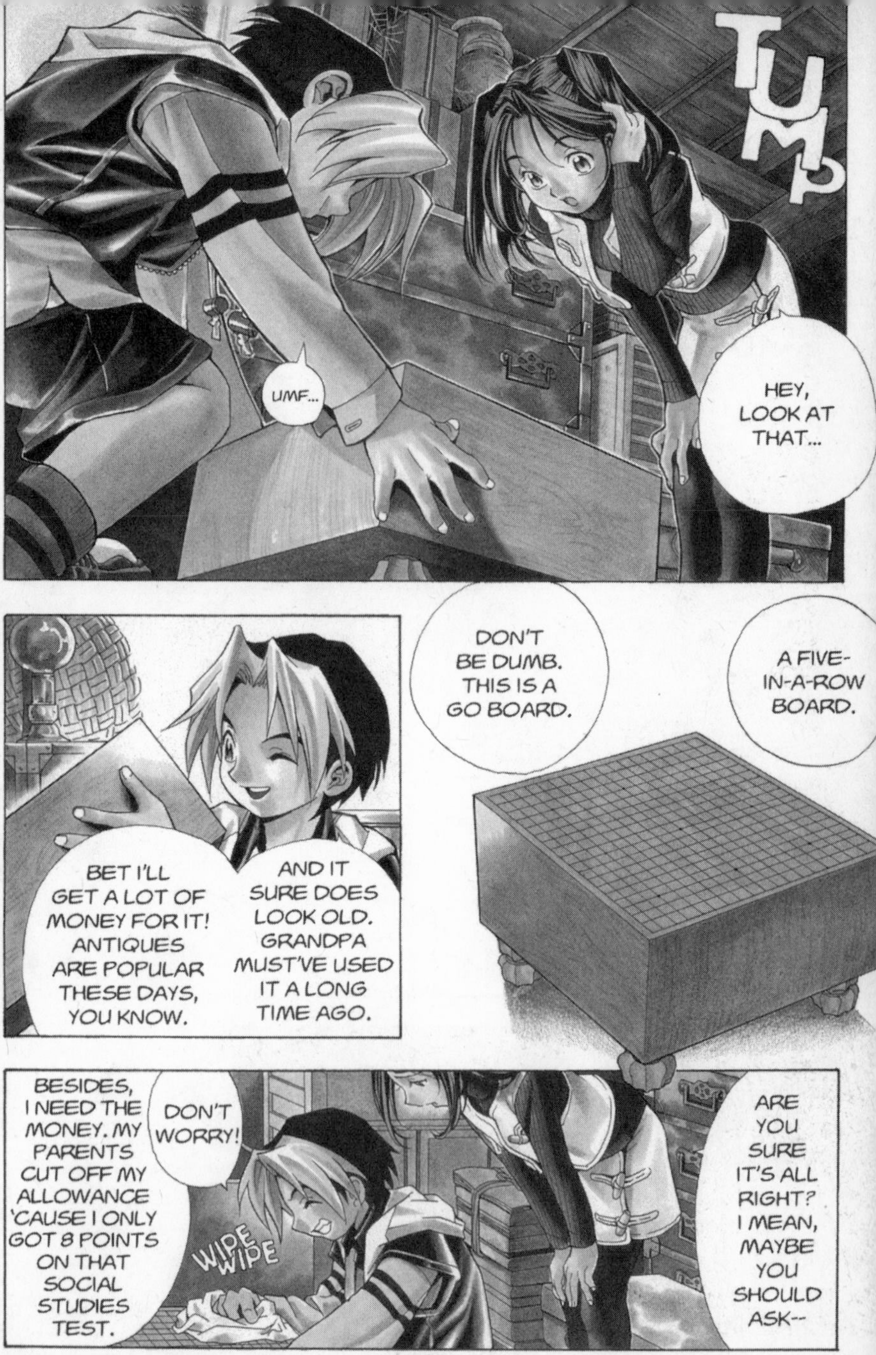
TUMP
HEY, LOOK AT THAT...
UMF...
A FIVE-IN-A-ROW BOARD.
DON'T BE DUMB. THIS IS A GO BOARD.
AND IT SURE DOES LOOK OLD. GRANDPA MUST'VE USED IT A LONG TIME AGO.
BET I'LL GET A LOT OF MONEY FOR IT! ANTIQUES ARE POPULAR THESE DAYS, YOU KNOW.
ARE YOU SURE IT'S ALL RIGHT? I MEAN, MAYBE YOU SHOULD ASK--
DON'T WORRY!
BESIDES, I NEED THE MONEY. MY PARENTS CUT OFF MY ALLOWANCE 'CAUSE I ONLY GOT 8 POINTS ON THAT SOCIAL STUDIES TEST.
WIPE WIPE

READ THIS WAY

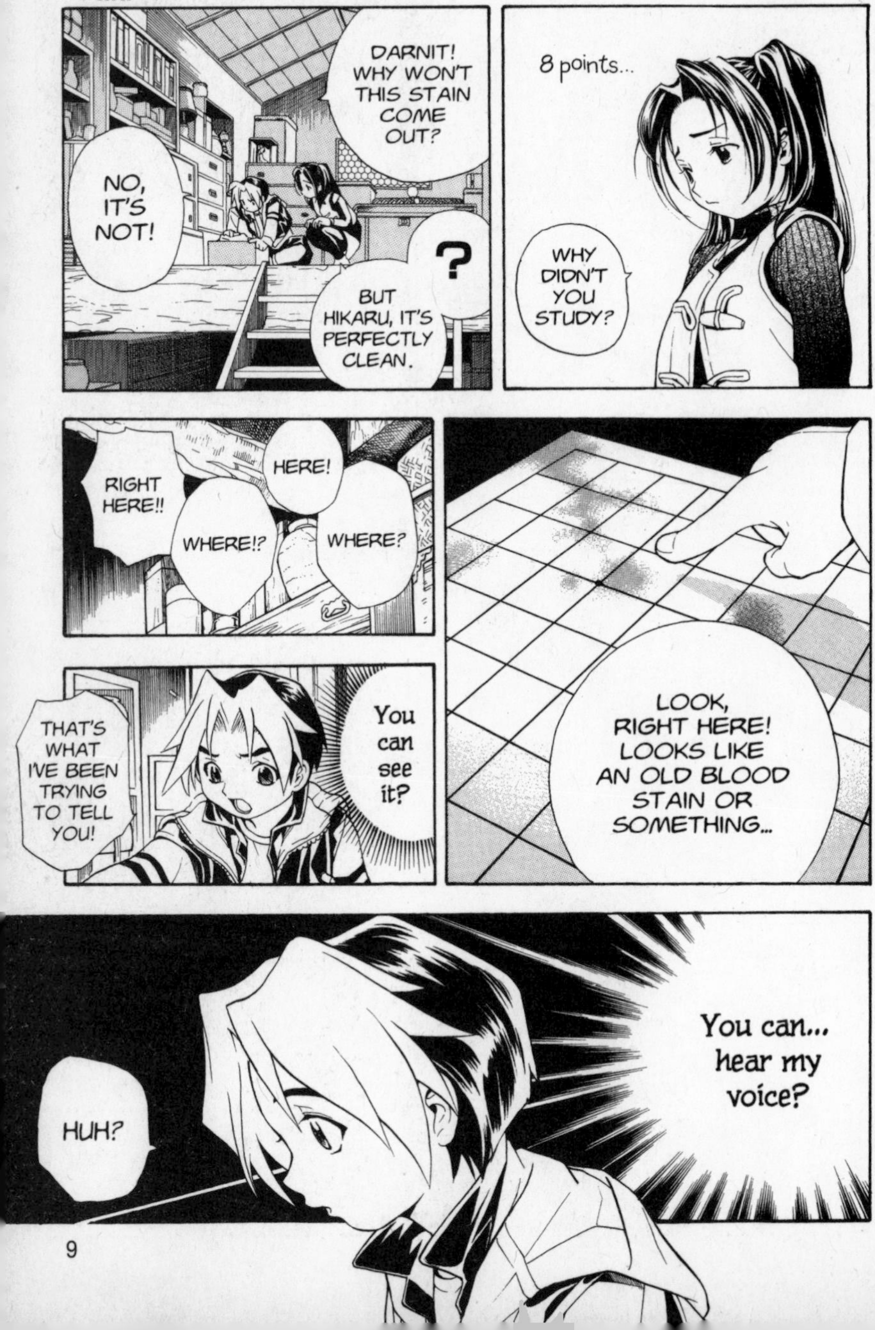
8 points...
WHY DIDN'T YOU STUDY?
DARNIT! WHY WON'T THIS STAIN COME OUT?
?
BUT HIKARU, IT'S PERFECTLY CLEAN.
NO, IT'S NOT!
LOOK, RIGHT HERE! LOOKS LIKE AN OLD BLOOD STAIN OR SOMETHING...
WHERE?
HERE!
WHERE!?
RIGHT HERE!!
You can see it?
THAT'S WHAT I'VE BEEN TRYING TO TELL YOU!
You can... hear my voice?
HUH?

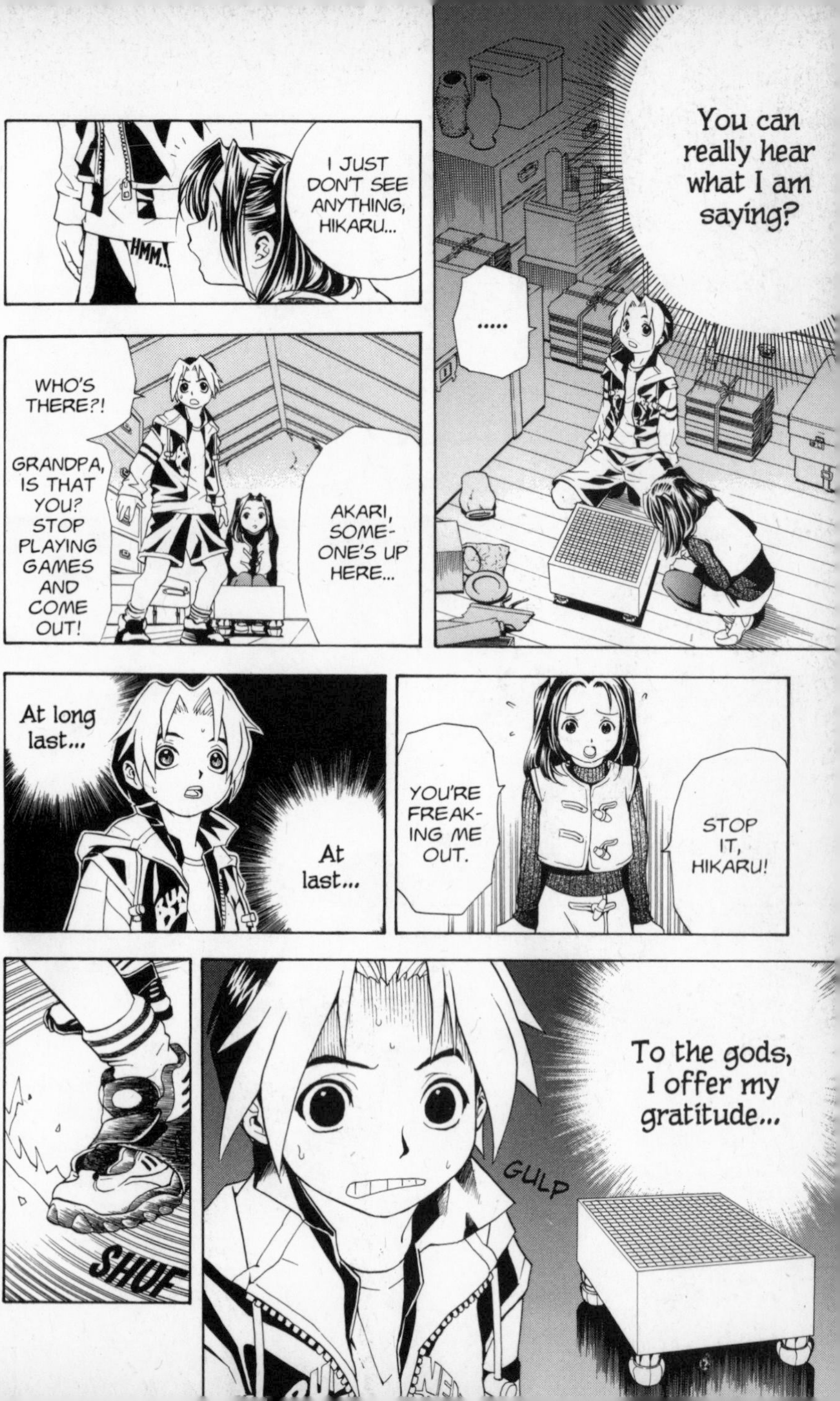
You can really hear what I am saying?
.....
HMM..
I JUST DON'T SEE ANYTHING, HIKARU...
AKARI, SOME-ONE'S UP HERE...
WHO'S THERE?!
GRANDPA, IS THAT YOU? STOP PLAYING GAMES AND COME OUT!
STOP IT, HIKARU!
YOU'RE FREAK-ING ME OUT.
At last...
At long last...
To the gods, I offer my gratitude...
GULP
SHUF

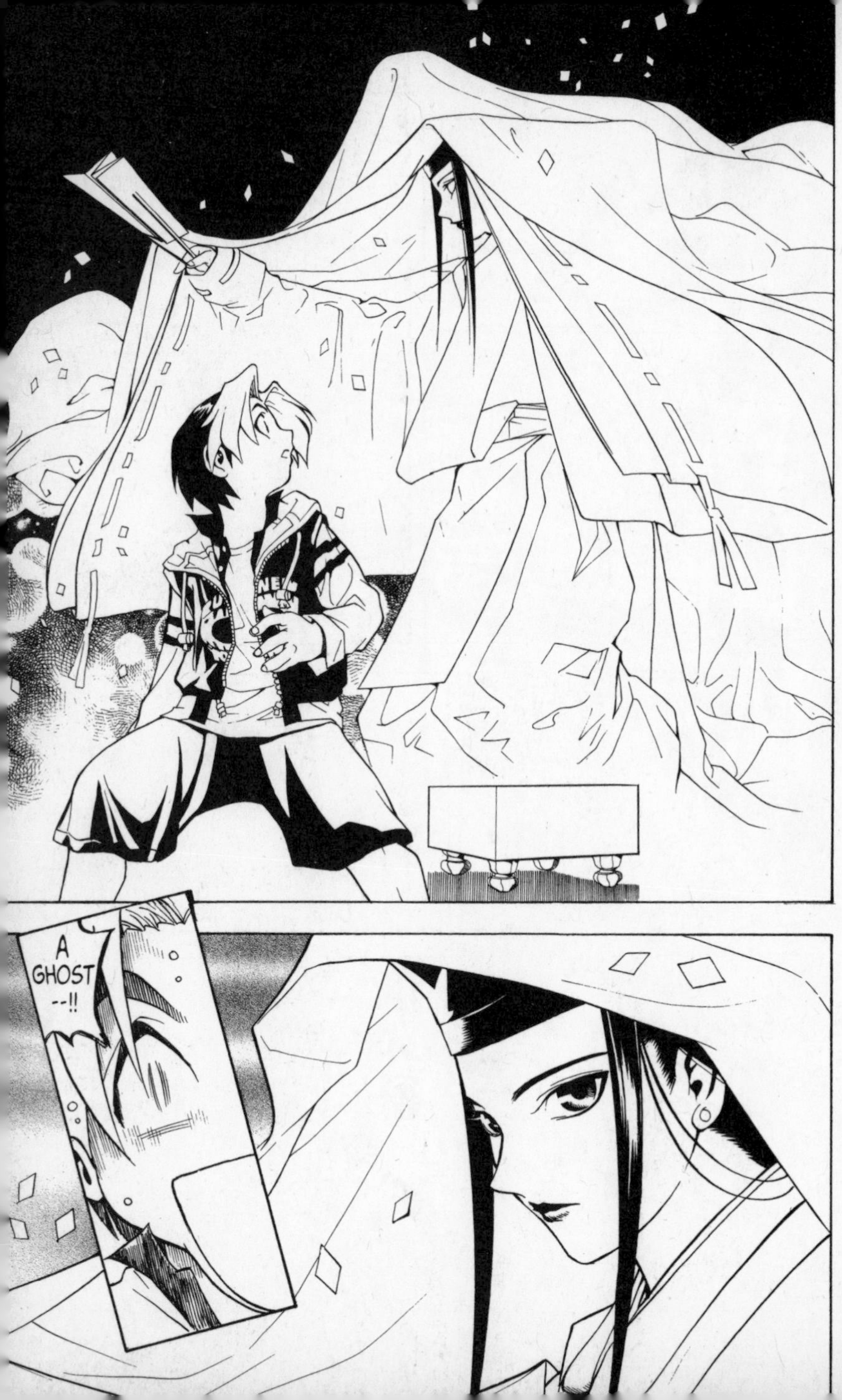
A GHOST --!!

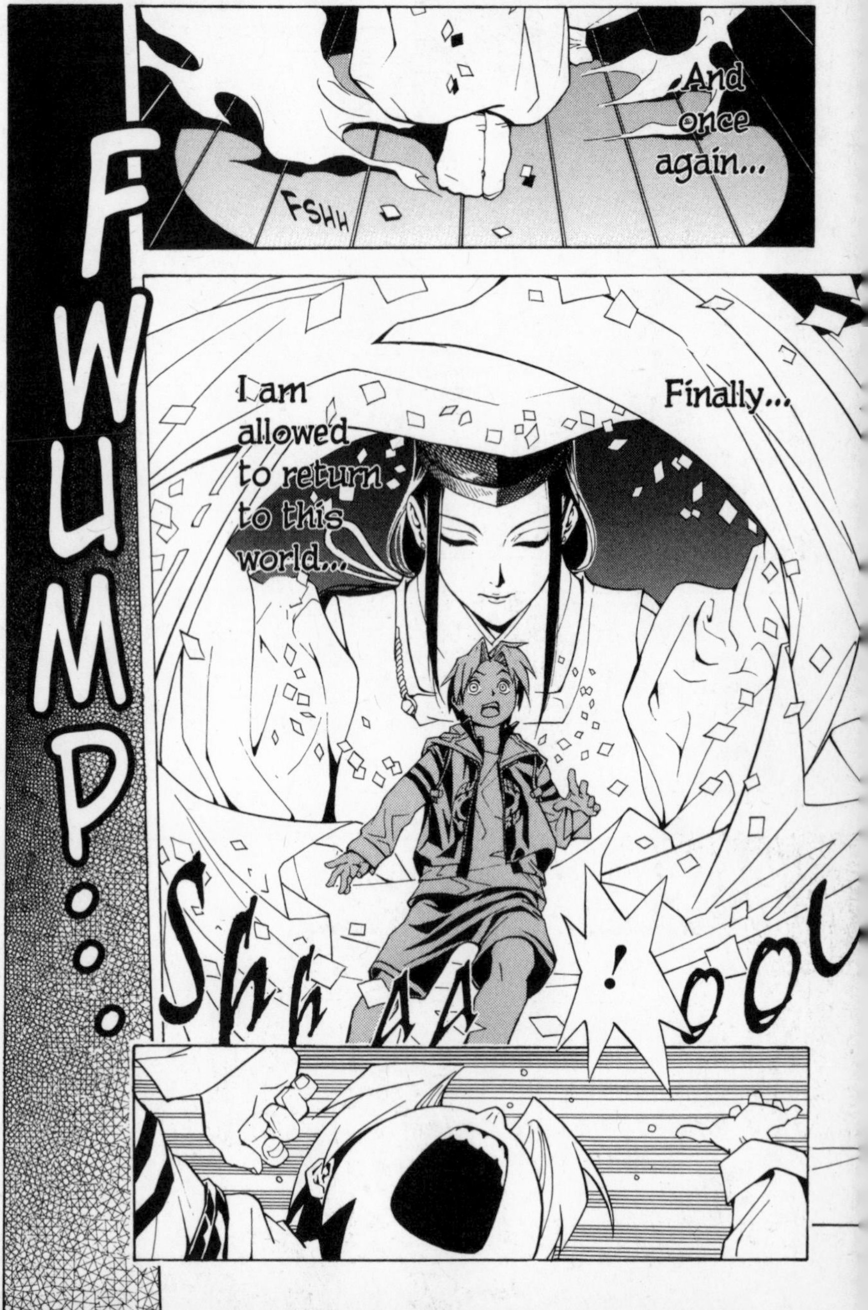
And once again...
FSHH
Finally...
I am allowed to return to this world...
FWUMP...
Shhaaooo

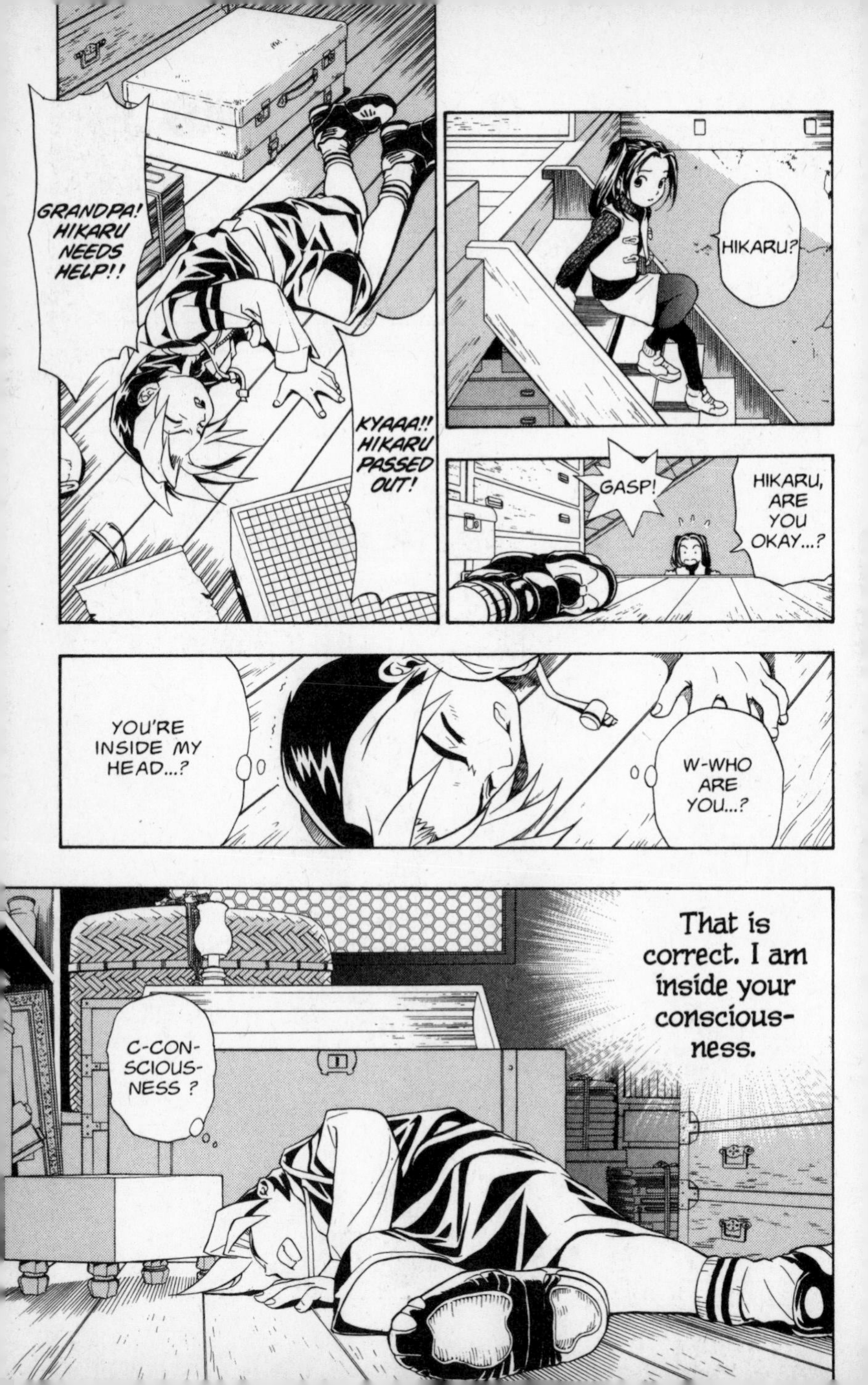
HIKARU?
HIKARU, ARE YOU OKAY...?
GASP!
KYAAA!! HIKARU PASSED OUT!
GRANDPA! HIKARU NEEDS HELP!!
W-WHO ARE YOU...?
YOU'RE INSIDE MY HEAD...?
That is correct. I am inside your conscious-ness.
C-CON-SCIOUS-NESS ?

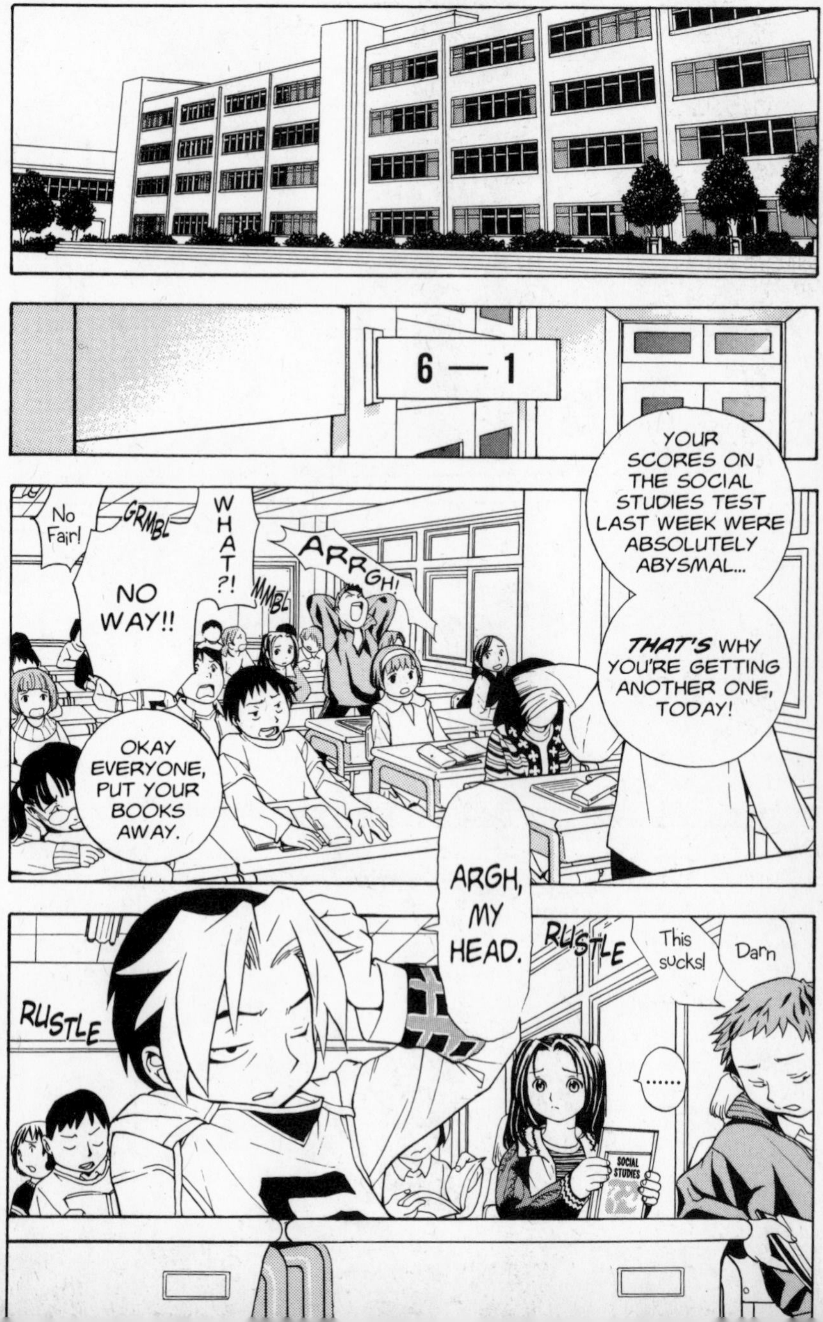
6 — 1
YOUR SCORES ON THE SOCIAL STUDIES TEST LAST WEEK WERE ABSOLUTELY ABYSMAL...
THAT'S WHY YOU'RE GETTING ANOTHER ONE, TODAY!
ARRGH!
WHAT?!
MMBL
GRMBL
NO WAY!!
No Fair!
OKAY EVERYONE, PUT YOUR BOOKS AWAY.
Darn
This sucks!
......
RUSTLE
ARGH, MY HEAD.
RUSTLE
SOCIAL STUDIES

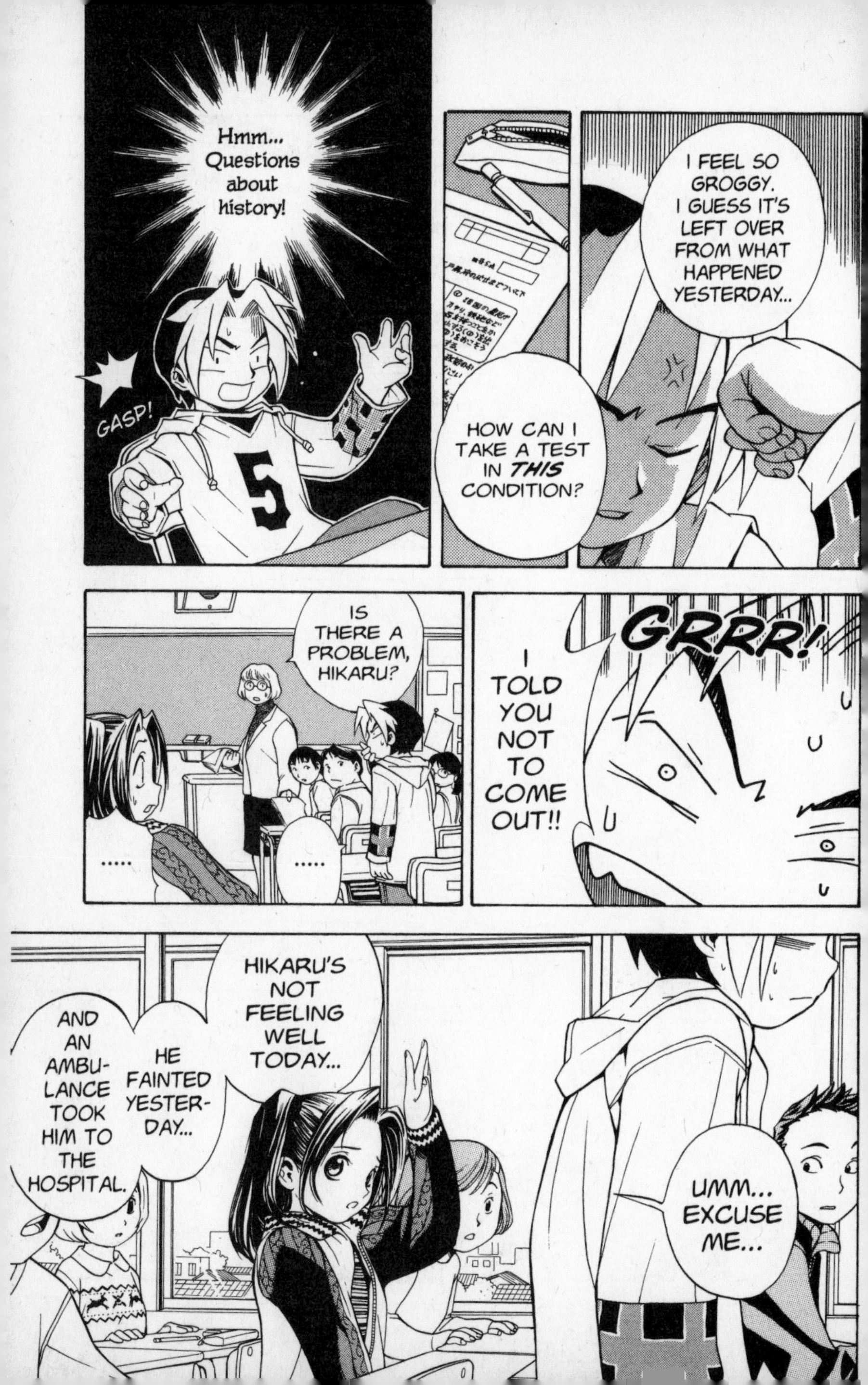
I FEEL SO GROGGY. I GUESS IT'S LEFT OVER FROM WHAT HAPPENED YESTERDAY...
HOW CAN I TAKE A TEST IN *THIS* CONDITION?
Hmm... Questions about history!
GASP!
GRRR!
I TOLD YOU NOT TO COME OUT!!
IS THERE A PROBLEM, HIKARU?
.....
.....
UMM... EXCUSE ME...
HIKARU'S NOT FEELING WELL TODAY...
HE FAINTED YESTER-DAY...
AND AN AMBU-LANCE TOOK HIM TO THE HOSPITAL.

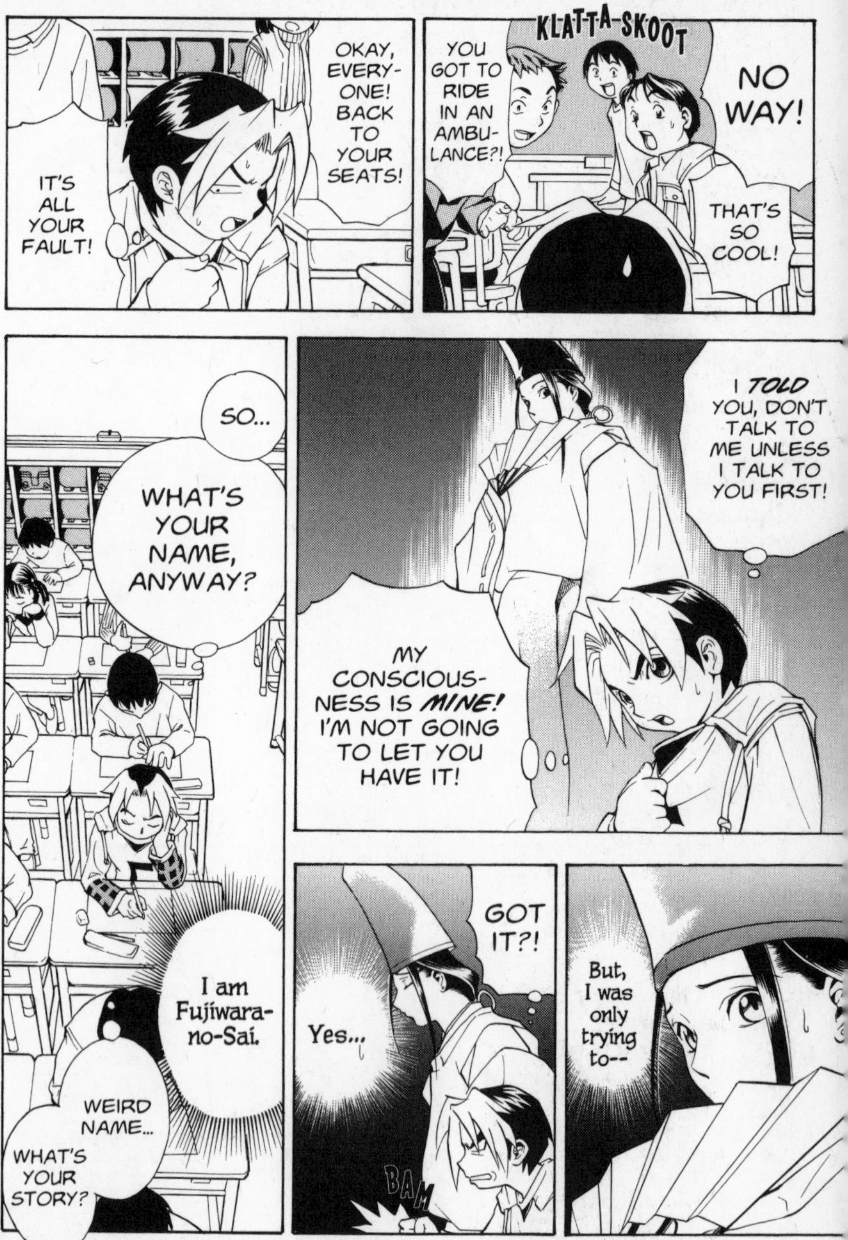
KLATT-A-SKOOT
NO WAY!
YOU GOT TO RIDE IN AN AMBULANCE?!
THAT'S SO COOL!
OKAY, EVERYONE! BACK TO YOUR SEATS!
IT'S ALL YOUR FAULT!
I TOLD YOU, DON'T TALK TO ME UNLESS I TALK TO YOU FIRST!
MY CONSCIOUSNESS IS MINE! I'M NOT GOING TO LET YOU HAVE IT!
But, I was only trying to--
GOT IT?!
Yes...
BAM
SO...
WHAT'S YOUR NAME, ANYWAY?
I am Fujiwara-no-Sai.
WEIRD NAME...
WHAT'S YOUR STORY?

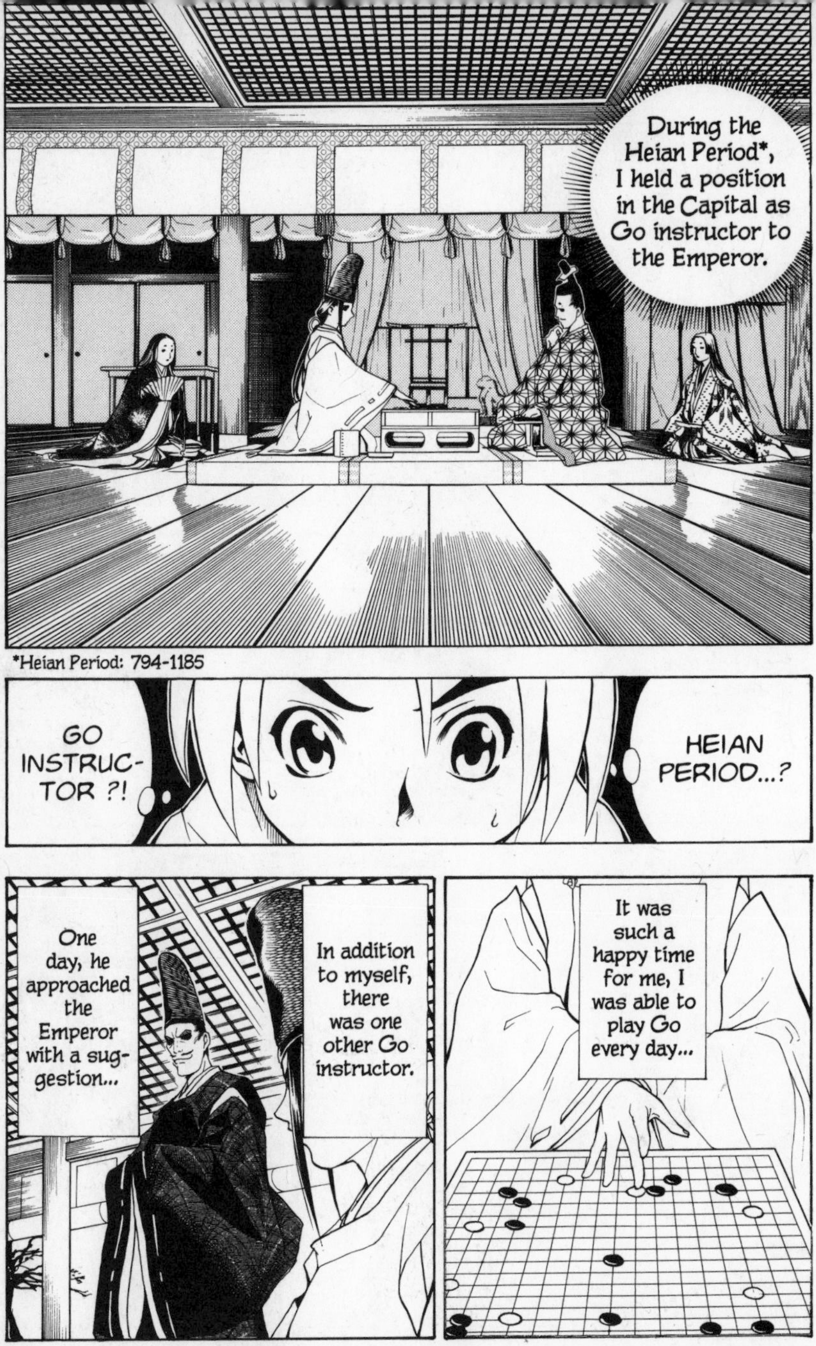
During the Heian Period*, I held a position in the Capital as Go instructor to the Emperor.
HEIAN PERIOD...?
GO INSTRUCTOR ?!
It was such a happy time for me, I was able to play Go every day...
In addition to myself, there was one other Go instructor.
One day, he approached the Emperor with a suggestion...
*Heian Period: 794-1185

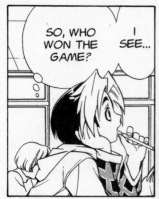

Sir, I believe that you have need for only one Go instructor.
Let us play a game to decide who shall keep his position.
I SEE...
SO, WHO WON THE GAME?
The game was dead even...
Everyone's attention was drawn to the board, it was only by mere chance that I saw it...
A single white stone lay in my opponent's Go bowl.*

*A container used to keep a player's stones

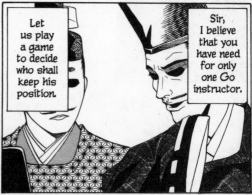

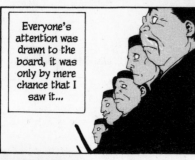

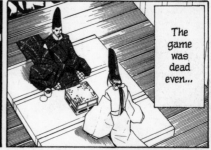

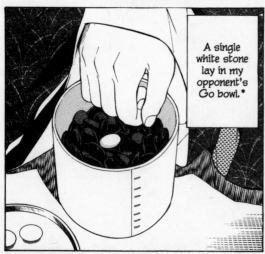

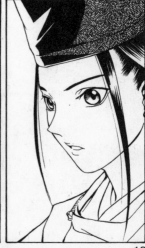

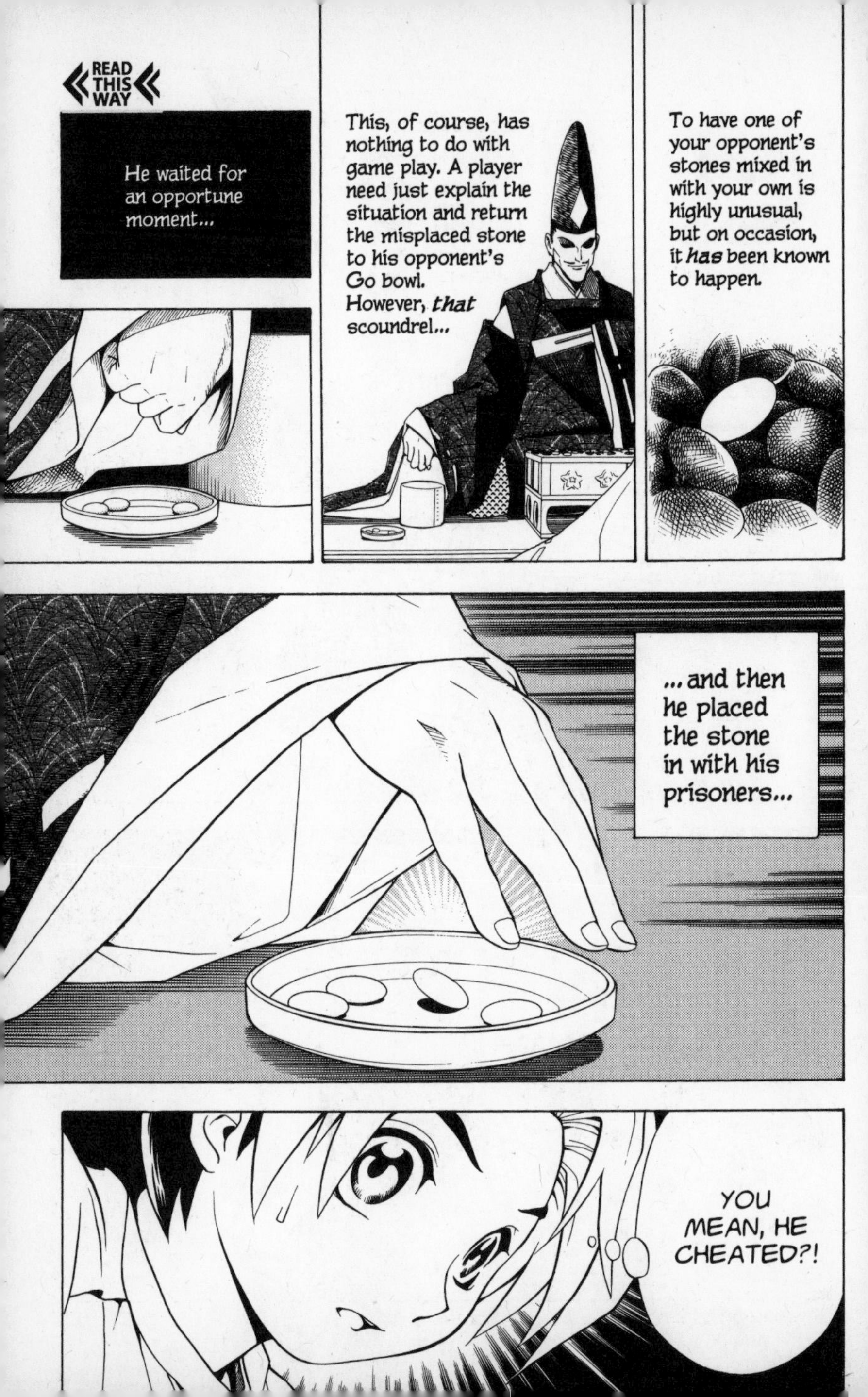
READ THIS WAY
To have one of your opponent's stones mixed in with your own is highly unusual, but on occasion, it *has* been known to happen.
This, of course, has nothing to do with game play. A player need just explain the situation and return the misplaced stone to his opponent's Go bowl. However, *that* scoundrel...
He waited for an opportune moment...
...and then he placed the stone in with his prisoners...
YOU MEAN, HE CHEATED?!

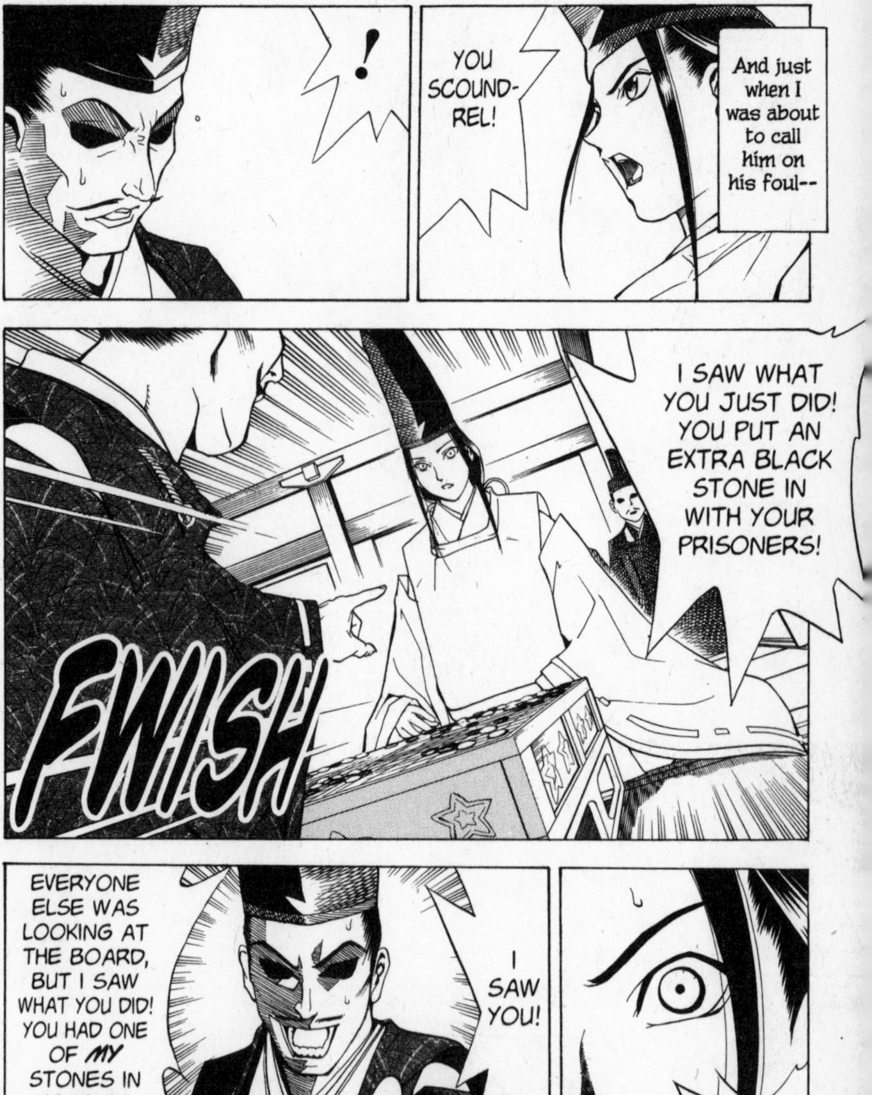

And just when I was about to call him on his foul--
YOU SCOUNDREL!
!
I SAW WHAT YOU JUST DID! YOU PUT AN EXTRA BLACK STONE IN WITH YOUR PRISONERS!
FWISH
WHAT?!
I SAW YOU!
EVERYONE ELSE WAS LOOKING AT THE BOARD, BUT I SAW WHAT YOU DID! YOU HAD ONE OF *MY* STONES IN YOUR GO BOWL AND YOU SLIPPED IT IN WITH YOUR PRISONERS!

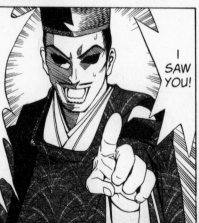

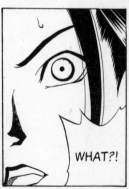

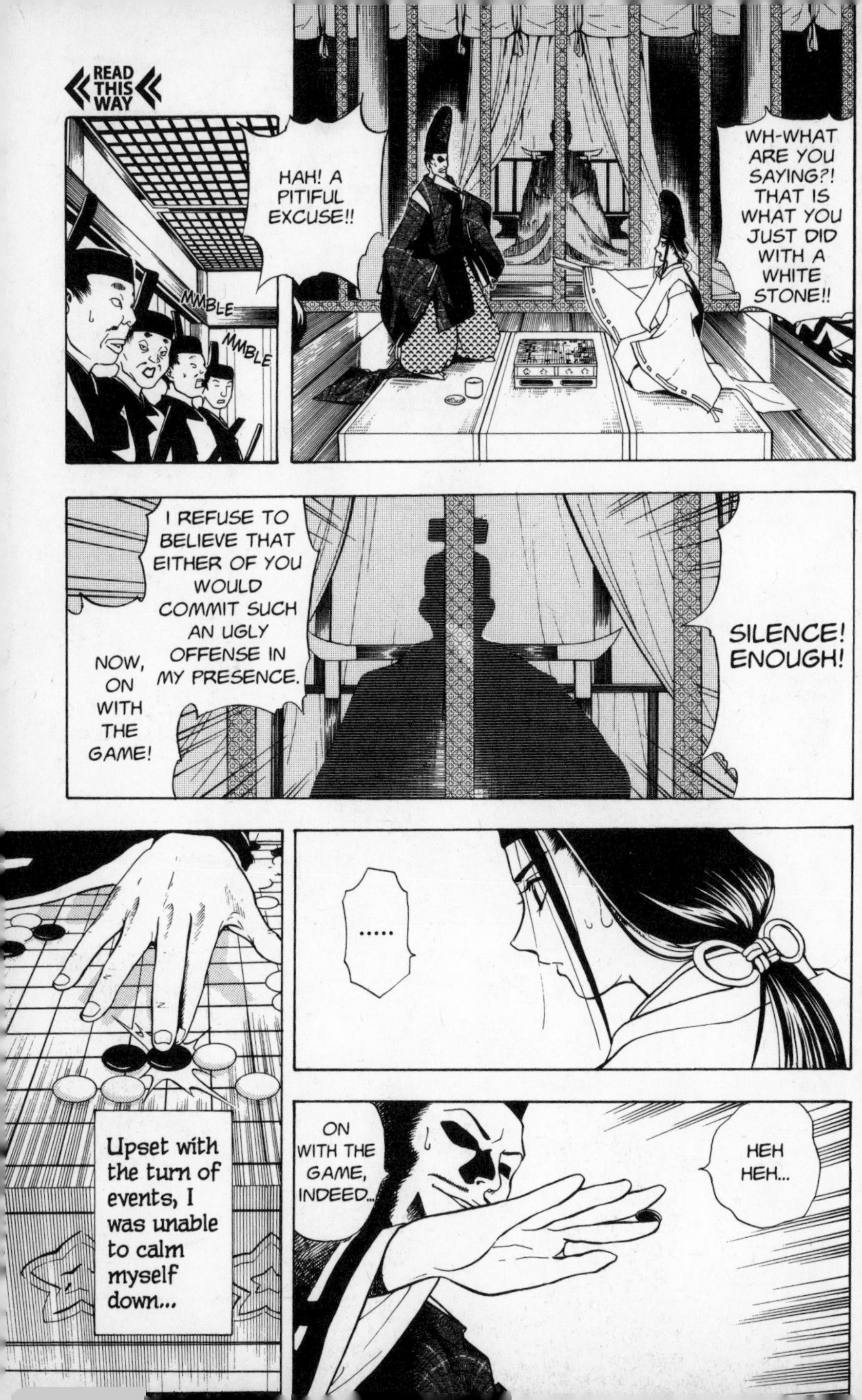
READ THIS WAY
WH-WHAT ARE YOU SAYING?! THAT IS WHAT YOU JUST DID WITH A WHITE STONE!!
HAH! A PITIFUL EXCUSE!!
MMBLE
MMBLE
SILENCE! ENOUGH!
I REFUSE TO BELIEVE THAT EITHER OF YOU WOULD COMMIT SUCH AN UGLY OFFENSE IN MY PRESENCE.
NOW, ON WITH THE GAME!
......
HEH HEH...
ON WITH THE GAME, INDEED...
Upset with the turn of events, I was unable to calm myself down...

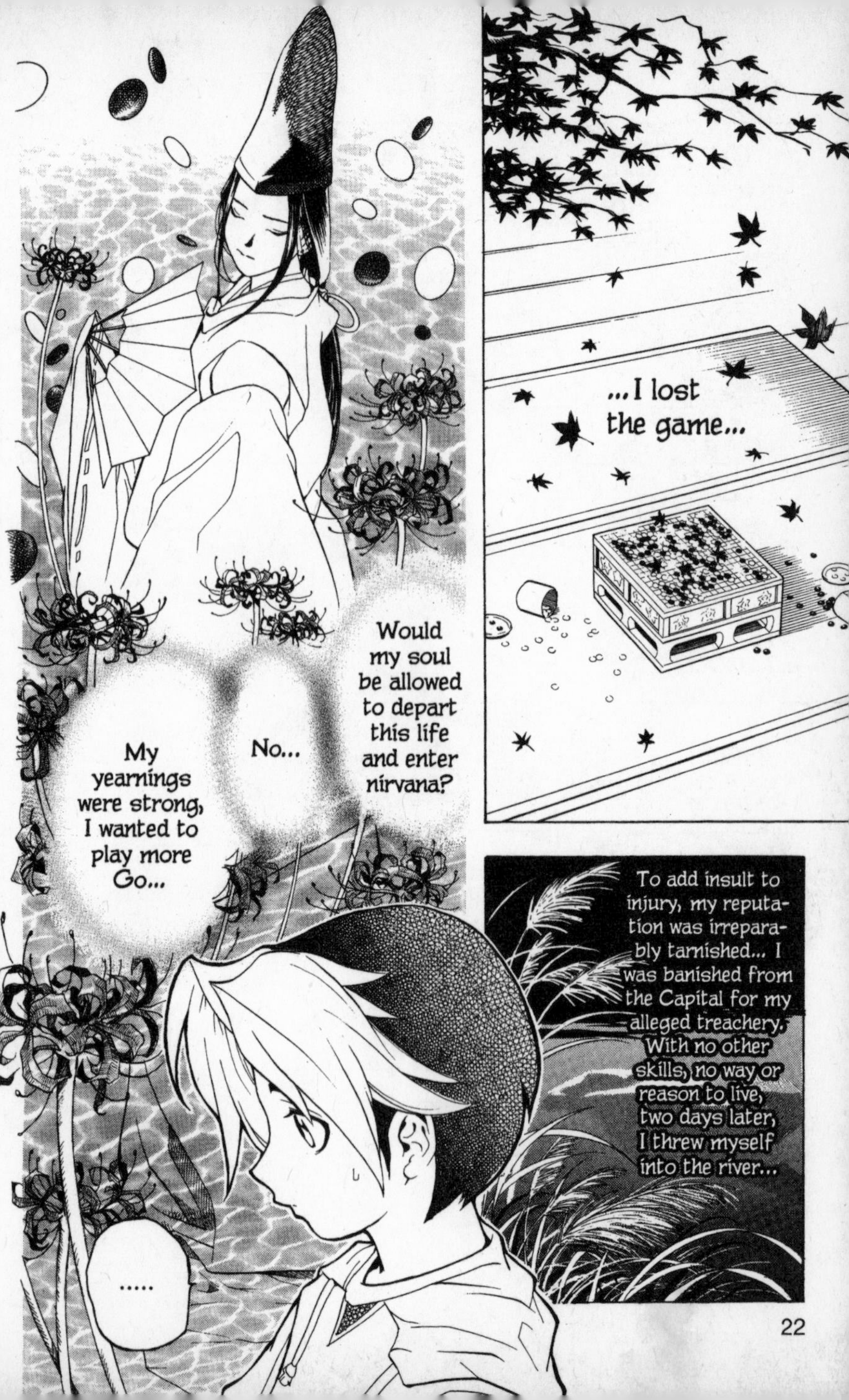
...I lost the game...
To add insult to injury, my reputation was irreparably tarnished... I was banished from the Capital for my alleged treachery. With no other skills, no way or reason to live, two days later, I threw myself into the river...
Would my soul be allowed to depart this life and enter nirvana?
No...
My yearnings were strong, I wanted to play more Go...
.....

READ THIS WAY

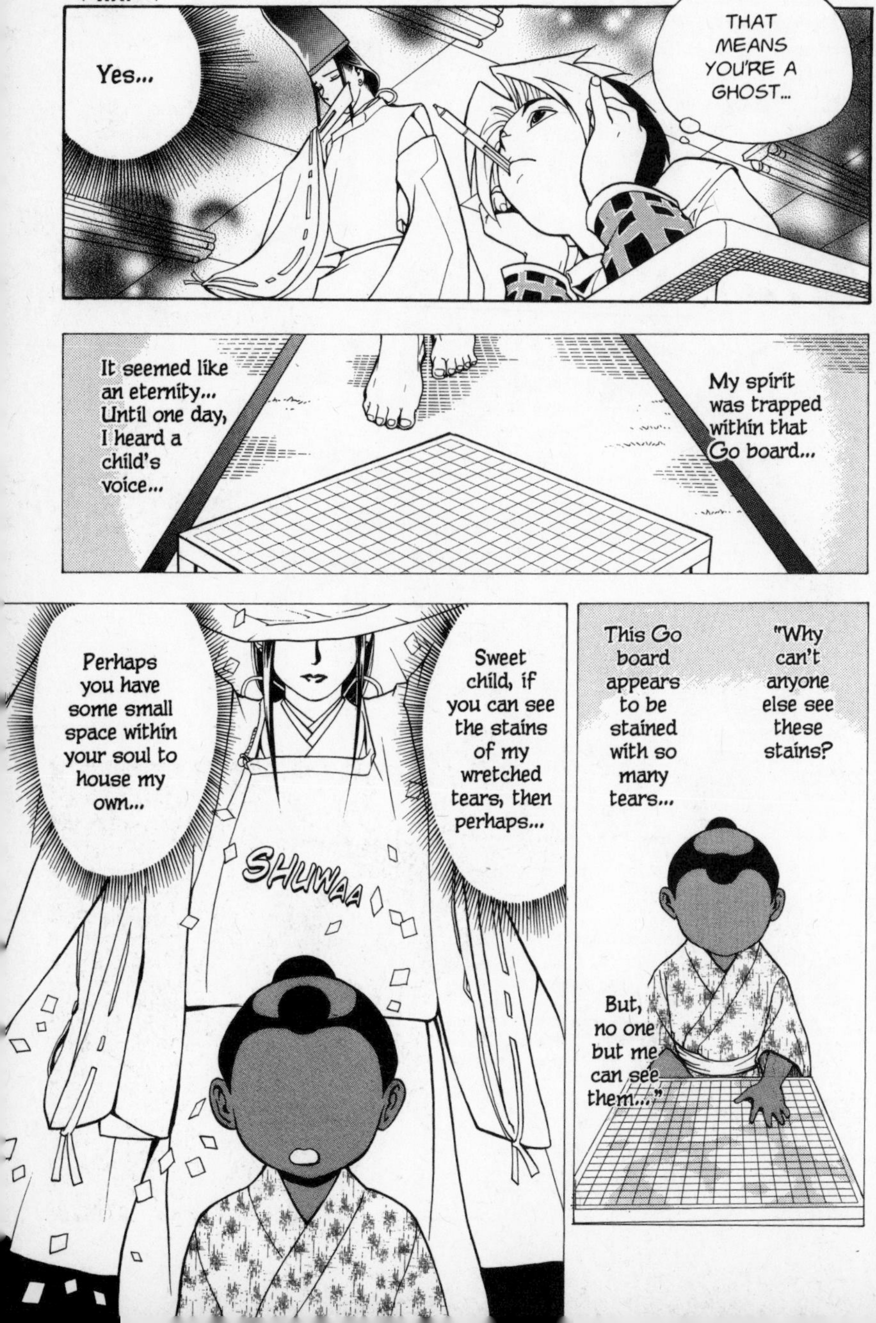
THAT MEANS YOU'RE A GHOST...
Yes...
My spirit was trapped within that Go board...
It seemed like an eternity... Until one day, I heard a child's voice...
"Why can't anyone else see these stains?
This Go board appears to be stained with so many tears...
But, no one but me can see them..."
Sweet child, if you can see the stains of my wretched tears, then perhaps...
Perhaps you have some small space within your soul to house my own...
SHUWAA

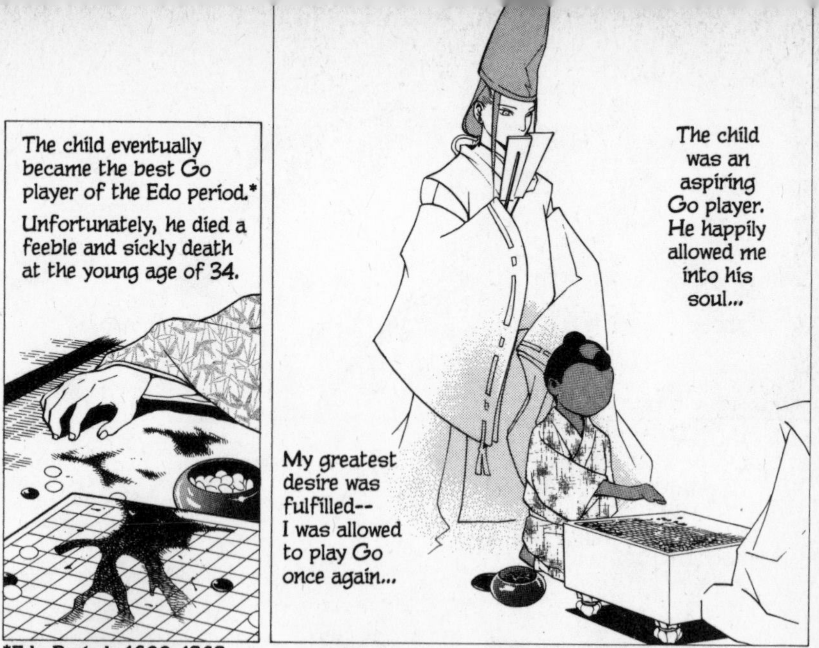
The child was an aspiring Go player. He happily allowed me into his soul...
My greatest desire was fulfilled-- I was allowed to play Go once again...
The child eventually became the best Go player of the Edo period.*
Unfortunately, he died a feeble and sickly death at the young age of 34.

*Edo Period: 1600-1868

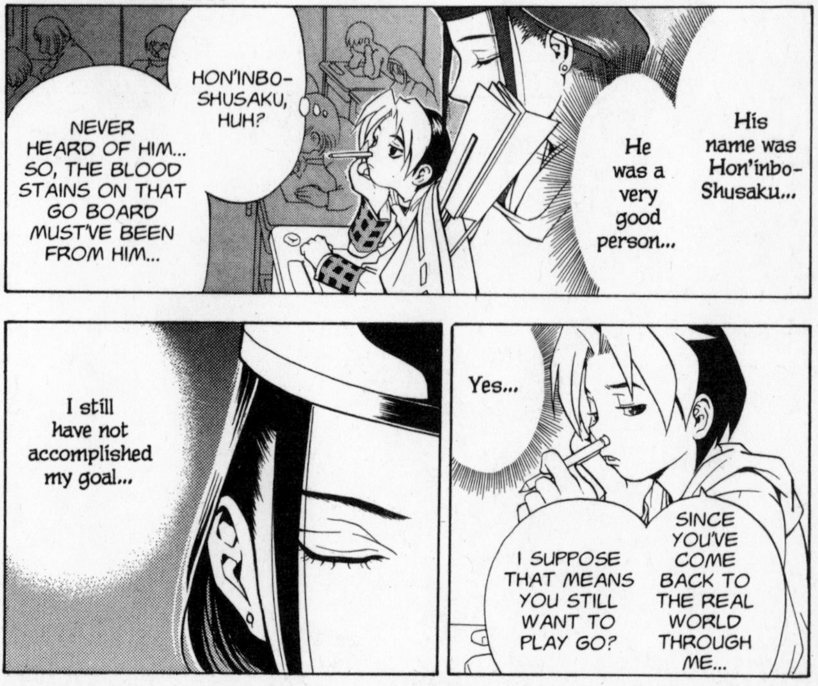
His name was Hon'inbo-Shusaku...
He was a very good person...
HON'INBO-SHUSAKU, HUH?
NEVER HEARD OF HIM... SO, THE BLOOD STAINS ON THAT GO BOARD MUST'VE BEEN FROM HIM...
Yes...
SINCE YOU'VE COME BACK TO THE REAL WORLD THROUGH ME...
I SUPPOSE THAT MEANS YOU STILL WANT TO PLAY GO?
I still have not accomplished my goal...

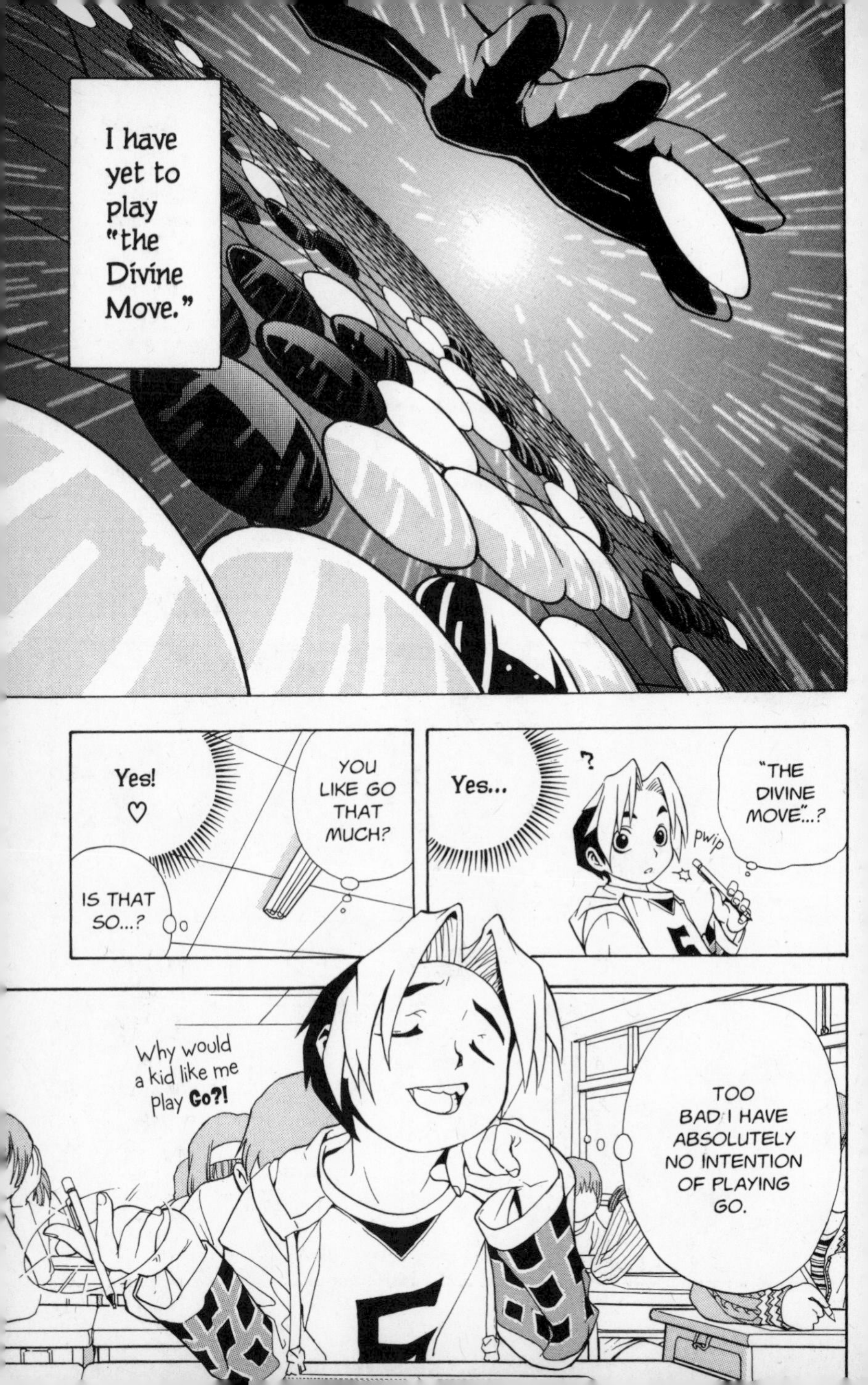
I have yet to play "the Divine Move."
"THE DIVINE MOVE"...?
?
Yes...
pwip
YOU LIKE GO THAT MUCH?
Yes! ♡
IS THAT SO...?
TOO BAD I HAVE ABSOLUTELY NO INTENTION OF PLAYING GO.
Why would a kid like me play Go?!

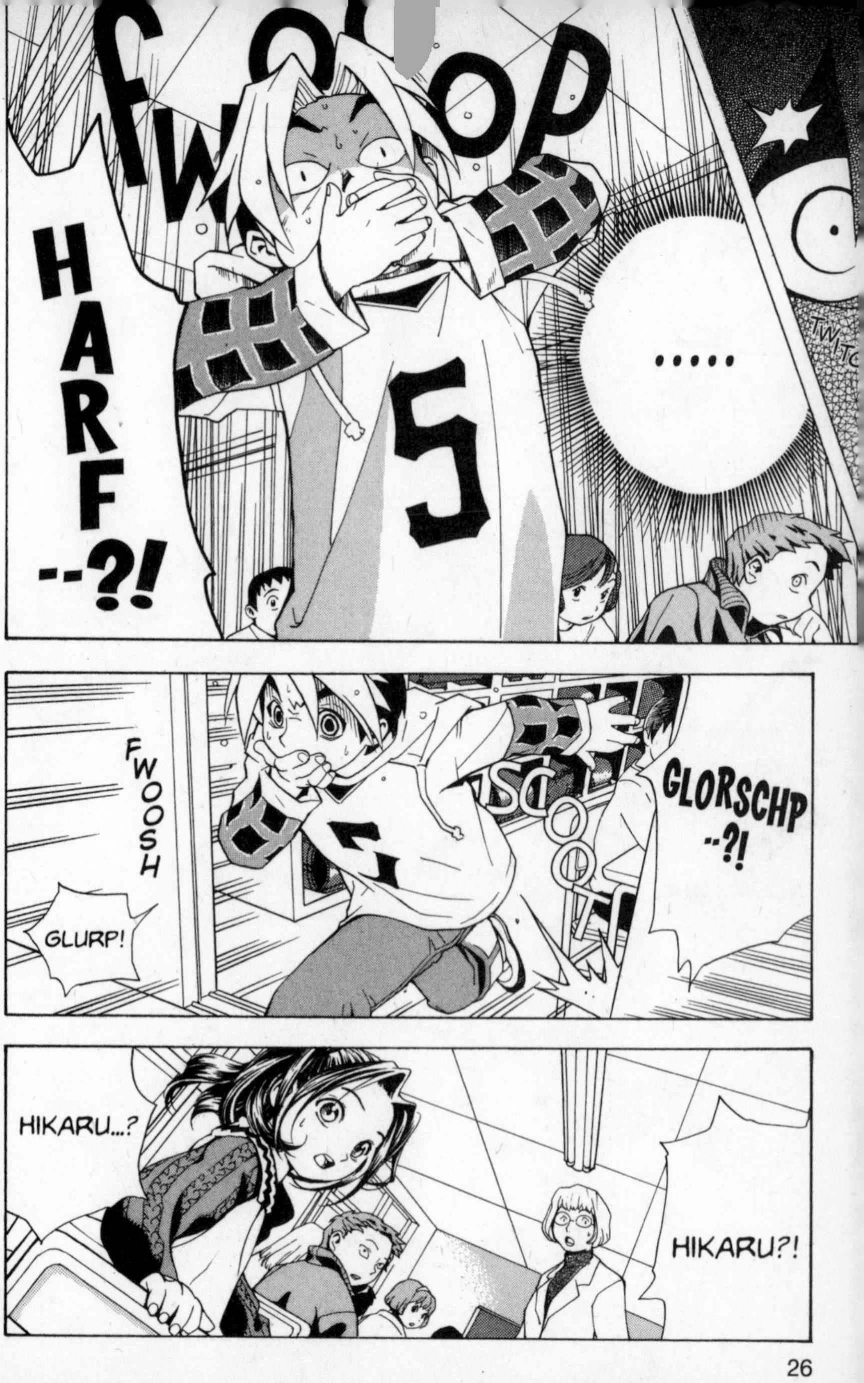
TWITC
.....
FWOOP
HARF--?!
GLORSCHP--?!
SCOOT
FWOOSH
GLURP!
HIKARU?!
HIKARU...?

READ THIS WAY

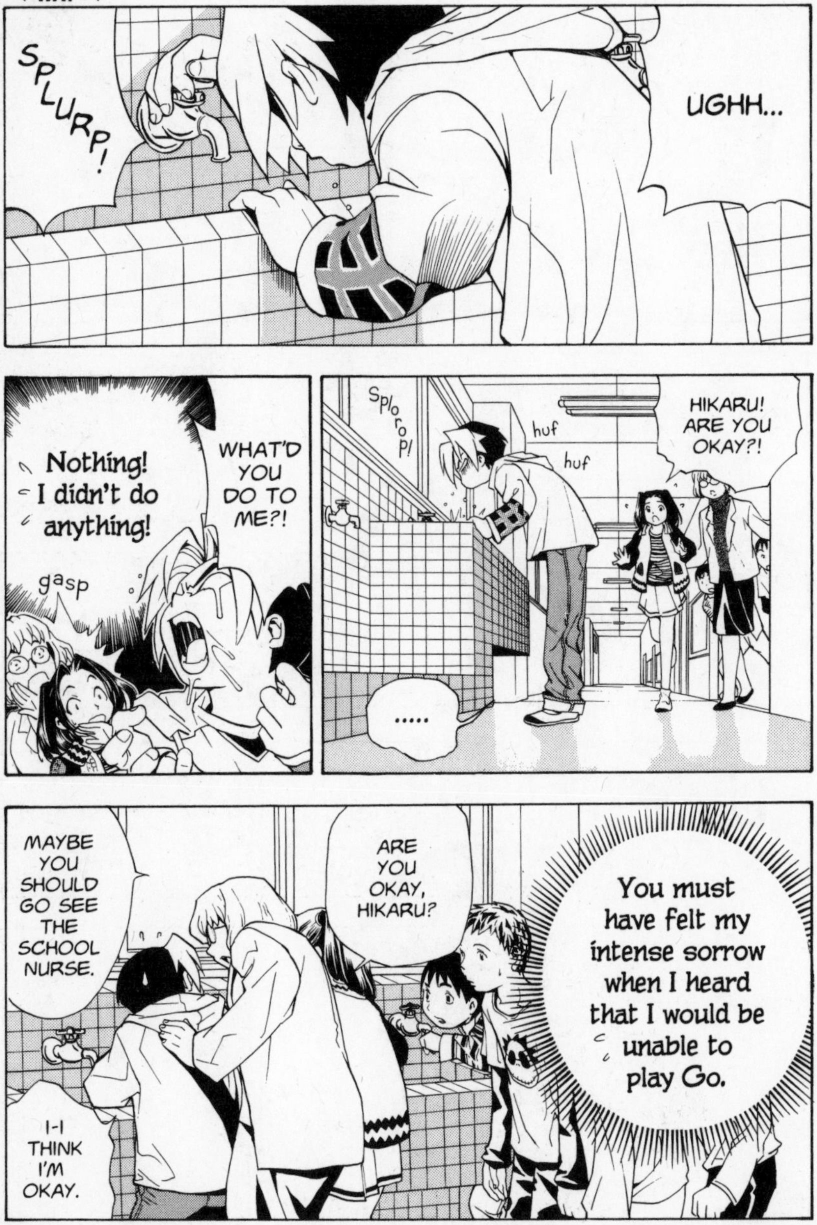
UGHH...
SPLURP!
HIKARU! ARE YOU OKAY?!
Splorop!
huf
huf
.....
WHAT'D YOU DO TO ME?!
Nothing! I didn't do anything!
gasp
You must have felt my intense sorrow when I heard that I would be unable to play Go.
ARE YOU OKAY, HIKARU?
MAYBE YOU SHOULD GO SEE THE SCHOOL NURSE.
I-I THINK I'M OKAY.

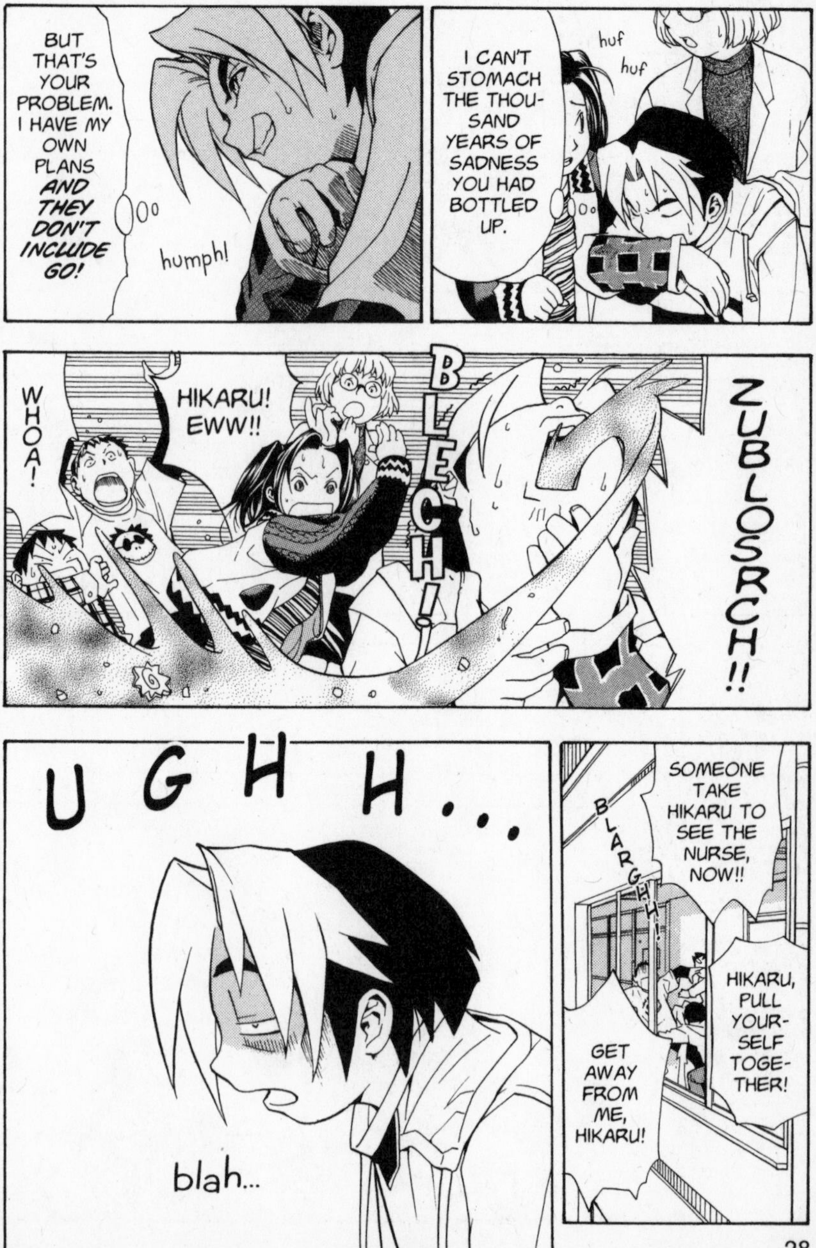
I CAN'T STOMACH THE THOU-SAND YEARS OF SADNESS YOU HAD BOTTLED UP.
huf
huf
BUT THAT'S YOUR PROBLEM. I HAVE MY OWN PLANS ***AND THEY DON'T INCLUDE GO!***
humph!
ZUBLOSRCH!!
BLECH!
HIKARU! EWW!!
WHOA!
SOMEONE TAKE HIKARU TO SEE THE NURSE, NOW!!
BLARGHH!
HIKARU, PULL YOUR-SELF TOGE-THER!
GET AWAY FROM ME, HIKARU!
UGHH...
blah...

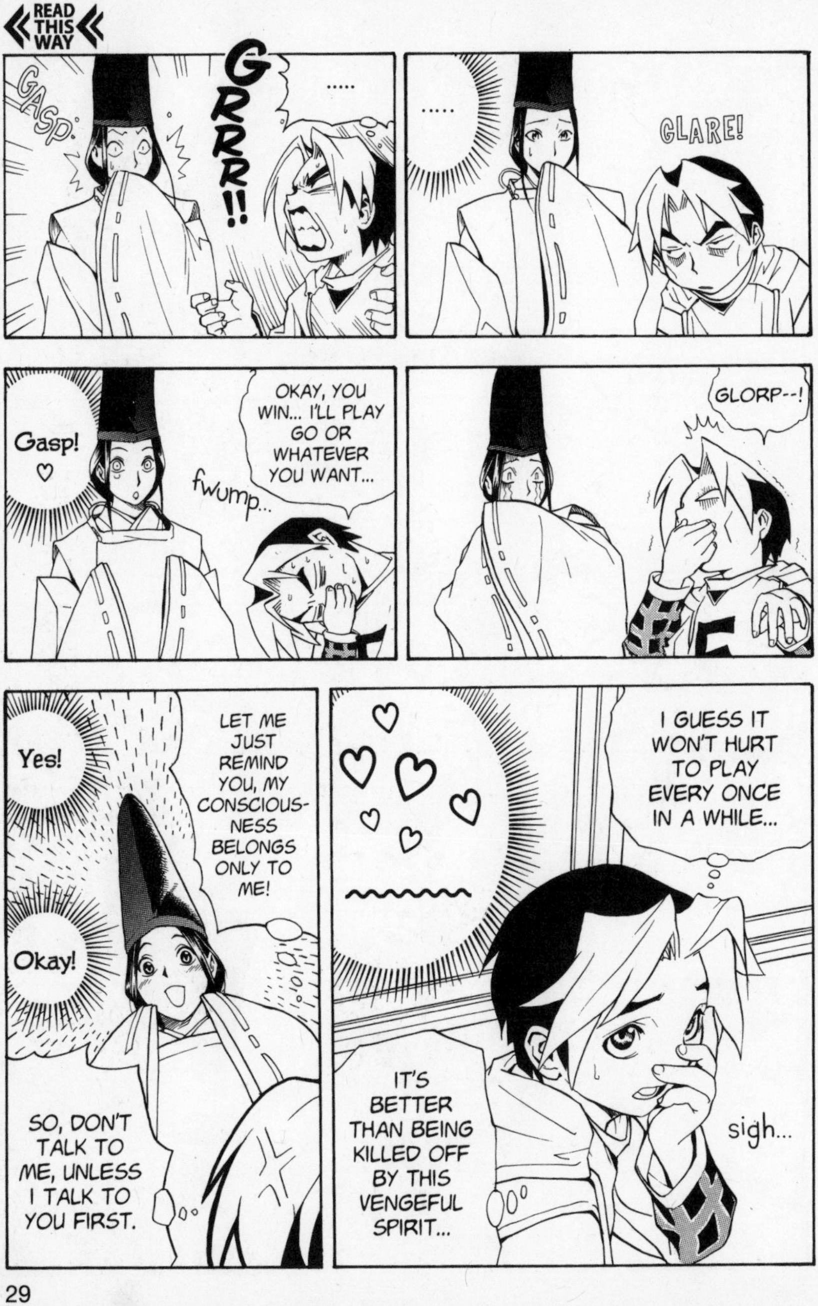

READ THIS WAY
GLARE!
.....
.....
GRRR!!
GASP
GLORP--!
OKAY, YOU WIN... I'LL PLAY GO OR WHATEVER YOU WANT...
fwump...
Gasp! ♡
I GUESS IT WON'T HURT TO PLAY EVERY ONCE IN A WHILE...
sigh...
IT'S BETTER THAN BEING KILLED OFF BY THIS VENGEFUL SPIRIT...
LET ME JUST REMIND YOU, MY CONSCIOUSNESS BELONGS ONLY TO ME!
Yes!
Okay!
SO, DON'T TALK TO ME, UNLESS I TALK TO YOU FIRST.

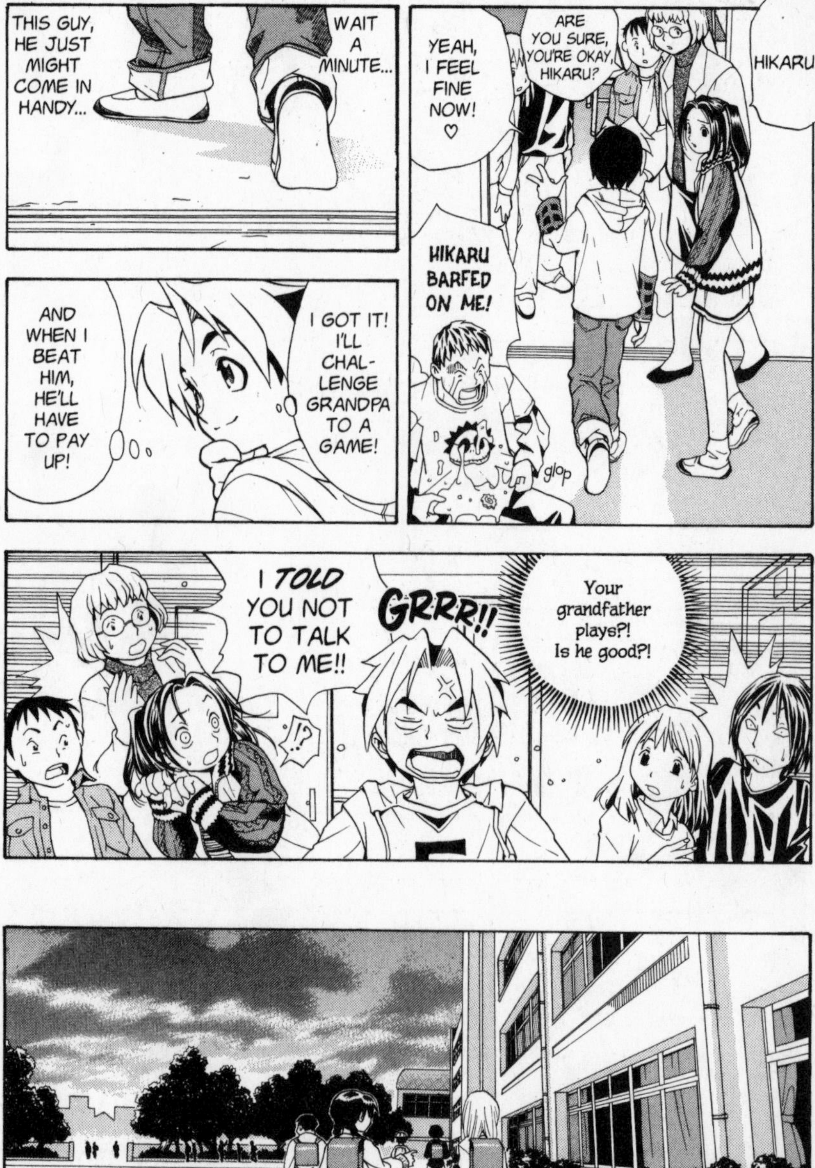
HIKARU...
ARE YOU SURE, YOU'RE OKAY, HIKARU?
YEAH, I FEEL FINE NOW! ♡
HIKARU BARFED ON ME!
glop
WAIT A MINUTE...
THIS GUY, HE JUST MIGHT COME IN HANDY...
I GOT IT! I'LL CHAL-LENGE GRANDPA TO A GAME!
AND WHEN I BEAT HIM, HE'LL HAVE TO PAY UP!
Your grandfather plays?! Is he good?!
GRRR!!
I TOLD YOU NOT TO TALK TO ME!!
!?

READ THIS WAY

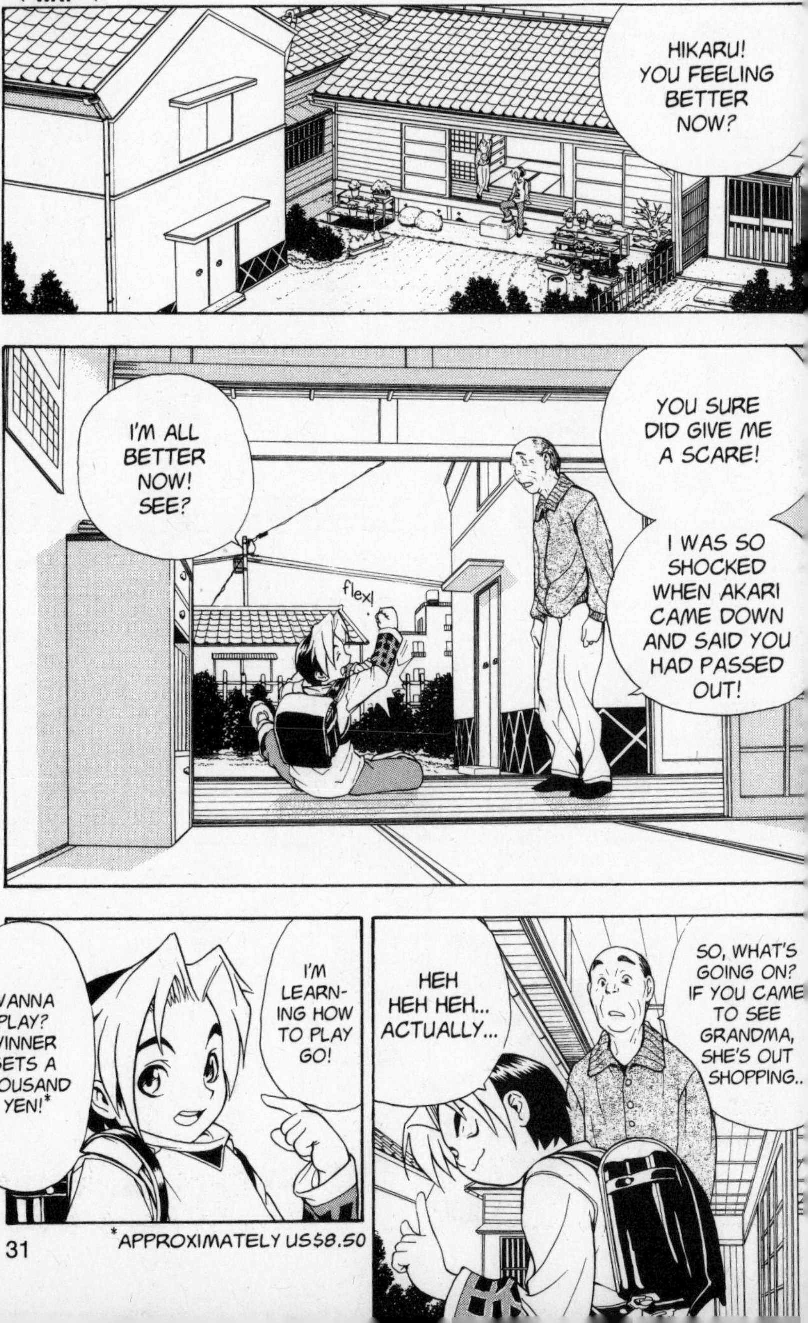
HIKARU! YOU FEELING BETTER NOW?
YOU SURE DID GIVE ME A SCARE!
I WAS SO SHOCKED WHEN AKARI CAME DOWN AND SAID YOU HAD PASSED OUT!
I'M ALL BETTER NOW! SEE?
flex!
SO, WHAT'S GOING ON? IF YOU CAME TO SEE GRANDMA, SHE'S OUT SHOPPING..
HEH HEH HEH... ACTUALLY...
I'M LEARNING HOW TO PLAY GO!
WANNA PLAY? WINNER GETS A THOUSAND YEN!*

*APPROXIMATELY US$8.50

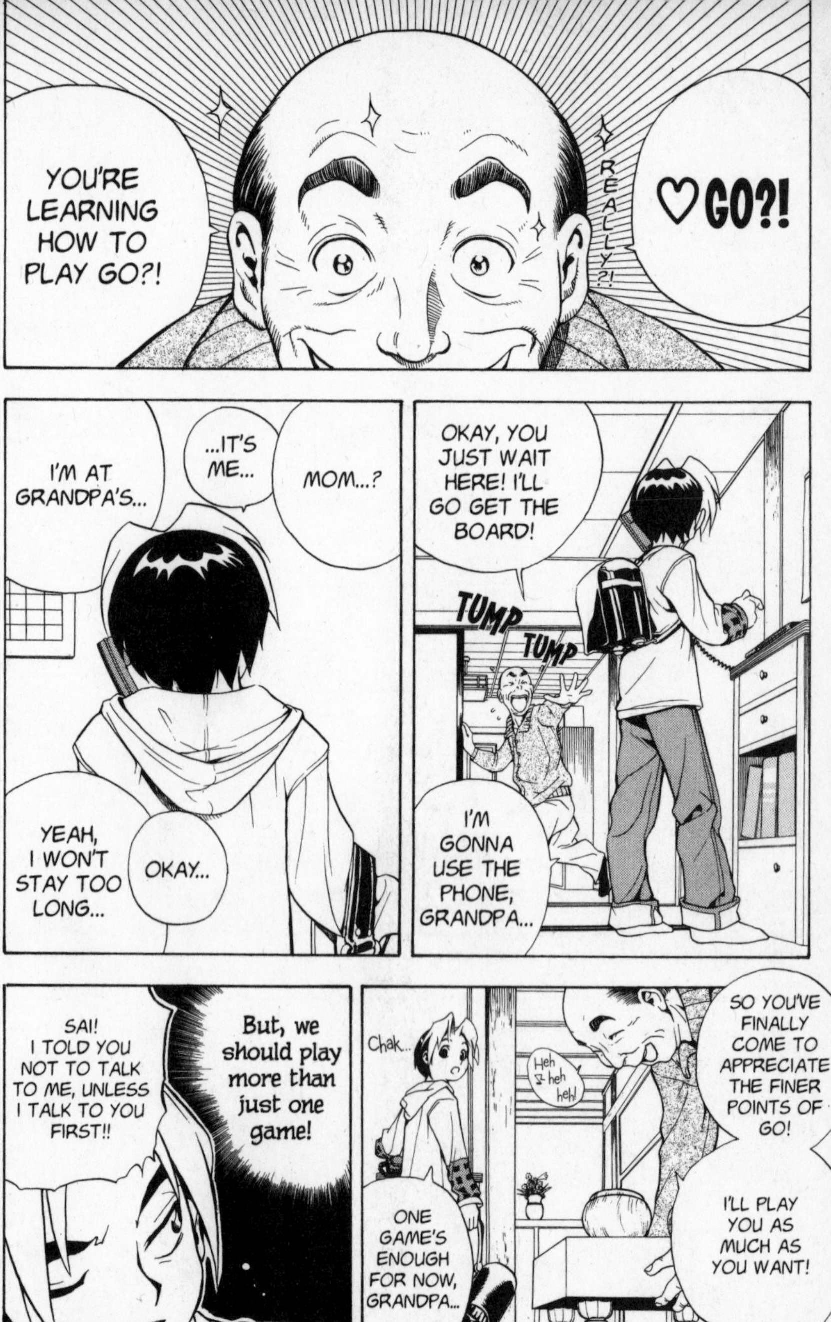
♡GO?!
REALLY?!
YOU'RE LEARNING HOW TO PLAY GO?!
OKAY, YOU JUST WAIT HERE! I'LL GO GET THE BOARD!
TUMP
TUMP
I'M GONNA USE THE PHONE, GRANDPA...
MOM...?
...IT'S ME...
I'M AT GRANDPA'S...
OKAY...
YEAH, I WON'T STAY TOO LONG...
SO YOU'VE FINALLY COME TO APPRECIATE THE FINER POINTS OF GO!
Heh heh heh!
Chak...
I'LL PLAY YOU AS MUCH AS YOU WANT!
ONE GAME'S ENOUGH FOR NOW, GRANDPA...
But, we should play more than just one game!
SAI! I TOLD YOU NOT TO TALK TO ME, UNLESS I TALK TO YOU FIRST!!

READ THIS WAY

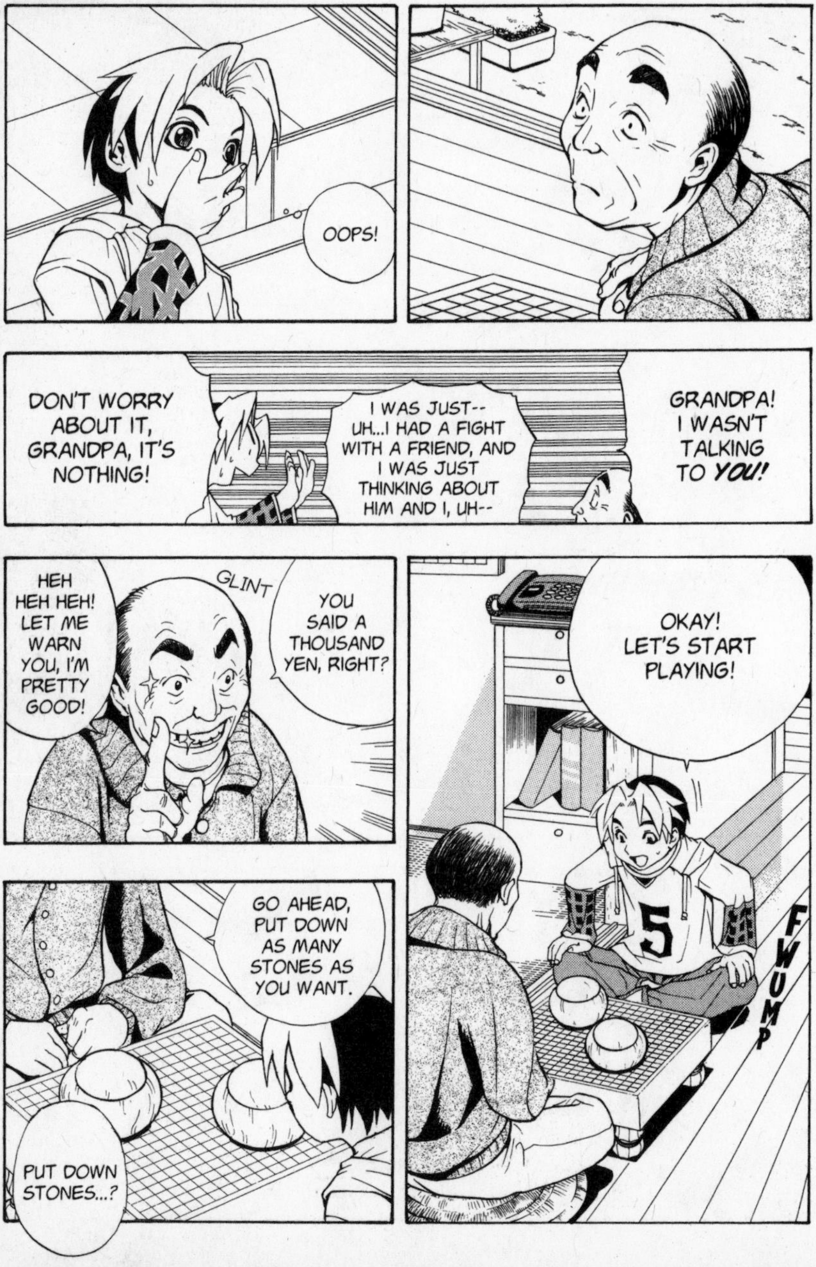
OOPS!
GRANDPA! I WASN'T TALKING TO ***YOU!***
I WAS JUST-- UH...I HAD A FIGHT WITH A FRIEND, AND I WAS JUST THINKING ABOUT HIM AND I, UH--
DON'T WORRY ABOUT IT, GRANDPA, IT'S NOTHING!
OKAY! LET'S START PLAYING!
FWUMP
YOU SAID A THOUSAND YEN, RIGHT?
GLINT
HEH HEH HEH! LET ME WARN YOU, I'M PRETTY GOOD!
GO AHEAD, PUT DOWN AS MANY STONES AS YOU WANT.
PUT DOWN STONES...?

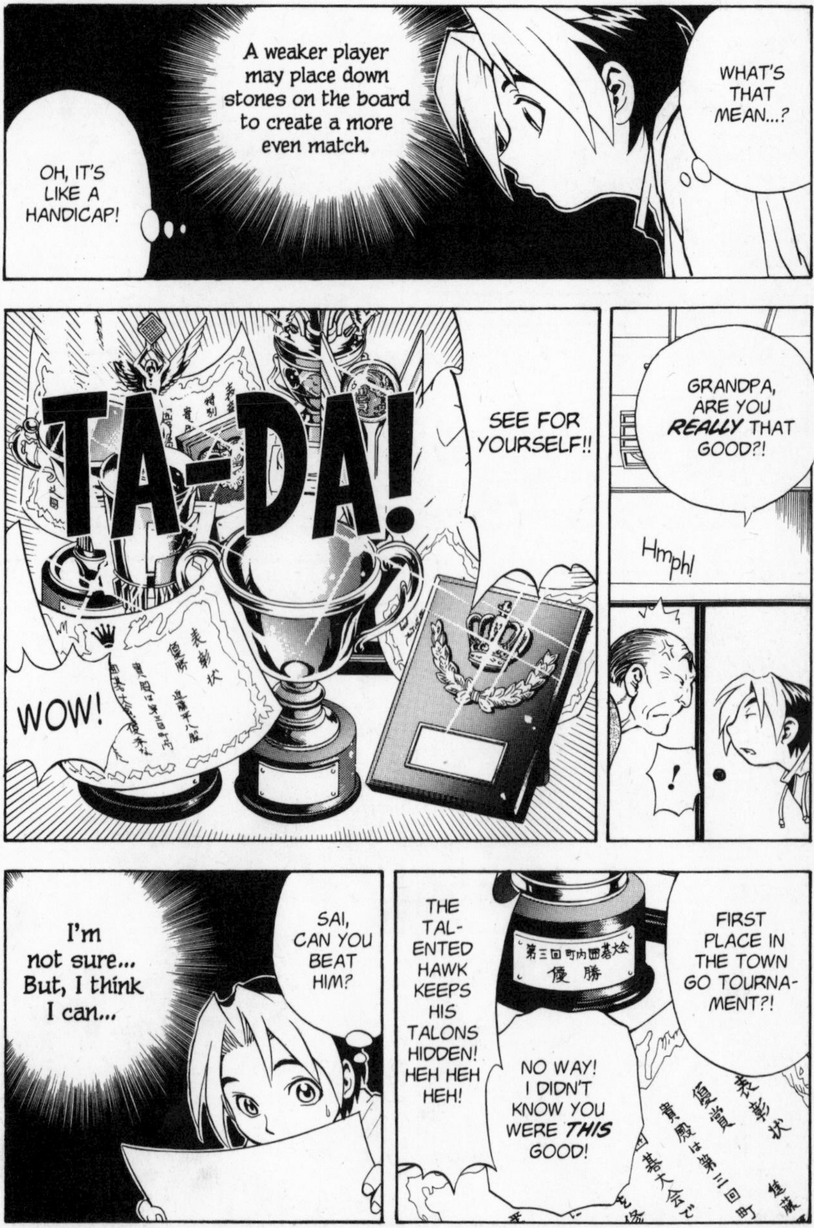
WHAT'S THAT MEAN...?
A weaker player may place down stones on the board to create a more even match.
OH, IT'S LIKE A HANDICAP!
GRANDPA, ARE YOU *REALLY* THAT GOOD?!
Hmph!
!
SEE FOR YOURSELF!!
TA-DA!
WOW!
FIRST PLACE IN THE TOWN GO TOURNA-MENT?!
第三回町内囲碁大会
優勝
THE TAL-ENTED HAWK KEEPS HIS TALONS HIDDEN! HEH HEH HEH!
NO WAY! I DIDN'T KNOW YOU WERE *THIS* GOOD!
SAI, CAN YOU BEAT HIM?
I'm not sure... But, I think I can...

READ THIS WAY

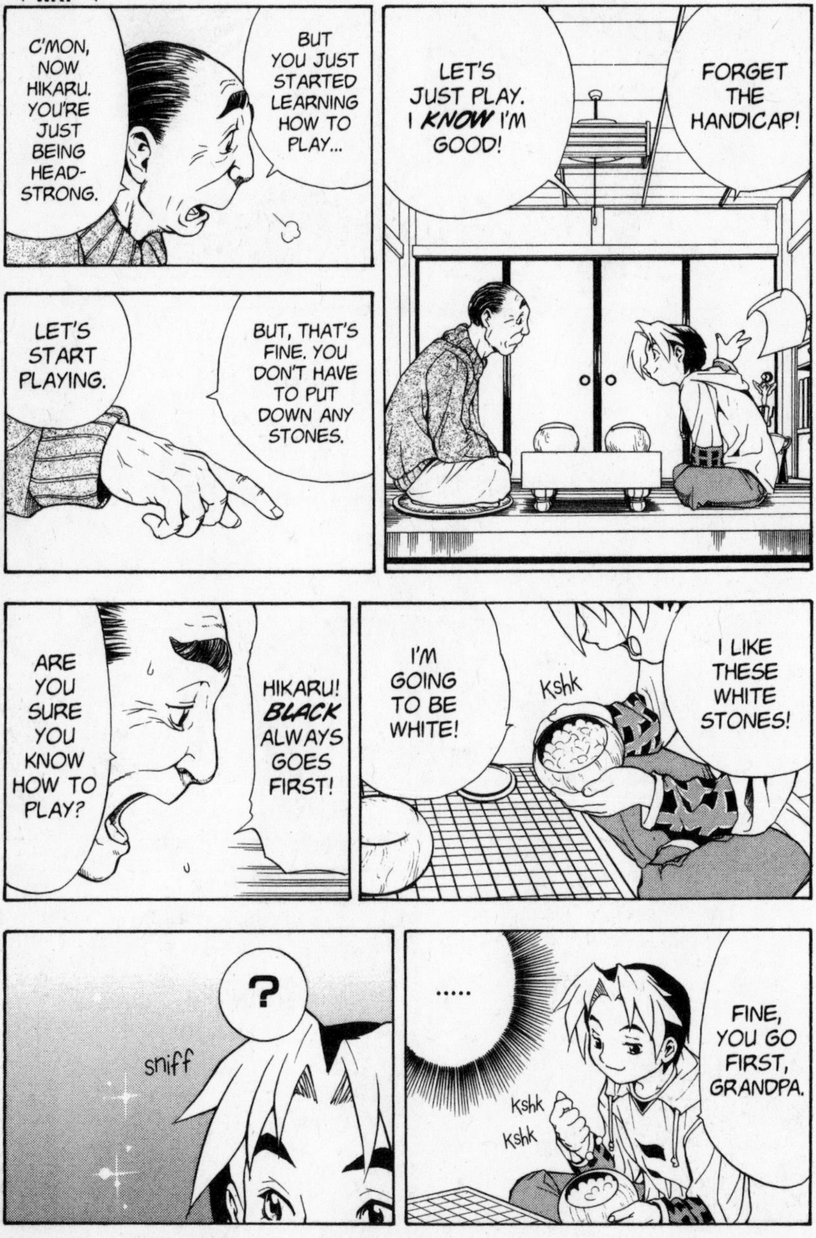
FORGET THE HANDICAP!
LET'S JUST PLAY. I *KNOW* I'M GOOD!
BUT YOU JUST STARTED LEARNING HOW TO PLAY...
C'MON, NOW HIKARU. YOU'RE JUST BEING HEAD-STRONG.
BUT, THAT'S FINE. YOU DON'T HAVE TO PUT DOWN ANY STONES.
LET'S START PLAYING.
I LIKE THESE WHITE STONES!
Kshk
I'M GOING TO BE WHITE!
HIKARU! *BLACK* ALWAYS GOES FIRST!
ARE YOU SURE YOU KNOW HOW TO PLAY?
FINE, YOU GO FIRST, GRANDPA.
Kshk
Kshk
.....
?
sniff

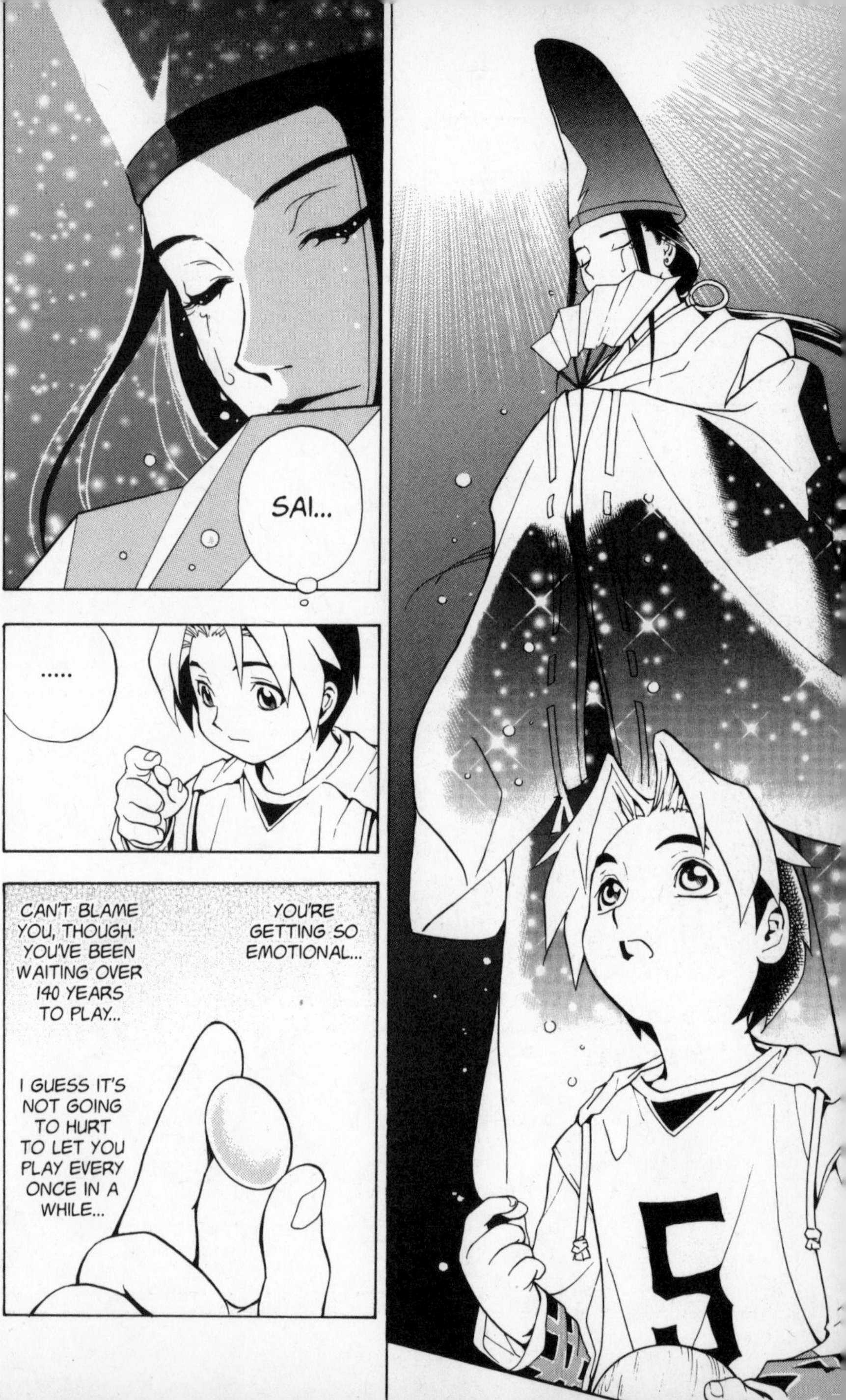
SAI...
.....
YOU'RE GETTING SO EMOTIONAL...
CAN'T BLAME YOU, THOUGH. YOU'VE BEEN WAITING OVER 140 YEARS TO PLAY...
I GUESS IT'S NOT GOING TO HURT TO LET YOU PLAY EVERY ONCE IN A WHILE...

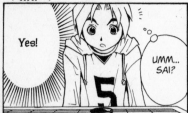

READ THIS WAY

OKAY HIKARU, HERE WE GO...
KLAK
UMM... SAI?
Yes!
A star point... on the first move...
STAR POINT?
Look at the board. There are nine points marked by black dots.
NINE BLACK DOTS...
They are called "Star Points."
In Shusaku's time, it was unheard of to play an opening move on a star point.
Hmm...
The game must have advanced quite a bit in the past 140 years...
!

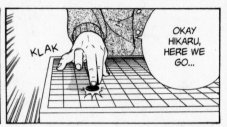

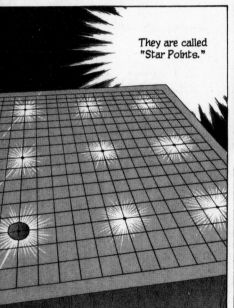

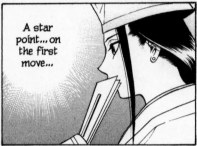

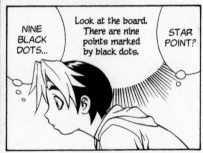

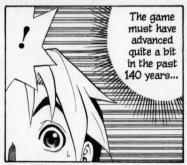

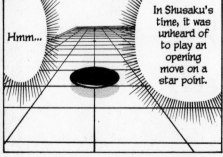

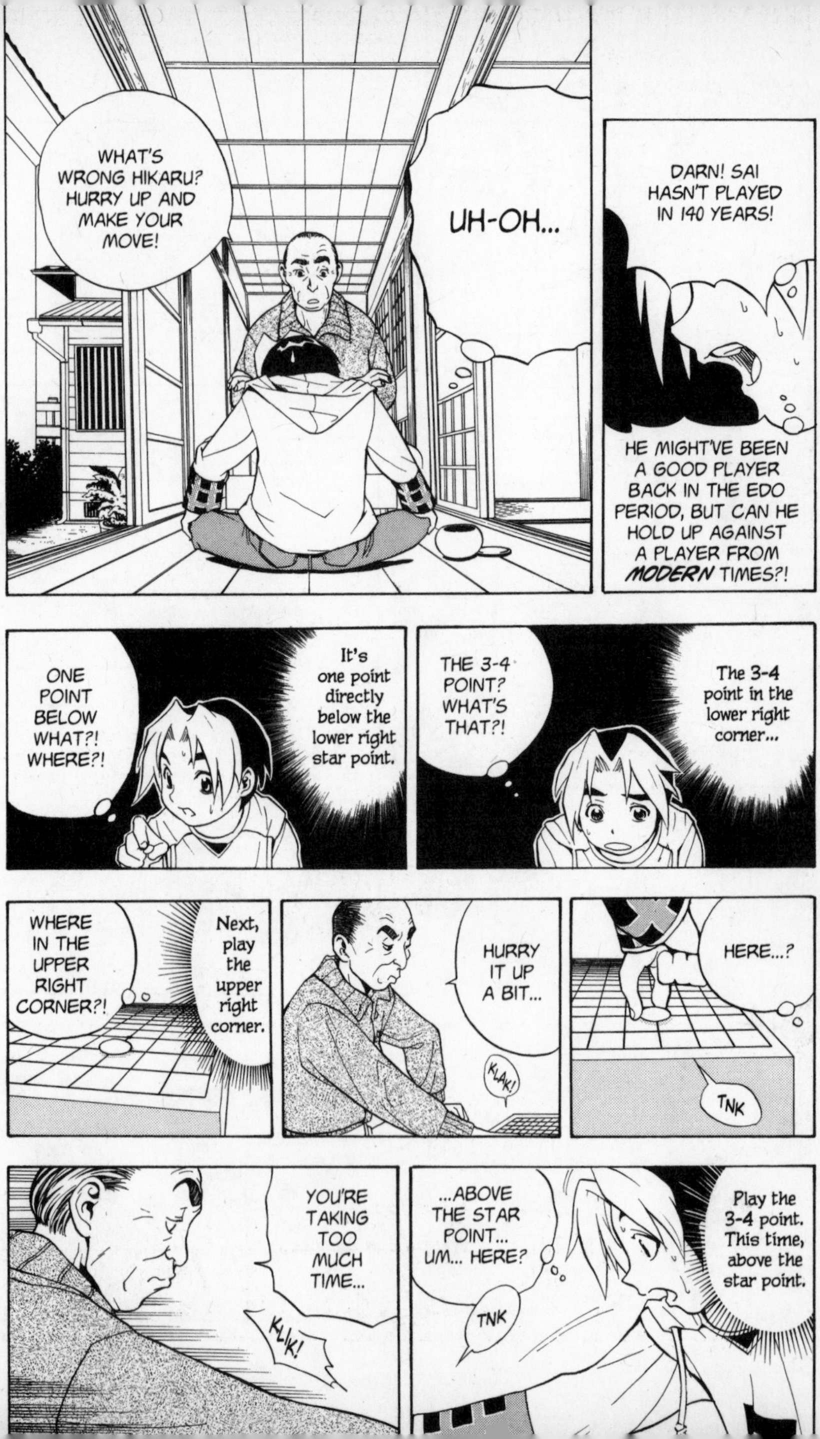
DARN! SAI HASN'T PLAYED IN 140 YEARS!
HE MIGHT'VE BEEN A GOOD PLAYER BACK IN THE EDO PERIOD, BUT CAN HE HOLD UP AGAINST A PLAYER FROM *MODERN* TIMES?!
UH-OH...
WHAT'S WRONG HIKARU? HURRY UP AND MAKE YOUR MOVE!
The 3-4 point in the lower right corner...
THE 3-4 POINT? WHAT'S THAT?!
It's one point directly below the lower right star point.
ONE POINT BELOW WHAT?! WHERE?!
HERE...?
TNK
HURRY IT UP A BIT...
KLAK!
Next, play the upper right corner.
WHERE IN THE UPPER RIGHT CORNER?!
Play the 3-4 point. This time, above the star point.
...ABOVE THE STAR POINT... UM... HERE?
TNK
YOU'RE TAKING TOO MUCH TIME...
KLIK!

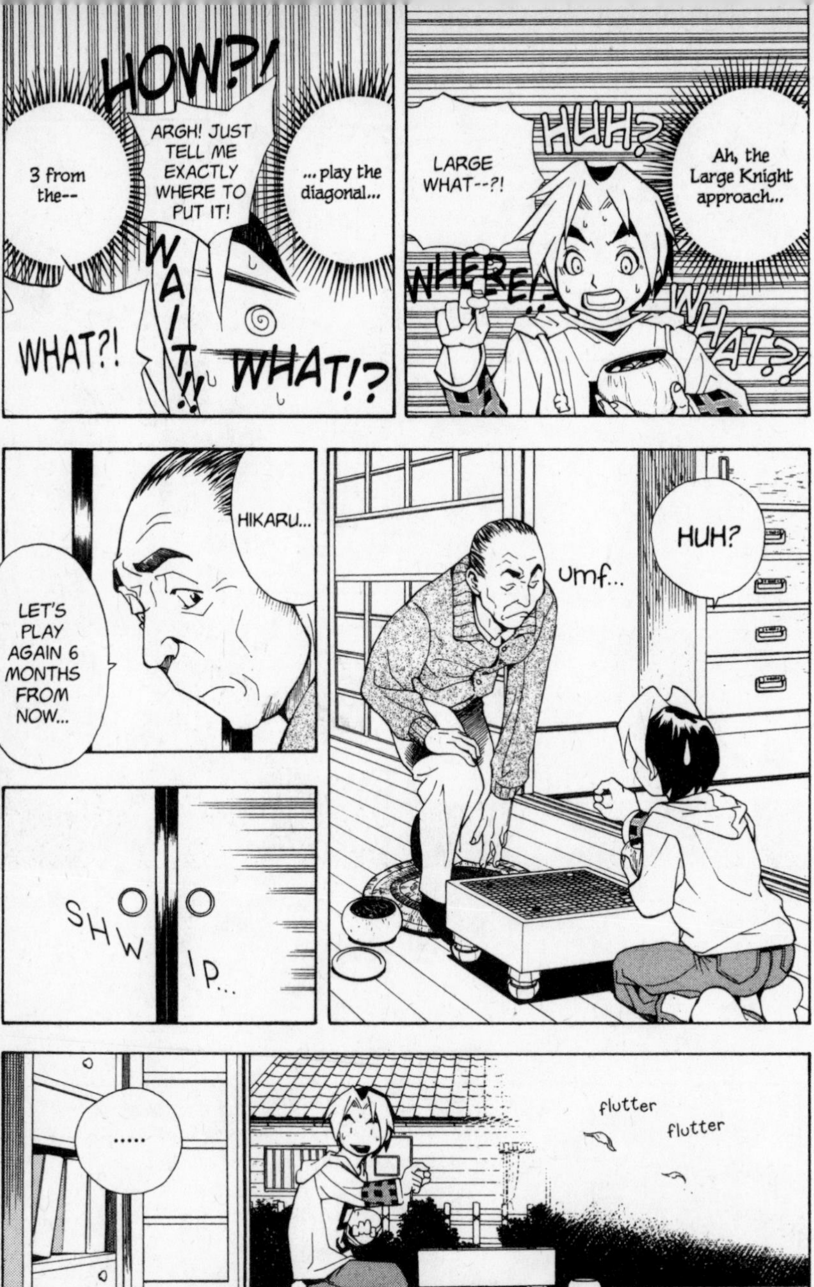
Ah, the Large Knight approach...
HUH?
LARGE WHAT--?!
WHAT?!
WHERE?!
... play the diagonal...
HOW?!
ARGH! JUST TELL ME EXACTLY WHERE TO PUT IT!
3 from the--
WHAT!?
WAIT!!
WHAT?!
HUH?
umf...
HIKARU...
LET'S PLAY AGAIN 6 MONTHS FROM NOW...
SHWIP...
flutter
flutter
......

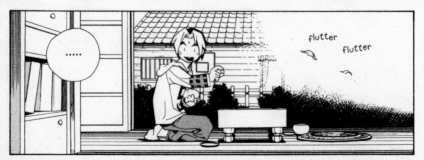

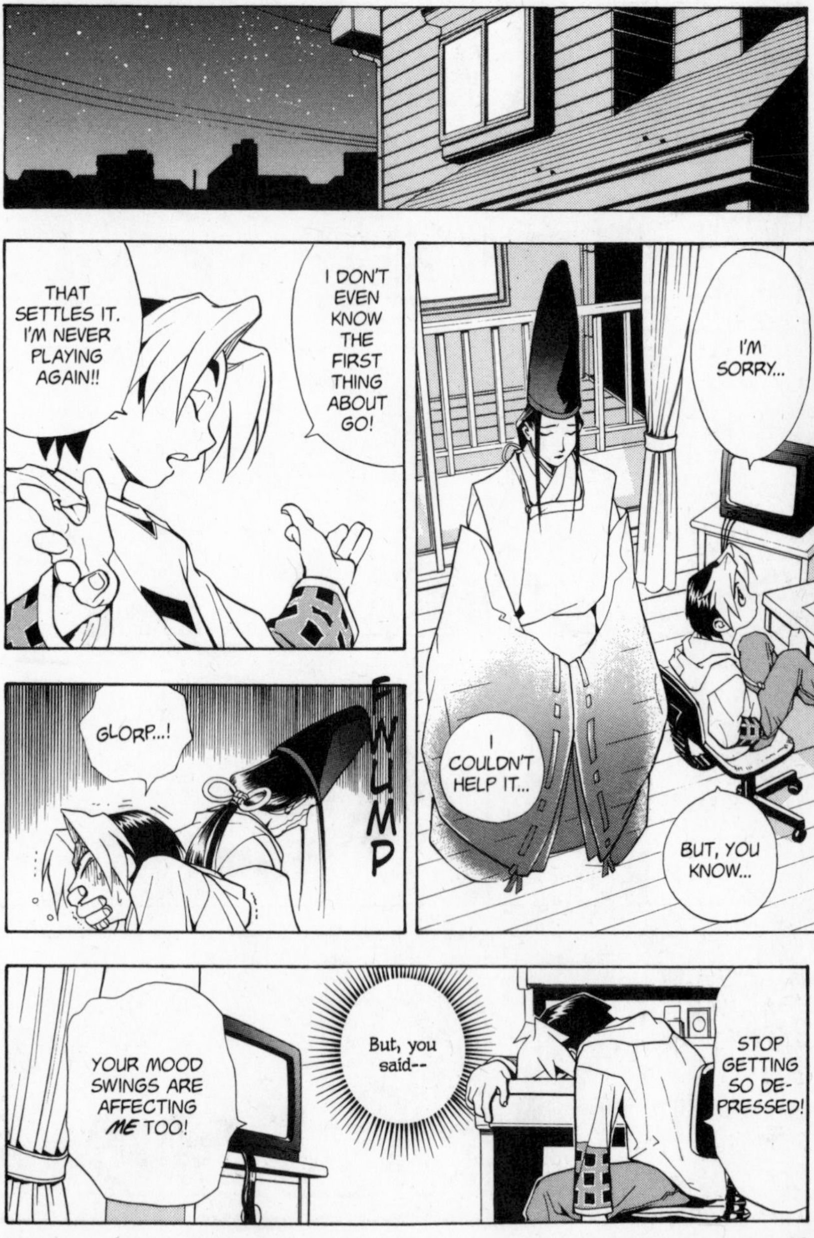
I'M SORRY...
I COULDN'T HELP IT...
BUT, YOU KNOW...
I DON'T EVEN KNOW THE FIRST THING ABOUT GO!
THAT SETTLES IT. I'M NEVER PLAYING AGAIN!!
FWUMP
GLORP...!
STOP GETTING SO DE-PRESSED!
But, you said--
YOUR MOOD SWINGS ARE AFFECTING ME TOO!

READ THIS WAY

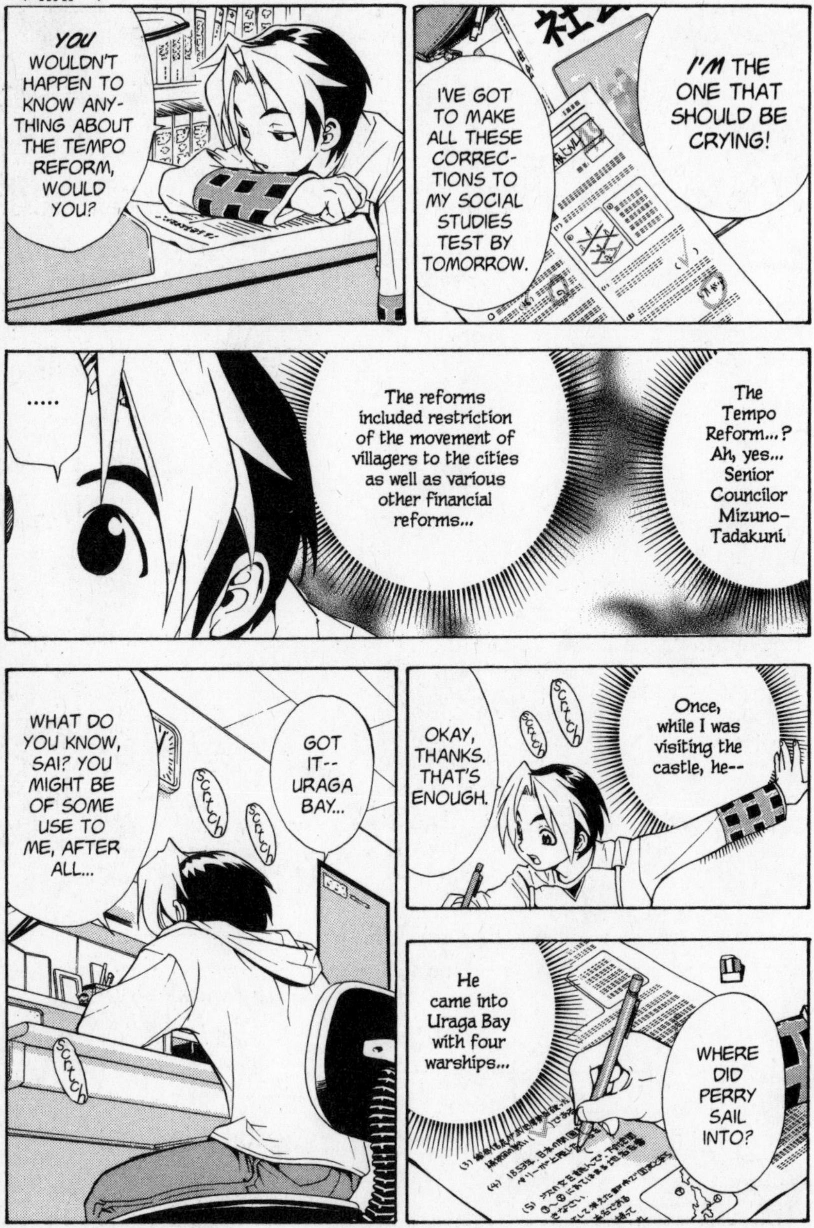

I'M THE ONE THAT SHOULD BE CRYING!
I'VE GOT TO MAKE ALL THESE CORRECTIONS TO MY SOCIAL STUDIES TEST BY TOMORROW.
YOU WOULDN'T HAPPEN TO KNOW ANYTHING ABOUT THE TEMPO REFORM, WOULD YOU?
The Tempo Reform...? Ah, yes... Senior Councilor Mizuno-Tadakuni.
The reforms included restriction of the movement of villagers to the cities as well as various other financial reforms...
.....
Once, while I was visiting the castle, he--
Scratch
Scratch
OKAY, THANKS. THAT'S ENOUGH.
WHERE DID PERRY SAIL INTO?
He came into Uraga Bay with four warships...
GOT IT-- URAGA BAY...
Scratch
Scratch
WHAT DO YOU KNOW, SAI? YOU MIGHT BE OF SOME USE TO ME, AFTER ALL...
Scratch

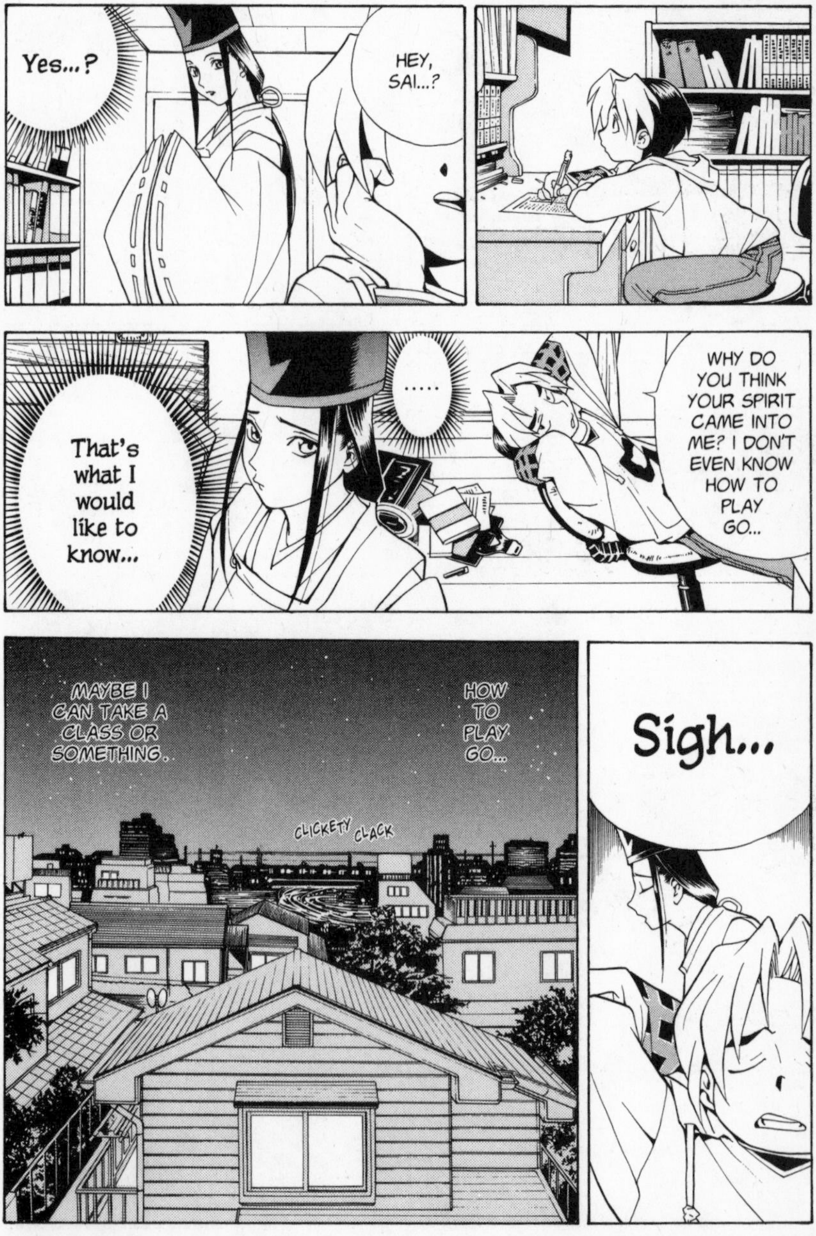
HEY, SAI...?
Yes...?
WHY DO YOU THINK YOUR SPIRIT CAME INTO ME? I DON'T EVEN KNOW HOW TO PLAY GO...
.....
That's what I would like to know...
Sigh...
HOW TO PLAY GO...
MAYBE I CAN TAKE A CLASS OR SOMETHING.
CLICKETY CLACK

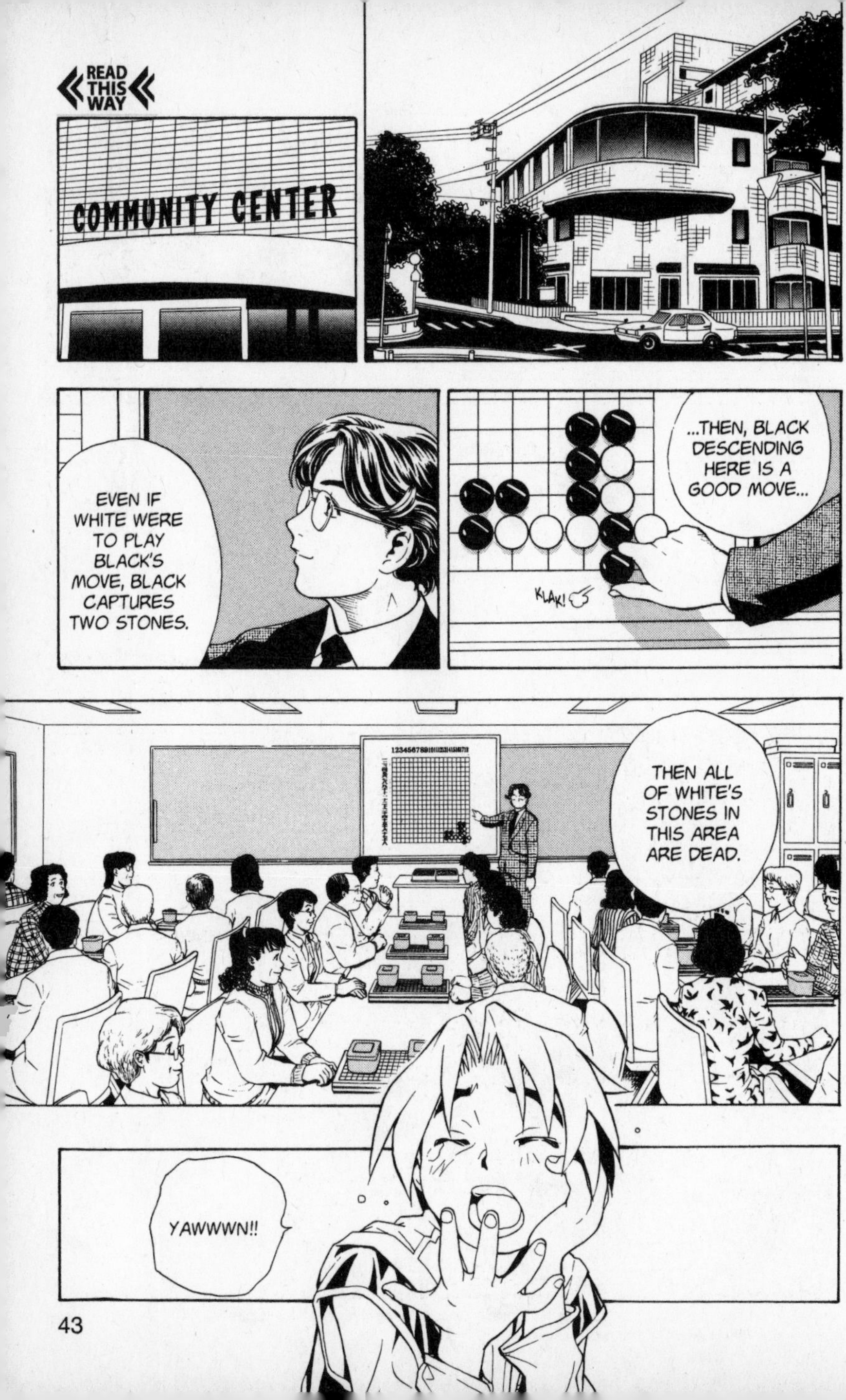
READ THIS WAY
COMMUNITY CENTER
...THEN, BLACK DESCENDING HERE IS A GOOD MOVE...
KLAK!
EVEN IF WHITE WERE TO PLAY BLACK'S MOVE, BLACK CAPTURES TWO STONES.
THEN ALL OF WHITE'S STONES IN THIS AREA ARE DEAD.
YAWWWN!!

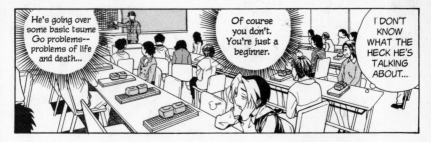

I DON'T KNOW WHAT THE HECK HE'S TALKING ABOUT...
Of course you don't. You're just a beginner.
He's going over some basic tsume Go problems--problems of life and death...
I wonder how good a player this instructor is...
HE'S A PRO...
A pro...?
YEAH, HE MAKES A LIVING OFF OF PLAYING GO.
THAT'S IT FOR MY LECTURE. LET'S START PLAYING SOME GAMES...
SKOOT
ONEGAISHIMASU...*
CLATTER
SKOOT
ONEGAISHIMASU...
CLATTER
YOU MUST BE HIKARU SHINDO...
HAVE YOU EVER PLAYED GO, BEFORE?
UMM...
NO, I DON'T KNOW A THING ABOUT GO...

*Onegaishimasu: a standard greeting to one's opponent before starting a game. Also, literally meaning, "to make a request."

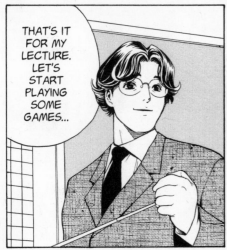

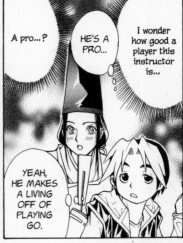

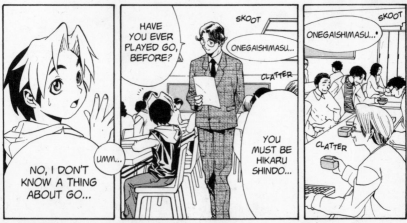

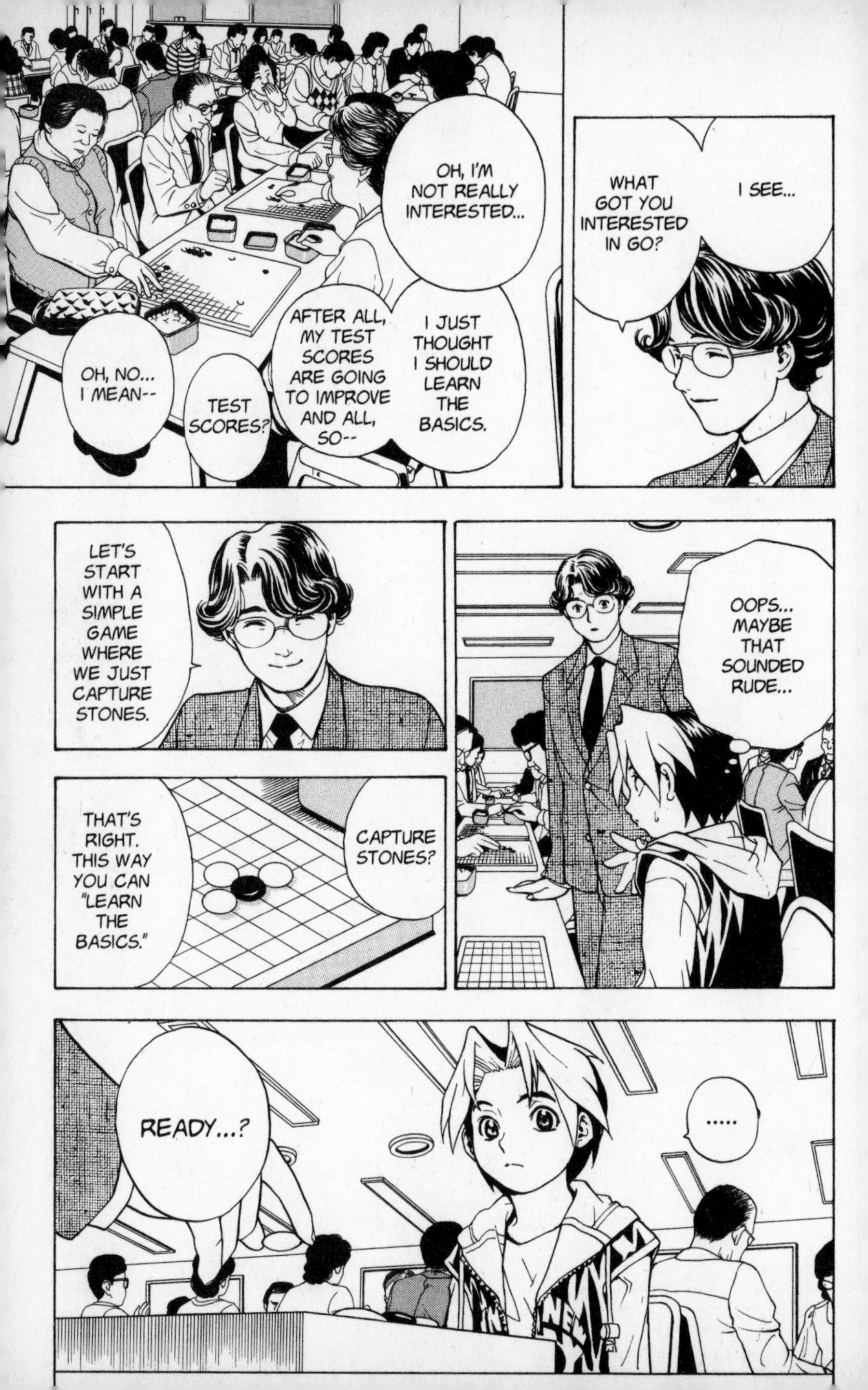
I SEE...
WHAT GOT YOU INTERESTED IN GO?
OH, I'M NOT REALLY INTERESTED...
I JUST THOUGHT I SHOULD LEARN THE BASICS.
AFTER ALL, MY TEST SCORES ARE GOING TO IMPROVE AND ALL, SO--
TEST SCORES?
OH, NO... I MEAN--
OOPS... MAYBE THAT SOUNDED RUDE...
LET'S START WITH A SIMPLE GAME WHERE WE JUST CAPTURE STONES.
CAPTURE STONES?
THAT'S RIGHT. THIS WAY YOU CAN "LEARN THE BASICS."
.....
READY...?

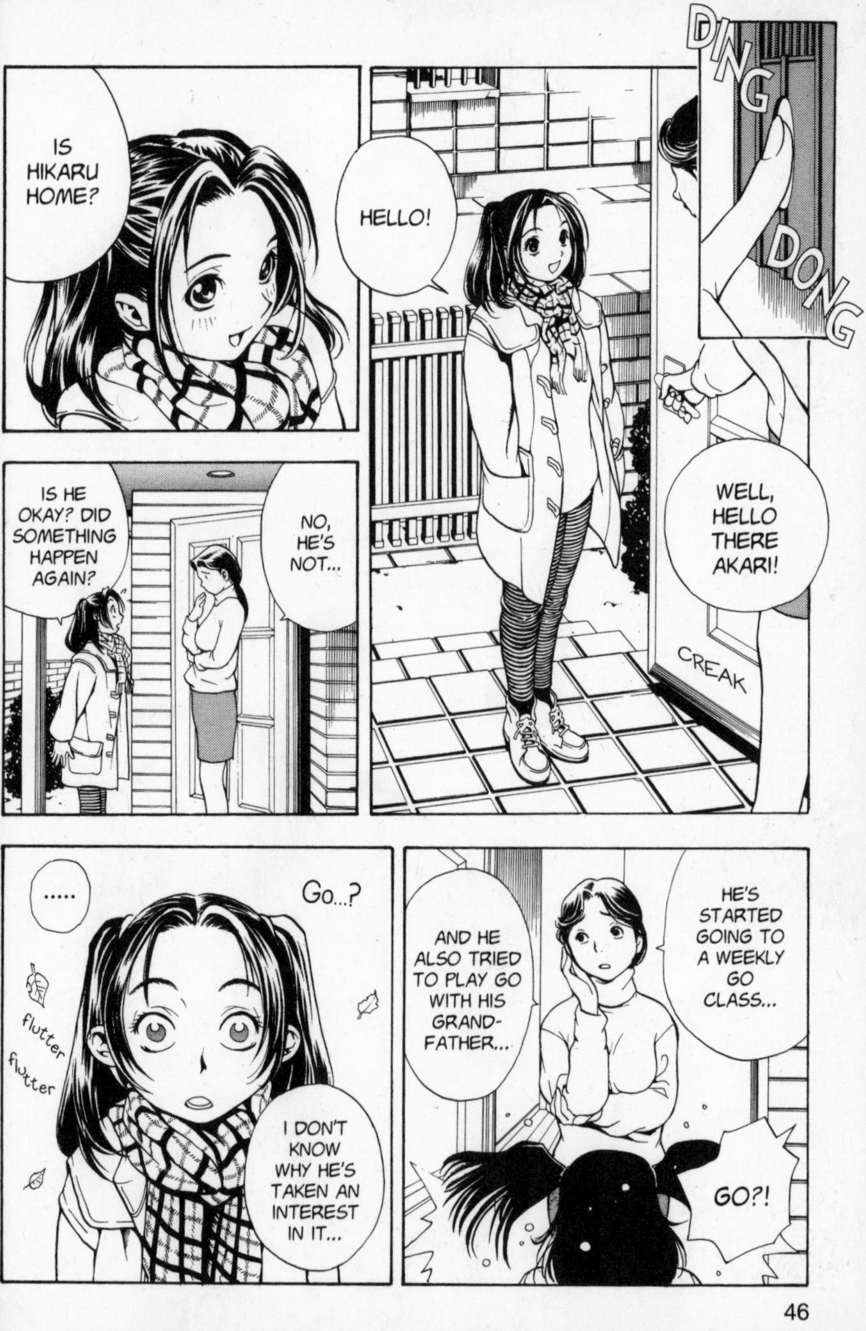
DING DONG
WELL, HELLO THERE AKARI!
HELLO!
CREAK
IS HIKARU HOME?
NO, HE'S NOT...
IS HE OKAY? DID SOMETHING HAPPEN AGAIN?
HE'S STARTED GOING TO A WEEKLY GO CLASS...
AND HE ALSO TRIED TO PLAY GO WITH HIS GRAND-FATHER...
GO?!
Go...?
.....
I DON'T KNOW WHY HE'S TAKEN AN INTEREST IN IT...
flutter
flutter

READ THIS WAY

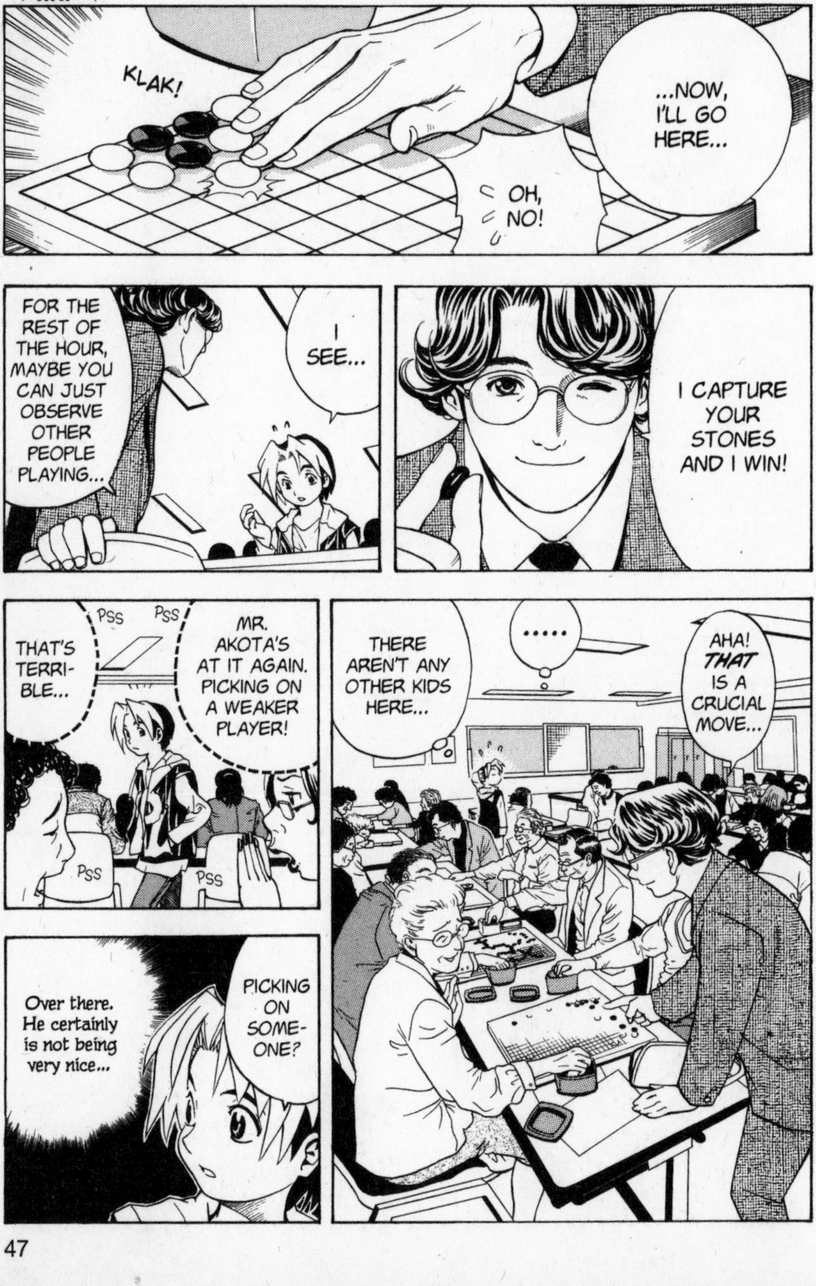
...NOW, I'LL GO HERE...
KLAK!
OH, NO!
I CAPTURE YOUR STONES AND I WIN!
I SEE...
FOR THE REST OF THE HOUR, MAYBE YOU CAN JUST OBSERVE OTHER PEOPLE PLAYING...
AHA! *THAT* IS A CRUCIAL MOVE...
......
THERE AREN'T ANY OTHER KIDS HERE...
PSS
PSS
MR. AKOTA'S AT IT AGAIN. PICKING ON A WEAKER PLAYER!
THAT'S TERRI-BLE...
PSS
PSS
PICKING ON SOME-ONE?
Over there. He certainly is not being very nice...

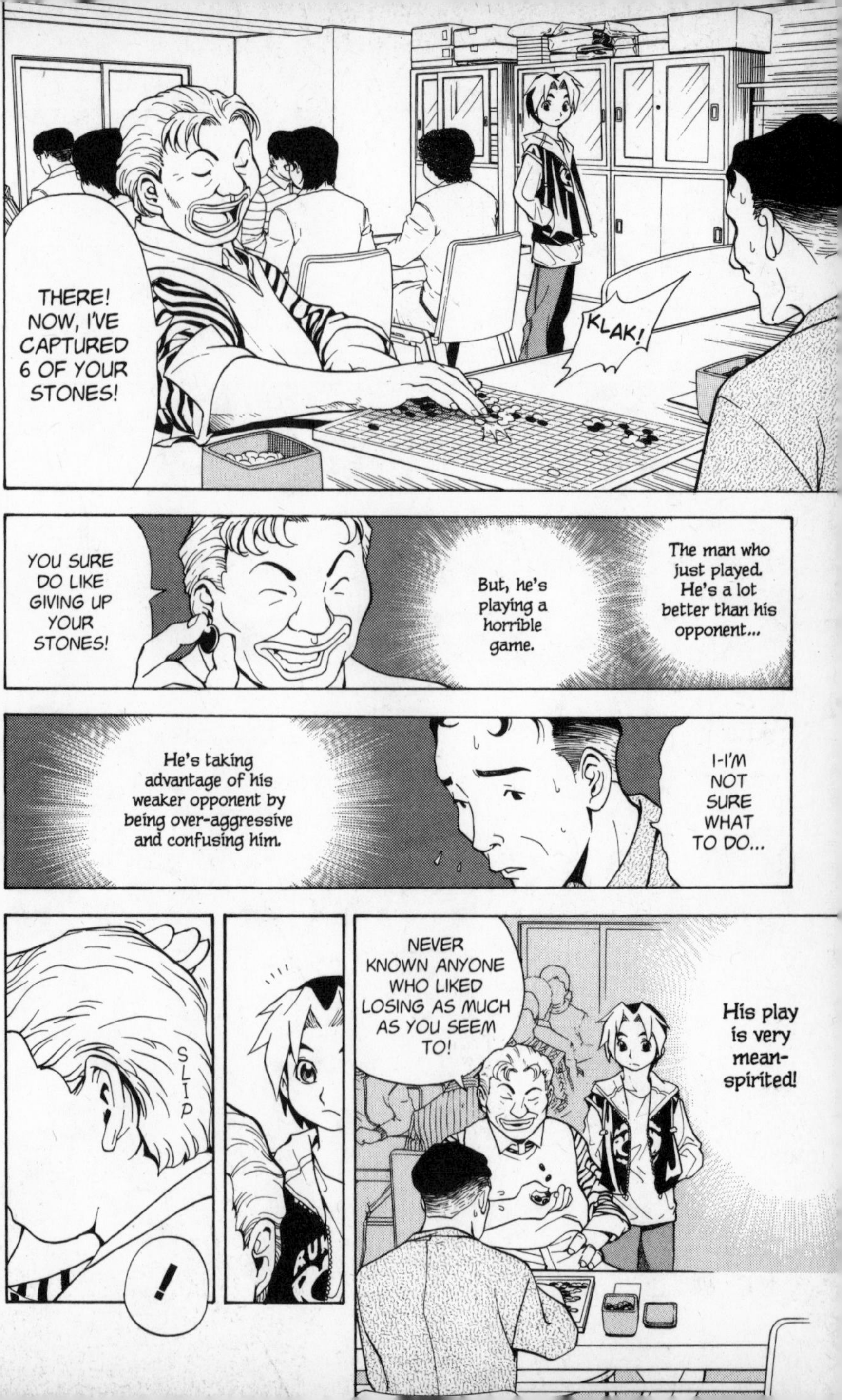
KLAK!
THERE! NOW, I'VE CAPTURED 6 OF YOUR STONES!
The man who just played. He's a lot better than his opponent...
But, he's playing a horrible game.
YOU SURE DO LIKE GIVING UP YOUR STONES!
I-I'M NOT SURE WHAT TO DO...
He's taking advantage of his weaker opponent by being over-aggressive and confusing him.
His play is very mean-spirited!
NEVER KNOWN ANYONE WHO LIKED LOSING AS MUCH AS YOU SEEM TO!
SLIP
!

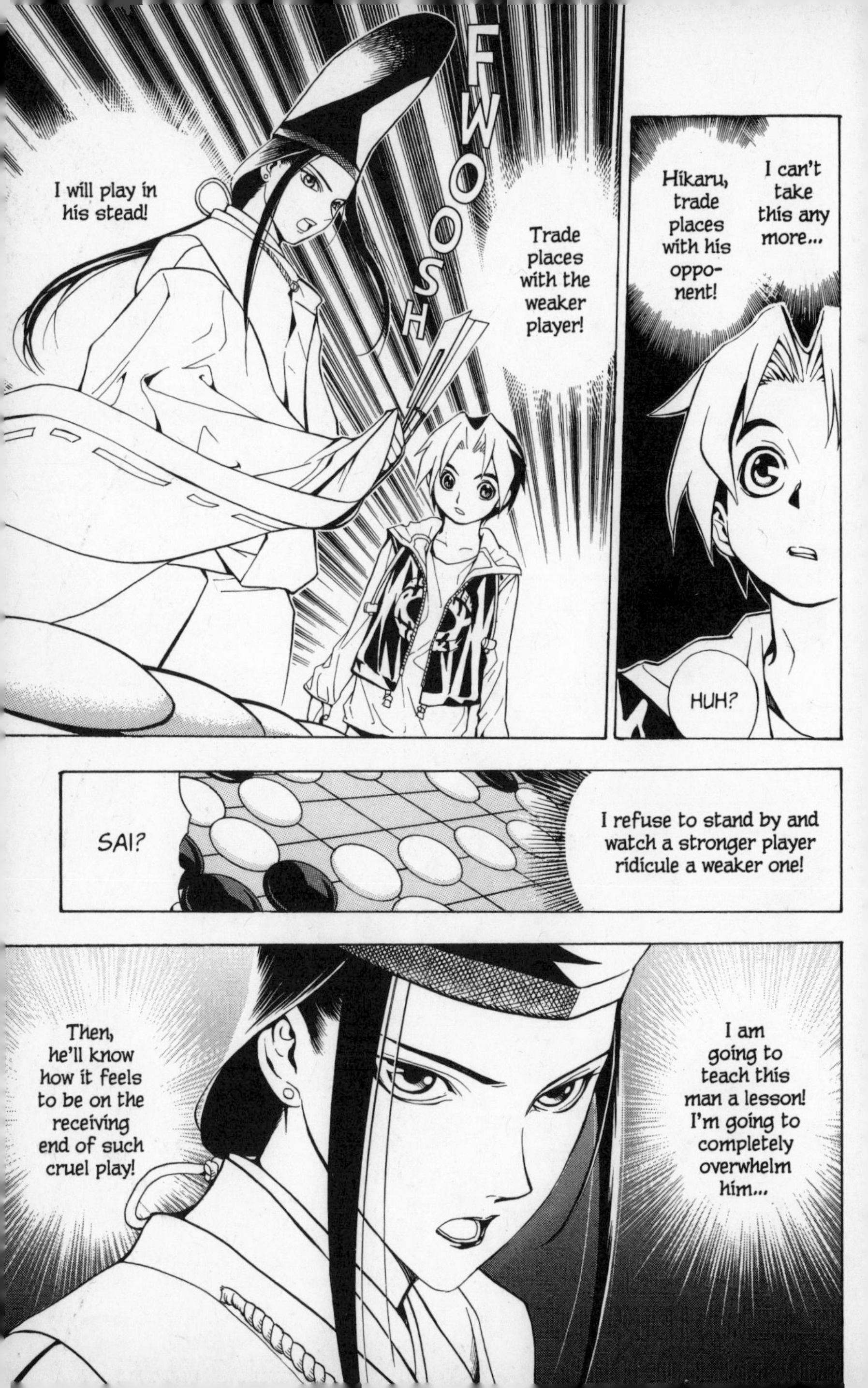
I can't take this any more...
Hikaru, trade places with his opponent!
HUH?
FWOOSH
Trade places with the weaker player!
I will play in his stead!
I refuse to stand by and watch a stronger player ridicule a weaker one!
SAI?
I am going to teach this man a lesson! I'm going to completely overwhelm him...
Then, he'll know how it feels to be on the receiving end of such cruel play!

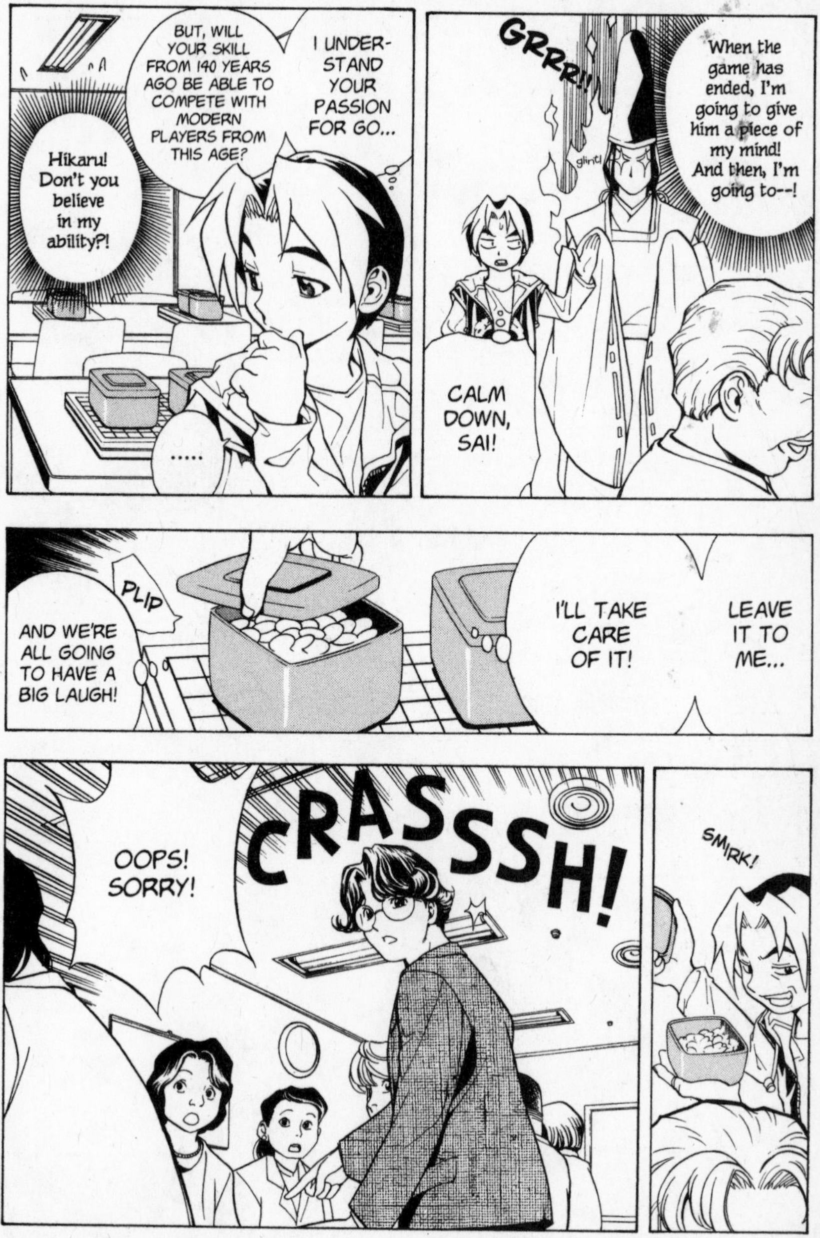
GRRRR!!
When the game has ended, I'm going to give him a piece of my mind! And then, I'm going to--!
glint!
CALM DOWN, SAI!
I UNDER-STAND YOUR PASSION FOR GO...
BUT, WILL YOUR SKILL FROM 140 YEARS AGO BE ABLE TO COMPETE WITH MODERN PLAYERS FROM THIS AGE?
Hikaru! Don't you believe in my ability?!
.....
LEAVE IT TO ME...
I'LL TAKE CARE OF IT!
PLIP
AND WE'RE ALL GOING TO HAVE A BIG LAUGH!
SMIRK!
CRASSSH!
OOPS! SORRY!

READ THIS WAY

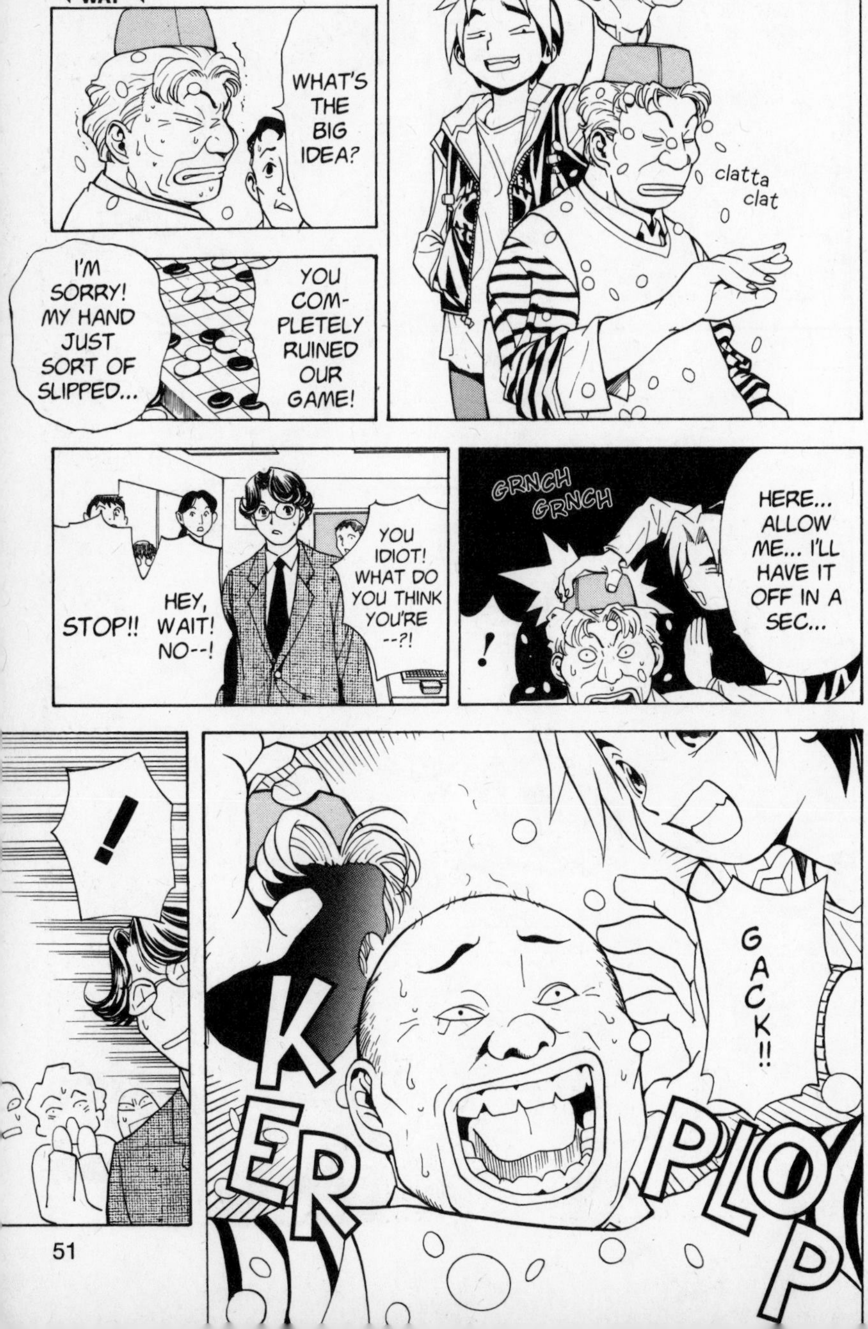
clatta clat
WHAT'S THE BIG IDEA?
YOU COMPLETELY RUINED OUR GAME!
I'M SORRY! MY HAND JUST SORT OF SLIPPED...
GRNCH GRNCH
HERE... ALLOW ME... I'LL HAVE IT OFF IN A SEC...
!
YOU IDIOT! WHAT DO YOU THINK YOU'RE --?!
HEY, WAIT! NO--!
STOP!!
GACK!!
KER PLOP
!

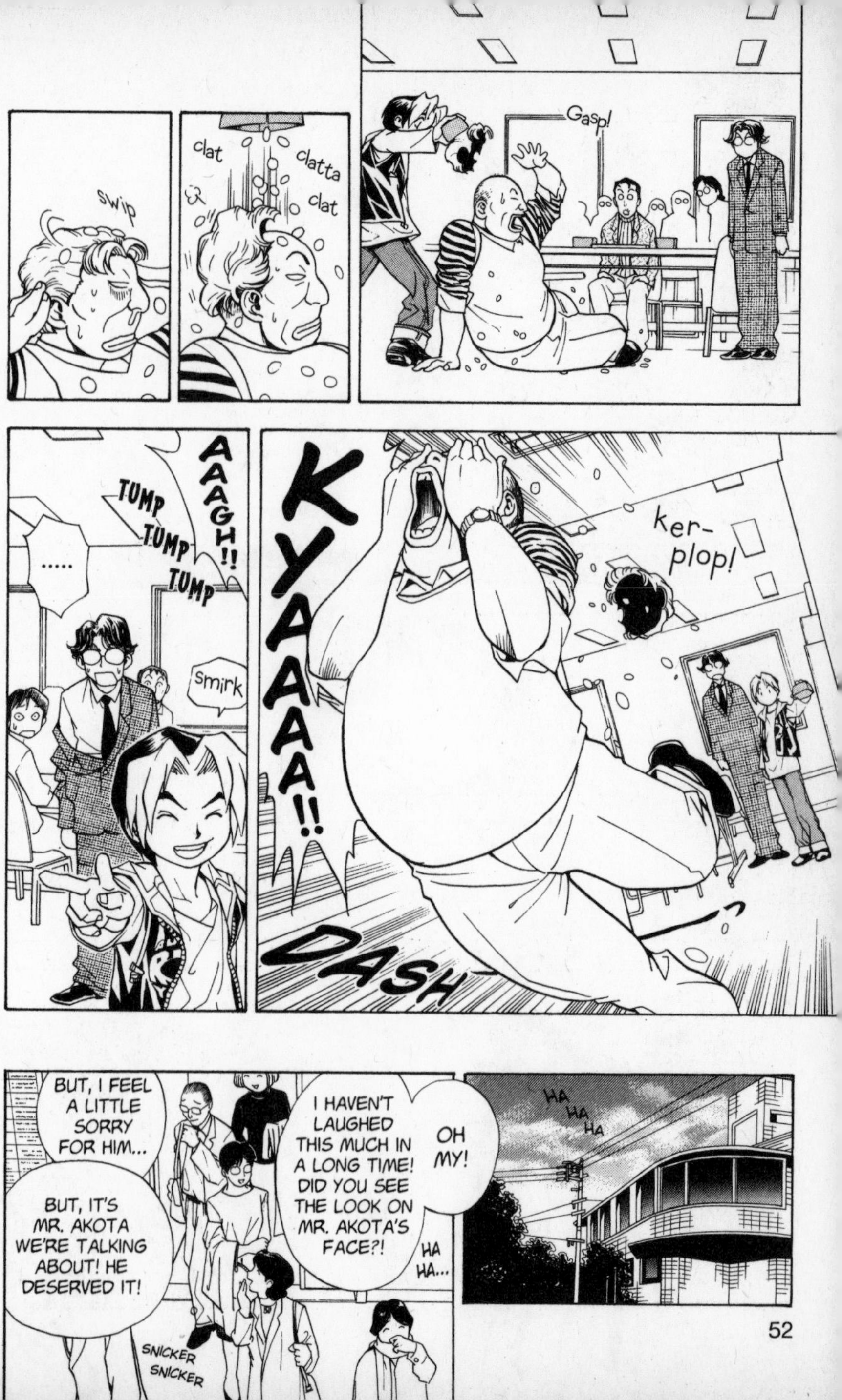
Gasp!
clat
clatta
clat
swip
KYAAAAA!!
DASH
ker-plop!
AAAGH!!
TUMP
TUMP
TUMP
.....
smirk
HA
HA
HA
OH MY!
I HAVEN'T LAUGHED THIS MUCH IN A LONG TIME! DID YOU SEE THE LOOK ON MR. AKOTA'S FACE?!
HA HA...
BUT, I FEEL A LITTLE SORRY FOR HIM...
BUT, IT'S MR. AKOTA WE'RE TALKING ABOUT! HE DESERVED IT!
SNICKER SNICKER

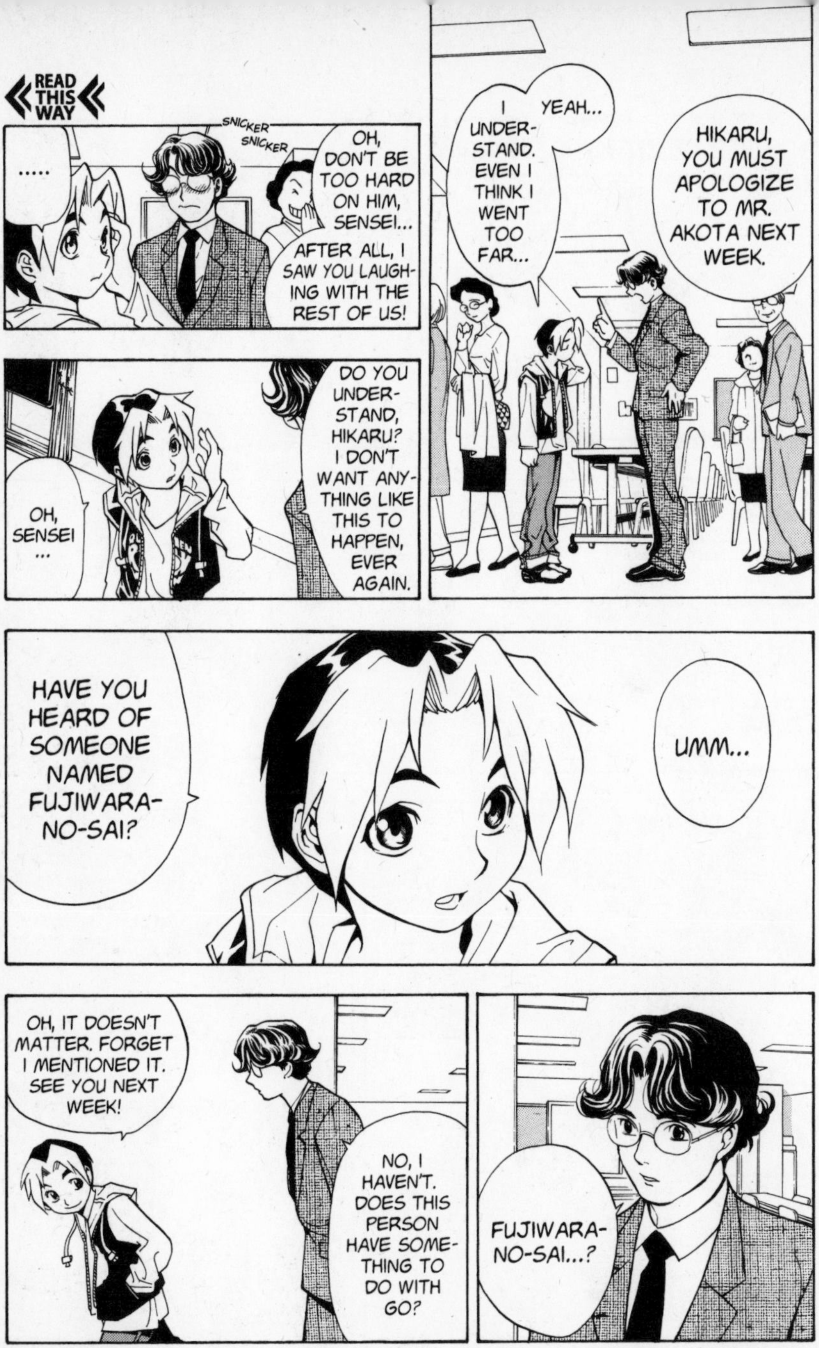
READ THIS WAY
HIKARU, YOU MUST APOLOGIZE TO MR. AKOTA NEXT WEEK.
YEAH...
I UNDERSTAND. EVEN I THINK I WENT TOO FAR...
OH, DON'T BE TOO HARD ON HIM, SENSEI...
AFTER ALL, I SAW YOU LAUGHING WITH THE REST OF US!
SNICKER SNICKER
......
DO YOU UNDERSTAND, HIKARU? I DON'T WANT ANYTHING LIKE THIS TO HAPPEN, EVER AGAIN.
OH, SENSEI ...
UMM...
HAVE YOU HEARD OF SOMEONE NAMED FUJIWARA-NO-SAI?
FUJIWARA-NO-SAI...?
NO, I HAVEN'T. DOES THIS PERSON HAVE SOMETHING TO DO WITH GO?
OH, IT DOESN'T MATTER. FORGET I MENTIONED IT. SEE YOU NEXT WEEK!

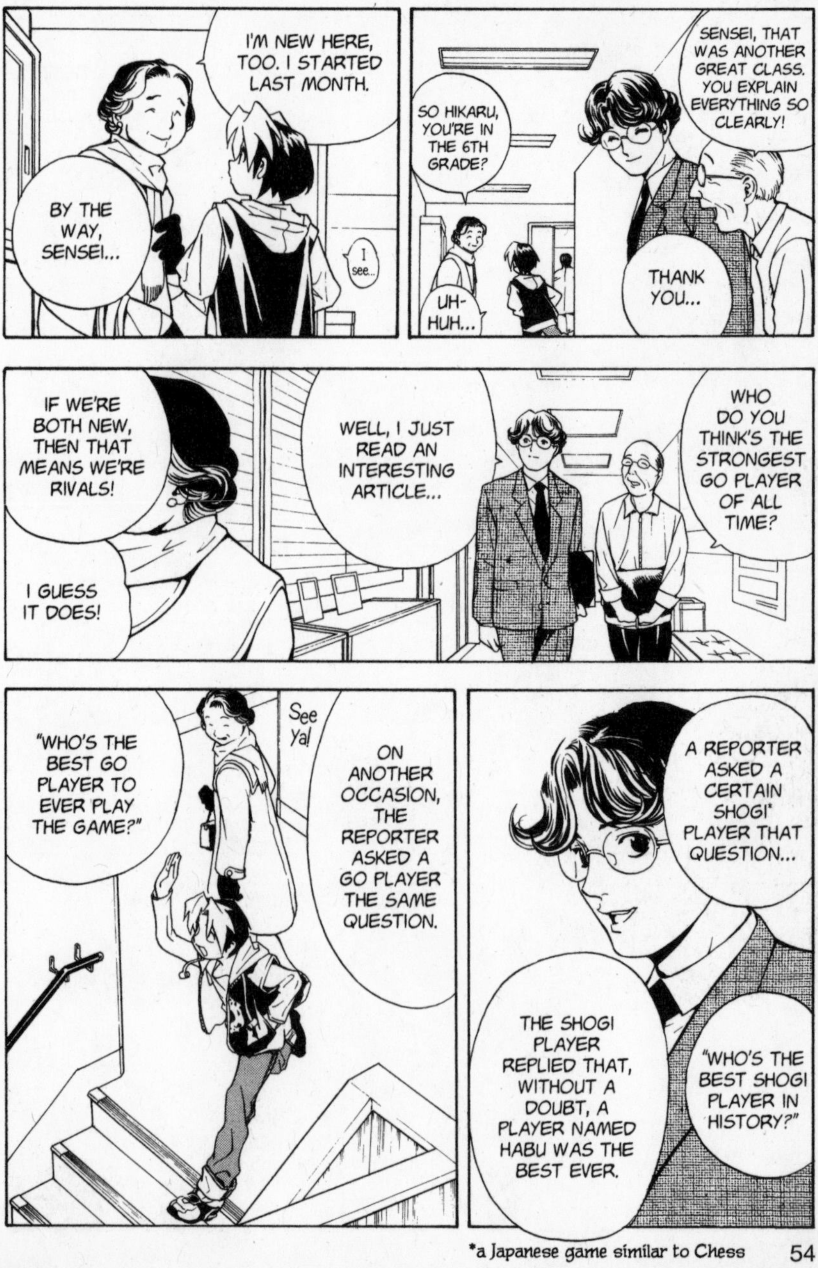
SENSEI, THAT WAS ANOTHER GREAT CLASS. YOU EXPLAIN EVERYTHING SO CLEARLY!
THANK YOU...
SO HIKARU, YOU'RE IN THE 6TH GRADE?
UH-HUH...
I'M NEW HERE, TOO. I STARTED LAST MONTH.
I see...
BY THE WAY, SENSEI...
WHO DO YOU THINK'S THE STRONGEST GO PLAYER OF ALL TIME?
WELL, I JUST READ AN INTERESTING ARTICLE...
IF WE'RE BOTH NEW, THEN THAT MEANS WE'RE RIVALS!
I GUESS IT DOES!
A REPORTER ASKED A CERTAIN SHOGI* PLAYER THAT QUESTION...
"WHO'S THE BEST SHOGI PLAYER IN HISTORY?"
THE SHOGI PLAYER REPLIED THAT, WITHOUT A DOUBT, A PLAYER NAMED HABU WAS THE BEST EVER.
See ya!
ON ANOTHER OCCASION, THE REPORTER ASKED A GO PLAYER THE SAME QUESTION.
"WHO'S THE BEST GO PLAYER TO EVER PLAY THE GAME?"

*a Japanese game similar to Chess

READ THIS WAY

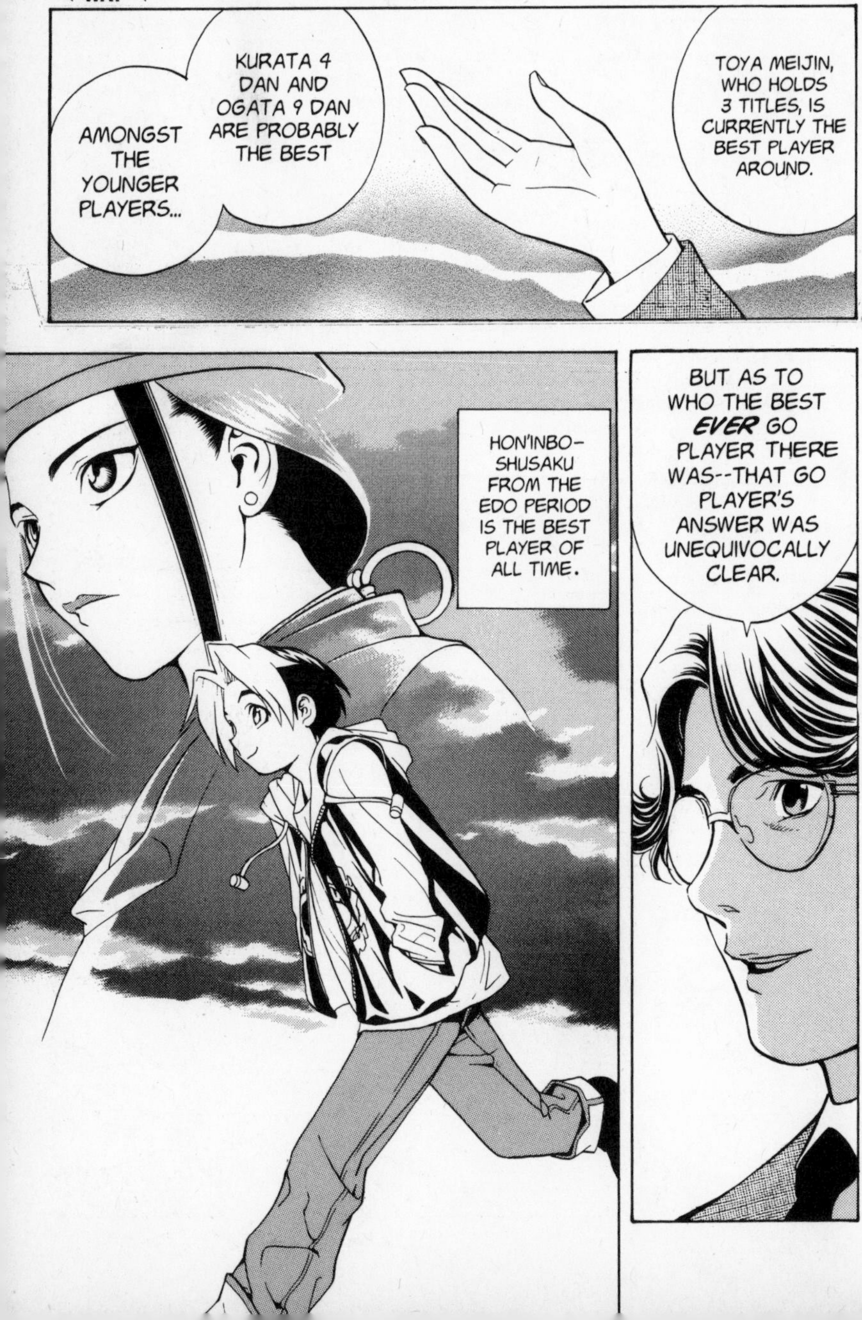
TOYA MEIJIN, WHO HOLDS 3 TITLES, IS CURRENTLY THE BEST PLAYER AROUND.
AMONGST THE YOUNGER PLAYERS...
KURATA 4 DAN AND OGATA 9 DAN ARE PROBABLY THE BEST
BUT AS TO WHO THE BEST *EVER* GO PLAYER THERE WAS--THAT GO PLAYER'S ANSWER WAS UNEQUIVOCALLY CLEAR.
HON'INBO-SHUSAKU FROM THE EDO PERIOD IS THE BEST PLAYER OF ALL TIME.

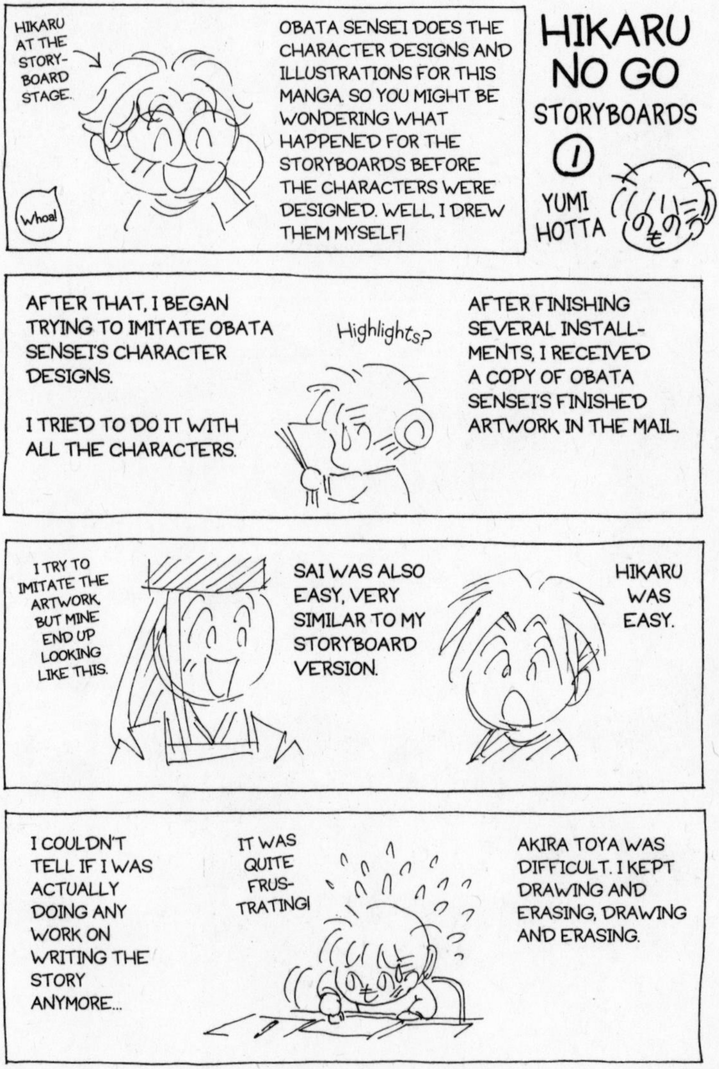
HIKARU NO GO
STORYBOARDS
1
YUMI HOTTA
OBATA SENSEI DOES THE CHARACTER DESIGNS AND ILLUSTRATIONS FOR THIS MANGA. SO YOU MIGHT BE WONDERING WHAT HAPPENED FOR THE STORYBOARDS BEFORE THE CHARACTERS WERE DESIGNED. WELL, I DREW THEM MYSELF!
HIKARU AT THE STORY-BOARD STAGE.
Whoa!
AFTER FINISHING SEVERAL INSTALL-MENTS, I RECEIVED A COPY OF OBATA SENSEI'S FINISHED ARTWORK IN THE MAIL.
Highlights?
AFTER THAT, I BEGAN TRYING TO IMITATE OBATA SENSEI'S CHARACTER DESIGNS.
I TRIED TO DO IT WITH ALL THE CHARACTERS.
HIKARU WAS EASY.
SAI WAS ALSO EASY, VERY SIMILAR TO MY STORYBOARD VERSION.
I TRY TO IMITATE THE ARTWORK, BUT MINE END UP LOOKING LIKE THIS.
AKIRA TOYA WAS DIFFICULT. I KEPT DRAWING AND ERASING, DRAWING AND ERASING.
IT WAS QUITE FRUS-TRATING!
I COULDN'T TELL IF I WAS ACTUALLY DOING ANY WORK ON WRITING THE STORY ANYMORE...

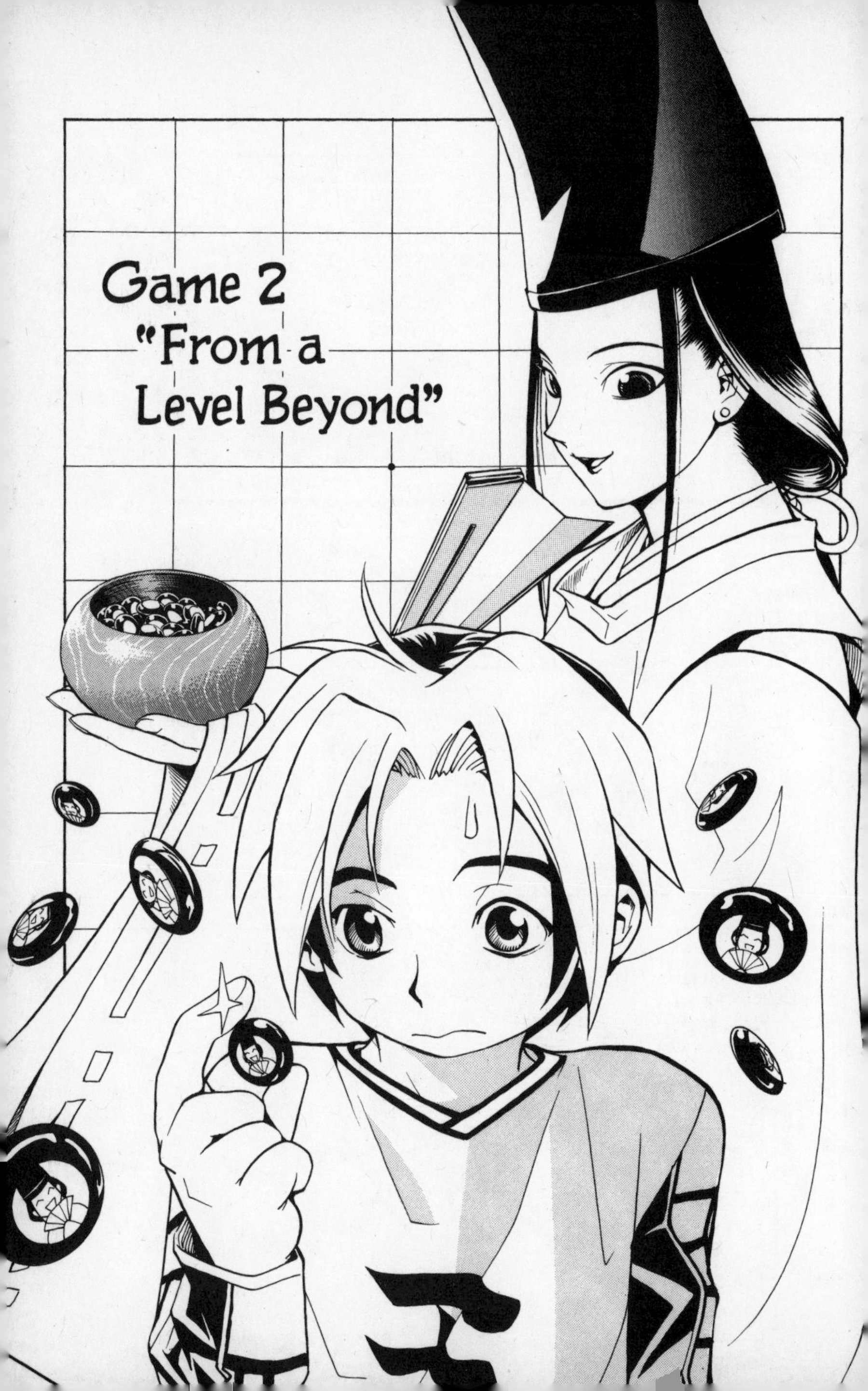

Game 2
"From a
Level Beyond"

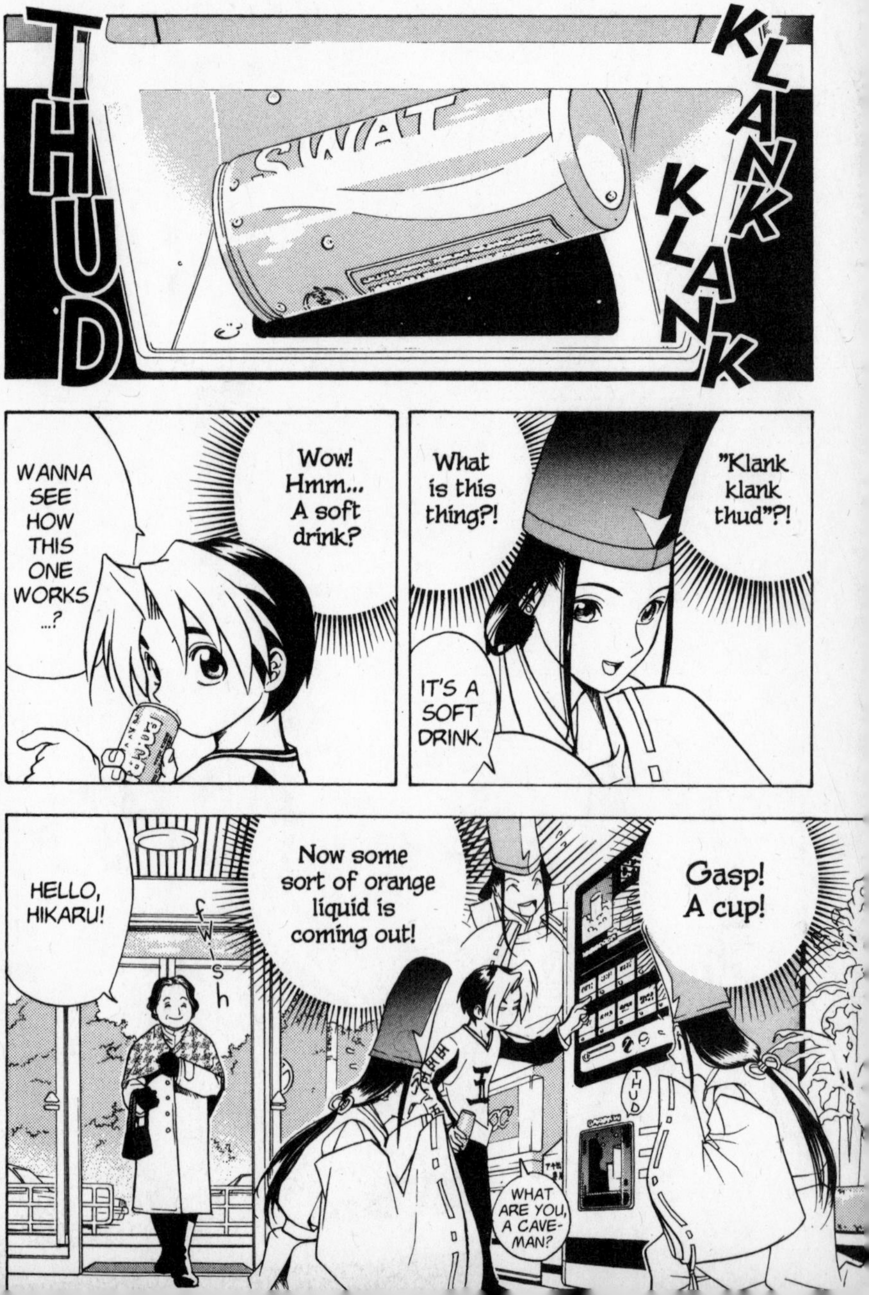
KLANK
KLANK
SWAT
THUD
"Klank klank thud"?!
What is this thing?!
IT'S A SOFT DRINK.
Wow! Hmm... A soft drink?
WANNA SEE HOW THIS ONE WORKS ...?
Gasp! A cup!
THUD
WHAT ARE YOU, A CAVE-MAN?
Now some sort of orange liquid is coming out!
fwish
HELLO, HIKARU!

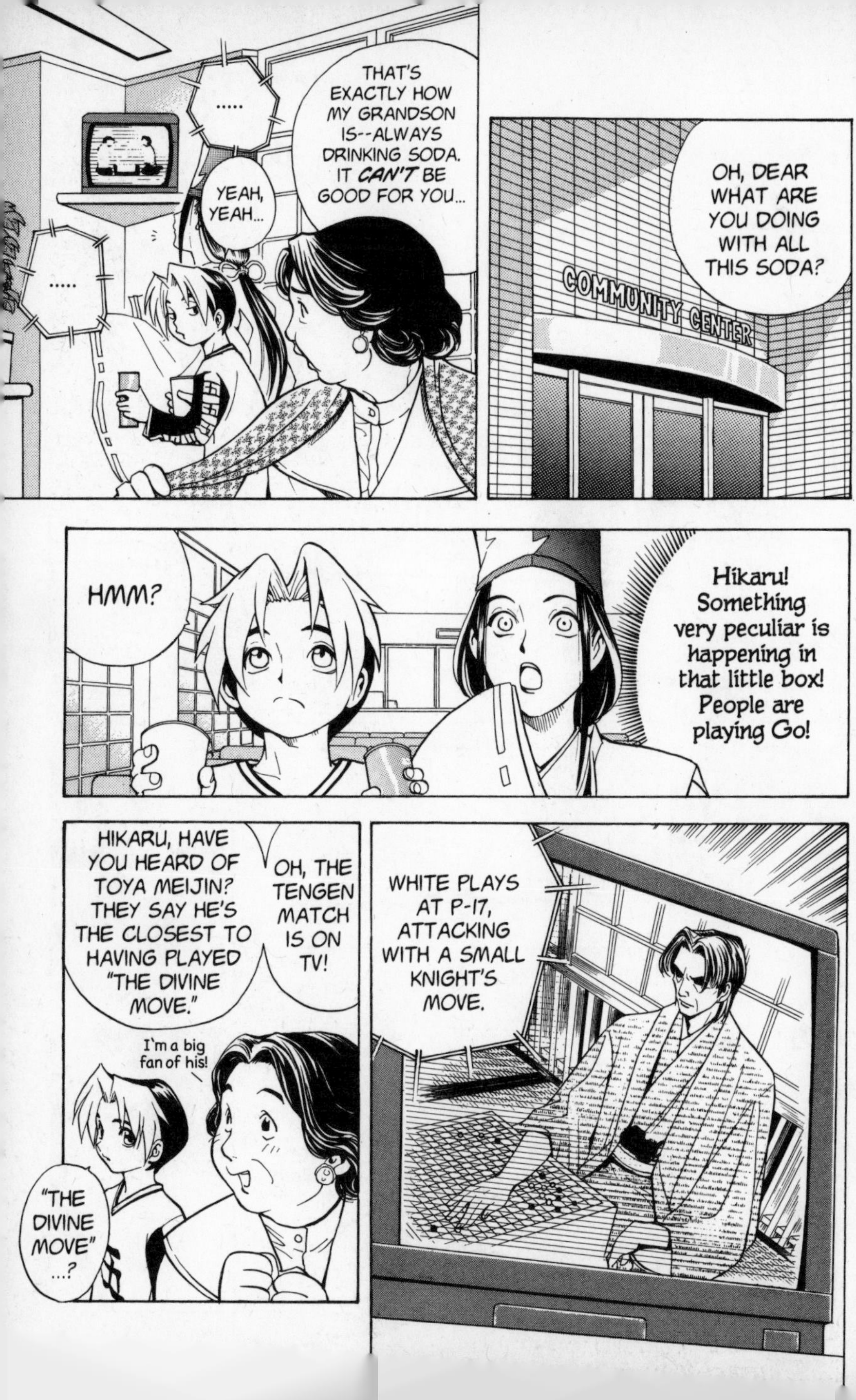

OH, DEAR WHAT ARE YOU DOING WITH ALL THIS SODA?
COMMUNITY CENTER
THAT'S EXACTLY HOW MY GRANDSON IS--ALWAYS DRINKING SODA. IT CAN'T BE GOOD FOR YOU...
.....
YEAH, YEAH...
.....
Hikaru! Something very peculiar is happening in that little box! People are playing Go!
HMM?
WHITE PLAYS AT P-17, ATTACKING WITH A SMALL KNIGHT'S MOVE.
OH, THE TENGEN MATCH IS ON TV!
HIKARU, HAVE YOU HEARD OF TOYA MEIJIN? THEY SAY HE'S THE CLOSEST TO HAVING PLAYED "THE DIVINE MOVE."
I'm a big fan of his!
"THE DIVINE MOVE" ...?

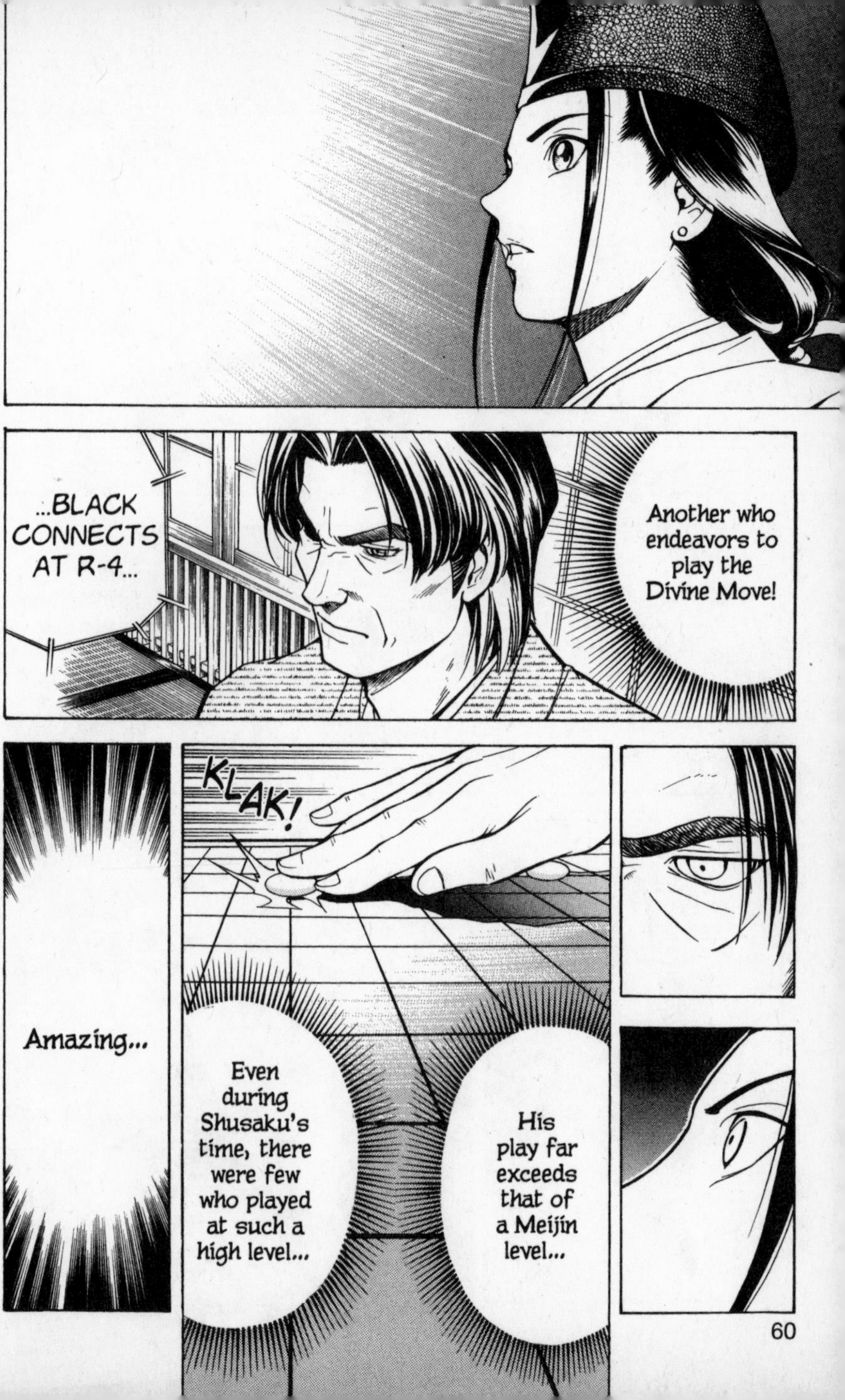
Another who endeavors to play the Divine Move!
...BLACK CONNECTS AT R-4...
KLAK!
His play far exceeds that of a Meijin level...
Even during Shusaku's time, there were few who played at such a high level...
Amazing...

READ THIS WAY

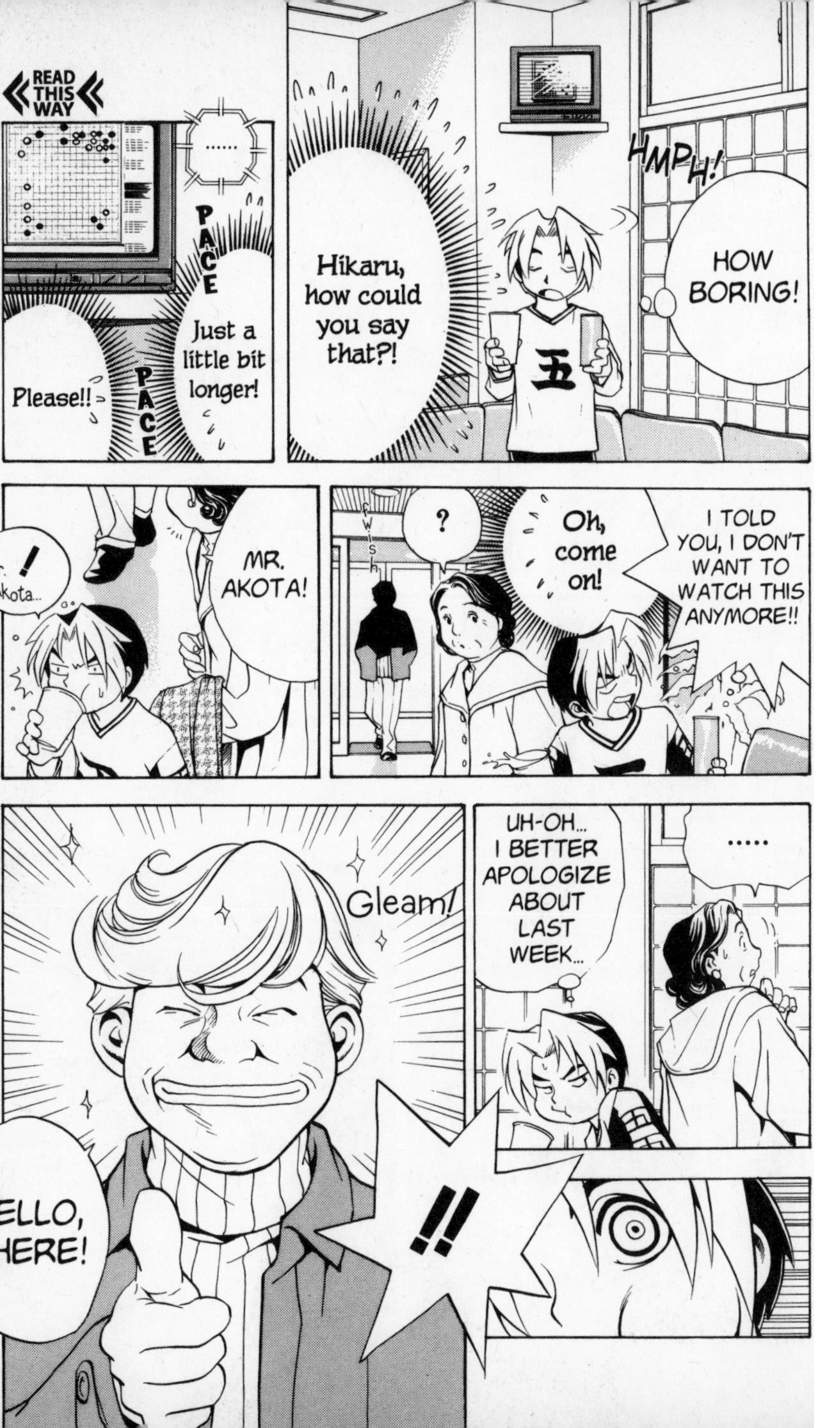
HMPH!
HOW BORING!
Hikaru, how could you say that?!
......
PACE
Just a little bit longer!
PACE
Please!!
I TOLD YOU, I DON'T WANT TO WATCH THIS ANYMORE!!
Oh, come on!
?
fwish
MR. AKOTA!
!
Mr. Akota...
UH-OH... I BETTER APOLOGIZE ABOUT LAST WEEK...
.....
!!
Gleam!
HELLO, THERE!

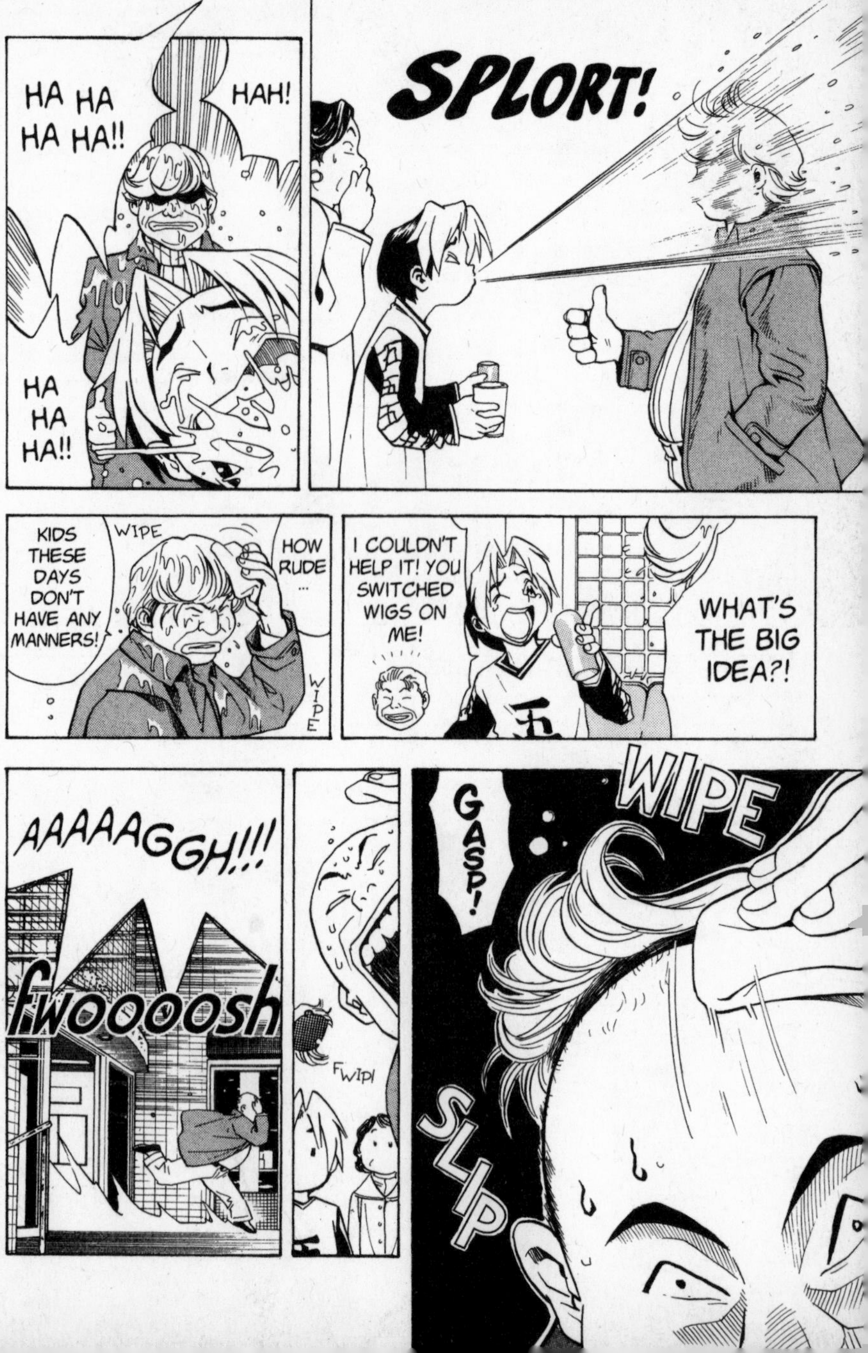
SPLORT!
HAH!
HA HA HA HA!!
HA HA HA!!
WHAT'S THE BIG IDEA?!
I COULDN'T HELP IT! YOU SWITCHED WIGS ON ME!
HOW RUDE ...
WIPE
KIDS THESE DAYS DON'T HAVE ANY MANNERS!
WIPE
WIPE
GASP!
SLIP
FWIP!
AAAAAGGH!!!
fwoooosh

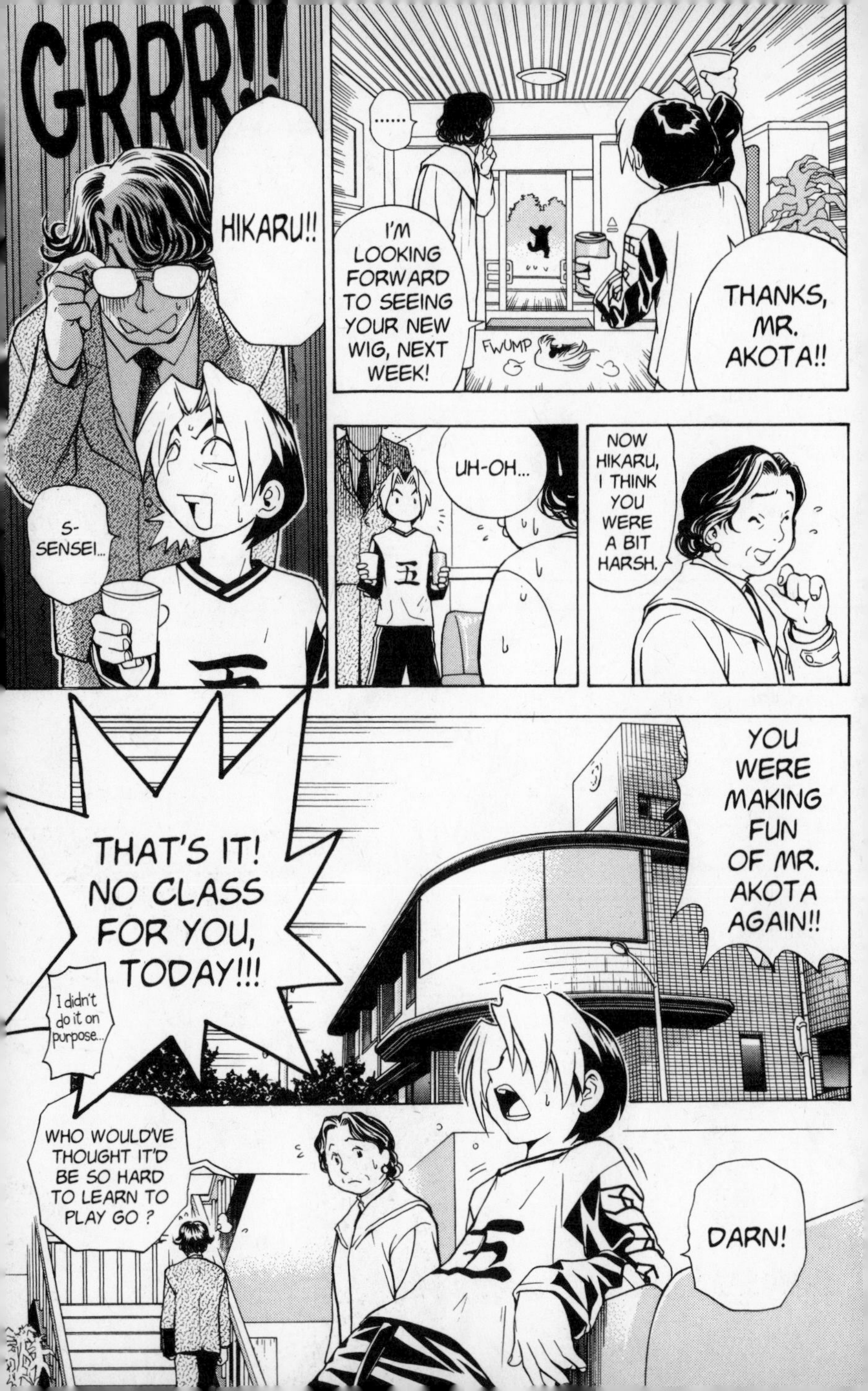

......
THANKS, MR. AKOTA!!
I'M LOOKING FORWARD TO SEEING YOUR NEW WIG, NEXT WEEK!
FWUMP
NOW HIKARU, I THINK YOU WERE A BIT HARSH.
UH-OH...
GRRR!!
HIKARU!!
S-SENSEI...
YOU WERE MAKING FUN OF MR. AKOTA AGAIN!!
THAT'S IT! NO CLASS FOR YOU, TODAY!!!
I didn't do it on purpose...
DARN!
WHO WOULD'VE THOUGHT IT'D BE SO HARD TO LEARN TO PLAY GO ?

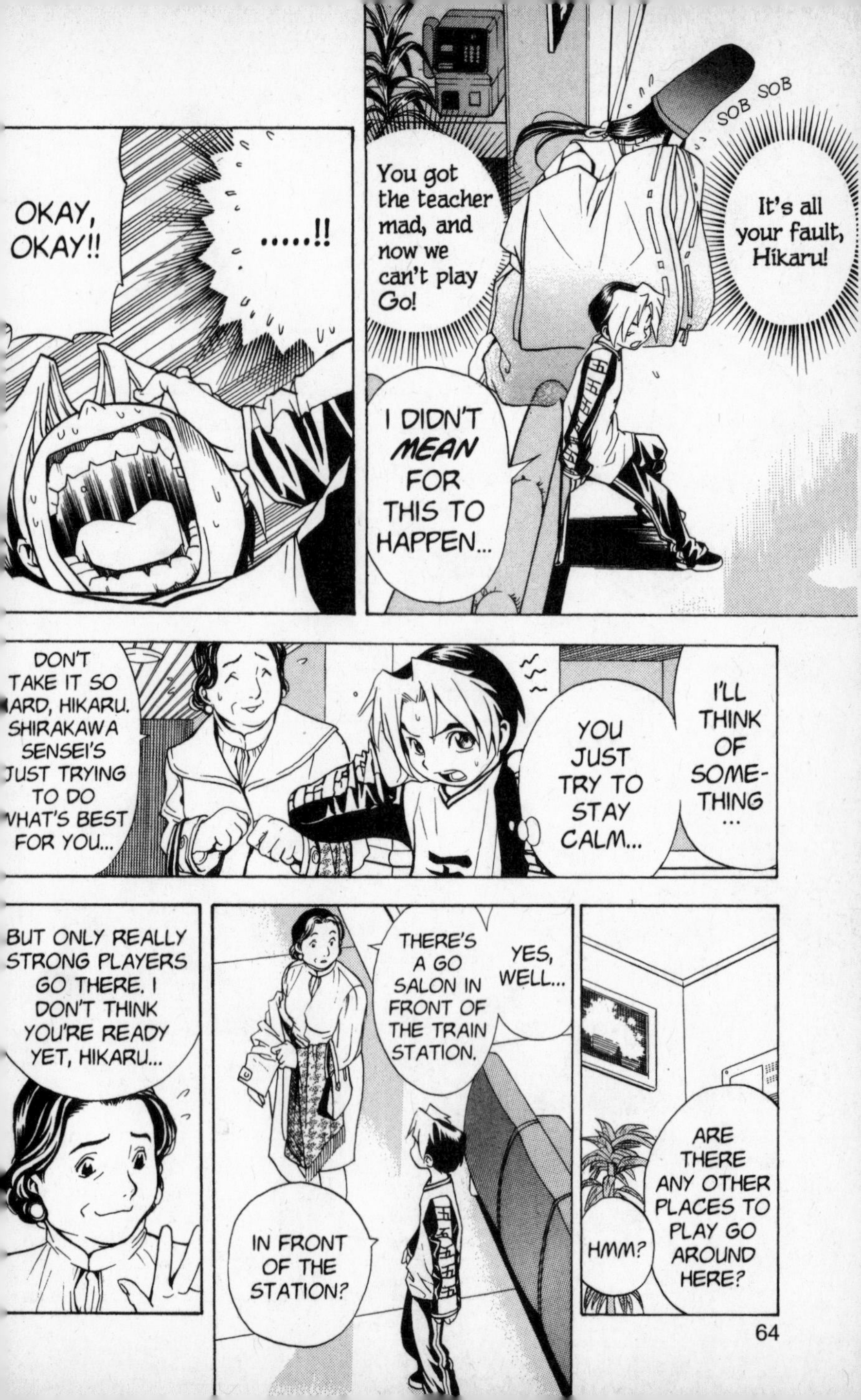
SOB SOB
It's all your fault, Hikaru!
You got the teacher mad, and now we can't play Go!
I DIDN'T MEAN FOR THIS TO HAPPEN...
.....!!
OKAY, OKAY!!
I'LL THINK OF SOME-THING ...
YOU JUST TRY TO STAY CALM...
DON'T TAKE IT SO ARD, HIKARU. SHIRAKAWA SENSEI'S JUST TRYING TO DO VHAT'S BEST FOR YOU...
ARE THERE ANY OTHER PLACES TO PLAY GO AROUND HERE?
HMM?
YES, WELL...
THERE'S A GO SALON IN FRONT OF THE TRAIN STATION.
IN FRONT OF THE STATION?
BUT ONLY REALLY STRONG PLAYERS GO THERE. I DON'T THINK YOU'RE READY YET, HIKARU...

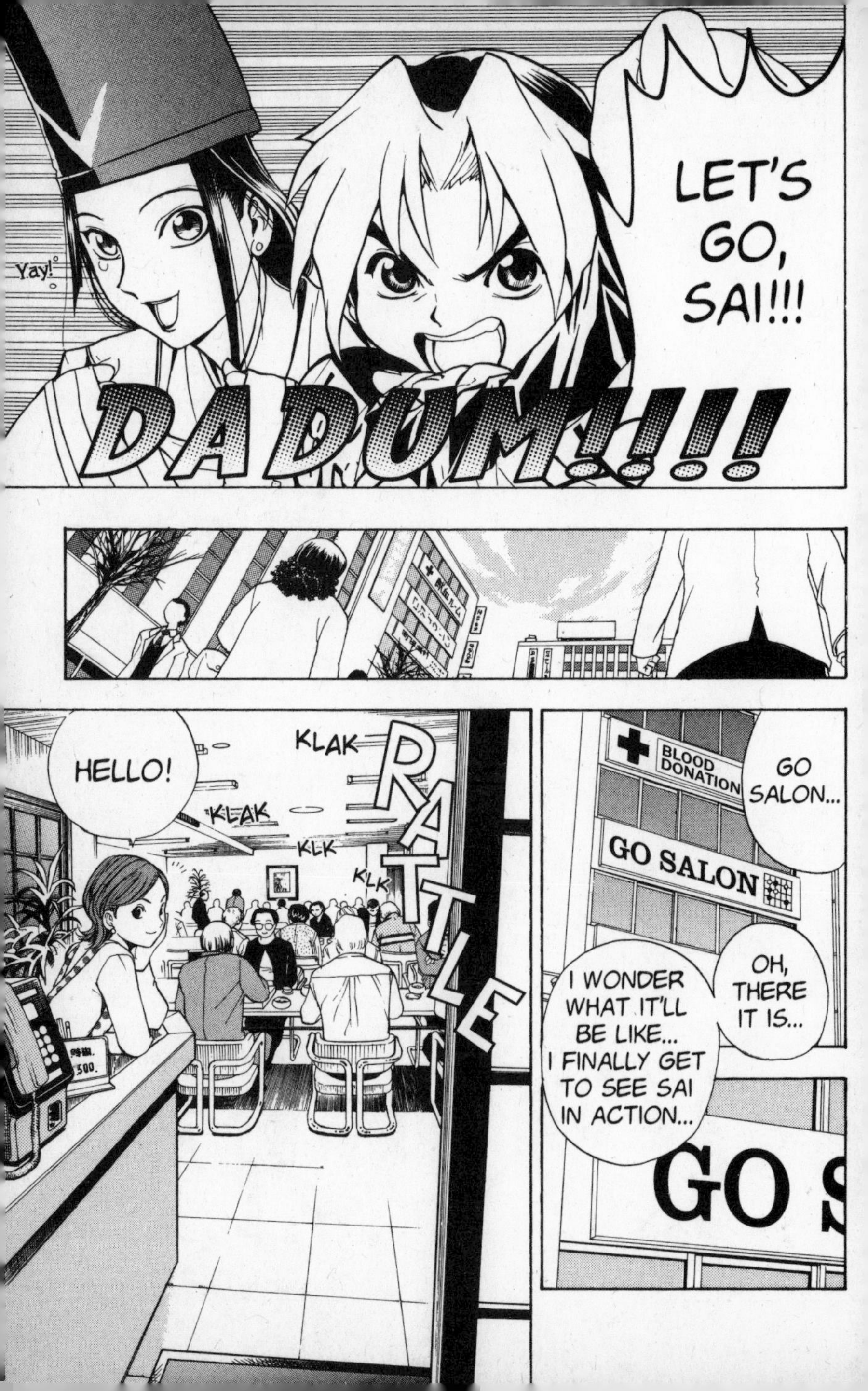

LET'S GO, SAI!!!
DADUM!!!!
Yay!
BLOOD DONATION
GO SALON
GO SALON...
OH, THERE IT IS...
I WONDER WHAT IT'LL BE LIKE... I FINALLY GET TO SEE SAI IN ACTION...
GO S
RATTLE
KLAK
KLAK
KLK
KLK
HELLO!
500.

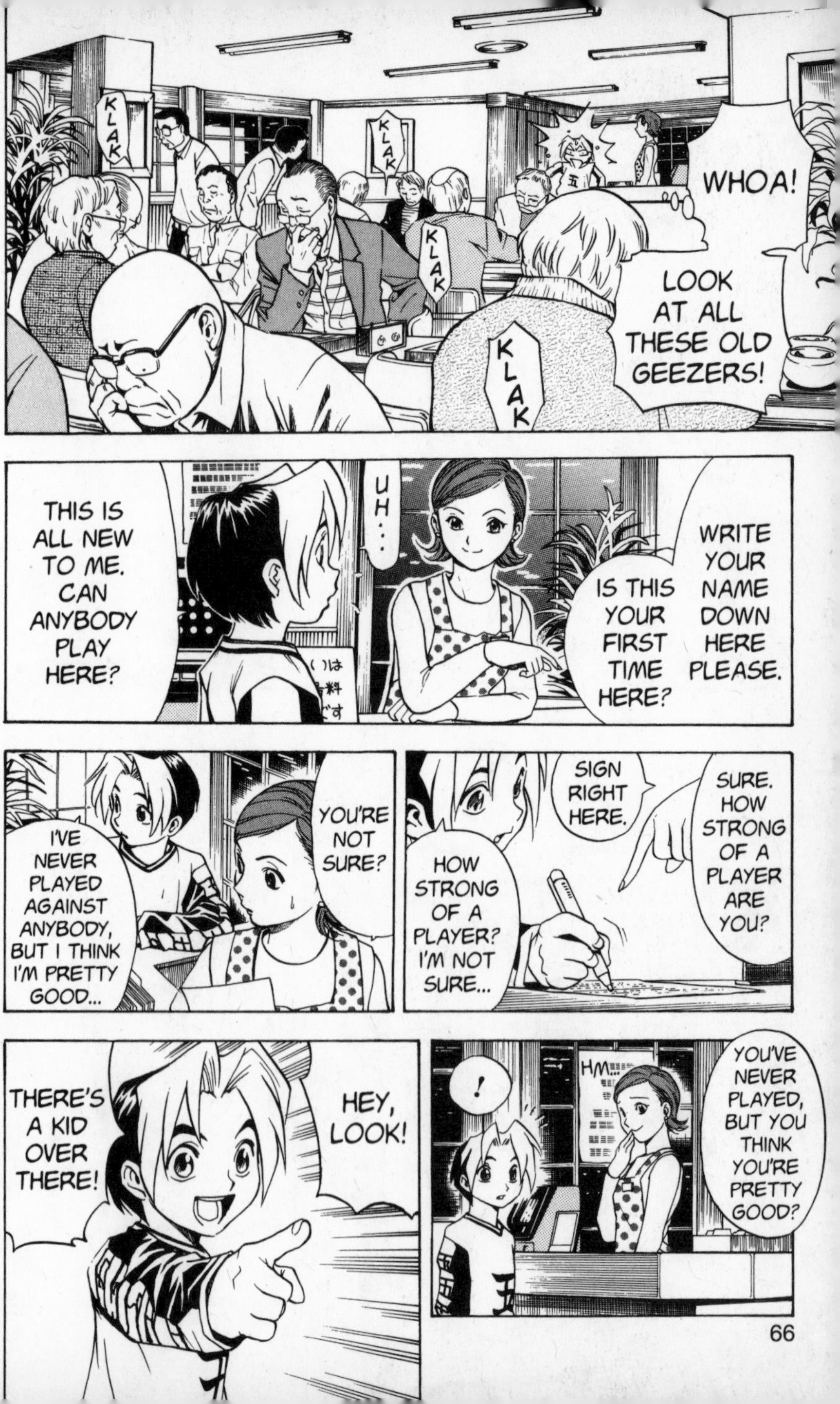
WHOA!
LOOK AT ALL THESE OLD GEEZERS!
KLAK
KLAK
KLAK
KLAK
KLAK
WRITE YOUR NAME DOWN HERE PLEASE.
IS THIS YOUR FIRST TIME HERE?
UH...
THIS IS ALL NEW TO ME. CAN ANYBODY PLAY HERE?
SURE. HOW STRONG OF A PLAYER ARE YOU?
SIGN RIGHT HERE.
HOW STRONG OF A PLAYER? I'M NOT SURE...
YOU'RE NOT SURE?
I'VE NEVER PLAYED AGAINST ANYBODY, BUT I THINK I'M PRETTY GOOD...
YOU'VE NEVER PLAYED, BUT YOU THINK YOU'RE PRETTY GOOD?
HM...
!
HEY, LOOK!
THERE'S A KID OVER THERE!

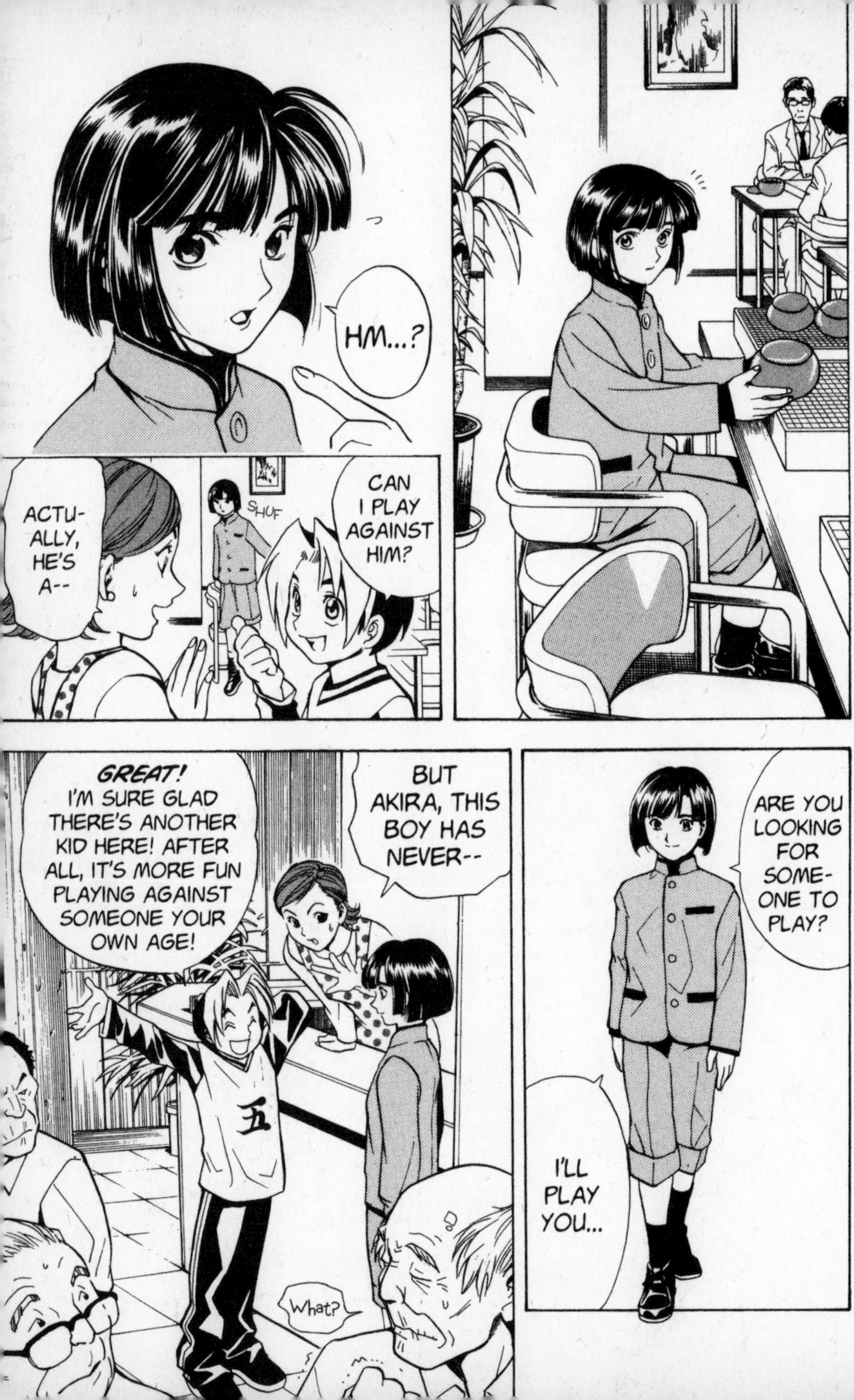
HM...?
SHUF
CAN I PLAY AGAINST HIM?
ACTU-ALLY, HE'S A--
ARE YOU LOOKING FOR SOME-ONE TO PLAY?
I'LL PLAY YOU...
BUT AKIRA, THIS BOY HAS NEVER--
GREAT! I'M SURE GLAD THERE'S ANOTHER KID HERE! AFTER ALL, IT'S MORE FUN PLAYING AGAINST SOMEONE YOUR OWN AGE!
What?

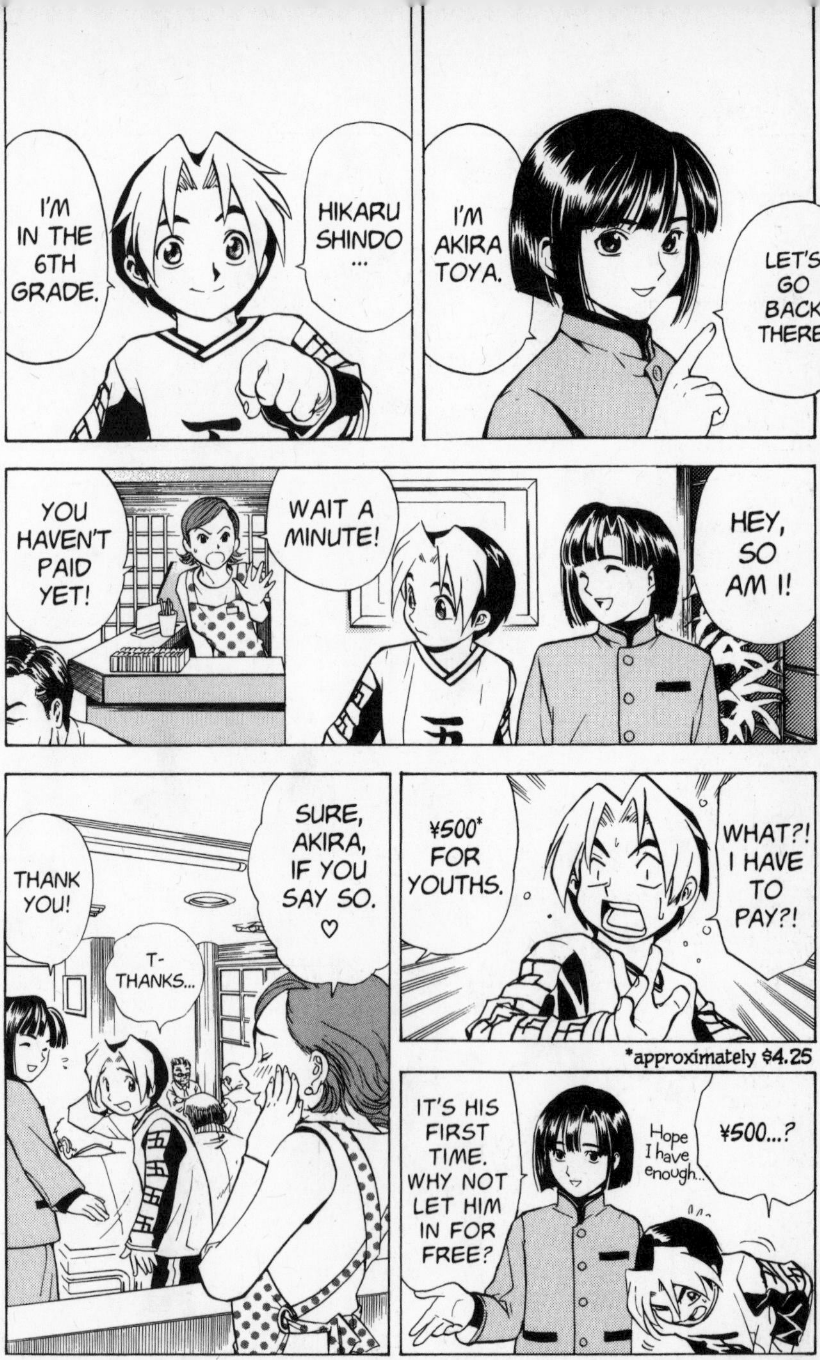
LET'S GO BACK THERE.
I'M AKIRA TOYA.
HIKARU SHINDO ...
I'M IN THE 6TH GRADE.
HEY, SO AM I!
WAIT A MINUTE!
YOU HAVEN'T PAID YET!
WHAT?! I HAVE TO PAY?!
¥500* FOR YOUTHS.
¥500...?
Hope I have enough...
IT'S HIS FIRST TIME. WHY NOT LET HIM IN FOR FREE?
SURE, AKIRA, IF YOU SAY SO. ♡
THANK YOU!
T-THANKS...

*approximately $4.25

READ THIS WAY

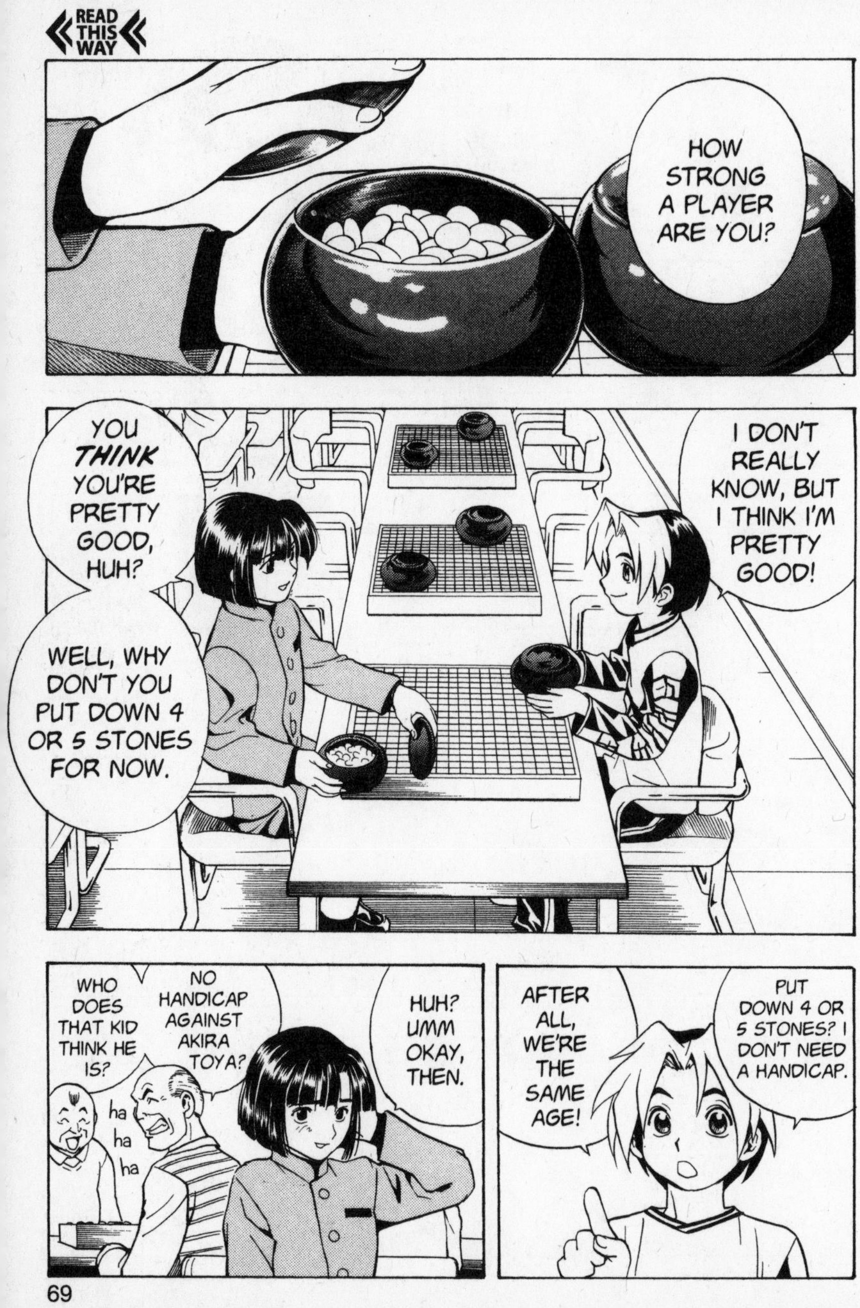
HOW STRONG A PLAYER ARE YOU?
I DON'T REALLY KNOW, BUT I THINK I'M PRETTY GOOD!
YOU *THINK* YOU'RE PRETTY GOOD, HUH?
WELL, WHY DON'T YOU PUT DOWN 4 OR 5 STONES FOR NOW.
PUT DOWN 4 OR 5 STONES? I DON'T NEED A HANDICAP.
AFTER ALL, WE'RE THE SAME AGE!
HUH? UMM OKAY, THEN.
NO HANDICAP AGAINST AKIRA TOYA?
WHO DOES THAT KID THINK HE IS?
ha ha ha

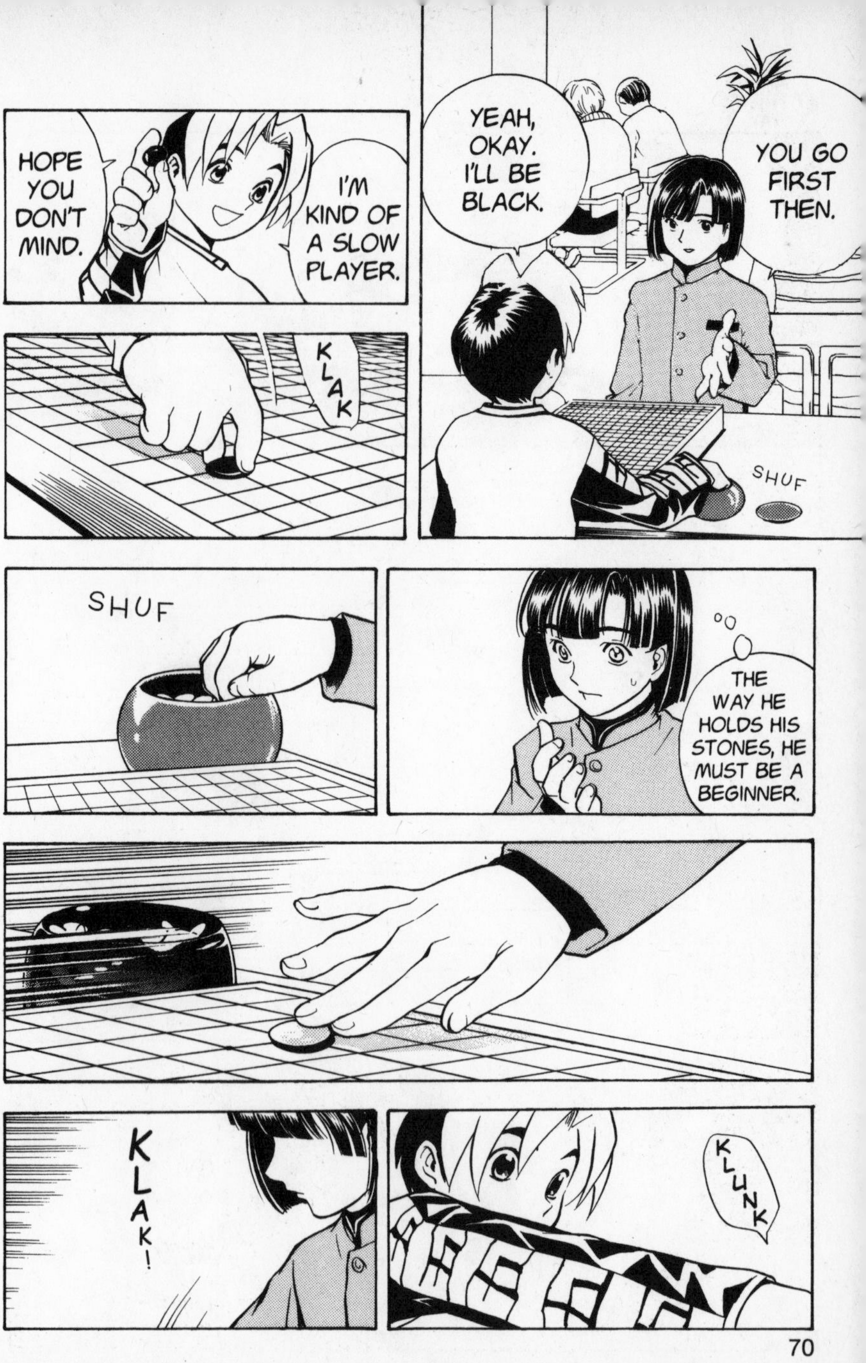
YOU GO FIRST THEN.
YEAH, OKAY. I'LL BE BLACK.
SHUF
HOPE YOU DON'T MIND.
I'M KIND OF A SLOW PLAYER.
KLAK
SHUF
THE WAY HE HOLDS HIS STONES, HE MUST BE A BEGINNER.
KLAK!
KLUNK

READ THIS WAY

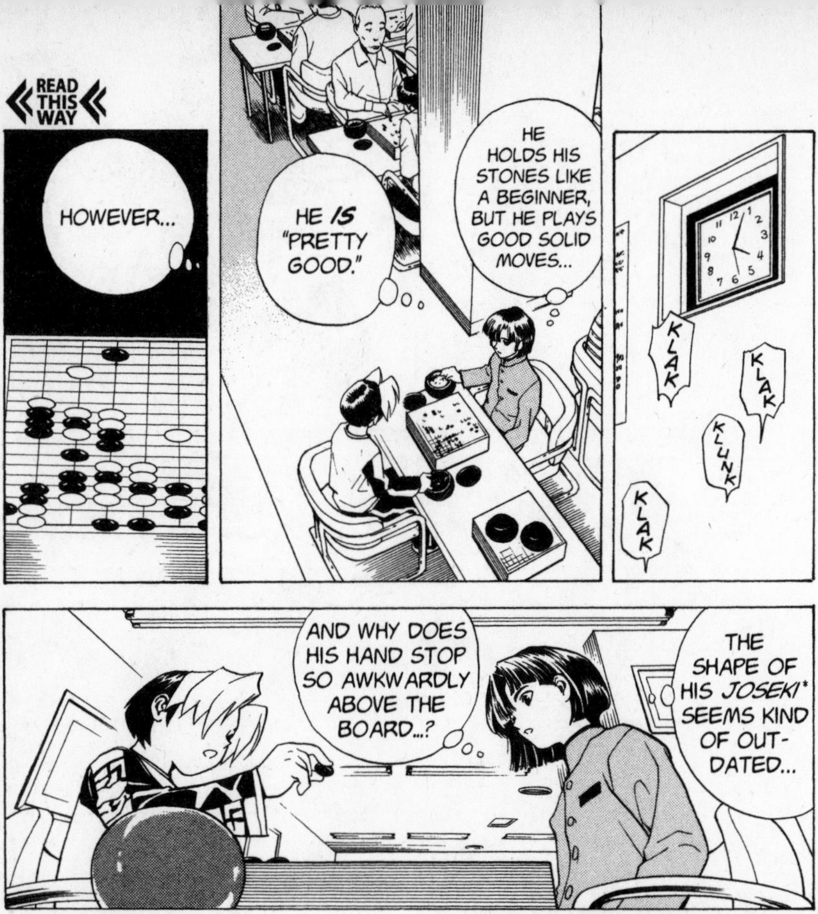
KLAK
KLAK
KLUNK
KLAK
HE HOLDS HIS STONES LIKE A BEGINNER, BUT HE PLAYS GOOD SOLID MOVES...
HE *IS* "PRETTY GOOD."
HOWEVER...
THE SHAPE OF HIS *JOSEKI** SEEMS KIND OF OUT-DATED...
AND WHY DOES HIS HAND STOP SO AWKWARDLY ABOVE THE BOARD...?

*joseki: a standardized set of plays.

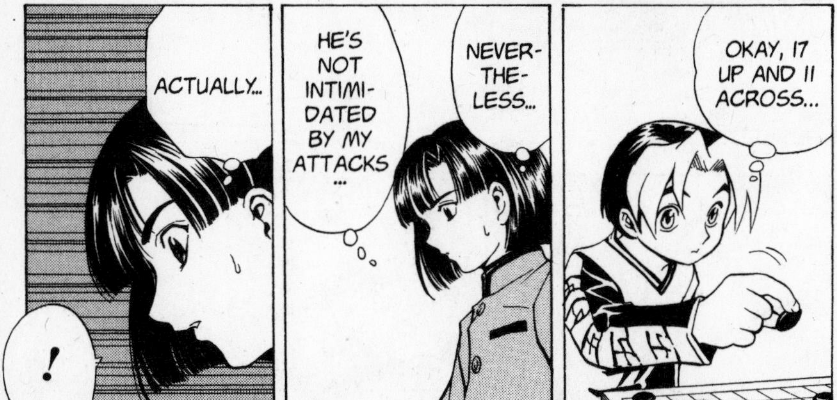
OKAY, 17 UP AND 11 ACROSS...
NEVER-THE-LESS...
HE'S NOT INTIMI-DATED BY MY ATTACKS...
ACTUALLY...
!

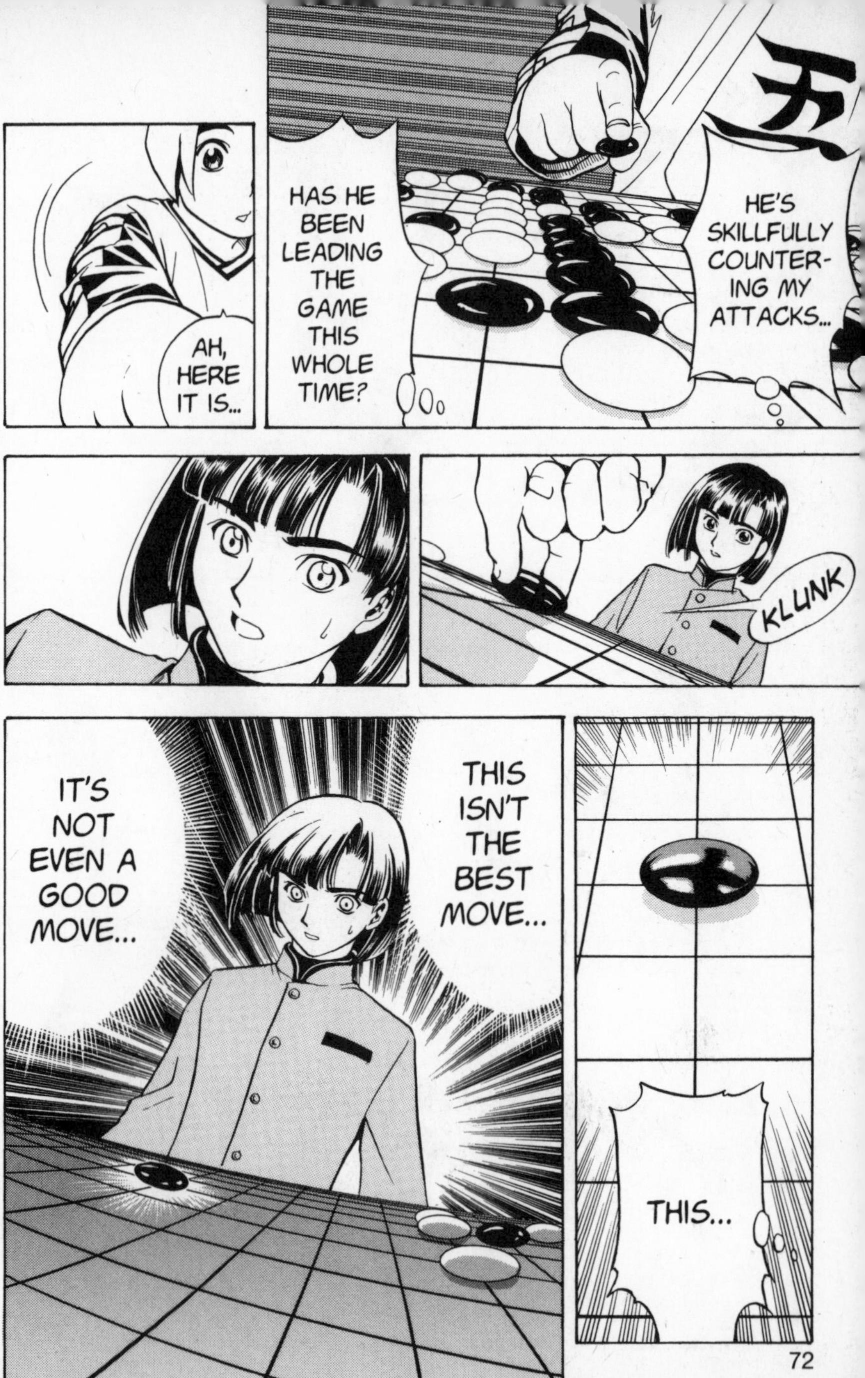
HE'S SKILLFULLY COUNTER-ING MY ATTACKS...
HAS HE BEEN LEADING THE GAME THIS WHOLE TIME?
AH, HERE IT IS...
KLUNK
THIS...
THIS ISN'T THE BEST MOVE...
IT'S NOT EVEN A GOOD MOVE...

READ THIS WAY

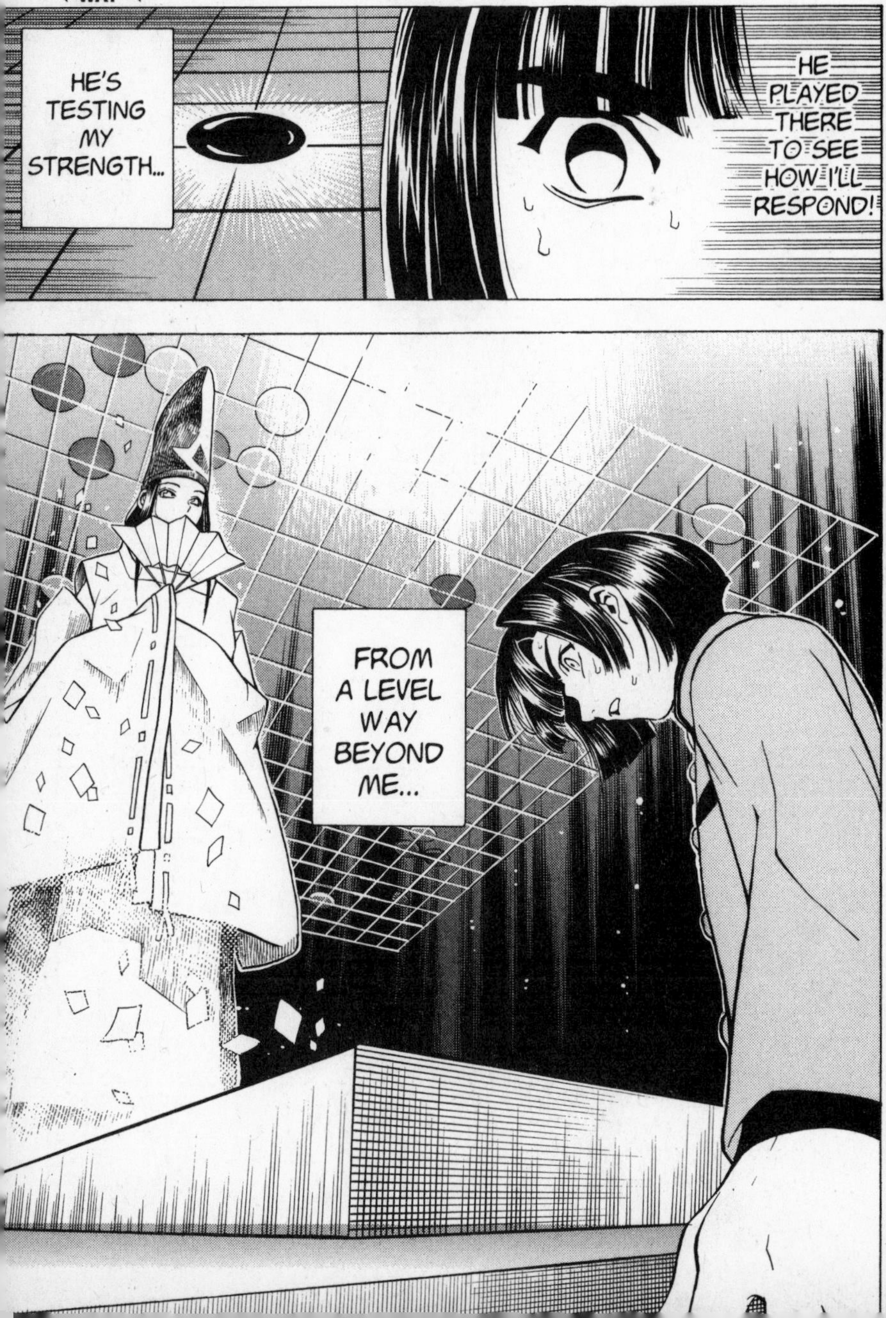
HE PLAYED THERE TO SEE HOW I'LL RESPOND!
HE'S TESTING MY STRENGTH...
FROM A LEVEL WAY BEYOND ME...

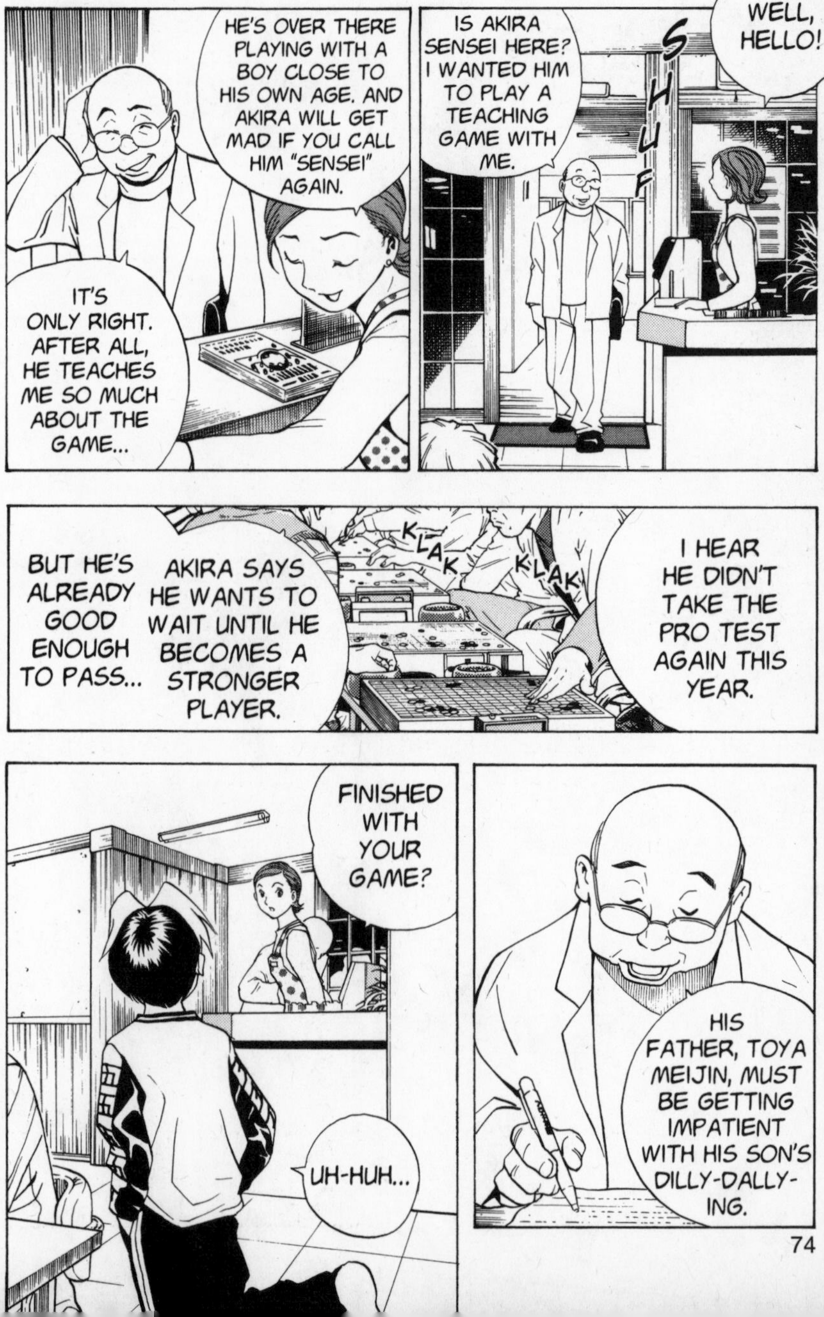
WELL, HELLO!
SHUF
IS AKIRA SENSEI HERE? I WANTED HIM TO PLAY A TEACHING GAME WITH ME.
HE'S OVER THERE PLAYING WITH A BOY CLOSE TO HIS OWN AGE. AND AKIRA WILL GET MAD IF YOU CALL HIM "SENSEI" AGAIN.
IT'S ONLY RIGHT. AFTER ALL, HE TEACHES ME SO MUCH ABOUT THE GAME...
I HEAR HE DIDN'T TAKE THE PRO TEST AGAIN THIS YEAR.
KLAK
KLAK
AKIRA SAYS HE WANTS TO WAIT UNTIL HE BECOMES A STRONGER PLAYER.
BUT HE'S ALREADY GOOD ENOUGH TO PASS...
HIS FATHER, TOYA MEIJIN, MUST BE GETTING IMPATIENT WITH HIS SON'S DILLY-DALLYING.
FINISHED WITH YOUR GAME?
UH-HUH...

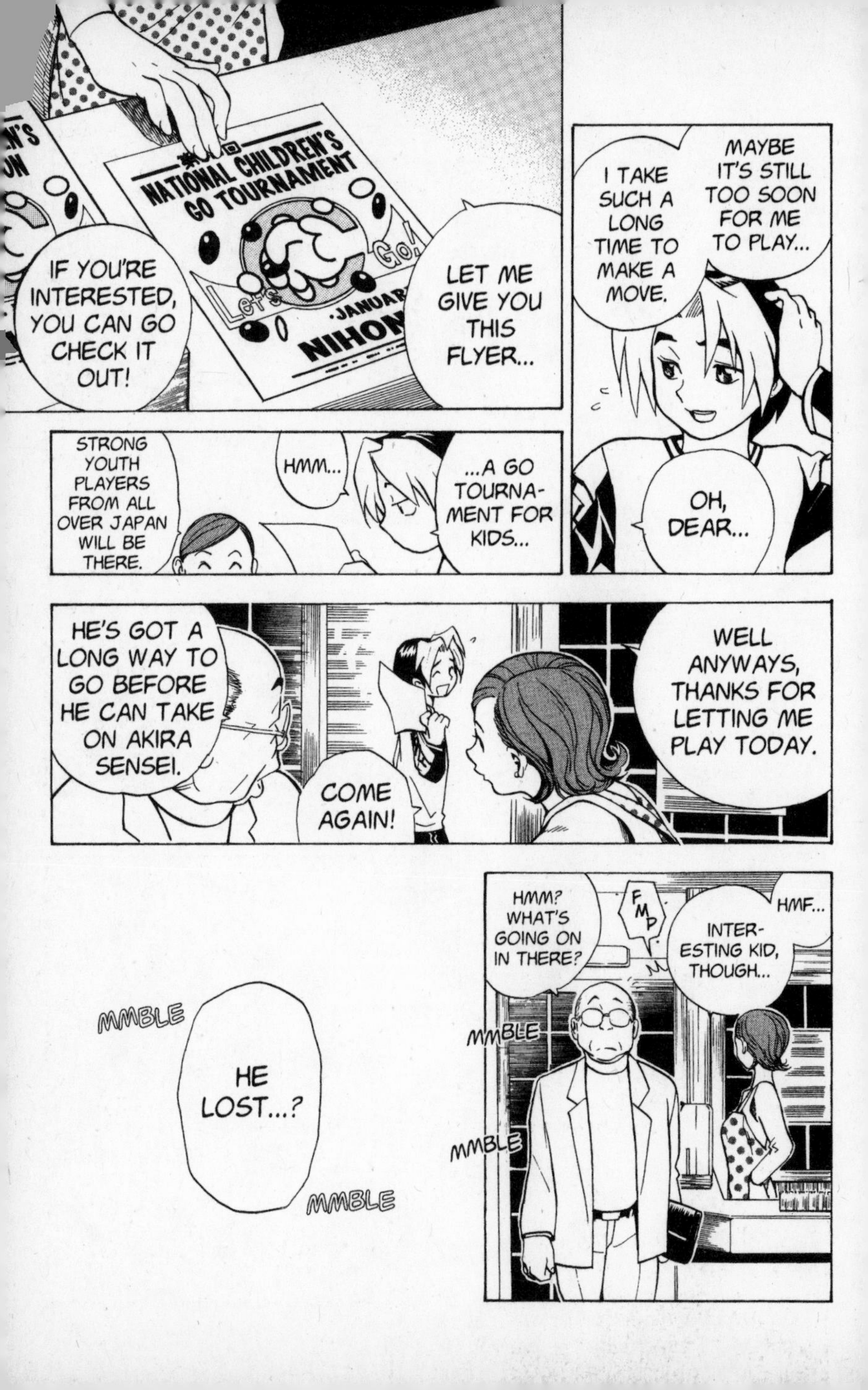
MAYBE IT'S STILL TOO SOON FOR ME TO PLAY...
I TAKE SUCH A LONG TIME TO MAKE A MOVE.
OH, DEAR...
NATIONAL CHILDREN'S GO TOURNAMENT
Let's Go!
LET ME GIVE YOU THIS FLYER...
IF YOU'RE INTERESTED, YOU CAN GO CHECK IT OUT!
...A GO TOURNAMENT FOR KIDS...
HMM...
STRONG YOUTH PLAYERS FROM ALL OVER JAPAN WILL BE THERE.
WELL ANYWAYS, THANKS FOR LETTING ME PLAY TODAY.
COME AGAIN!
HE'S GOT A LONG WAY TO GO BEFORE HE CAN TAKE ON AKIRA SENSEI.
HMF...
INTERESTING KID, THOUGH...
FMP
HMM? WHAT'S GOING ON IN THERE?
MMBLE
MMBLE
MMBLE
HE LOST...?
MMBLE

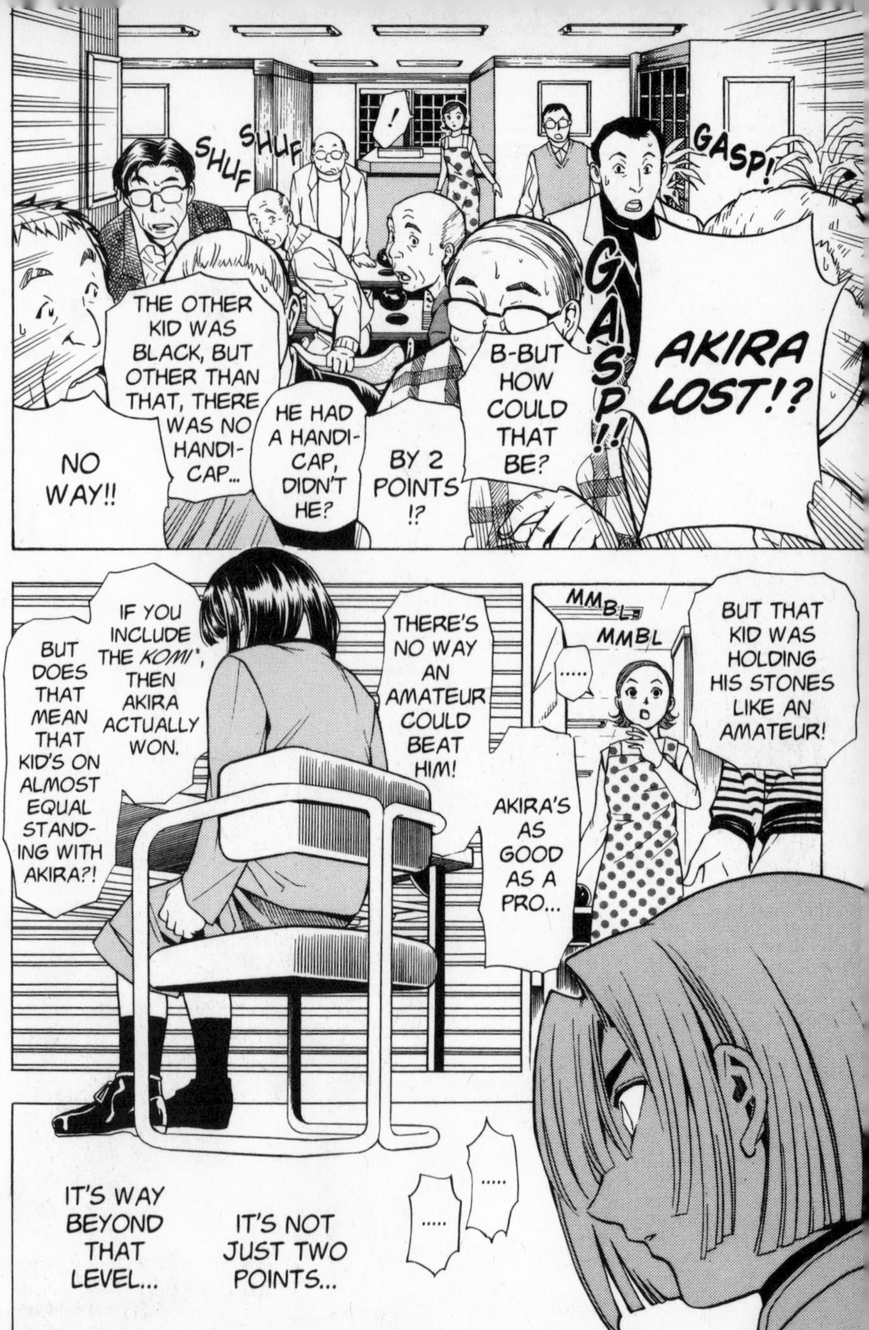
GASP!
AKIRA LOST!?
GASP!!
B-BUT HOW COULD THAT BE?
BY 2 POINTS!?
HE HAD A HANDICAP, DIDN'T HE?
THE OTHER KID WAS BLACK, BUT OTHER THAN THAT, THERE WAS NO HANDICAP...
!
SHUF SHUF
NO WAY!!
BUT THAT KID WAS HOLDING HIS STONES LIKE AN AMATEUR!
MMBL MMBL
.....
AKIRA'S AS GOOD AS A PRO...
THERE'S NO WAY AN AMATEUR COULD BEAT HIM!
IF YOU INCLUDE THE *KOMI**, THEN AKIRA ACTUALLY WON.
BUT DOES THAT MEAN THAT KID'S ON ALMOST EQUAL STANDING WITH AKIRA?!
.....
.....
IT'S NOT JUST TWO POINTS...
IT'S WAY BEYOND THAT LEVEL...

*komi - points awarded to white at the end of a game to compensate for black's first move

READ THIS WAY

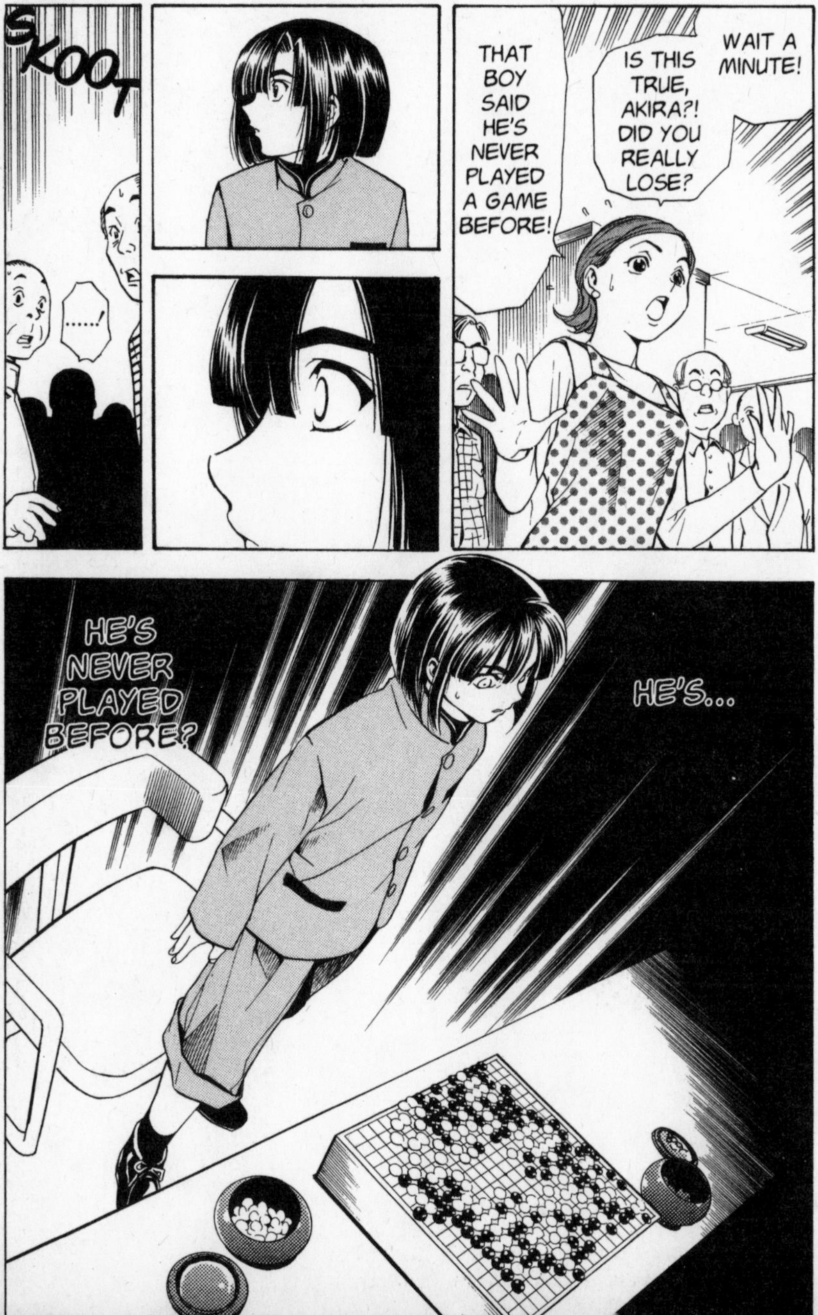
WAIT A MINUTE!
IS THIS TRUE, AKIRA?! DID YOU REALLY LOSE?
THAT BOY SAID HE'S NEVER PLAYED A GAME BEFORE!
SKOOT
......!
HE'S...
HE'S NEVER PLAYED BEFORE?

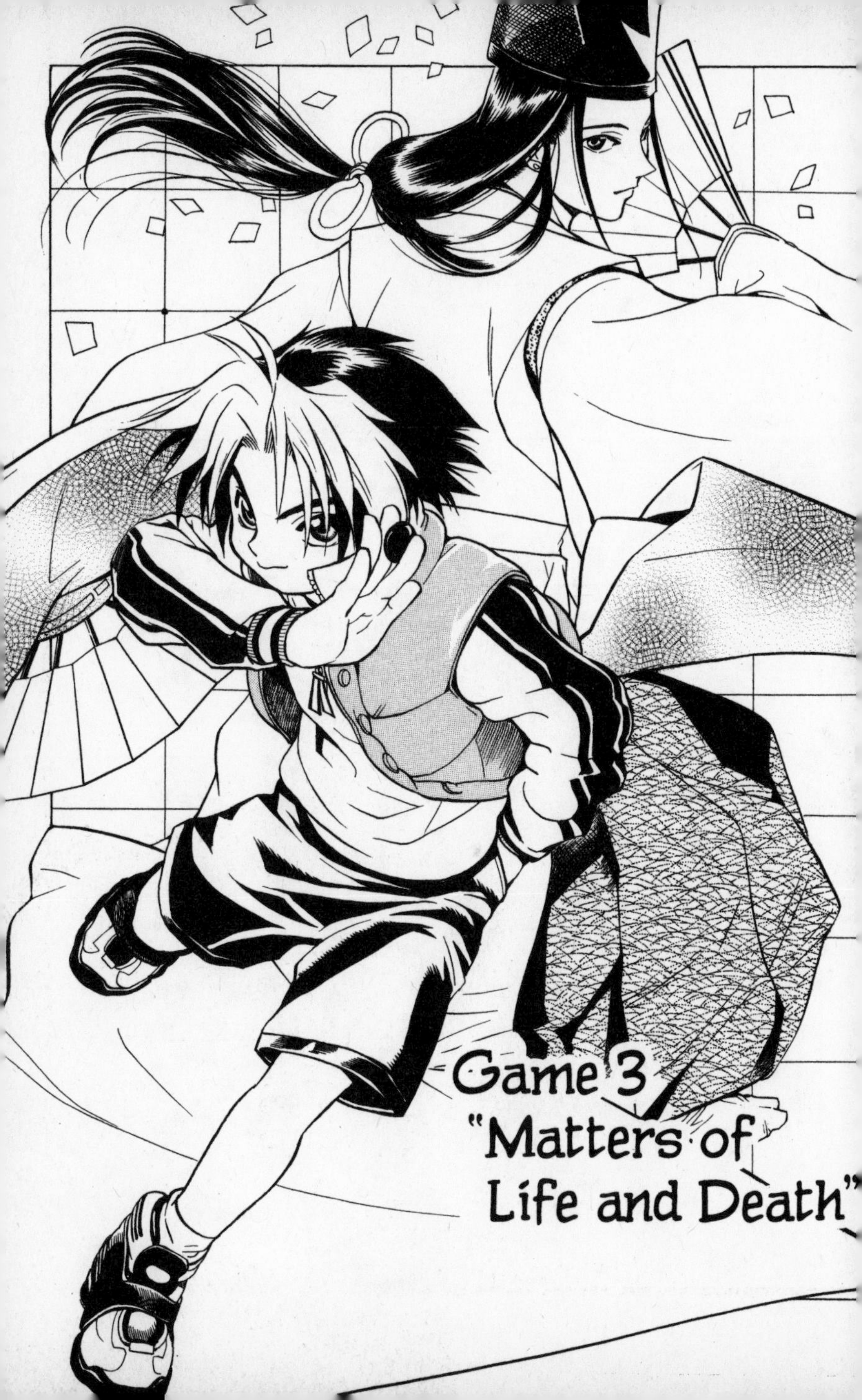
Game 3
"Matters of
Life and Death"

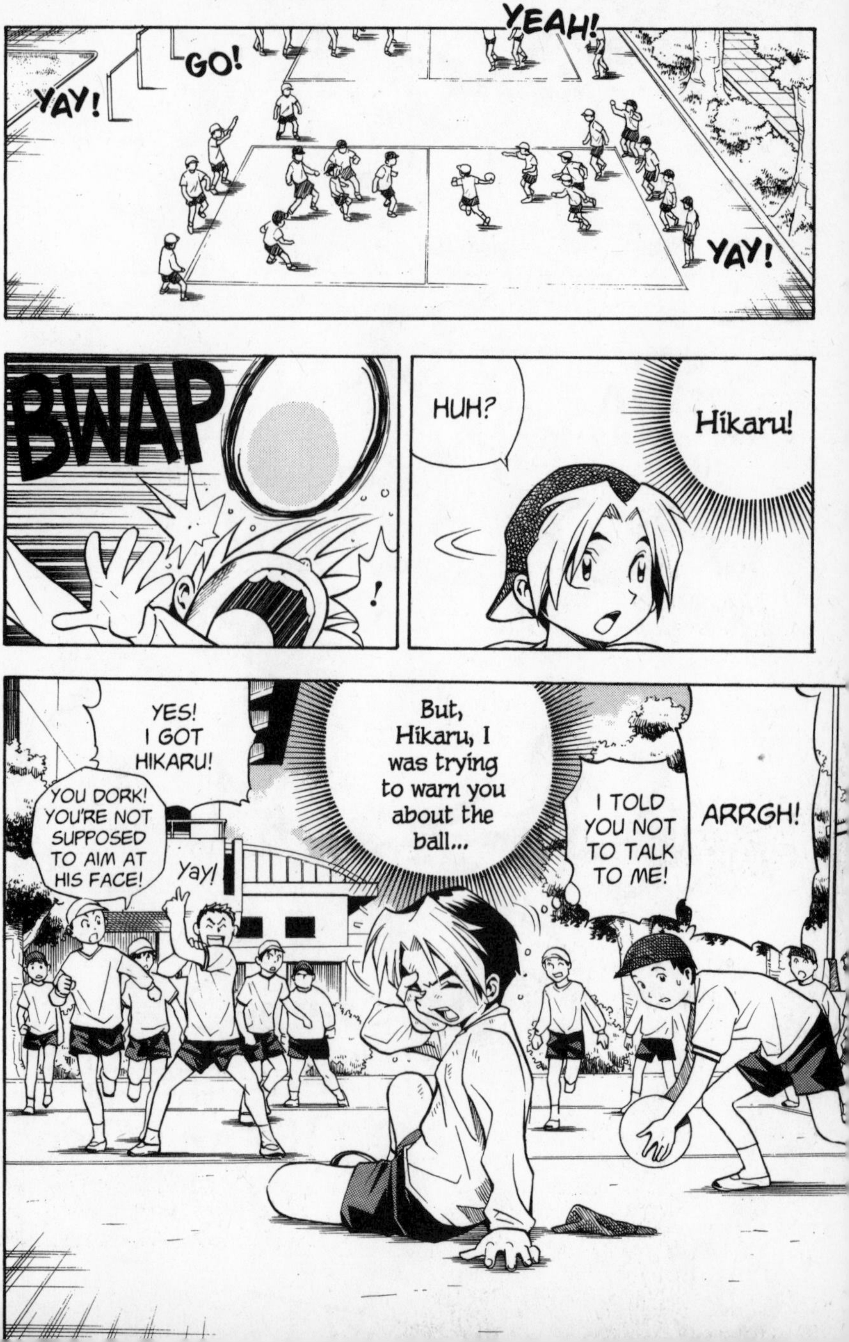
YEAH!
GO!
YAY!
YAY!
Hikaru!
HUH?
BWAP
ARRGH!
I TOLD YOU NOT TO TALK TO ME!
But, Hikaru, I was trying to warn you about the ball...
YES! I GOT HIKARU!
YOU DORK! YOU'RE NOT SUPPOSED TO AIM AT HIS FACE!
Yay!

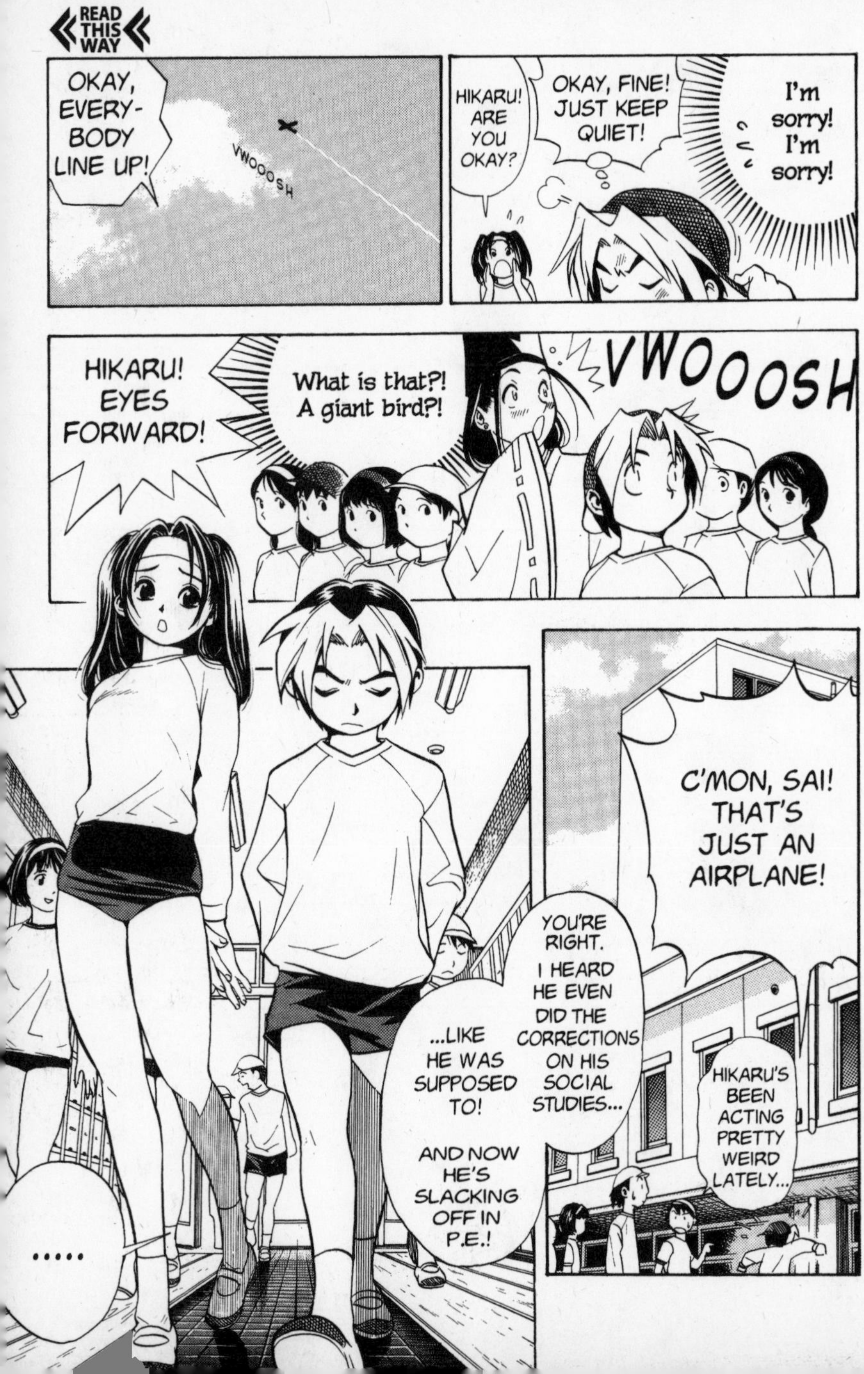
READ THIS WAY
I'm sorry! I'm sorry!
OKAY, FINE! JUST KEEP QUIET!
HIKARU! ARE YOU OKAY?
OKAY, EVERY-BODY LINE UP!
VWOOOSH
VWOOOSH
What is that?! A giant bird?!
HIKARU! EYES FORWARD!
C'MON, SAI! THAT'S JUST AN AIRPLANE!
HIKARU'S BEEN ACTING PRETTY WEIRD LATELY...
YOU'RE RIGHT. I HEARD HE EVEN DID THE CORRECTIONS ON HIS SOCIAL STUDIES...
...LIKE HE WAS SUPPOSED TO!
AND NOW HE'S SLACKING OFF IN P.E.!
.....

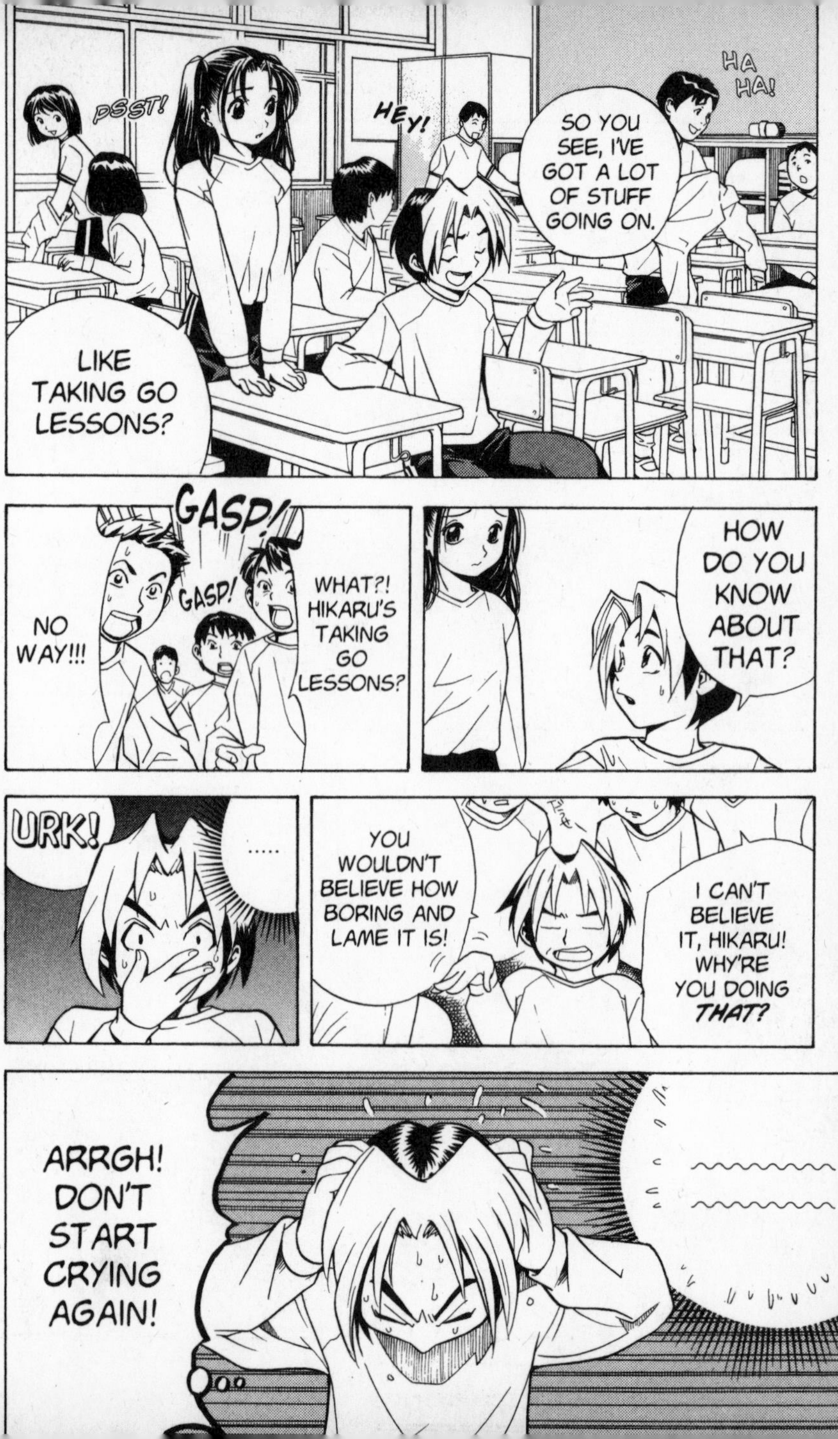
HA HA!
SO YOU SEE, I'VE GOT A LOT OF STUFF GOING ON.
HEY!
PSST!
LIKE TAKING GO LESSONS?
HOW DO YOU KNOW ABOUT THAT?
WHAT?! HIKARU'S TAKING GO LESSONS?
GASP!
GASP!
NO WAY!!!
I CAN'T BELIEVE IT, HIKARU! WHY'RE YOU DOING *THAT?*
YOU WOULDN'T BELIEVE HOW BORING AND LAME IT IS!
.....
URK!
ARRGH! DON'T START CRYING AGAIN!

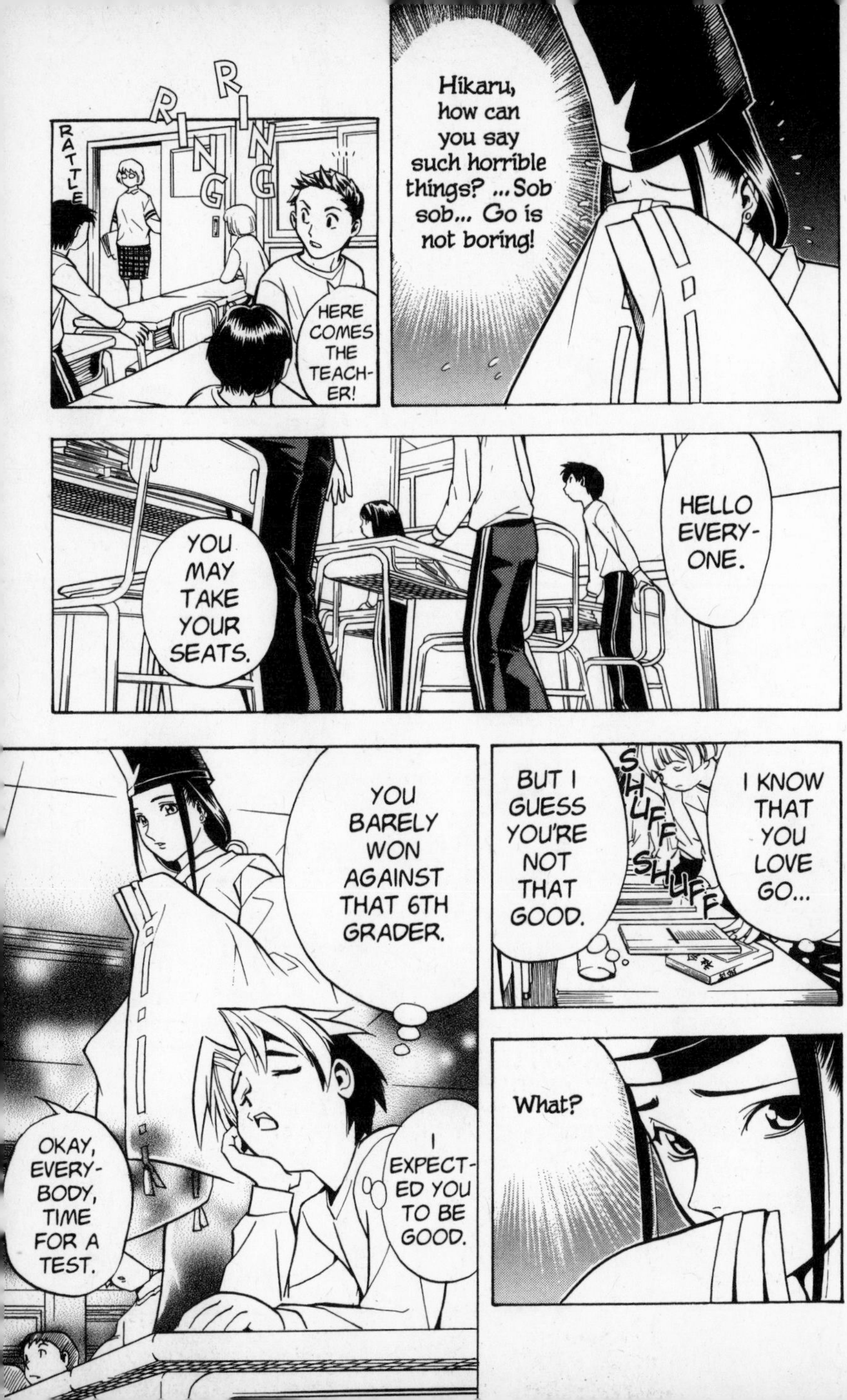
Hikaru, how can you say such horrible things? ...Sob sob... Go is not boring!
RING RING
RATTLE
HERE COMES THE TEACHER!
HELLO EVERY-ONE.
YOU MAY TAKE YOUR SEATS.
I KNOW THAT YOU LOVE GO...
SHUFF SHUFF
BUT I GUESS YOU'RE NOT THAT GOOD.
What?
YOU BARELY WON AGAINST THAT 6TH GRADER.
I EXPECT-ED YOU TO BE GOOD.
OKAY, EVERY-BODY, TIME FOR A TEST.

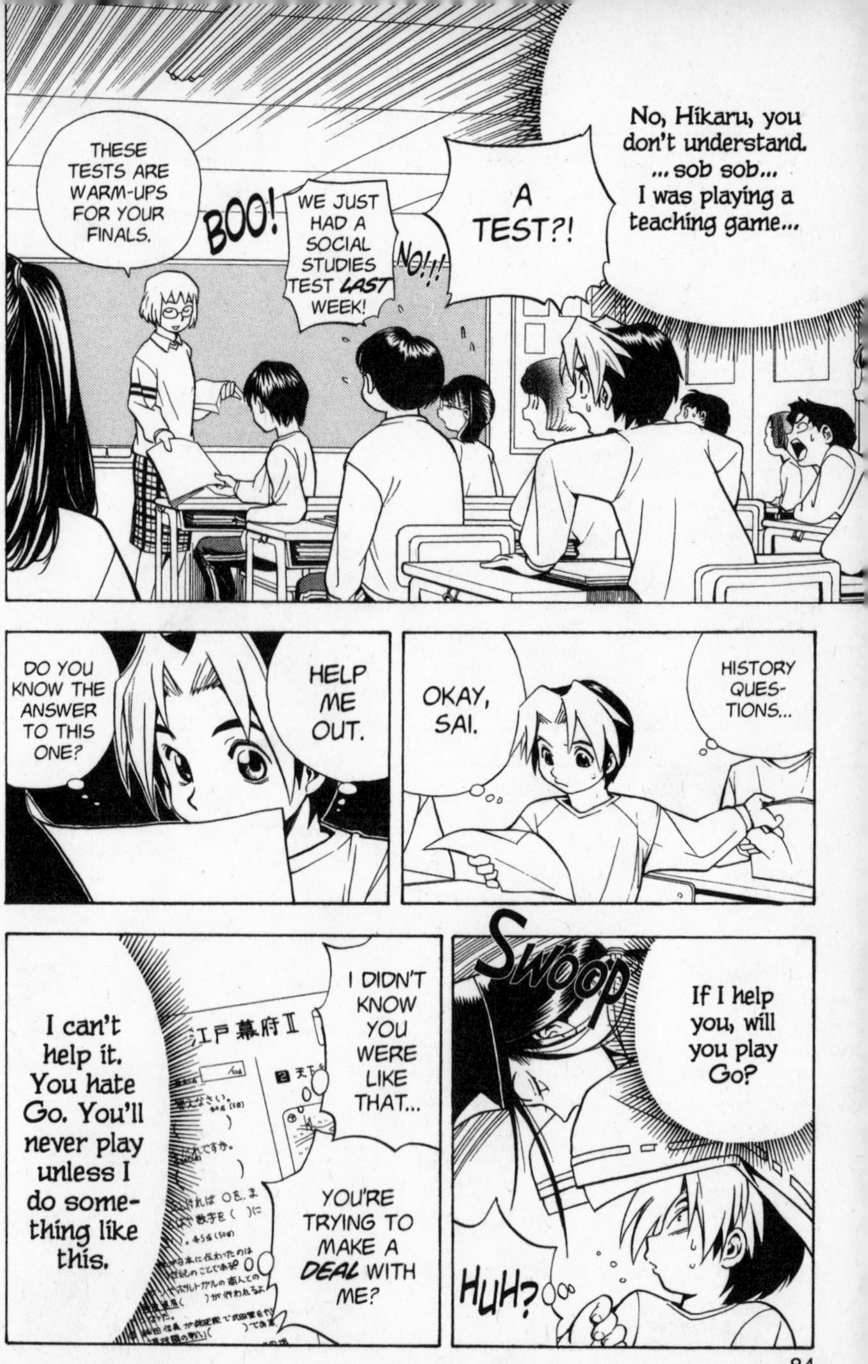

No, Hikaru, you don't understand. ... sob sob... I was playing a teaching game...
A TEST?!
NO!!!
WE JUST HAD A SOCIAL STUDIES TEST LAST WEEK!
BOO!
THESE TESTS ARE WARM-UPS FOR YOUR FINALS.
HISTORY QUES-TIONS...
OKAY, SAI.
HELP ME OUT.
DO YOU KNOW THE ANSWER TO THIS ONE?
SWOOP
If I help you, will you play Go?
HUH?
I DIDN'T KNOW YOU WERE LIKE THAT...
江戸幕府II
YOU'RE TRYING TO MAKE A DEAL WITH ME?
I can't help it. You hate Go. You'll never play unless I do some-thing like this.

READ THIS WAY

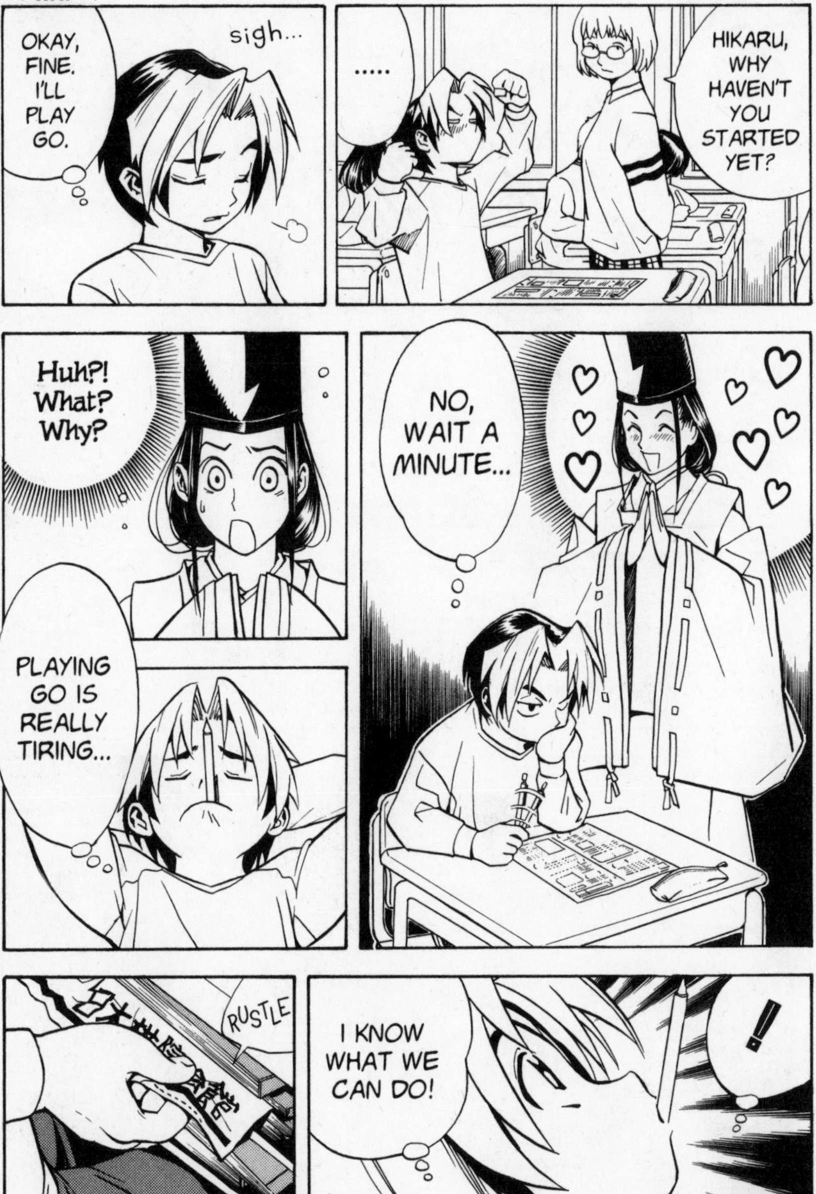

HIKARU, WHY HAVEN'T YOU STARTED YET?
.....
sigh...
OKAY, FINE. I'LL PLAY GO.
NO, WAIT A MINUTE...
Huh?! What? Why?
PLAYING GO IS REALLY TIRING...
!
I KNOW WHAT WE CAN DO!
RUSTLE

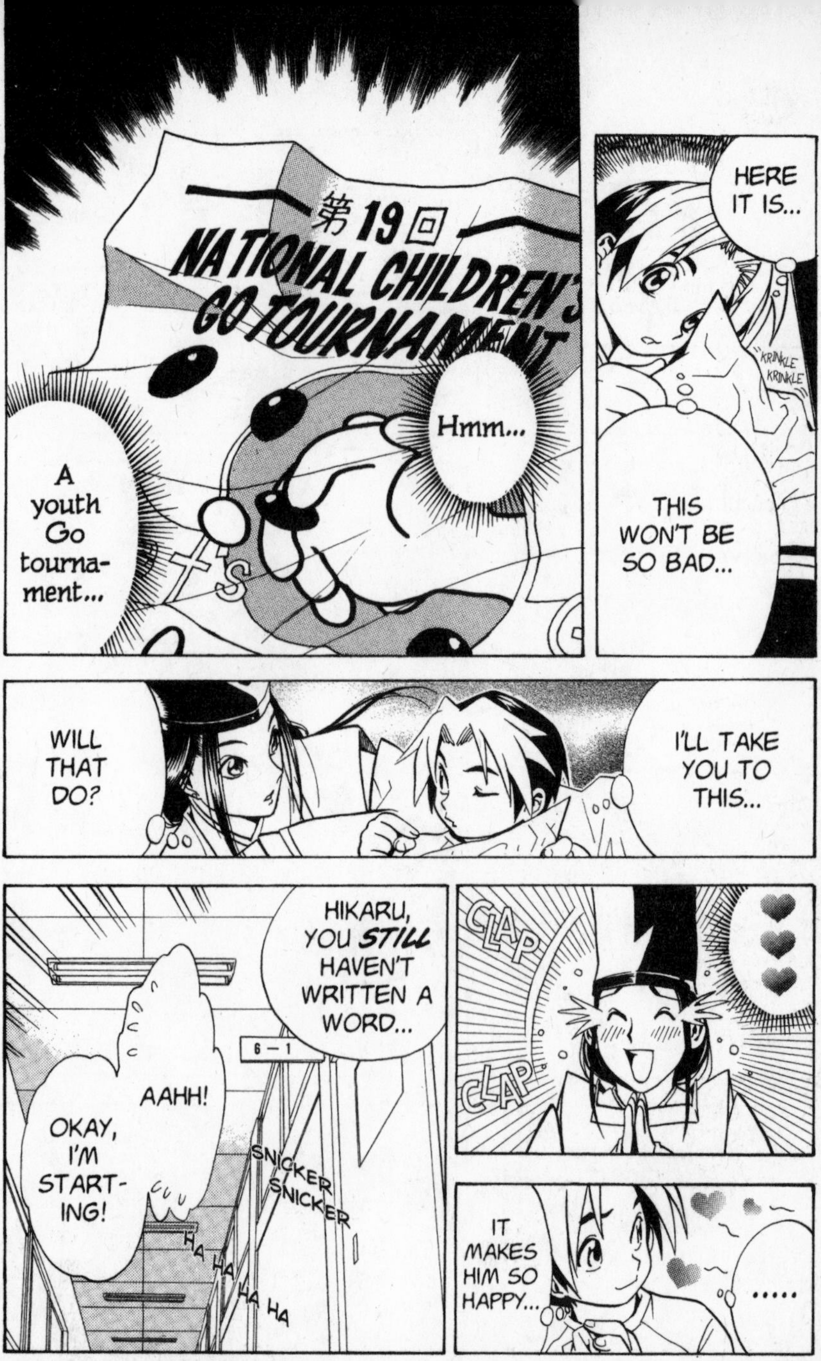
HERE IT IS...
KRINKLE KRINKLE
THIS WON'T BE SO BAD...
第19回
NATIONAL CHILDREN'S GO TOURNAMENT
Hmm...
A youth Go tourna-ment...
I'LL TAKE YOU TO THIS...
WILL THAT DO?
CLAP
CLAP
IT MAKES HIM SO HAPPY...
.....
HIKARU, YOU STILL HAVEN'T WRITTEN A WORD...
6-1
AAHH!
OKAY, I'M START-ING!
SNICKER SNICKER
HA HA HA HA

READ THIS WAY

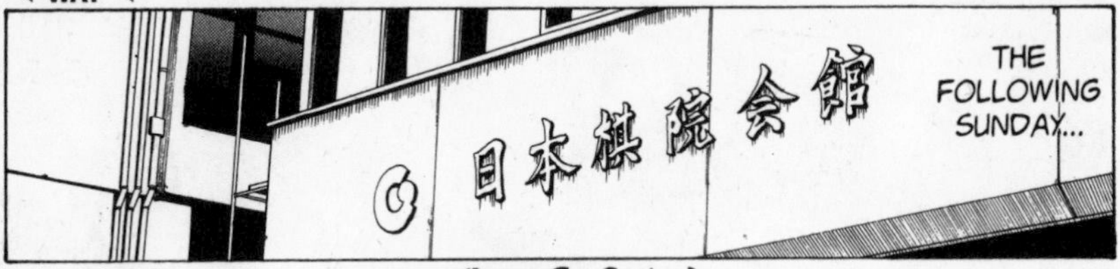
THE FOLLOWING SUNDAY...
日本棋院会館

(Japan Go Center)

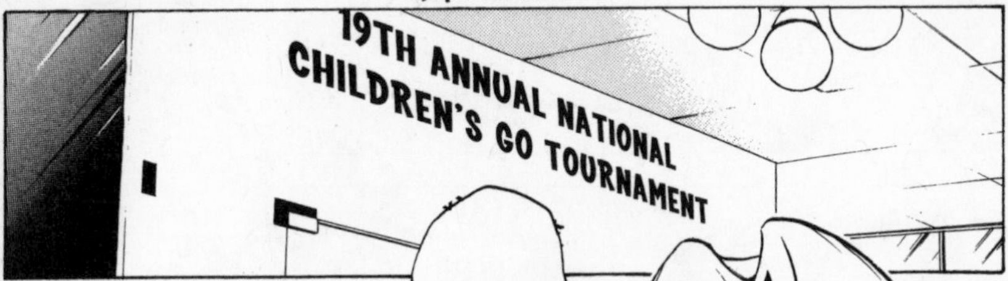
19TH ANNUAL NATIONAL CHILDREN'S GO TOURNAMENT

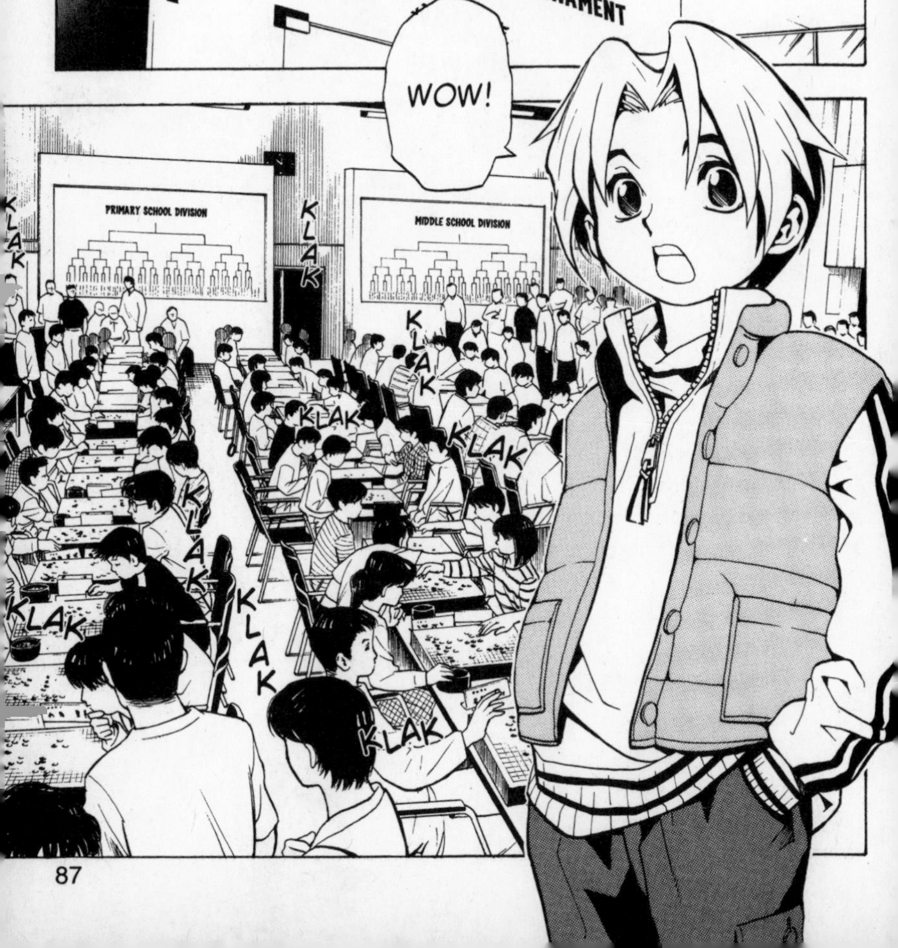
WOW!
MIDDLE SCHOOL DIVISION
PRIMARY SCHOOL DIVISION
KLAK
KLAK
KLAK
KLAK
KLAK
KLAK
KLAK
KLAK
KLAK
KLAK

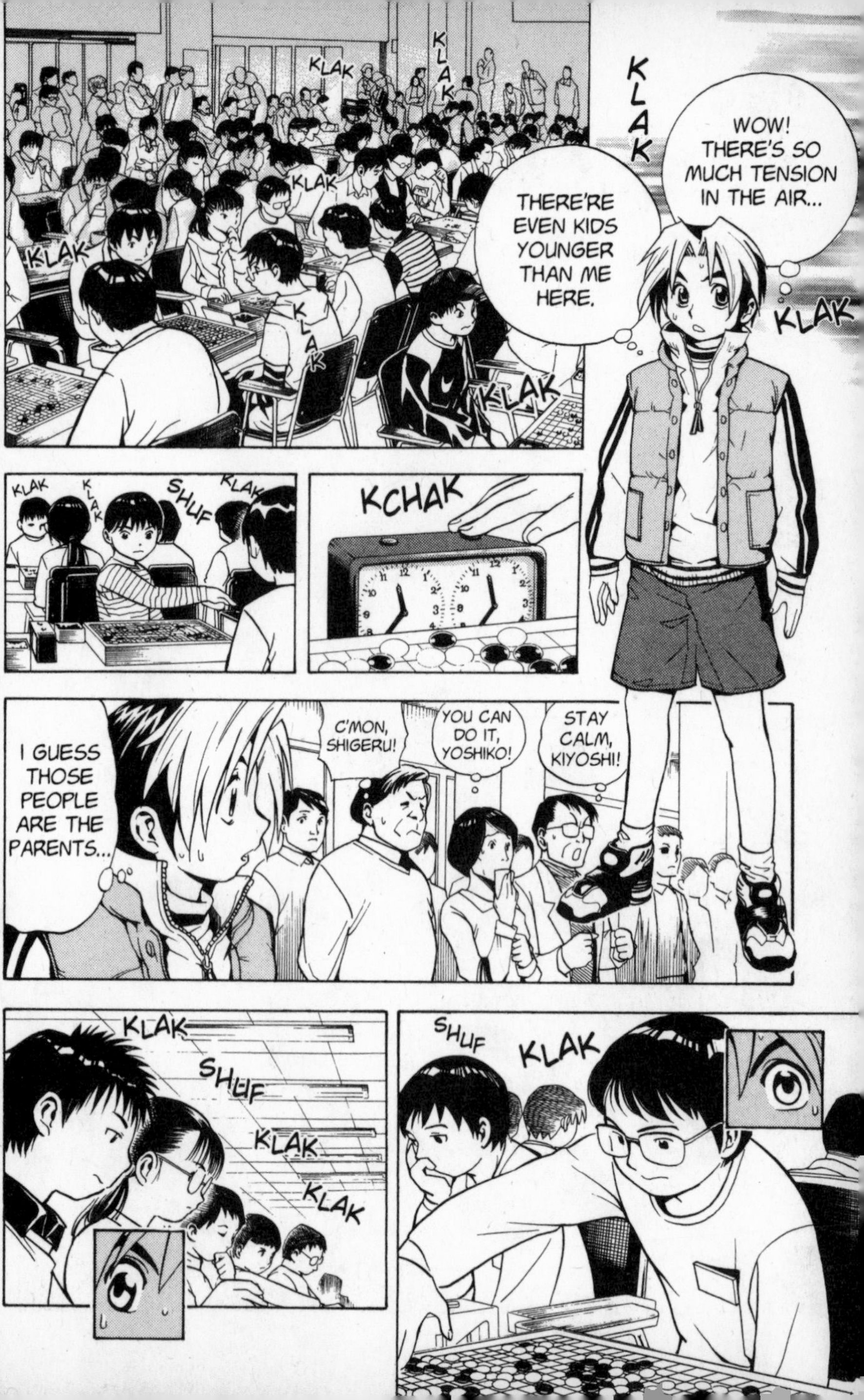
KLAK
WOW! THERE'S SO MUCH TENSION IN THE AIR...
KLAK
THERE'RE EVEN KIDS YOUNGER THAN ME HERE.
KLAK
KLAK
KLAK
KLAK
KLAK
KLAK
KLAK
KCHAK
KLAK
SHUF
KLAK
KLAK
STAY CALM, KIYOSHI!
YOU CAN DO IT, YOSHIKO!
C'MON, SHIGERU!
I GUESS THOSE PEOPLE ARE THE PARENTS...
KLAK
SHUF
KLAK
SHUF
KLAK
KLAK

READ THIS WAY

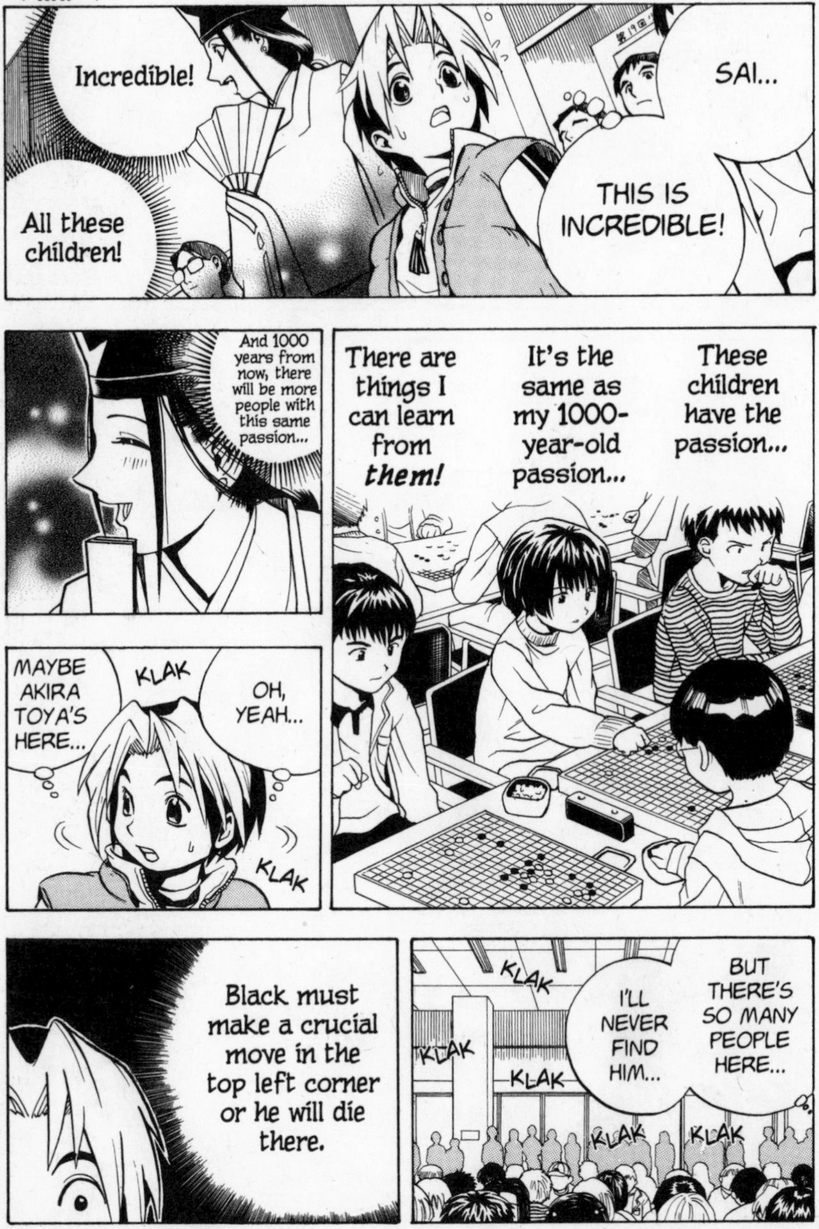
SAI...
THIS IS INCREDIBLE!
Incredible!
All these children!
These children have the passion...
It's the same as my 1000-year-old passion...
There are things I can learn from *them!*
And 1000 years from now, there will be more people with this same passion...
OH, YEAH...
KLAK
MAYBE AKIRA TOYA'S HERE...
KLAK
BUT THERE'S SO MANY PEOPLE HERE...
I'LL NEVER FIND HIM...
KLAK
KLAK
KLAK
KLAK
KLAK
Black must make a crucial move in the top left corner or he will die there.

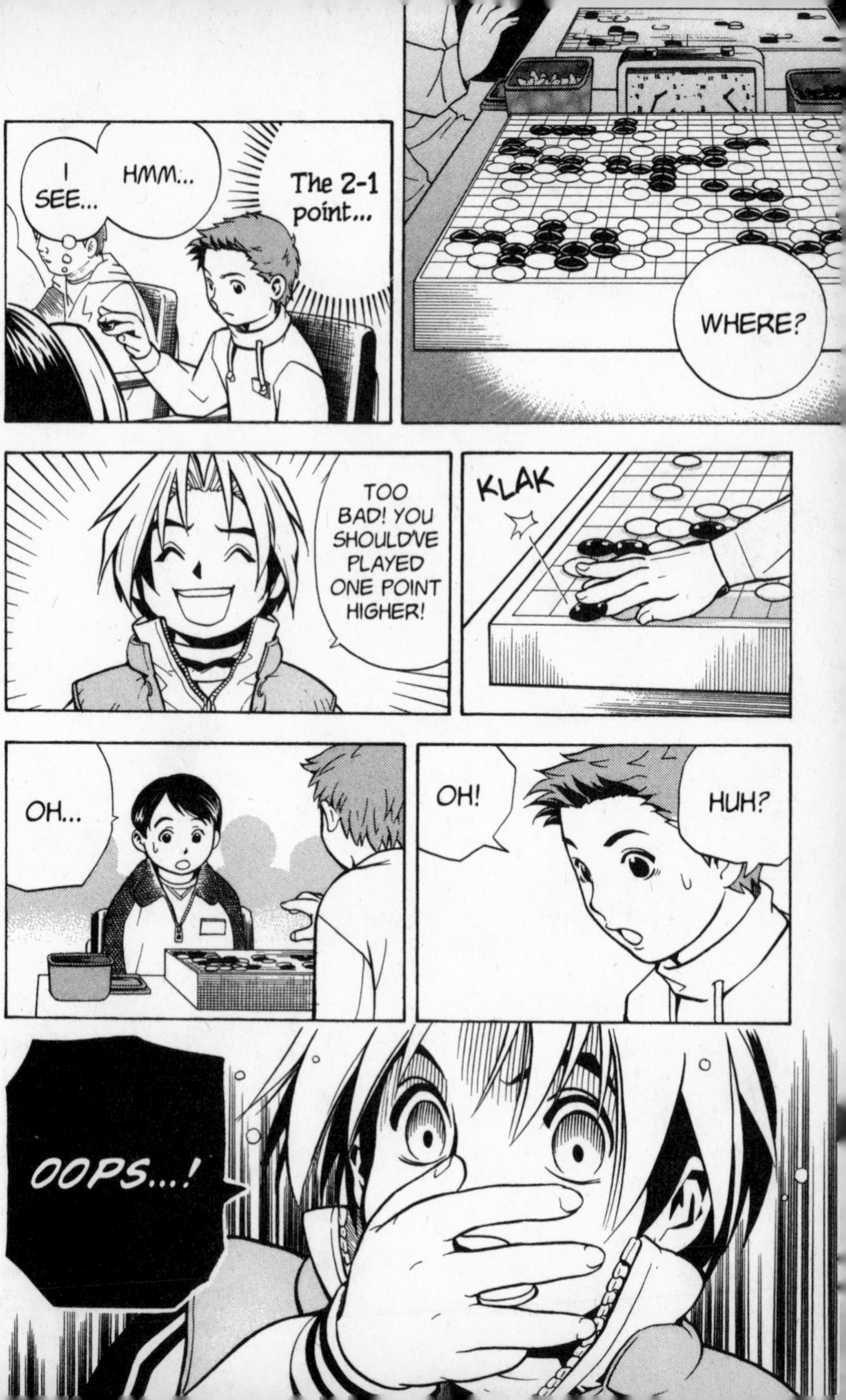
WHERE?
The 2-1 point...
HMM...
I SEE...
KLAK
TOO BAD! YOU SHOULD'VE PLAYED ONE POINT HIGHER!
HUH?
OH!
OH...
OOPS...!

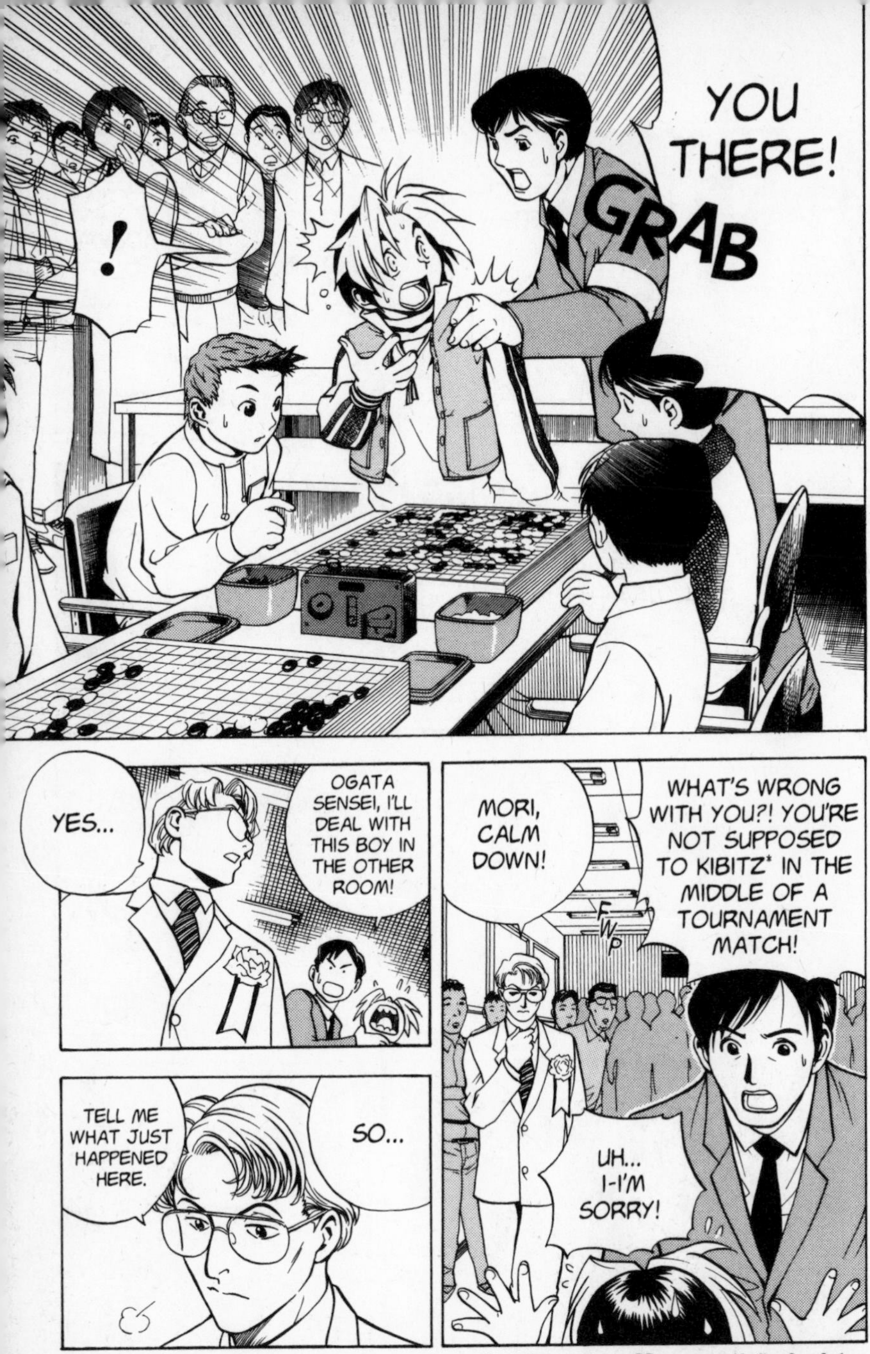
YOU THERE!
GRAB
!
WHAT'S WRONG WITH YOU?! YOU'RE NOT SUPPOSED TO KIBITZ* IN THE MIDDLE OF A TOURNAMENT MATCH!
FWP
MORI, CALM DOWN!
UH... I-I'M SORRY!
OGATA SENSEI, I'LL DEAL WITH THIS BOY IN THE OTHER ROOM!
YES...
SO...
TELL ME WHAT JUST HAPPENED HERE.

*kibitz - to offer unsolicited advice

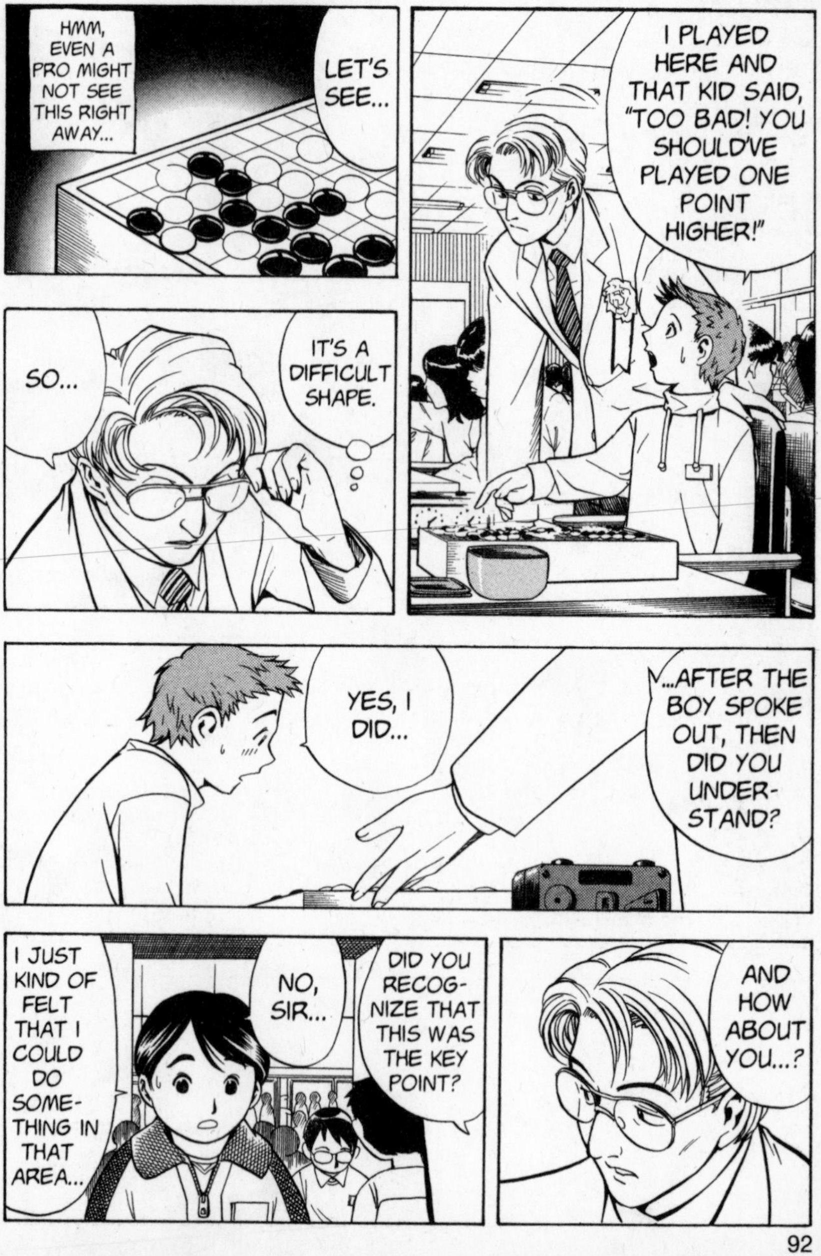
I PLAYED HERE AND THAT KID SAID, "TOO BAD! YOU SHOULD'VE PLAYED ONE POINT HIGHER!"
LET'S SEE...
HMM, EVEN A PRO MIGHT NOT SEE THIS RIGHT AWAY...
IT'S A DIFFICULT SHAPE.
SO...
...AFTER THE BOY SPOKE OUT, THEN DID YOU UNDER-STAND?
YES, I DID...
AND HOW ABOUT YOU...?
DID YOU RECOG-NIZE THAT THIS WAS THE KEY POINT?
NO, SIR...
I JUST KIND OF FELT THAT I COULD DO SOME-THING IN THAT AREA...

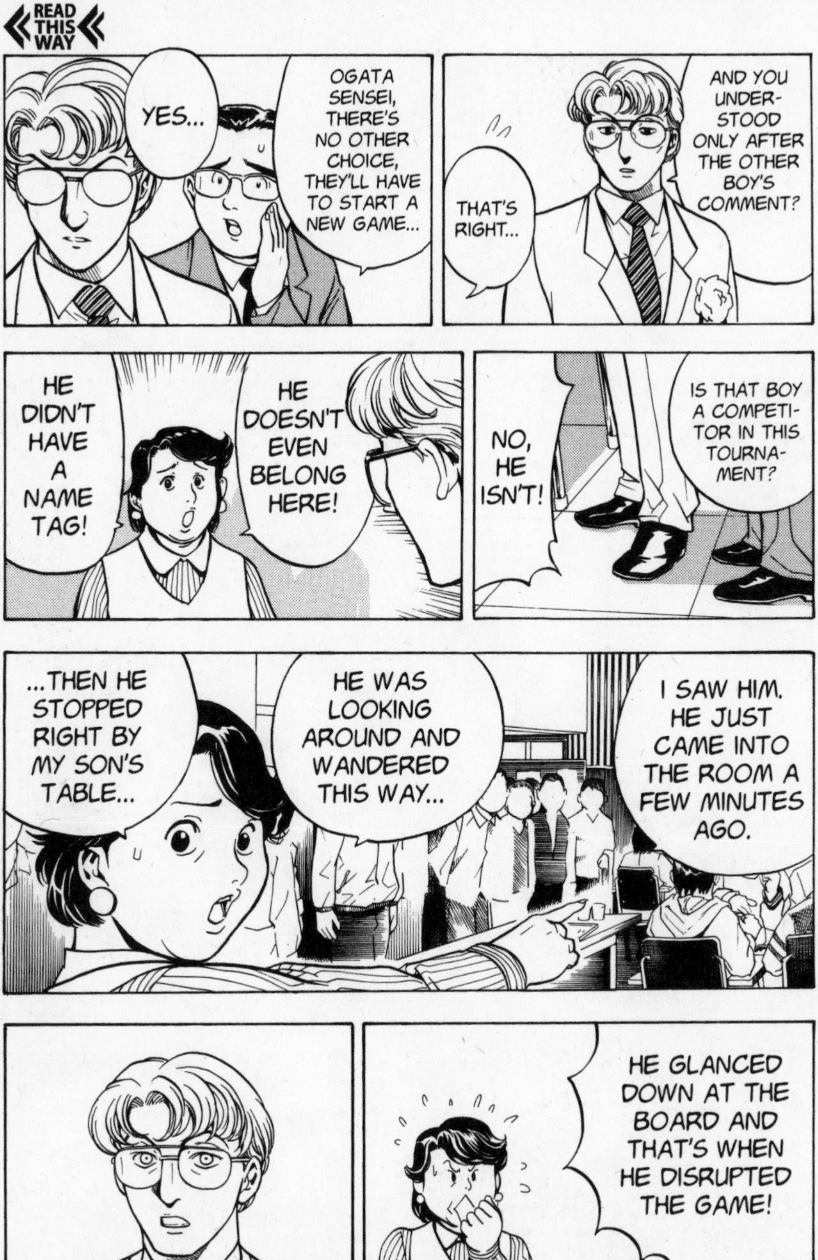
READ THIS WAY
AND YOU UNDERSTOOD ONLY AFTER THE OTHER BOY'S COMMENT?
THAT'S RIGHT...
OGATA SENSEI, THERE'S NO OTHER CHOICE, THEY'LL HAVE TO START A NEW GAME...
YES...
IS THAT BOY A COMPETITOR IN THIS TOURNAMENT?
NO, HE ISN'T!
HE DOESN'T EVEN BELONG HERE!
HE DIDN'T HAVE A NAME TAG!
I SAW HIM. HE JUST CAME INTO THE ROOM A FEW MINUTES AGO.
HE WAS LOOKING AROUND AND WANDERED THIS WAY...
...THEN HE STOPPED RIGHT BY MY SON'S TABLE...
HE GLANCED DOWN AT THE BOARD AND THAT'S WHEN HE DISRUPTED THE GAME!

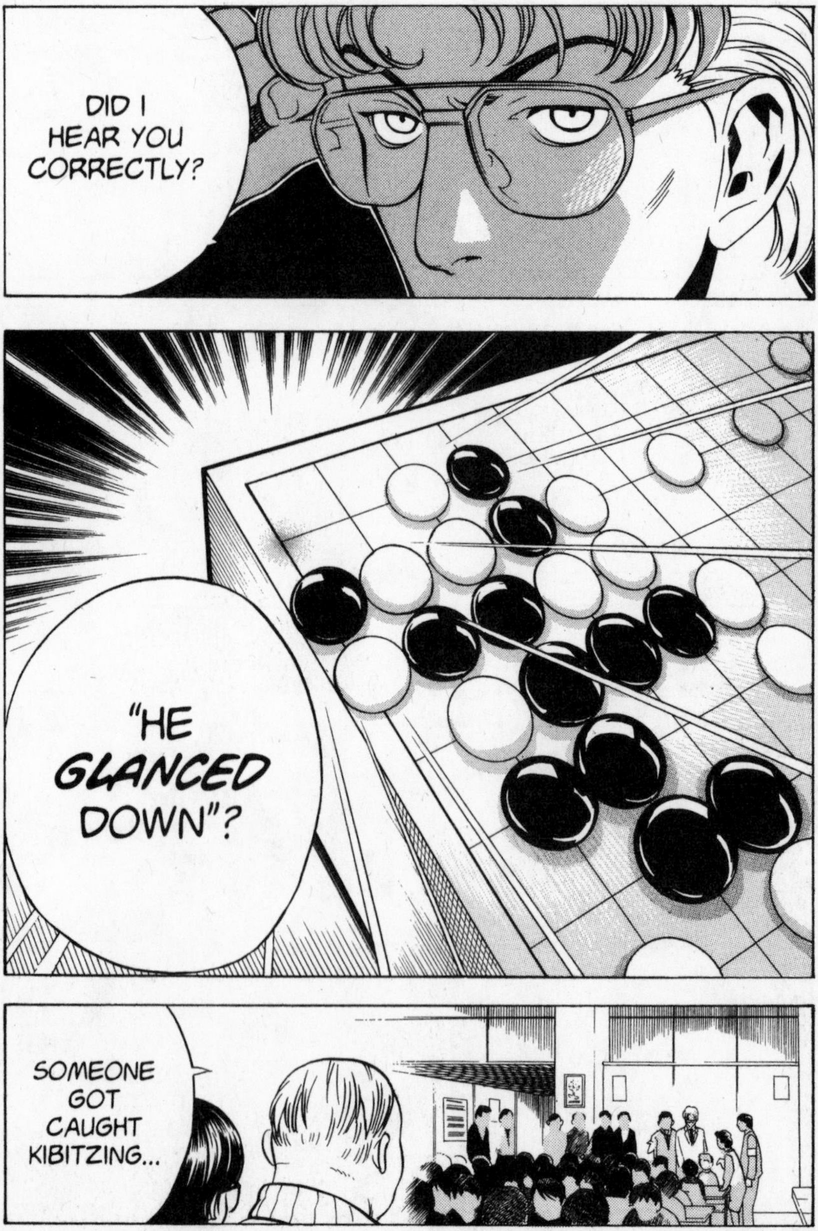
DID I HEAR YOU CORRECTLY?
"HE *GLANCED* DOWN"?
SOMEONE GOT CAUGHT KIBITZING...

READ THIS WAY

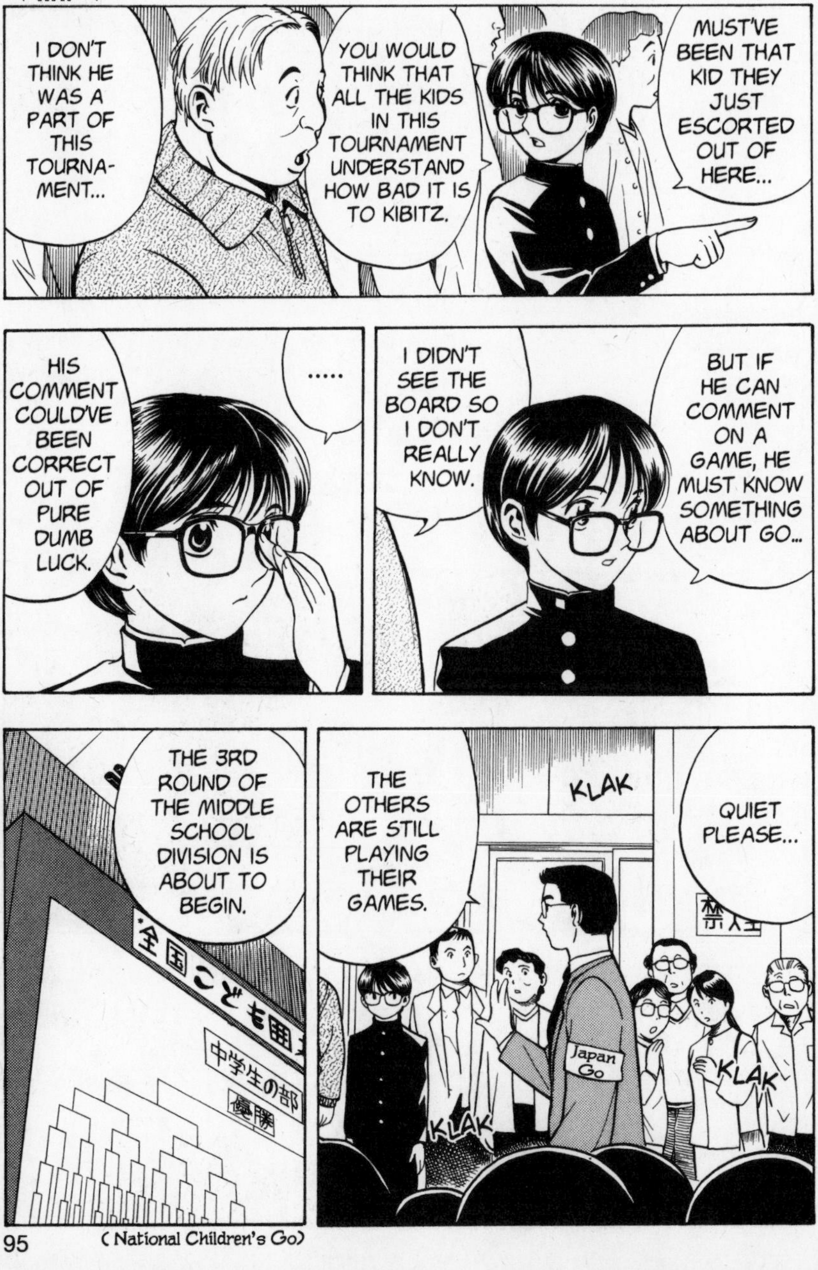

MUST'VE BEEN THAT KID THEY JUST ESCORTED OUT OF HERE...
YOU WOULD THINK THAT ALL THE KIDS IN THIS TOURNAMENT UNDERSTAND HOW BAD IT IS TO KIBITZ.
I DON'T THINK HE WAS A PART OF THIS TOURNA-MENT...
BUT IF HE CAN COMMENT ON A GAME, HE MUST KNOW SOMETHING ABOUT GO...
I DIDN'T SEE THE BOARD SO I DON'T REALLY KNOW.
.....
HIS COMMENT COULD'VE BEEN CORRECT OUT OF PURE DUMB LUCK.
QUIET PLEASE...
KLAK
THE OTHERS ARE STILL PLAYING THEIR GAMES.
Japan Go
KLAK
KLAK
THE 3RD ROUND OF THE MIDDLE SCHOOL DIVISION IS ABOUT TO BEGIN.
全国こども囲
中学生の部
優勝

(National Children's Go)

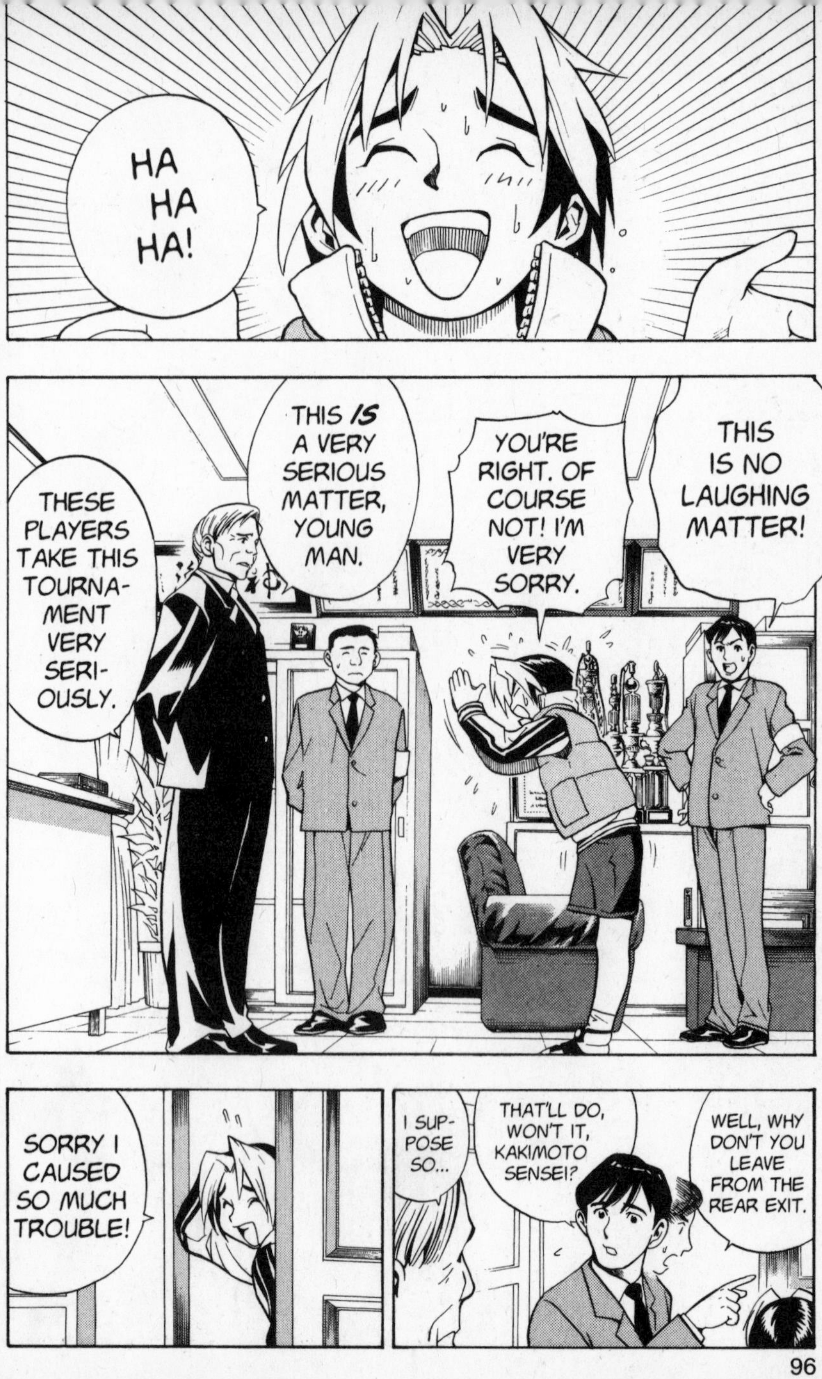
HA HA HA!
THIS IS NO LAUGHING MATTER!
YOU'RE RIGHT. OF COURSE NOT! I'M VERY SORRY.
THIS *IS* A VERY SERIOUS MATTER, YOUNG MAN.
THESE PLAYERS TAKE THIS TOURNAMENT VERY SERIOUSLY.
WELL, WHY DON'T YOU LEAVE FROM THE REAR EXIT.
THAT'LL DO, WON'T IT, KAKIMOTO SENSEI?
I SUPPOSE SO...
SORRY I CAUSED SO MUCH TROUBLE!

READ THIS WAY

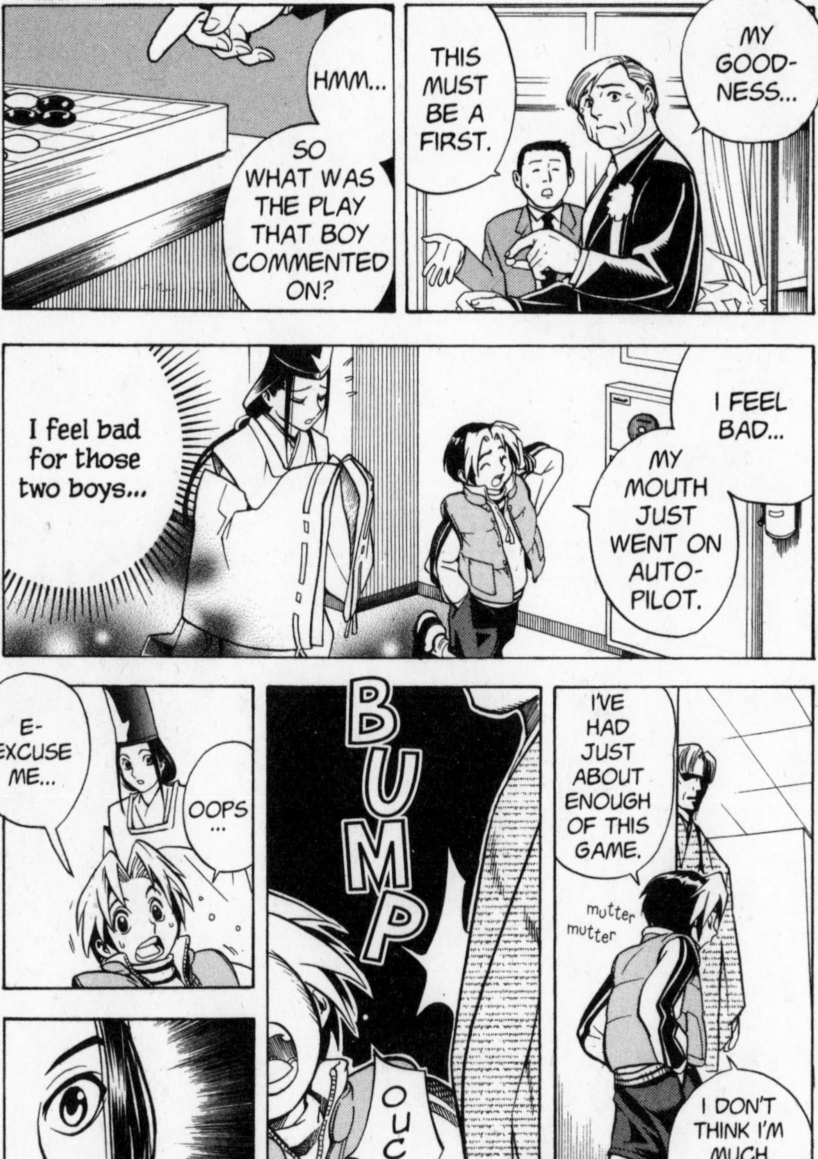
MY GOODNESS...
THIS MUST BE A FIRST.
HMM...
SO WHAT WAS THE PLAY THAT BOY COMMENTED ON?
I FEEL BAD...
MY MOUTH JUST WENT ON AUTO-PILOT.
I feel bad for those two boys...
I'VE HAD JUST ABOUT ENOUGH OF THIS GAME.
mutter mutter
I DON'T THINK I'M MUCH SUITED FOR IT.
BUMP
OUCH!
OOPS...
E-EXCUSE ME...

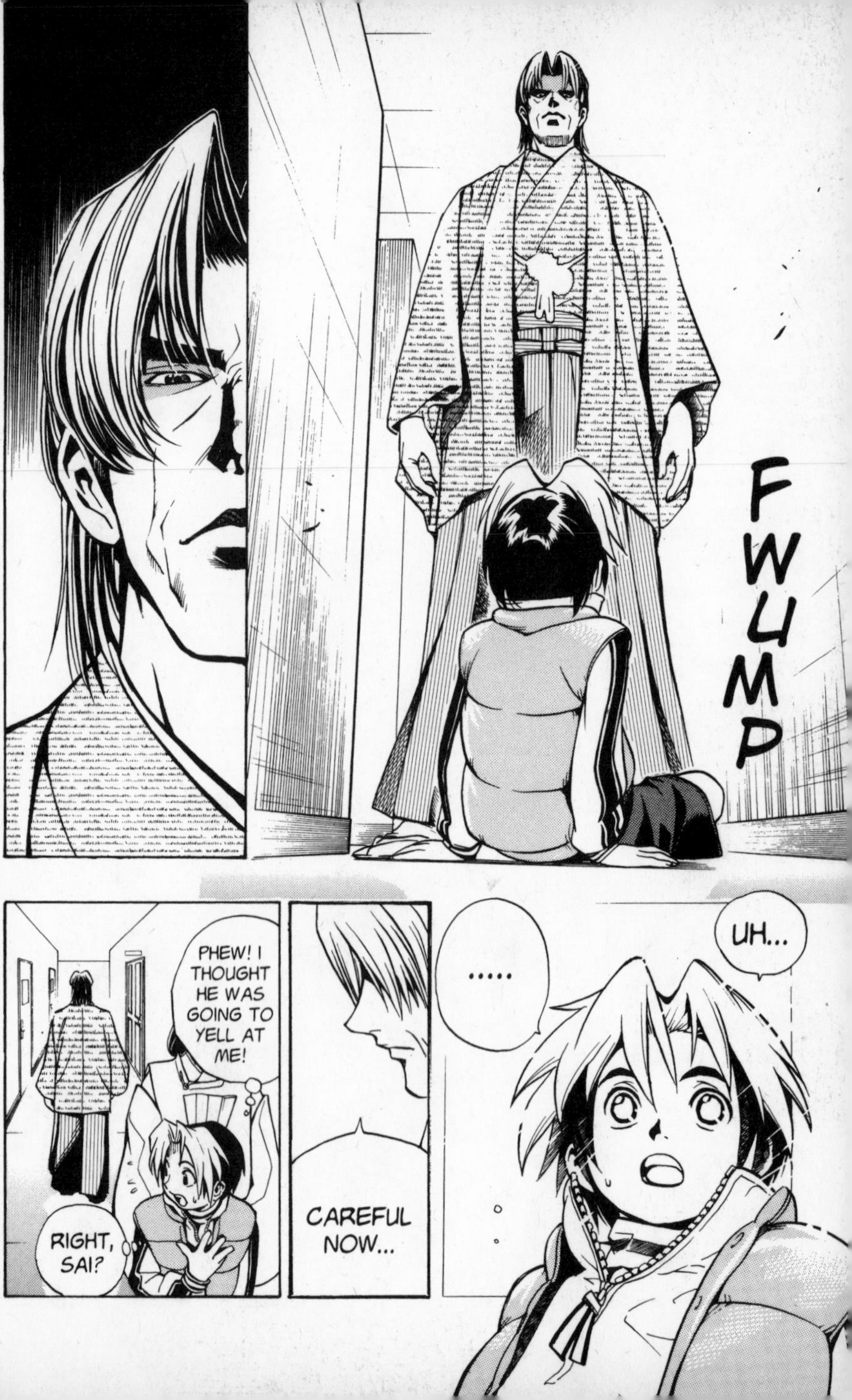
FWUMP
UH...
.....
CAREFUL NOW...
PHEW! I THOUGHT HE WAS GOING TO YELL AT ME!
RIGHT, SAI?

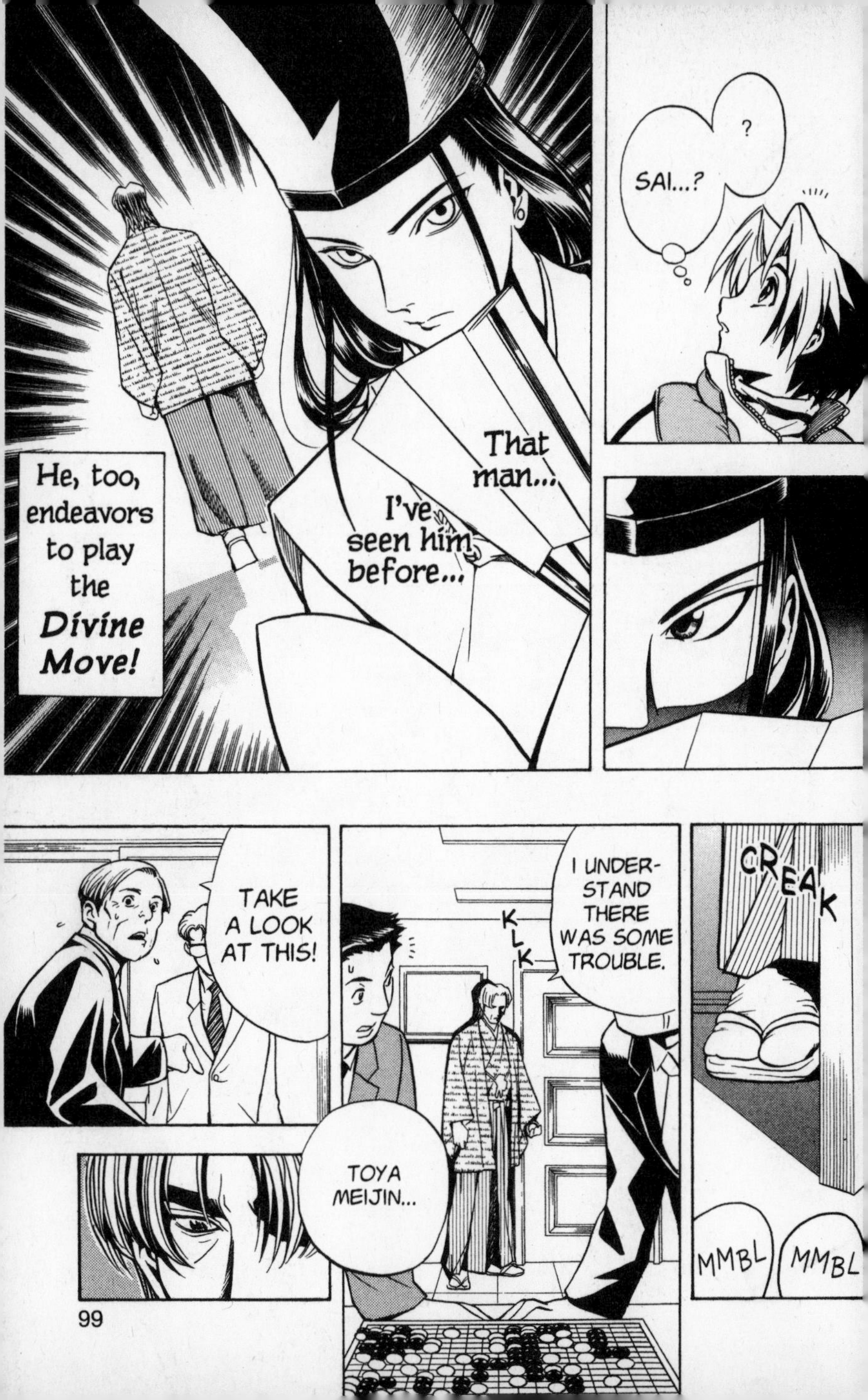
?
SAI...?
That man...
I've seen him before...
He, too, endeavors to play the *Divine Move!*
CREAK
MMBL
MMBL
I UNDERSTAND THERE WAS SOME TROUBLE.
KLK
TOYA MEIJIN...
TAKE A LOOK AT THIS!

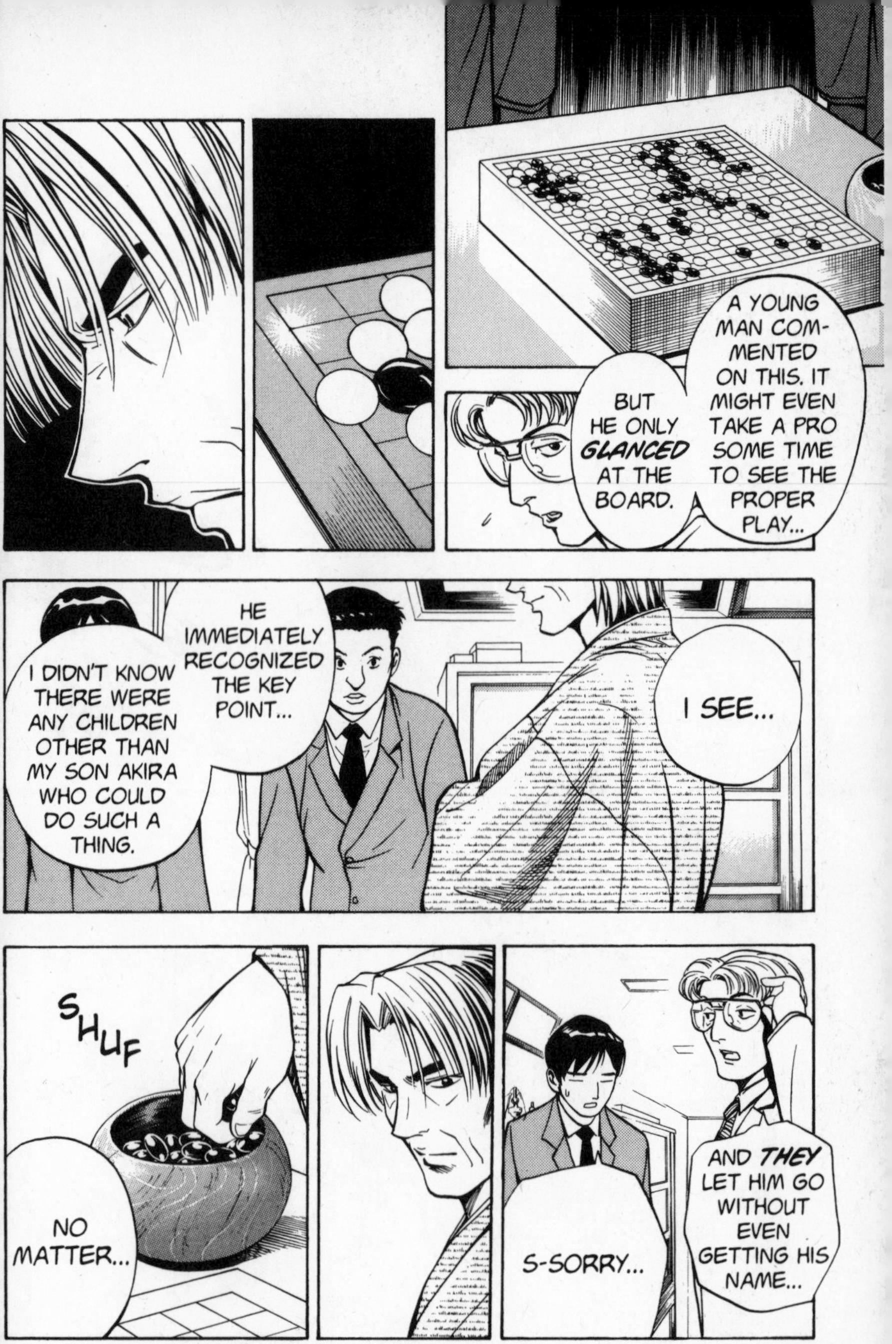

A YOUNG MAN COMMENTED ON THIS. IT MIGHT EVEN TAKE A PRO SOME TIME TO SEE THE PROPER PLAY...
BUT HE ONLY GLANCED AT THE BOARD.
I SEE...
HE IMMEDIATELY RECOGNIZED THE KEY POINT...
I DIDN'T KNOW THERE WERE ANY CHILDREN OTHER THAN MY SON AKIRA WHO COULD DO SUCH A THING.
AND THEY LET HIM GO WITHOUT EVEN GETTING HIS NAME...
S-SORRY...
SHUF
NO MATTER...

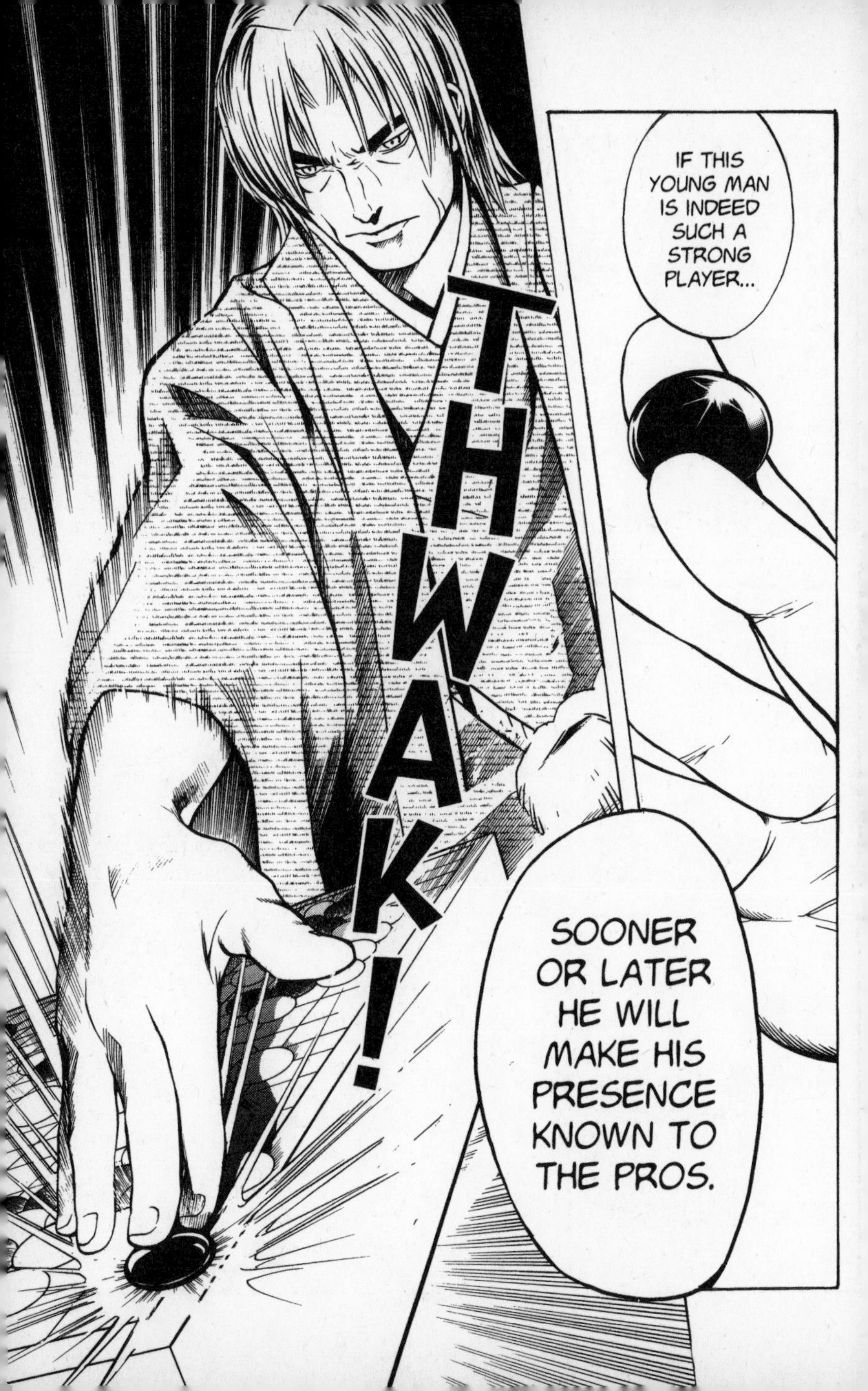
IF THIS YOUNG MAN IS INDEED SUCH A STRONG PLAYER...
SOONER OR LATER HE WILL MAKE HIS PRESENCE KNOWN TO THE PROS.
THWAK!

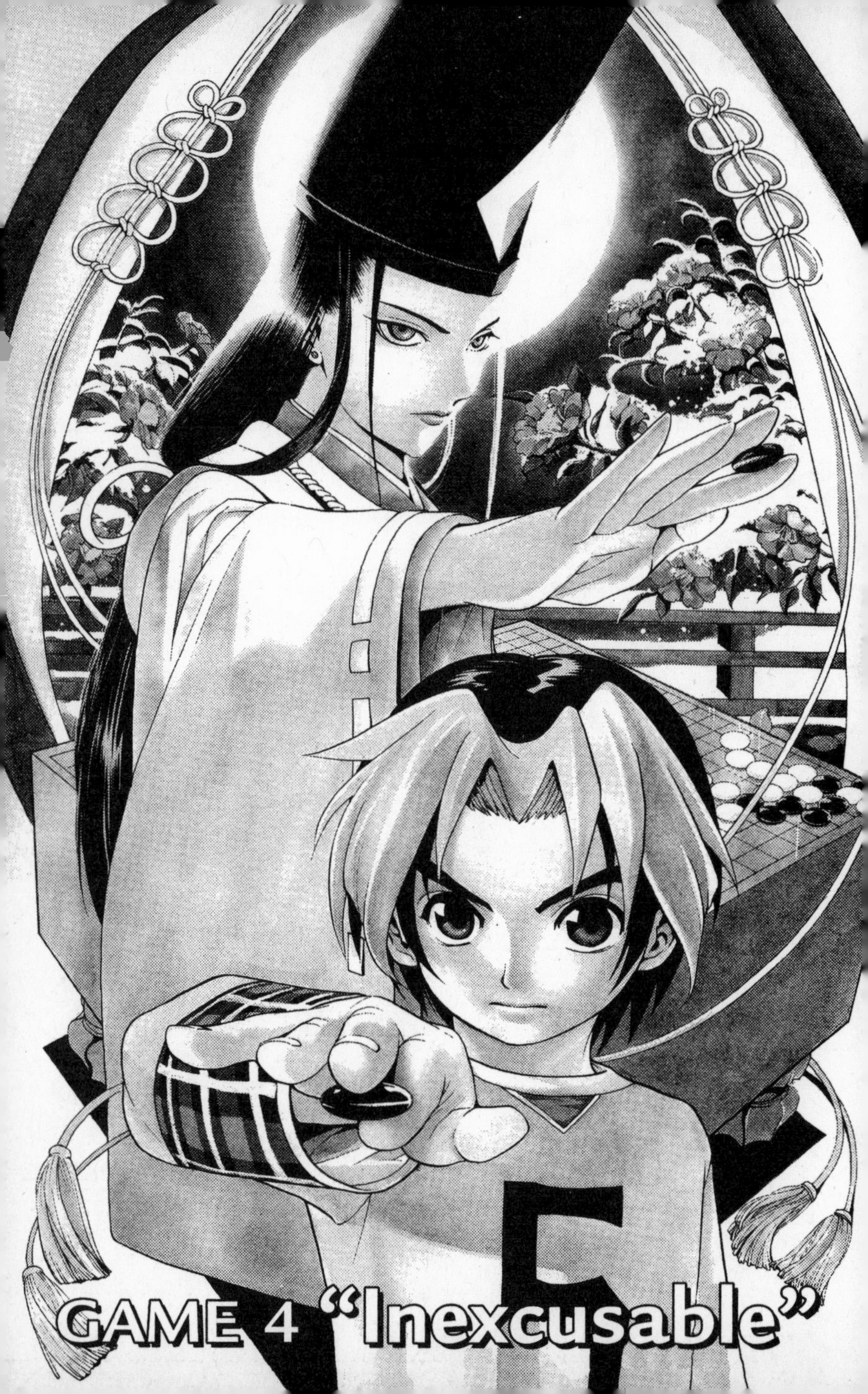

GAME 4 "Inexcusable"

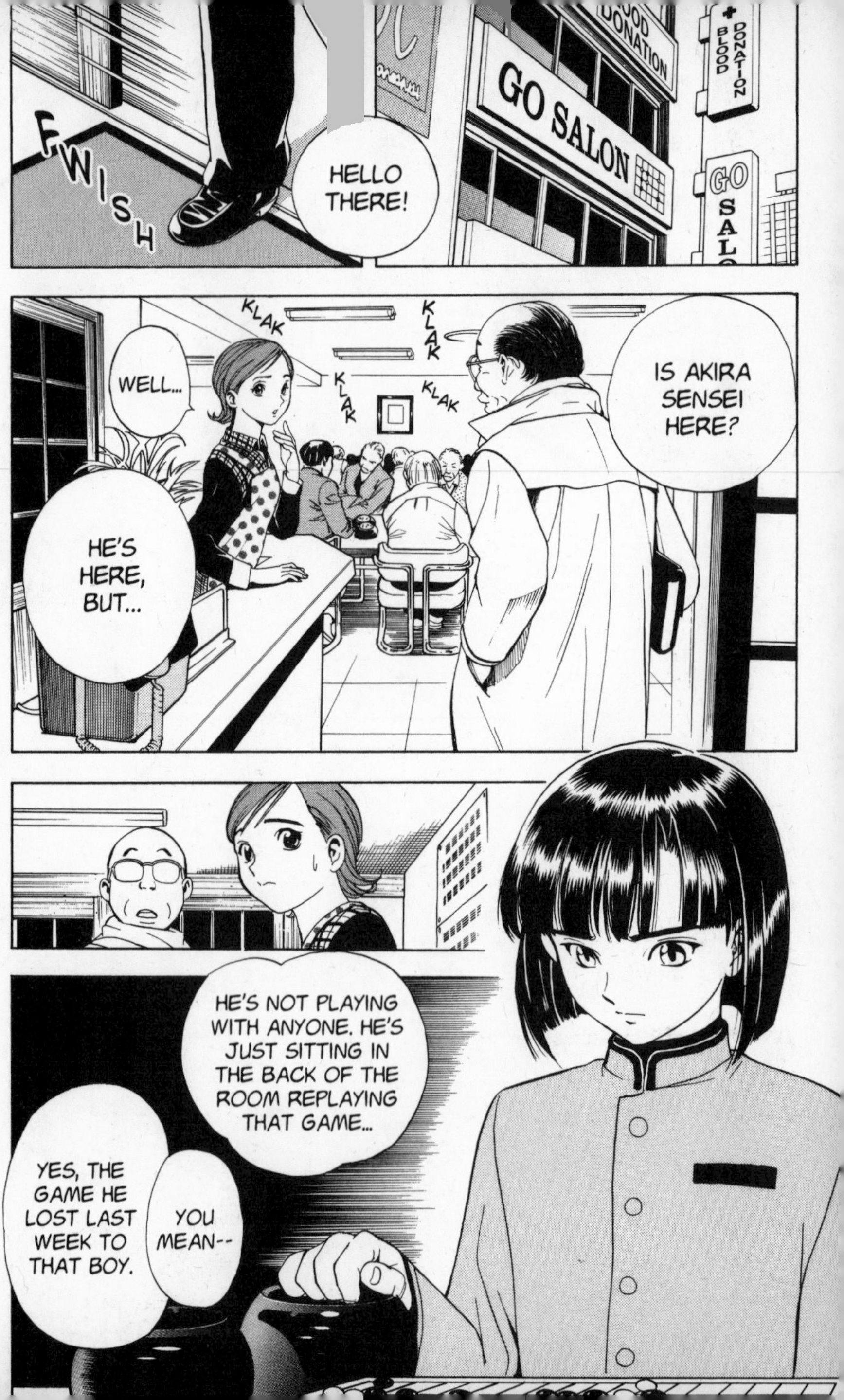
BLOOD DONATION
GO SALON
HELLO THERE!
FWISH
IS AKIRA SENSEI HERE?
KLAK
KLAK
KLAK
KLAK
WELL...
HE'S HERE, BUT...
HE'S NOT PLAYING WITH ANYONE. HE'S JUST SITTING IN THE BACK OF THE ROOM REPLAYING THAT GAME...
YOU MEAN--
YES, THE GAME HE LOST LAST WEEK TO THAT BOY.

READ THIS WAY

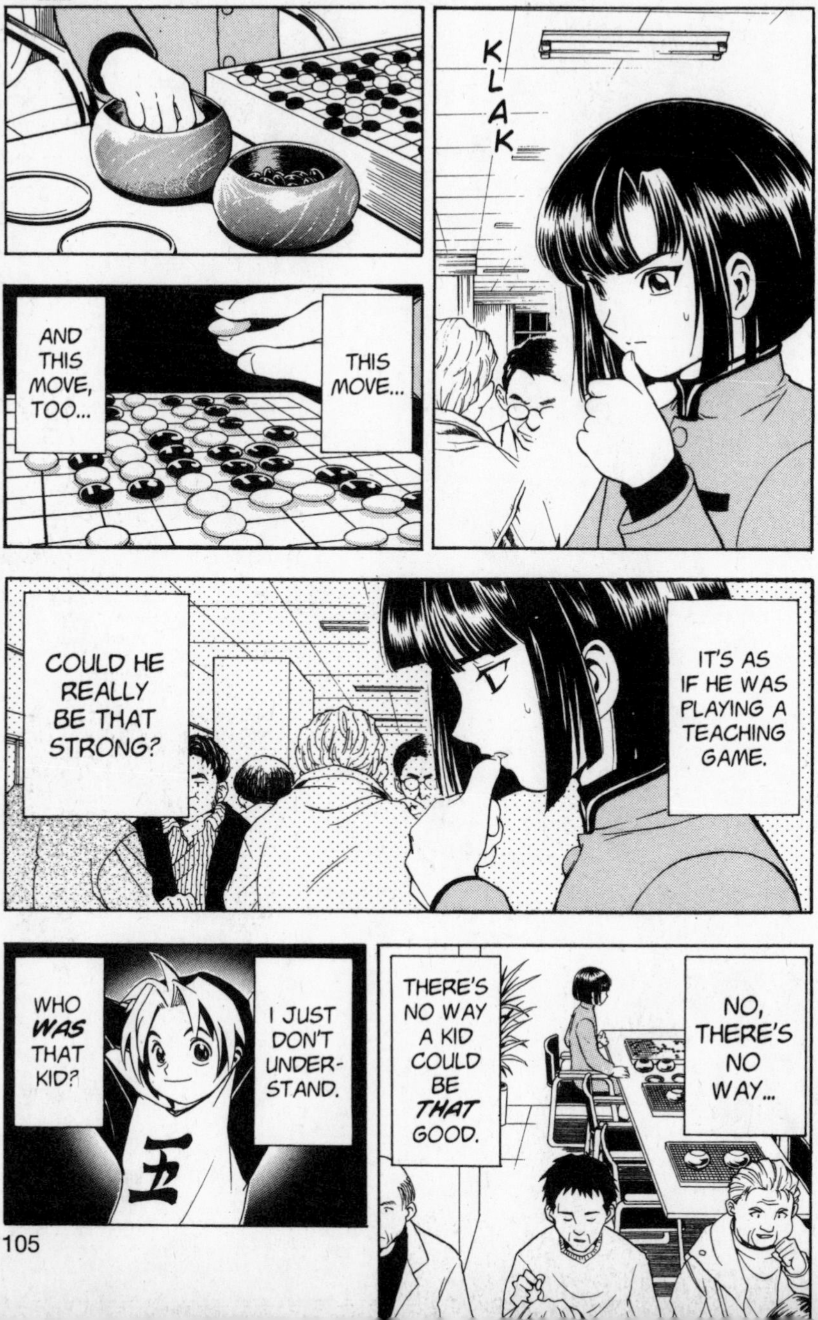
KLAK
THIS MOVE...
AND THIS MOVE, TOO...
IT'S AS IF HE WAS PLAYING A TEACHING GAME.
COULD HE REALLY BE THAT STRONG?
NO, THERE'S NO WAY...
THERE'S NO WAY A KID COULD BE *THAT* GOOD.
I JUST DON'T UNDER-STAND.
WHO *WAS* THAT KID?

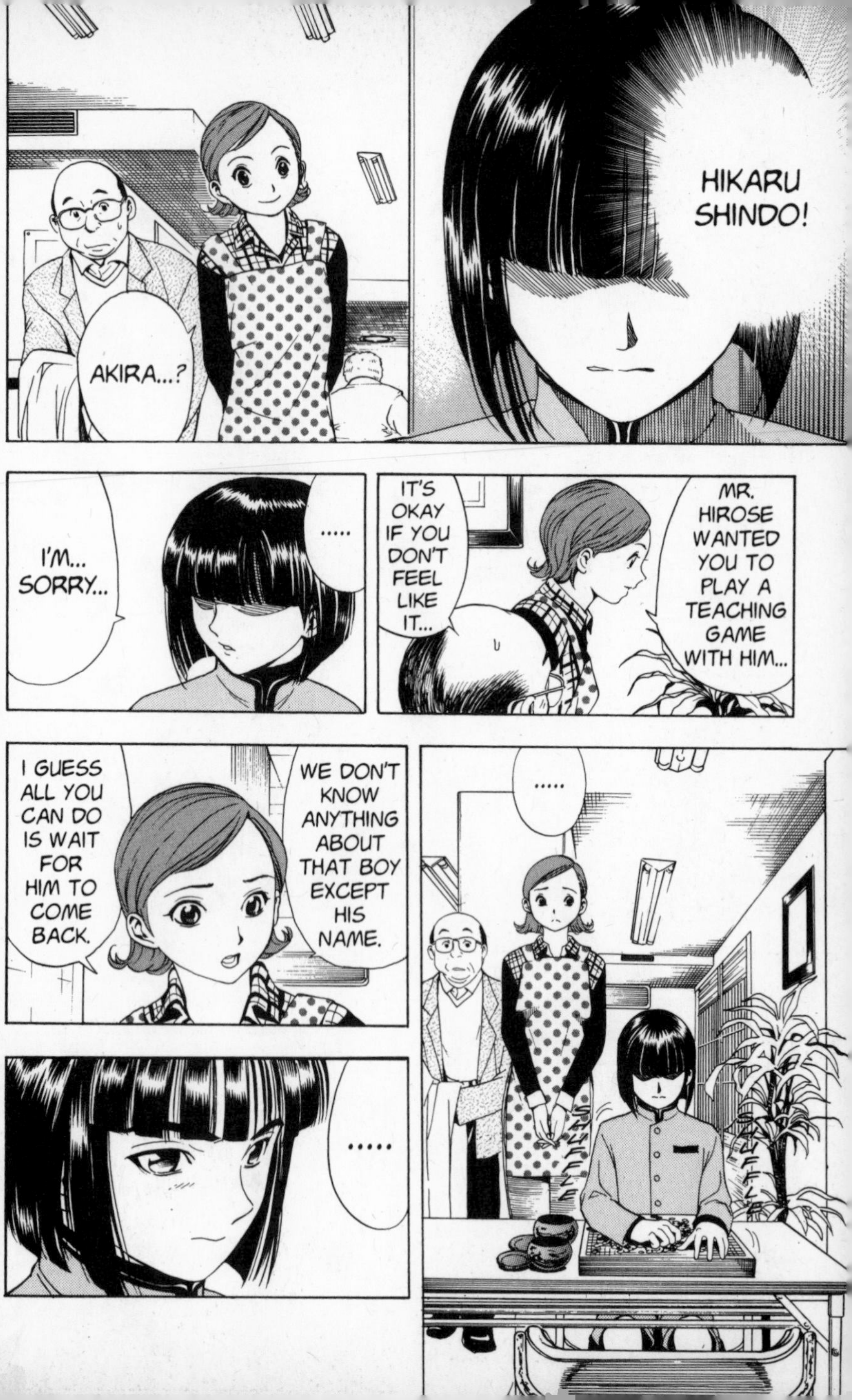
HIKARU SHINDO!
AKIRA...?
MR. HIROSE WANTED YOU TO PLAY A TEACHING GAME WITH HIM...
IT'S OKAY IF YOU DON'T FEEL LIKE IT...
.....
I'M... SORRY...
.....
SHUFFLE
SHUFFLE
WE DON'T KNOW ANYTHING ABOUT THAT BOY EXCEPT HIS NAME.
I GUESS ALL YOU CAN DO IS WAIT FOR HIM TO COME BACK.
.....

READ THIS WAY

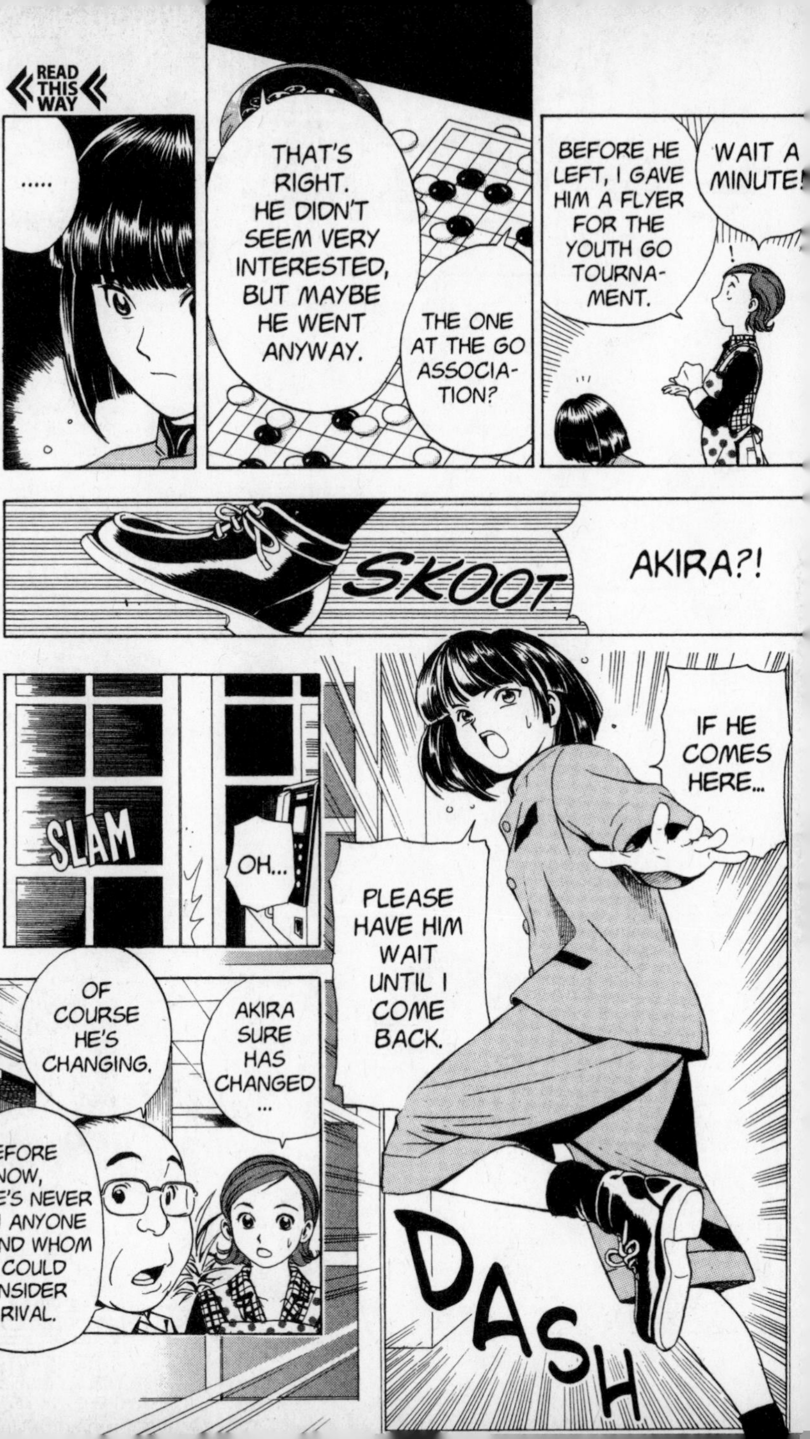
WAIT A MINUTE!
BEFORE HE LEFT, I GAVE HIM A FLYER FOR THE YOUTH GO TOURNAMENT.
THE ONE AT THE GO ASSOCIATION?
THAT'S RIGHT. HE DIDN'T SEEM VERY INTERESTED, BUT MAYBE HE WENT ANYWAY.
.....
AKIRA?!
SKOOT
IF HE COMES HERE...
PLEASE HAVE HIM WAIT UNTIL I COME BACK.
DASH
OH...
SLAM
AKIRA SURE HAS CHANGED...
OF COURSE HE'S CHANGING.
BEFORE NOW, THERE'S NEVER BEEN ANYONE AROUND WHOM HE COULD CONSIDER A RIVAL.

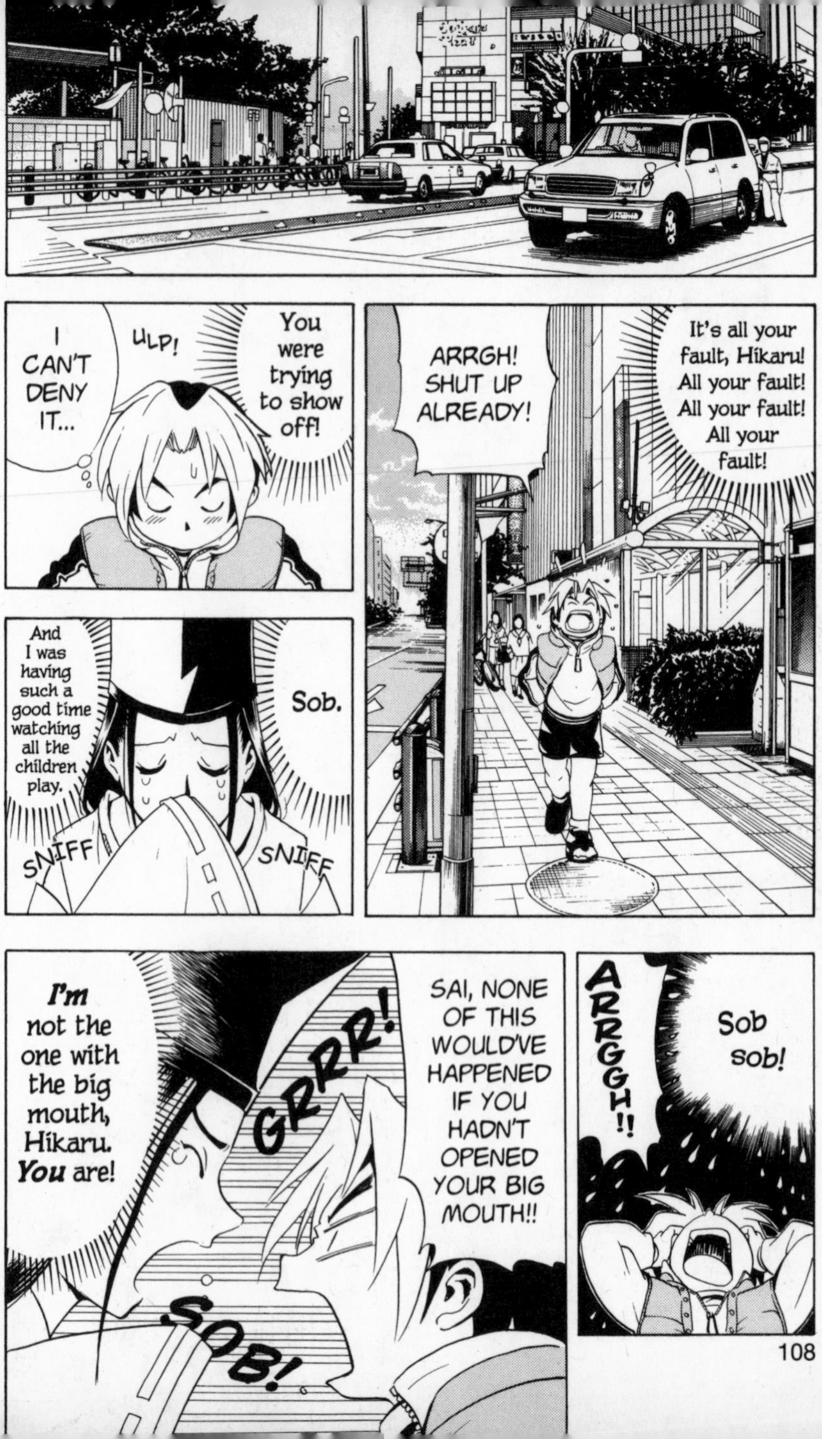

It's all your fault, Hikaru! All your fault! All your fault! All your fault!
ARRGH! SHUT UP ALREADY!
You were trying to show off!
ULP!
I CAN'T DENY IT...
Sob.
And I was having such a good time watching all the children play.
SNIFF
SNIFF
Sob sob!
ARRGGH!!
SAI, NONE OF THIS WOULD'VE HAPPENED IF YOU HADN'T OPENED YOUR BIG MOUTH!!
GRRR!
I'm not the one with the big mouth, Hikaru. *You* are!
SOB!

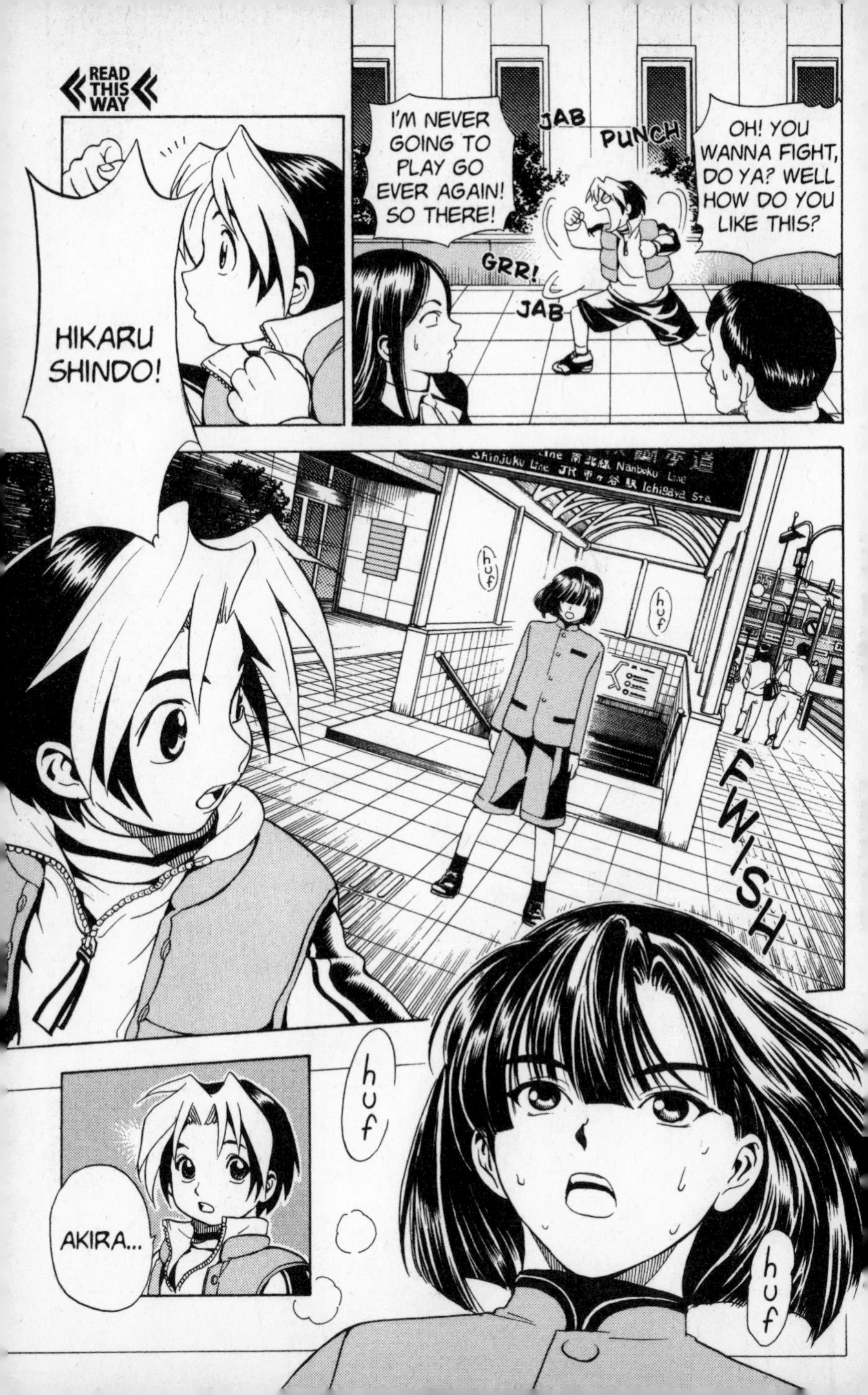
READ THIS WAY
OH! YOU WANNA FIGHT, DO YA? WELL HOW DO YOU LIKE THIS?
PUNCH
JAB
I'M NEVER GOING TO PLAY GO EVER AGAIN! SO THERE!
GRR!
JAB
HIKARU SHINDO!
Nanboku Line
Ichigaya Sta
huf
huf
FWISH
huf
huf
AKIRA...

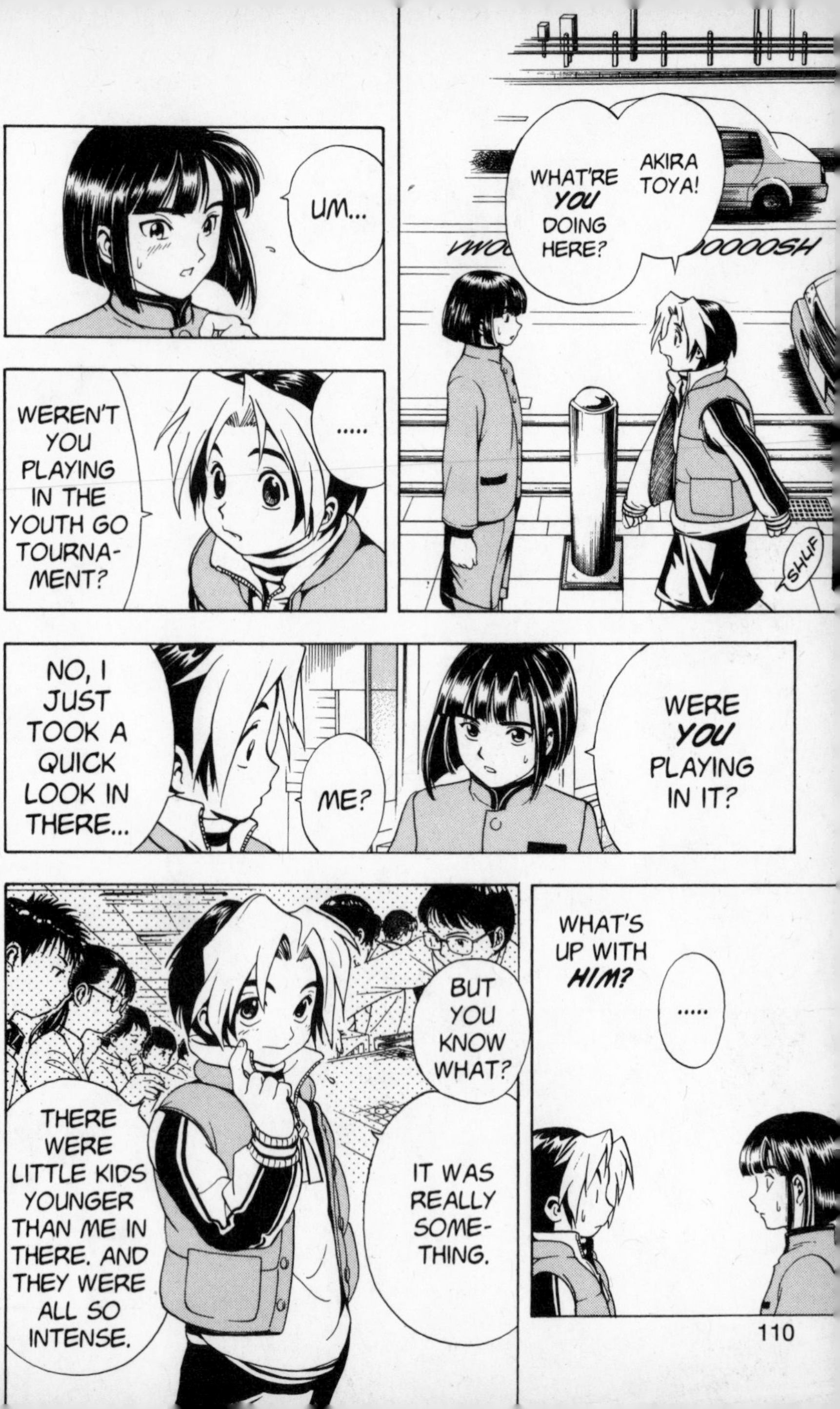
AKIRA TOYA!
WHAT'RE YOU DOING HERE?
VWOO
OOOOOSH
SHUF
UM...
.....
WEREN'T YOU PLAYING IN THE YOUTH GO TOURNAMENT?
WERE YOU PLAYING IN IT?
ME?
NO, I JUST TOOK A QUICK LOOK IN THERE...
WHAT'S UP WITH HIM?
.....
BUT YOU KNOW WHAT?
IT WAS REALLY SOMETHING.
THERE WERE LITTLE KIDS YOUNGER THAN ME IN THERE. AND THEY WERE ALL SO INTENSE.

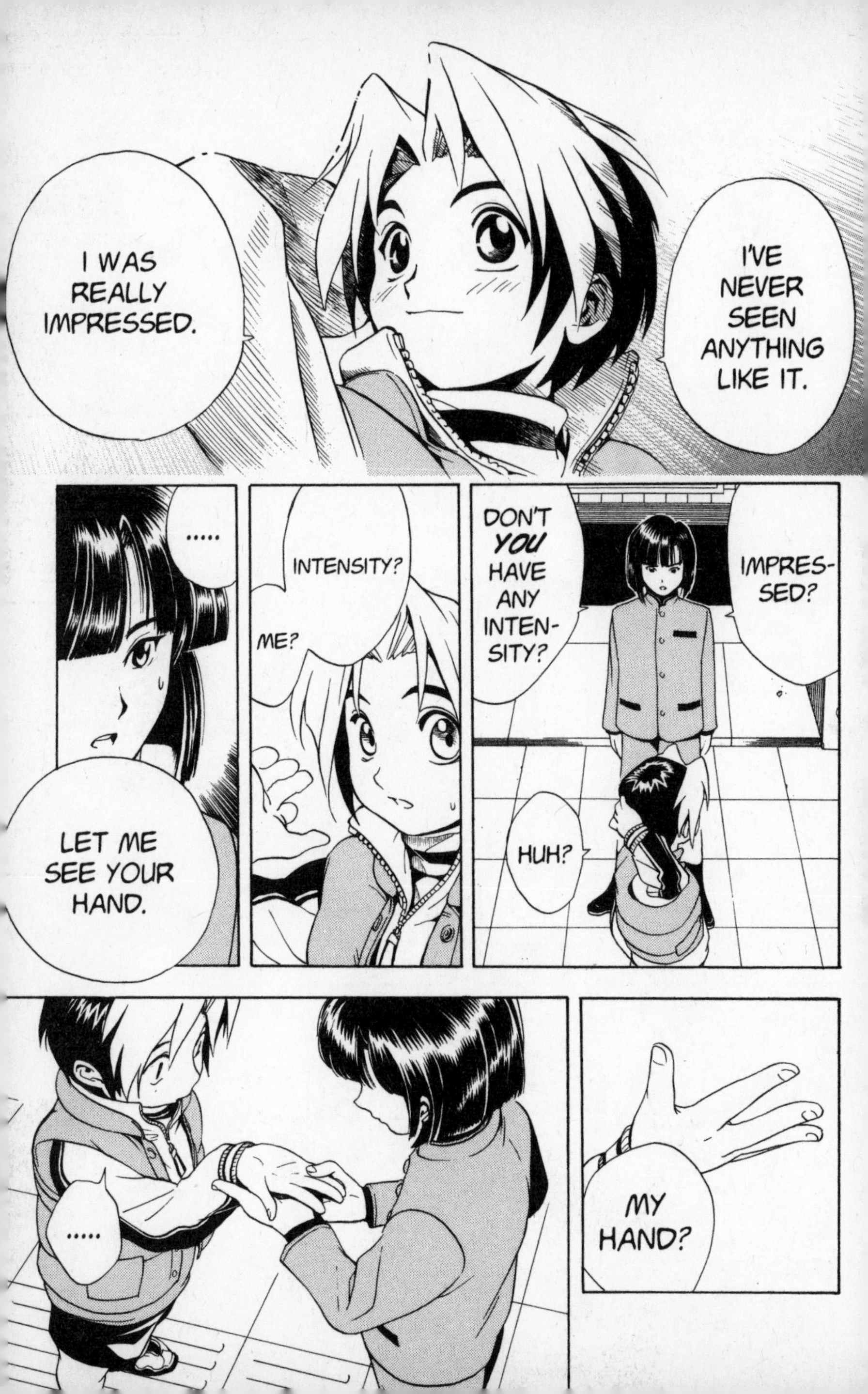
I'VE NEVER SEEN ANYTHING LIKE IT.
I WAS REALLY IMPRESSED.
IMPRESSED?
DON'T YOU HAVE ANY INTEN-SITY?
HUH?
INTENSITY?
ME?
.....
LET ME SEE YOUR HAND.
MY HAND?
.....

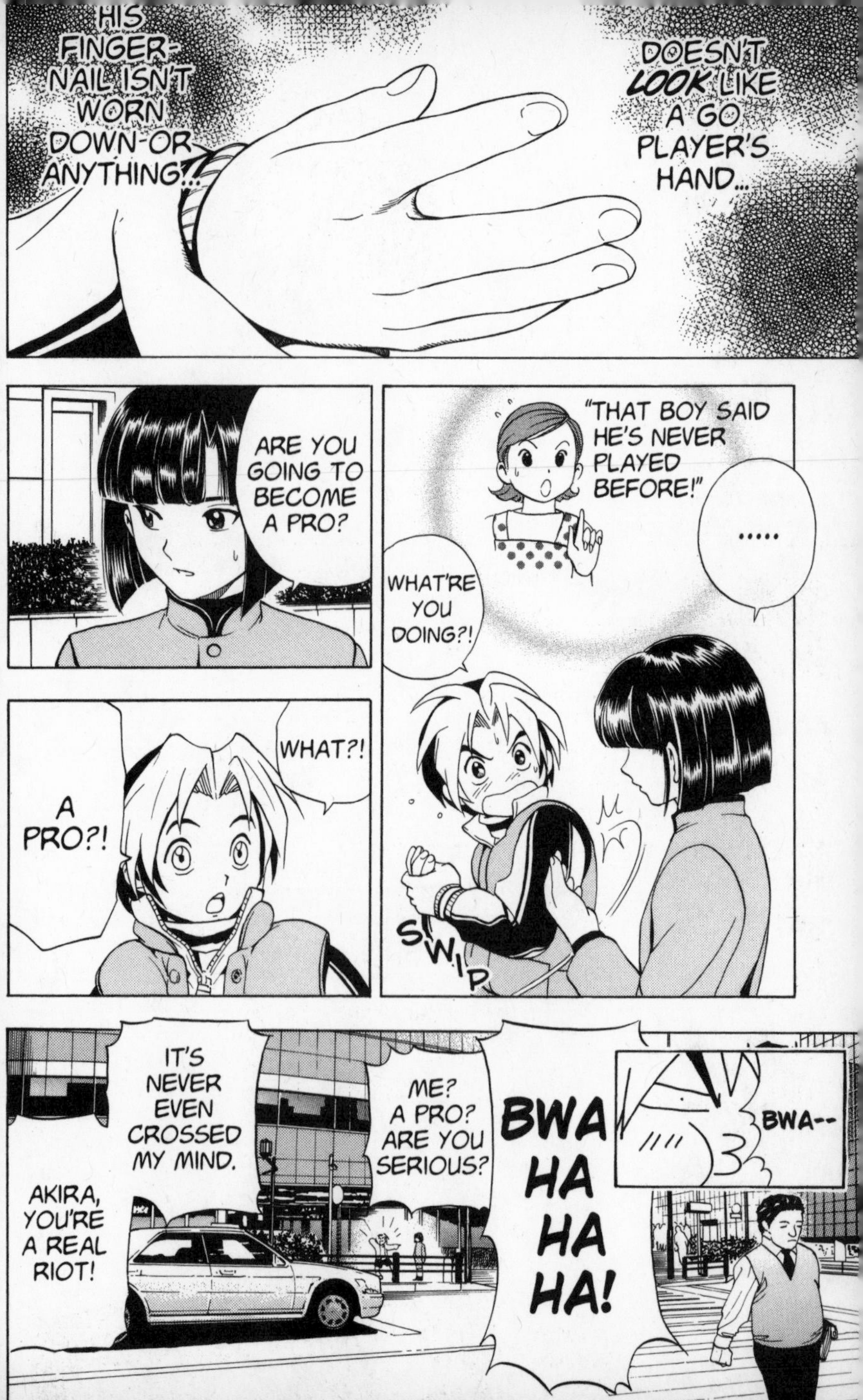
DOESN'T *LOOK* LIKE A GO PLAYER'S HAND...
HIS FINGER-NAIL ISN'T WORN DOWN-OR ANYTHING...
"THAT BOY SAID HE'S NEVER PLAYED BEFORE!"
.....
WHAT'RE YOU DOING?!
SWIP
ARE YOU GOING TO BECOME A PRO?
WHAT?!
A PRO?!
BWA--
BWA HA HA HA HA!
ME? A PRO? ARE YOU SERIOUS?
IT'S NEVER EVEN CROSSED MY MIND.
AKIRA, YOU'RE A REAL RIOT!

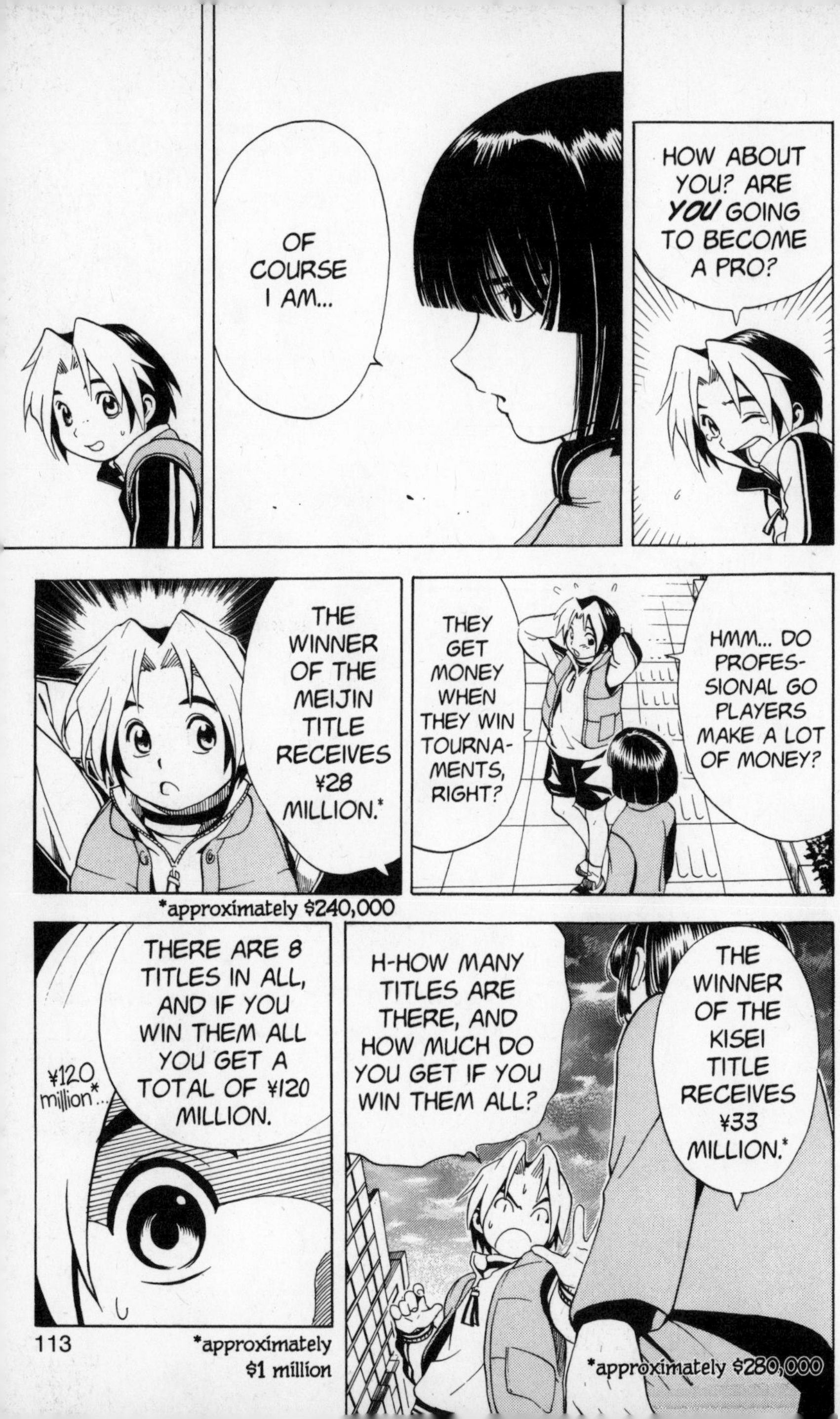
HOW ABOUT YOU? ARE ***YOU*** GOING TO BECOME A PRO?
OF COURSE I AM...
HMM... DO PROFES-SIONAL GO PLAYERS MAKE A LOT OF MONEY?
THEY GET MONEY WHEN THEY WIN TOURNA-MENTS, RIGHT?
THE WINNER OF THE MEIJIN TITLE RECEIVES ¥28 MILLION.*
THE WINNER OF THE KISEI TITLE RECEIVES ¥33 MILLION.*
H-HOW MANY TITLES ARE THERE, AND HOW MUCH DO YOU GET IF YOU WIN THEM ALL?
THERE ARE 8 TITLES IN ALL, AND IF YOU WIN THEM ALL YOU GET A TOTAL OF ¥120 MILLION.
¥120 million*...

*approximately $240,000

*approximately $280,000

*approximately $1 million

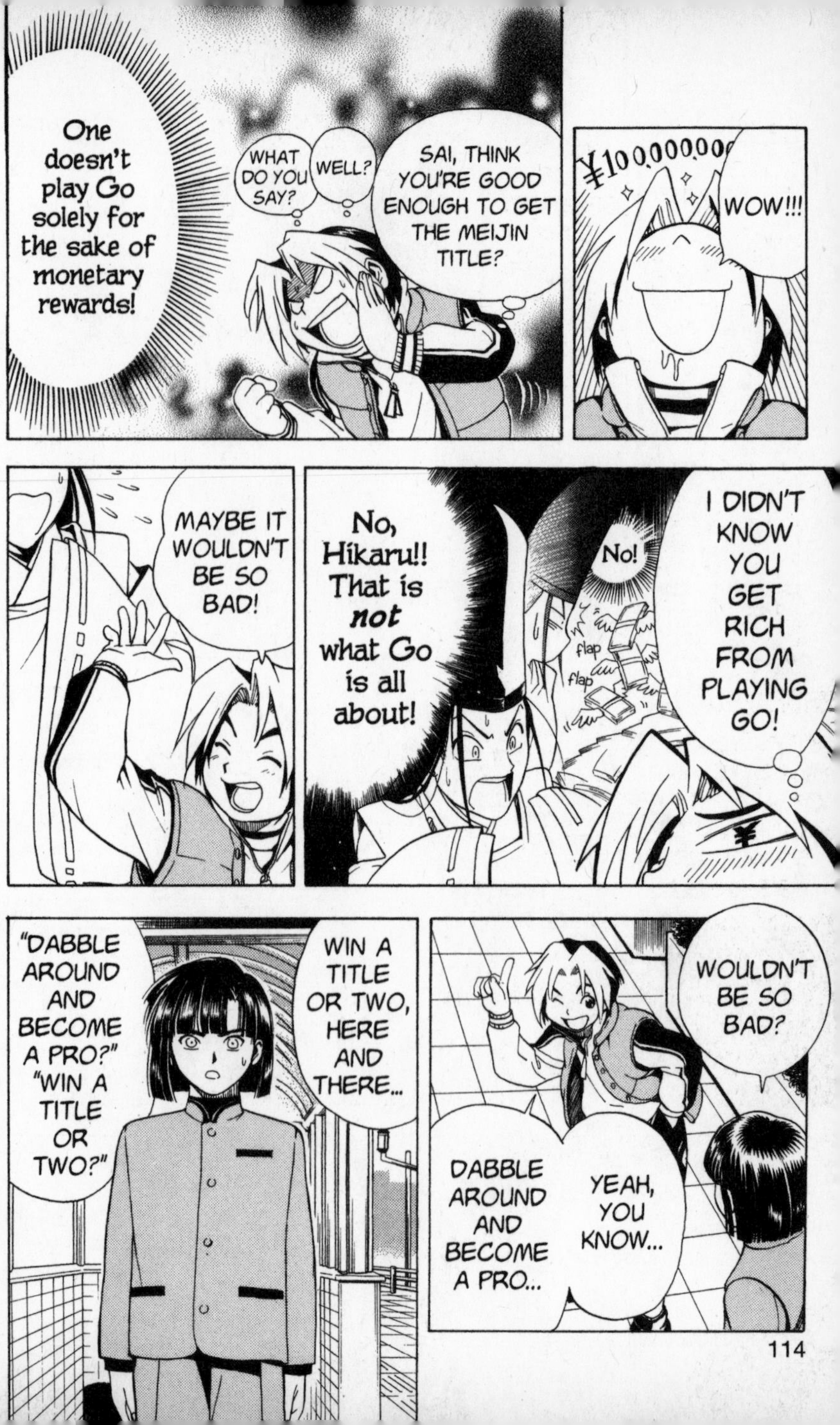

¥100,000,00
WOW!!!
SAI, THINK YOU'RE GOOD ENOUGH TO GET THE MEIJIN TITLE?
WELL?
WHAT DO YOU SAY?
One doesn't play Go solely for the sake of monetary rewards!
I DIDN'T KNOW YOU GET RICH FROM PLAYING GO!
No!
flap
flap
No, Hikaru!! That is *not* what Go is all about!
MAYBE IT WOULDN'T BE SO BAD!
WOULDN'T BE SO BAD?
YEAH, YOU KNOW...
DABBLE AROUND AND BECOME A PRO...
WIN A TITLE OR TWO, HERE AND THERE...
"DABBLE AROUND AND BECOME A PRO?" "WIN A TITLE OR TWO?"

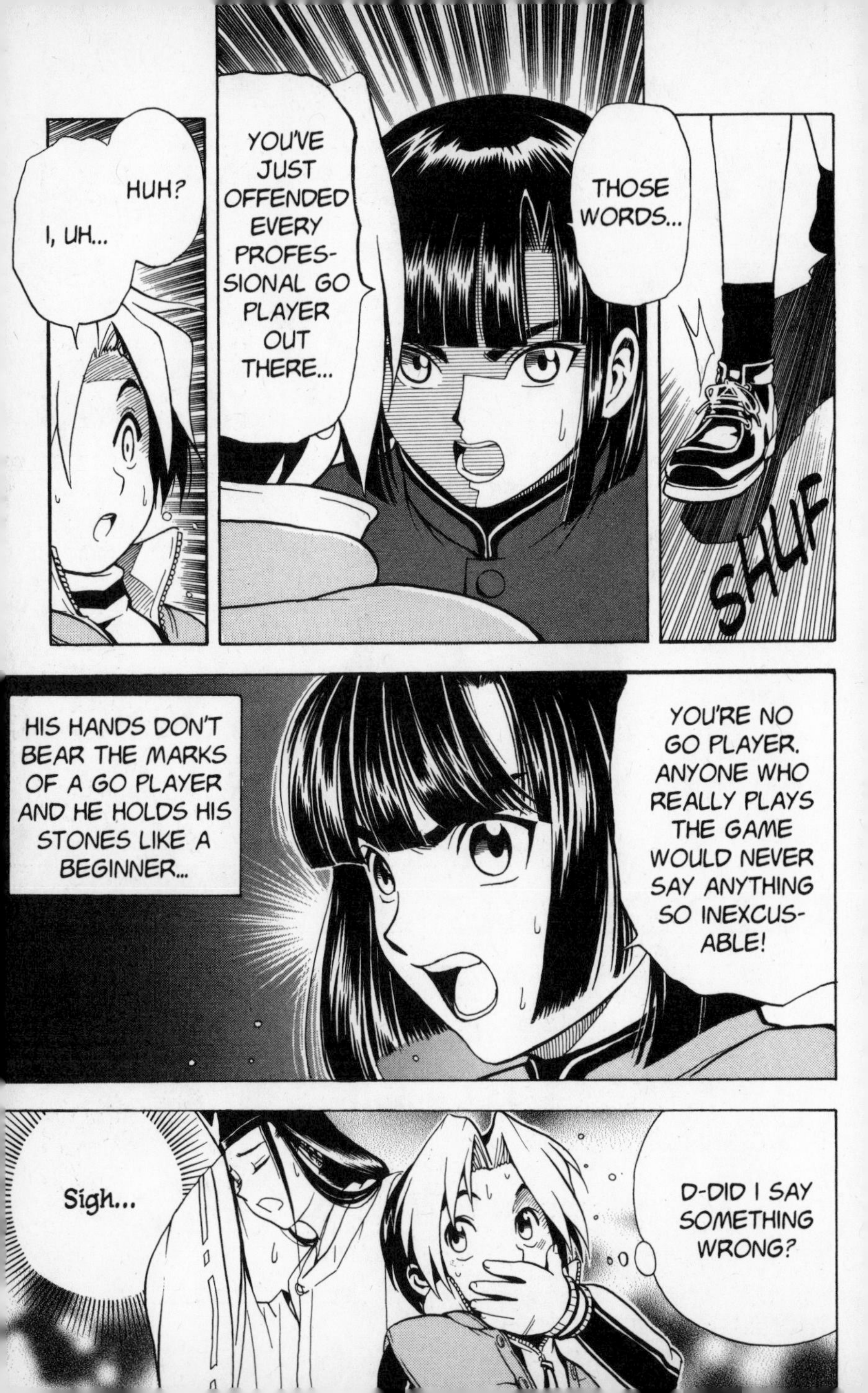
THOSE WORDS...
SHUF
YOU'VE JUST OFFENDED EVERY PROFES-SIONAL GO PLAYER OUT THERE...
HUH?
I, UH...
YOU'RE NO GO PLAYER. ANYONE WHO REALLY PLAYS THE GAME WOULD NEVER SAY ANYTHING SO INEXCUS-ABLE!
HIS HANDS DON'T BEAR THE MARKS OF A GO PLAYER AND HE HOLDS HIS STONES LIKE A BEGINNER...
D-DID I SAY SOMETHING WRONG?
Sigh...

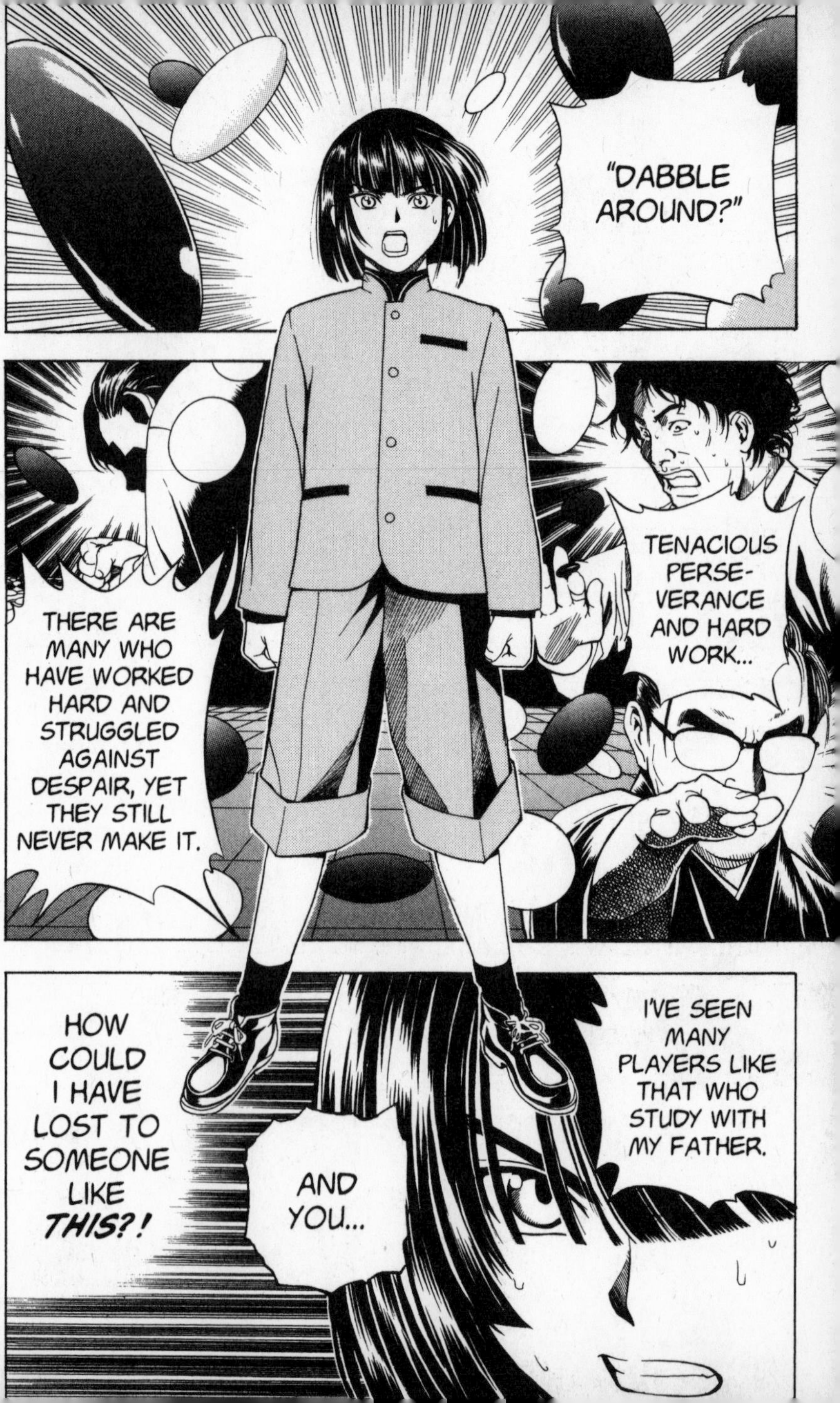
"DABBLE AROUND?"
TENACIOUS PERSEVERANCE AND HARD WORK...
THERE ARE MANY WHO HAVE WORKED HARD AND STRUGGLED AGAINST DESPAIR, YET THEY STILL NEVER MAKE IT.
I'VE SEEN MANY PLAYERS LIKE THAT WHO STUDY WITH MY FATHER.
AND YOU...
HOW COULD I HAVE LOST TO SOMEONE LIKE *THIS?!*

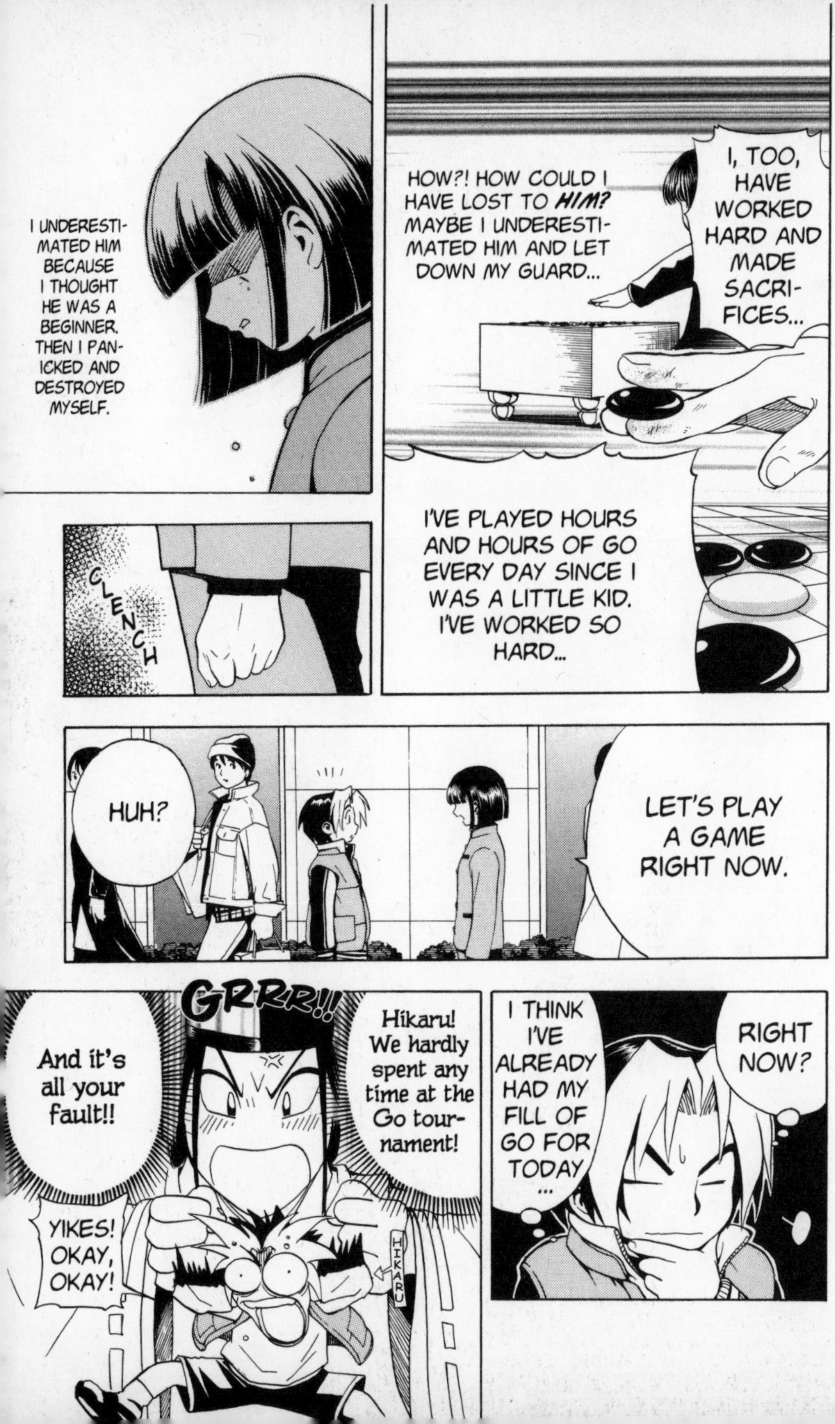
I, TOO, HAVE WORKED HARD AND MADE SACRIFICES...
HOW?! HOW COULD I HAVE LOST TO *HIM?* MAYBE I UNDERESTIMATED HIM AND LET DOWN MY GUARD...
I'VE PLAYED HOURS AND HOURS OF GO EVERY DAY SINCE I WAS A LITTLE KID. I'VE WORKED SO HARD...
I UNDERESTIMATED HIM BECAUSE I THOUGHT HE WAS A BEGINNER. THEN I PANICKED AND DESTROYED MYSELF.
CLENCH
LET'S PLAY A GAME RIGHT NOW.
HUH?
RIGHT NOW?
I THINK I'VE ALREADY HAD MY FILL OF GO FOR TODAY ...
GRRRR!!
Hikaru! We hardly spent any time at the Go tournament!
And it's all your fault!!
YIKES! OKAY, OKAY!
HIKARU

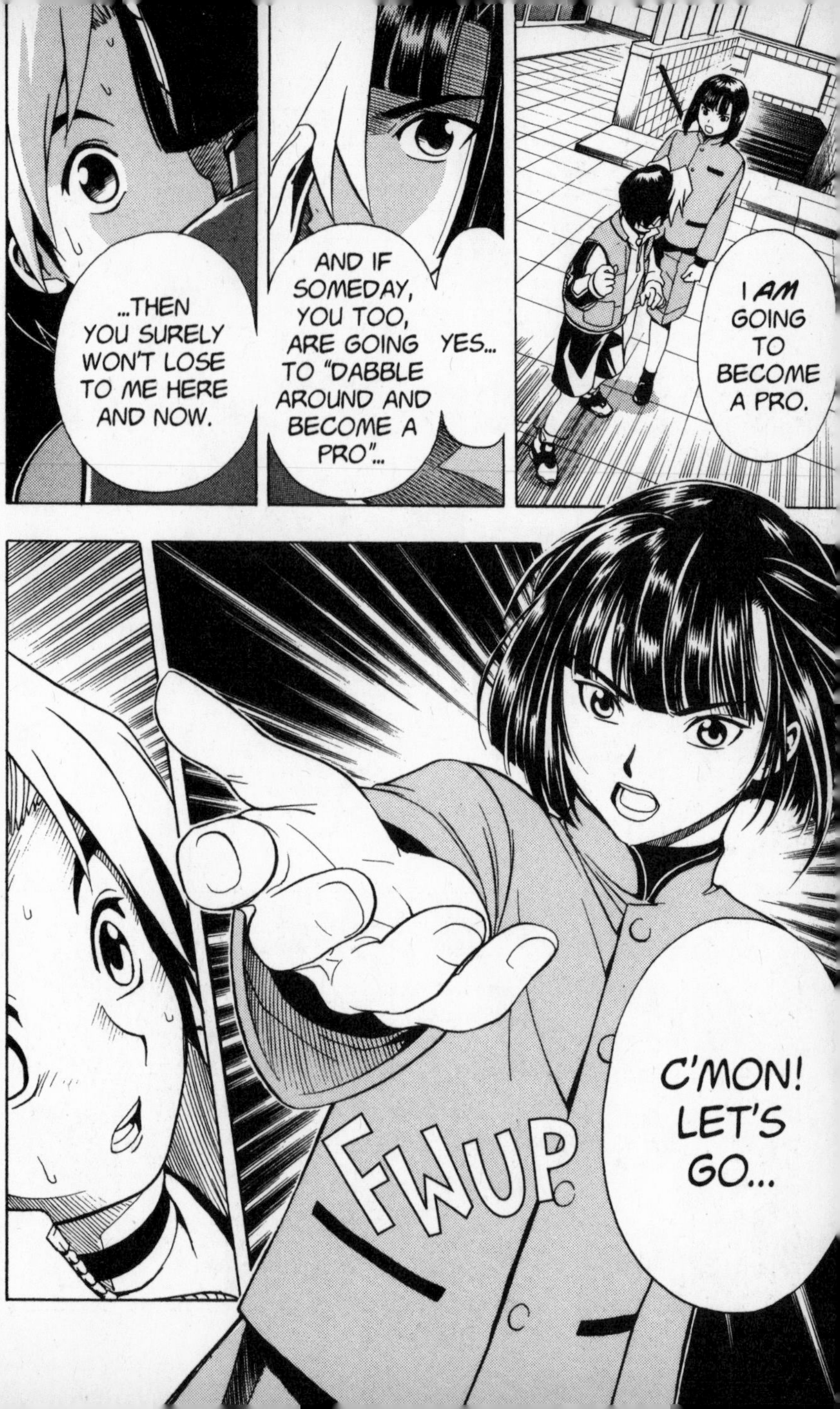
I AM GOING TO BECOME A PRO.
YES...
AND IF SOMEDAY, YOU TOO, ARE GOING TO "DABBLE AROUND AND BECOME A PRO"...
...THEN YOU SURELY WON'T LOSE TO ME HERE AND NOW.
C'MON! LET'S GO...
FWUP

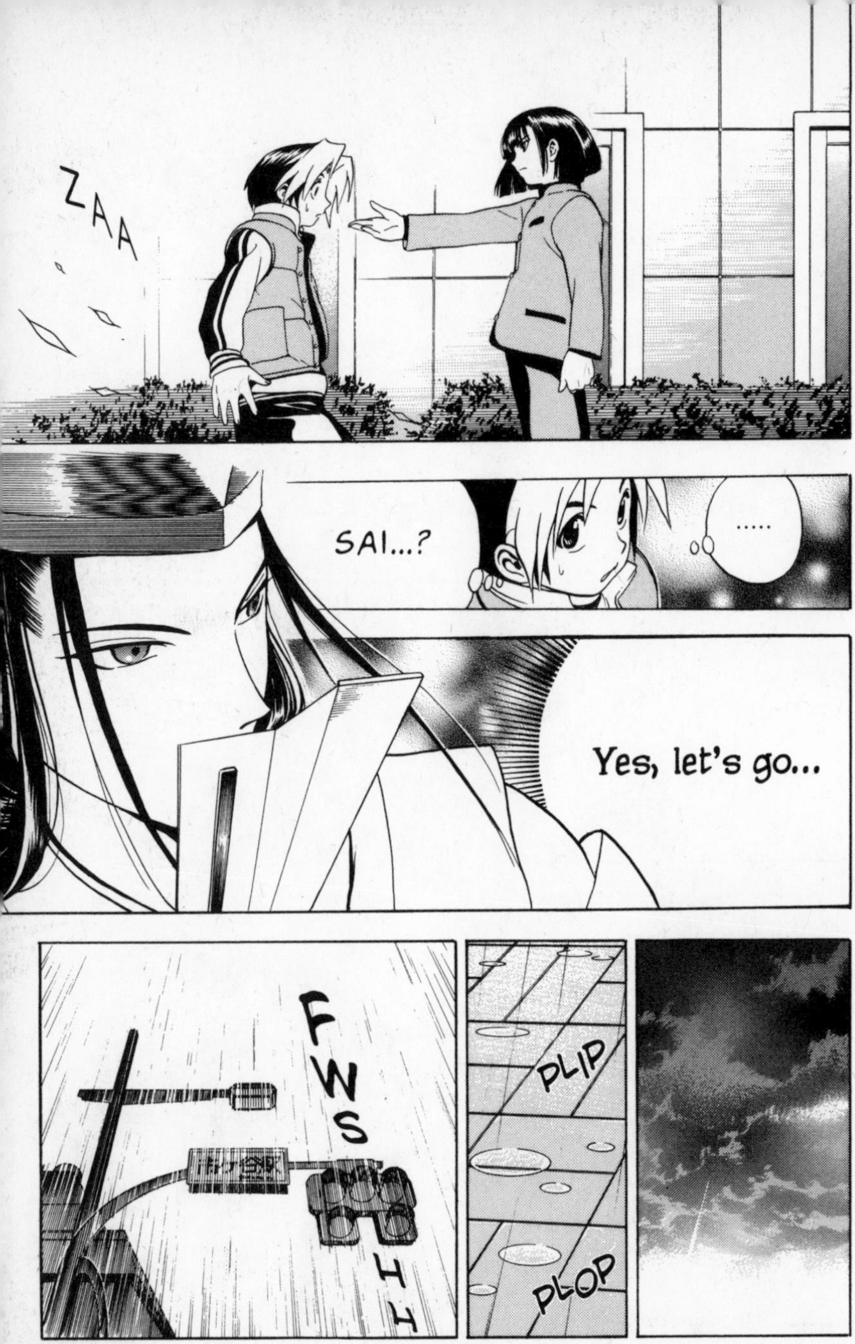
ZAA
SAI...?
.....
Yes, let's go...
PLIP
PLOP
FWSHH

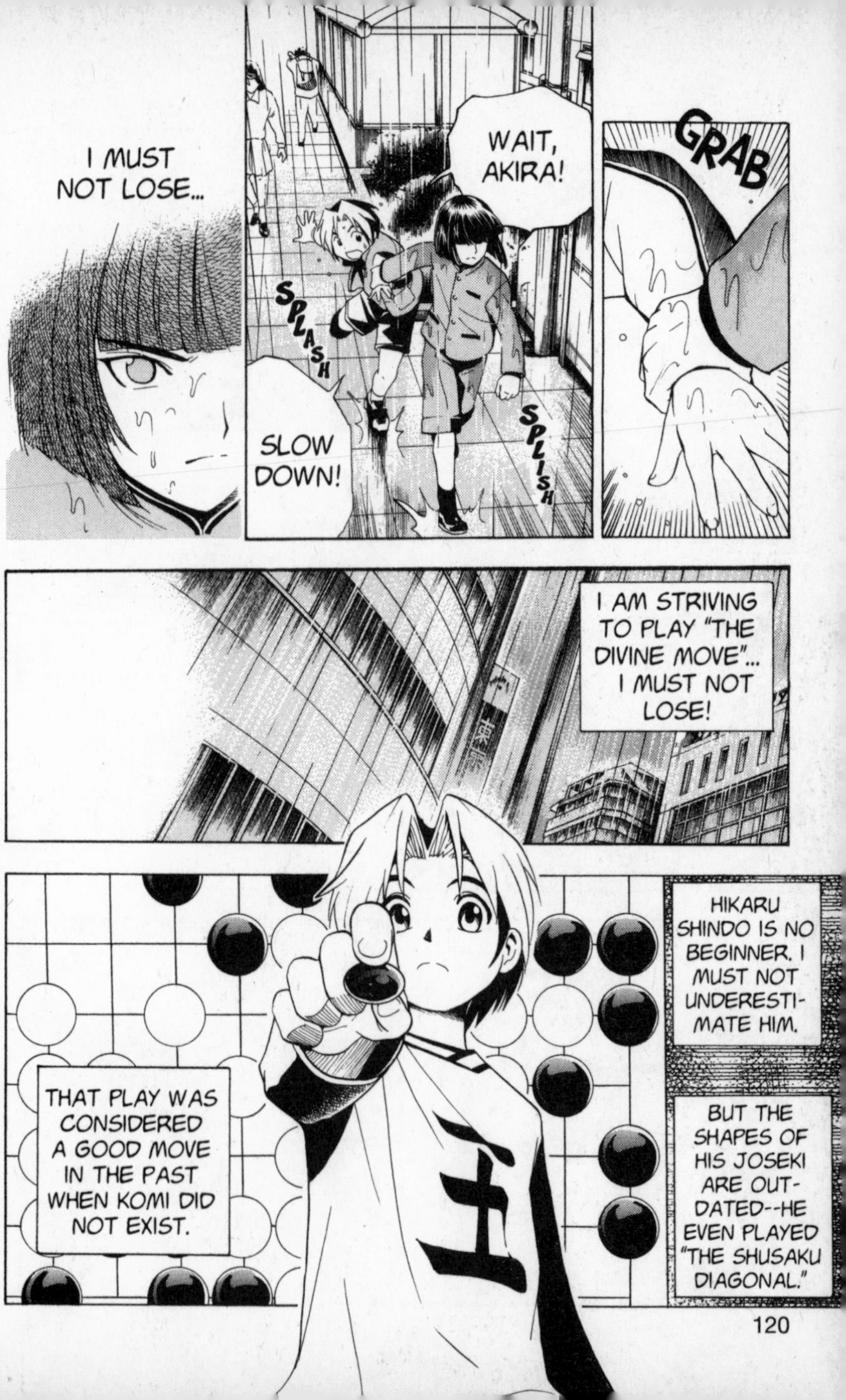
GRAB
WAIT, AKIRA!
SPLASH
SPLISH
SLOW DOWN!
I MUST NOT LOSE...
I AM STRIVING TO PLAY "THE DIVINE MOVE"... I MUST NOT LOSE!
HIKARU SHINDO IS NO BEGINNER. I MUST NOT UNDERESTIMATE HIM.
BUT THE SHAPES OF HIS JOSEKI ARE OUTDATED--HE EVEN PLAYED "THE SHUSAKU DIAGONAL."
THAT PLAY WAS CONSIDERED A GOOD MOVE IN THE PAST WHEN KOMI DID NOT EXIST.

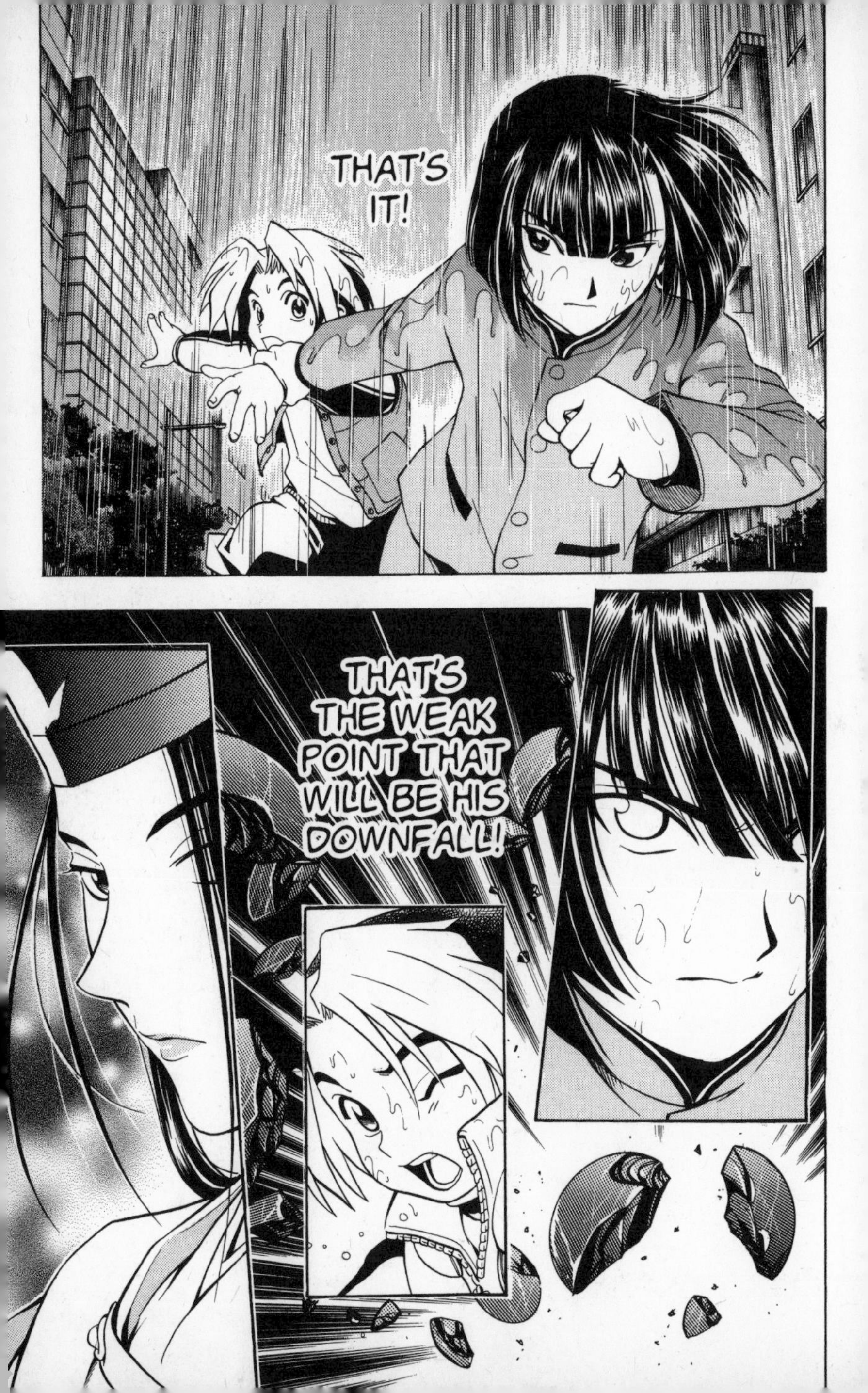
THAT'S IT!
THAT'S THE WEAK POINT THAT WILL BE HIS DOWNFALL!

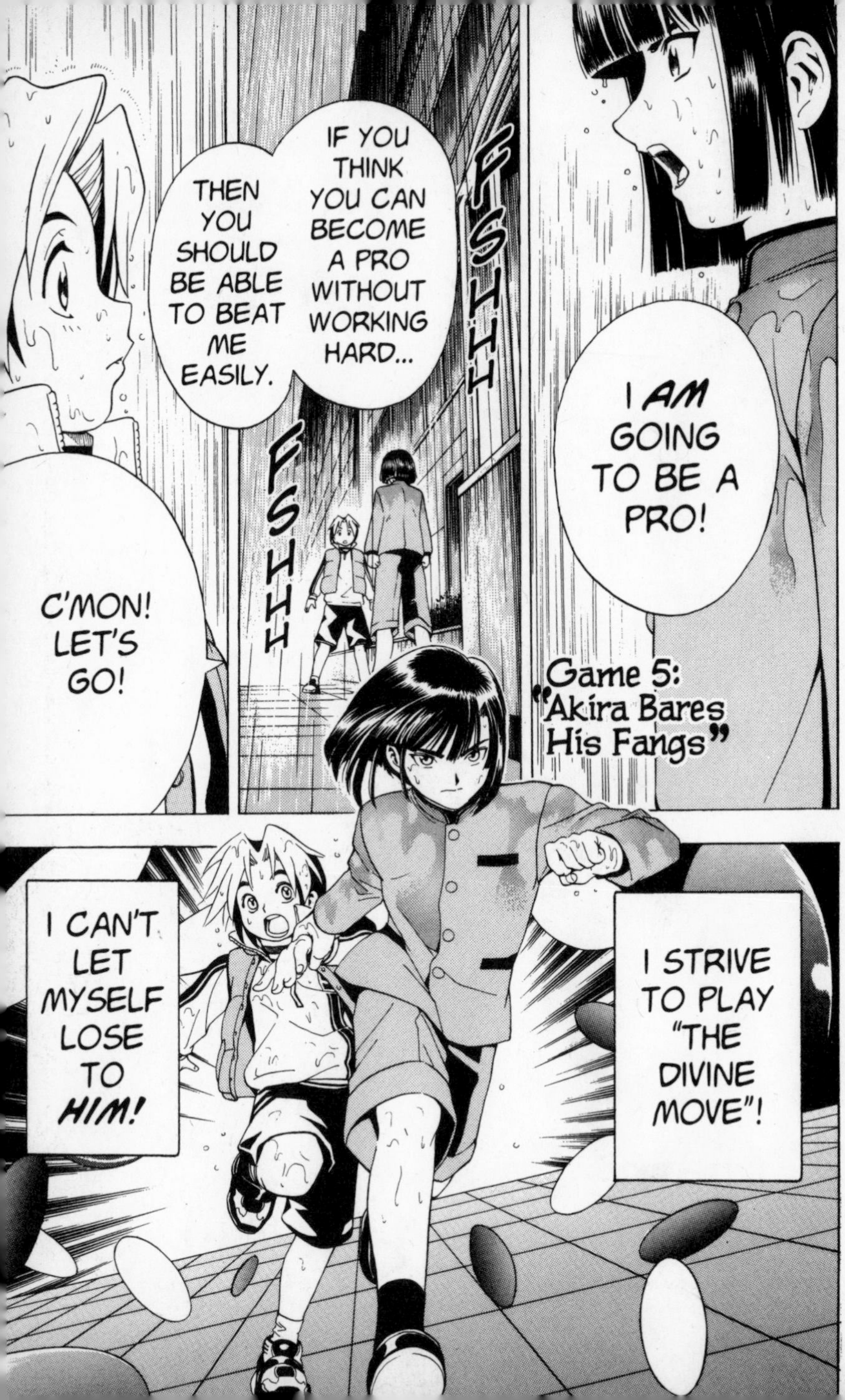
I AM GOING TO BE A PRO!
Game 5: "Akira Bares His Fangs"
IF YOU THINK YOU CAN BECOME A PRO WITHOUT WORKING HARD...
THEN YOU SHOULD BE ABLE TO BEAT ME EASILY.
FSHHH
FSHHH
C'MON! LET'S GO!
I STRIVE TO PLAY "THE DIVINE MOVE"!
I CAN'T LET MYSELF LOSE TO HIM!

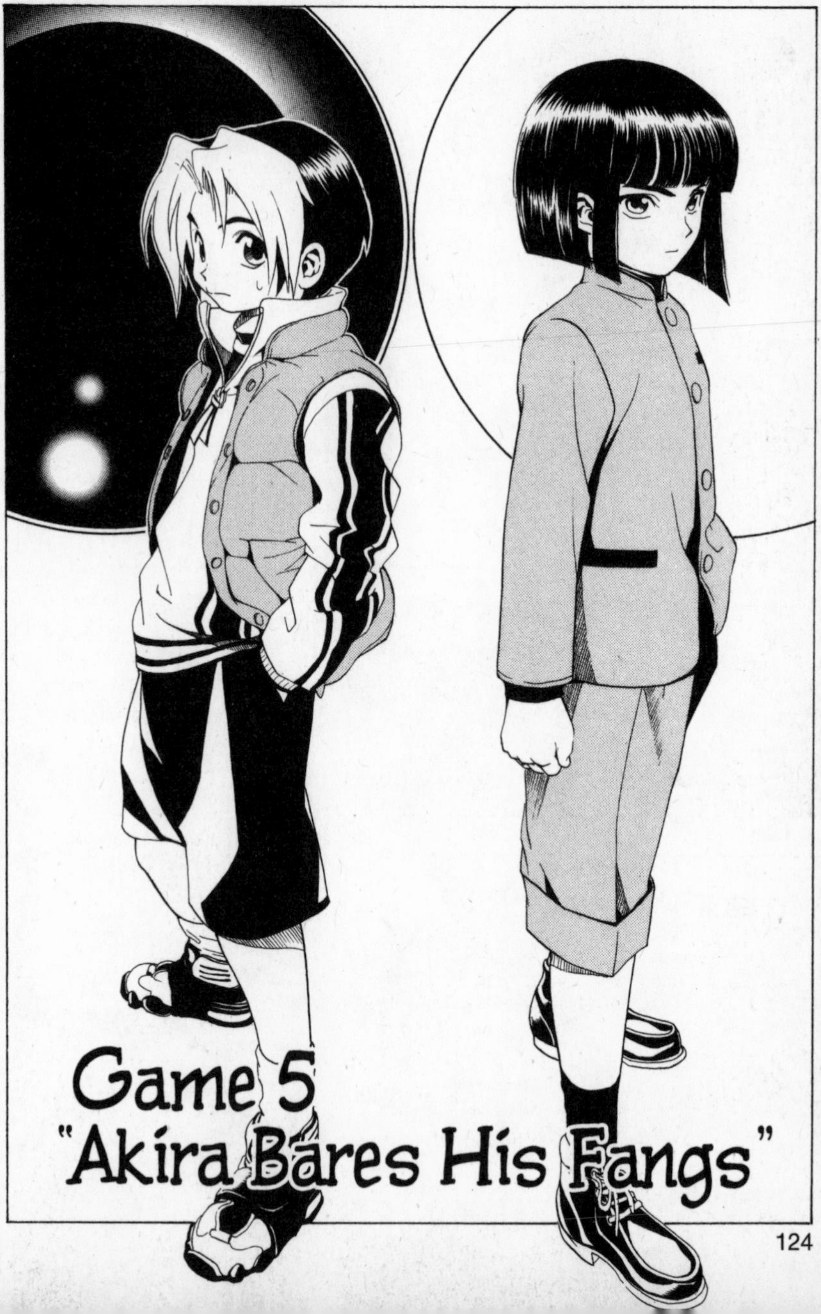

Game 5 "Akira Bares His Fangs"

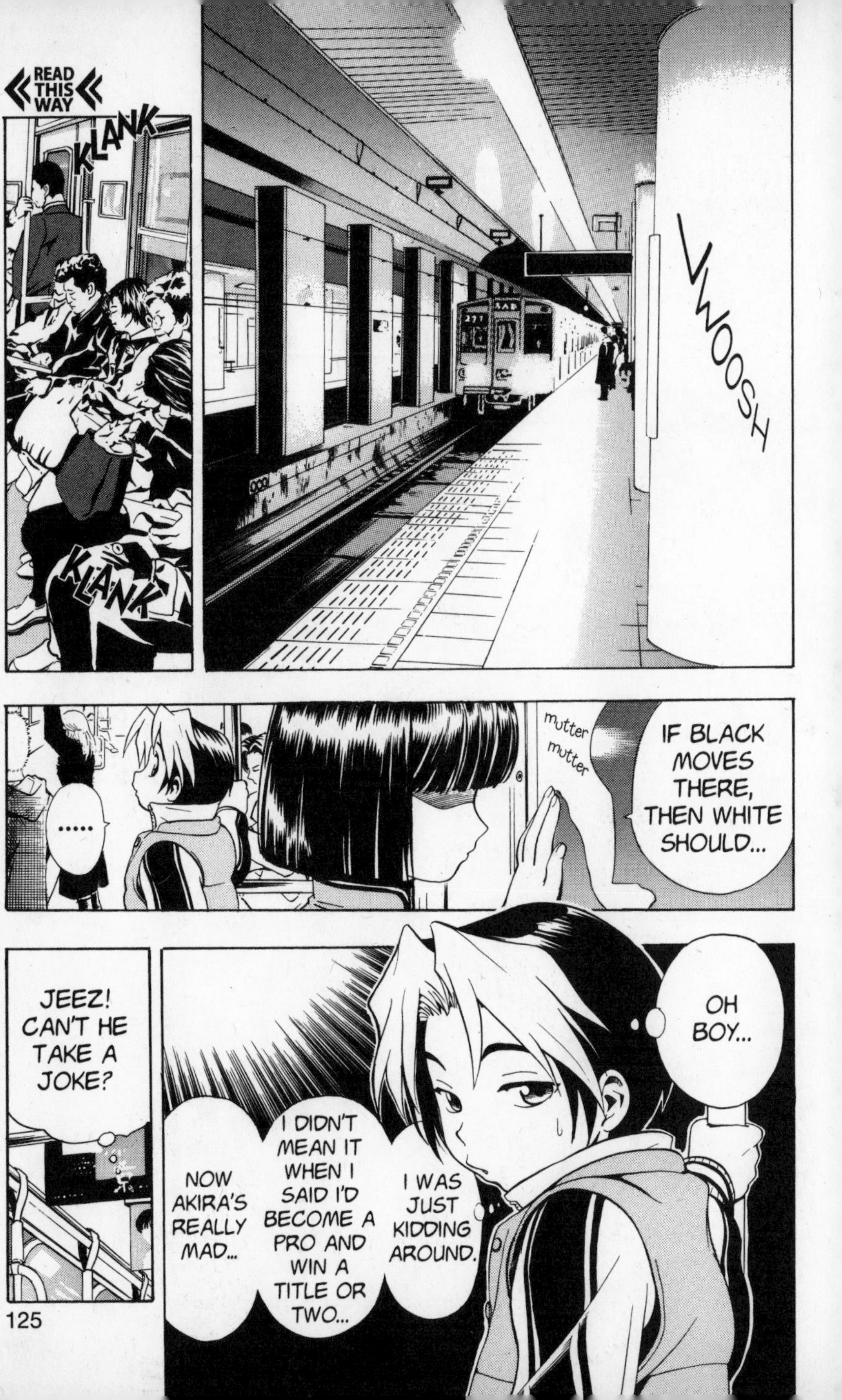
READ THIS WAY
VWOOSH
KLANK
KLANK
IF BLACK MOVES THERE, THEN WHITE SHOULD...
mutter mutter
.....
OH BOY...
I WAS JUST KIDDING AROUND.
I DIDN'T MEAN IT WHEN I SAID I'D BECOME A PRO AND WIN A TITLE OR TWO...
NOW AKIRA'S REALLY MAD...
JEEZ! CAN'T HE TAKE A JOKE?

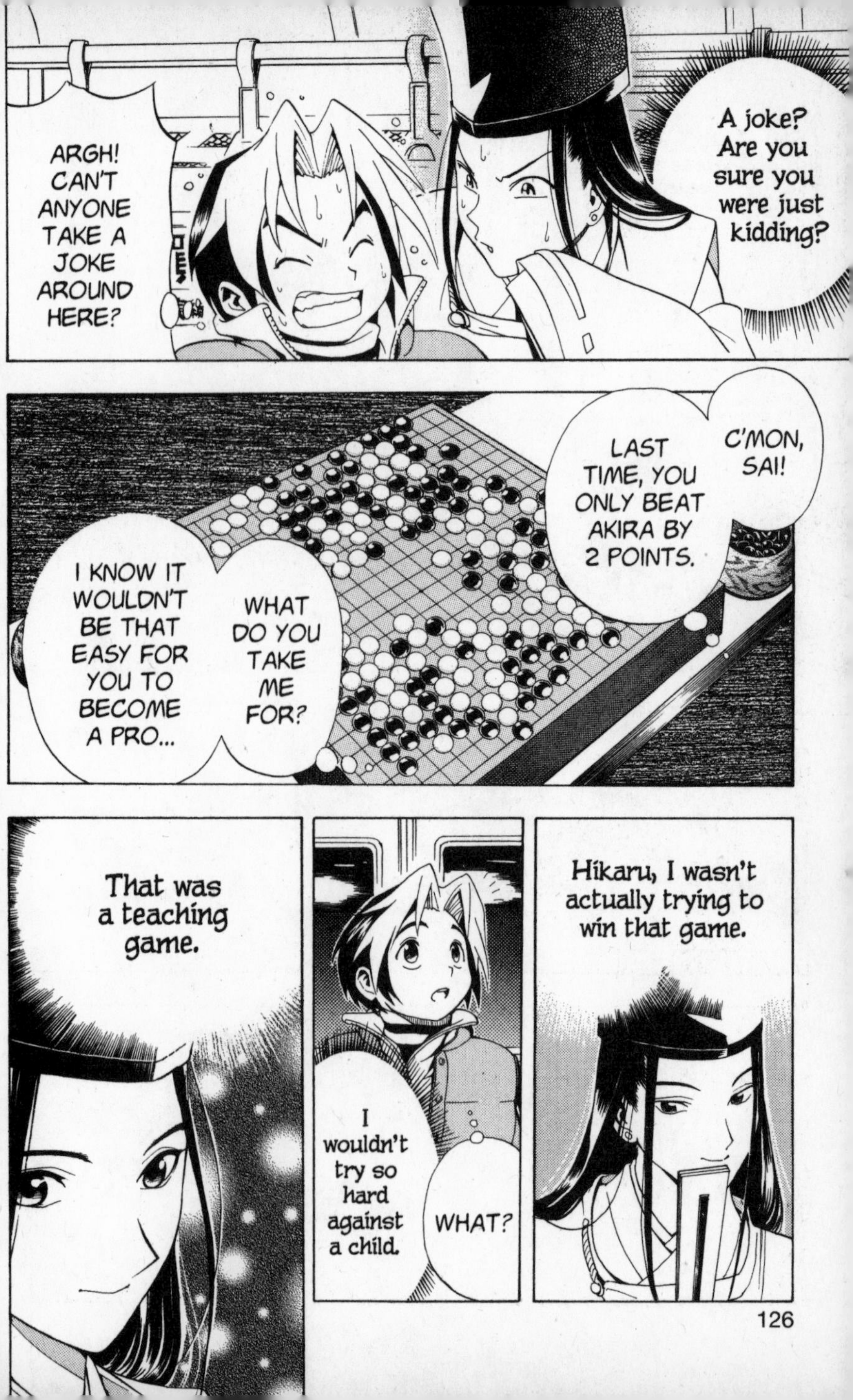
A joke? Are you sure you were just kidding?
ARGH! CAN'T ANYONE TAKE A JOKE AROUND HERE?
C'MON, SAI!
LAST TIME, YOU ONLY BEAT AKIRA BY 2 POINTS.
WHAT DO YOU TAKE ME FOR?
I KNOW IT WOULDN'T BE THAT EASY FOR YOU TO BECOME A PRO...
Hikaru, I wasn't actually trying to win that game.
WHAT?
I wouldn't try so hard against a child.
That was a teaching game.

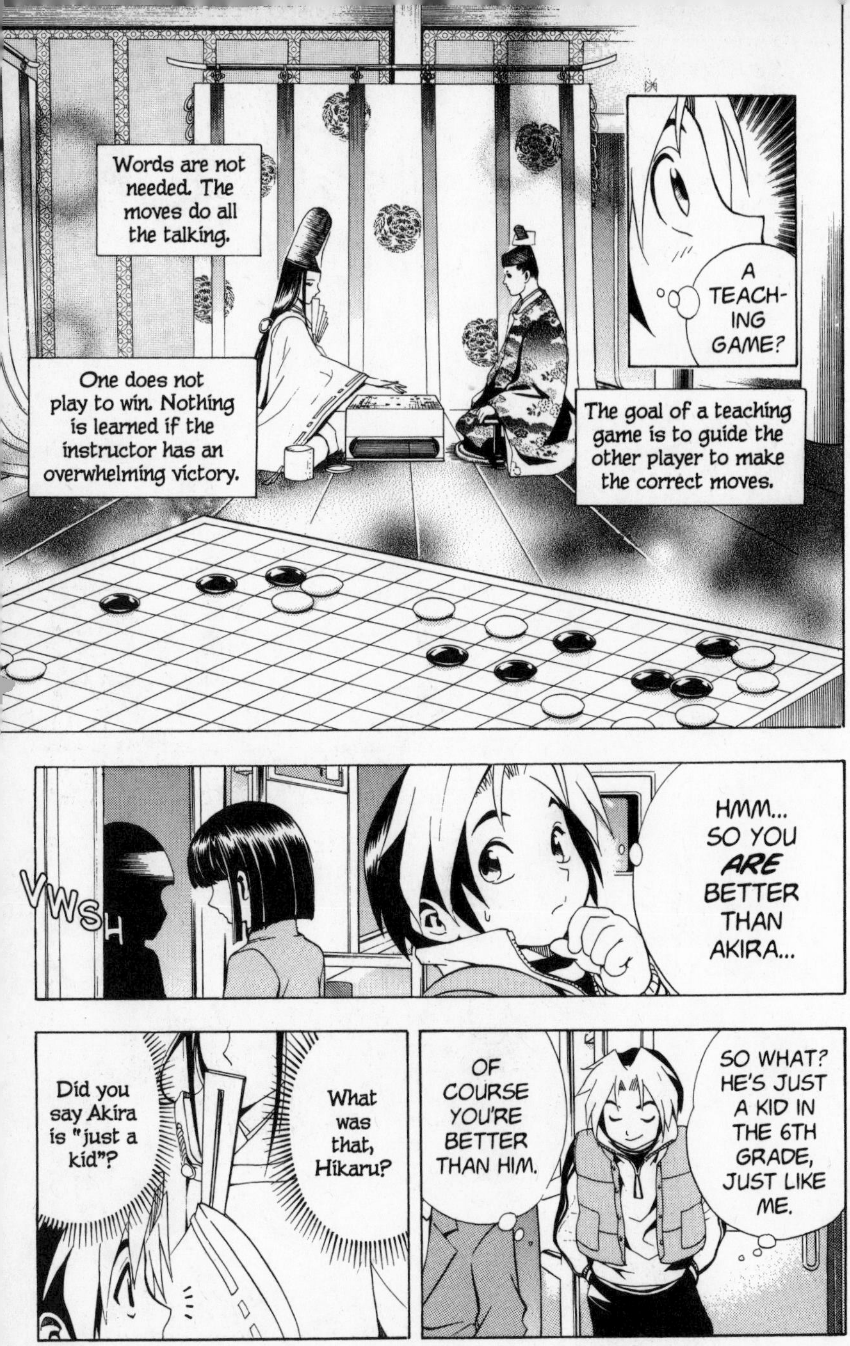
A TEACHING-ING GAME?
Words are not needed. The moves do all the talking.
The goal of a teaching game is to guide the other player to make the correct moves.
One does not play to win. Nothing is learned if the instructor has an overwhelming victory.
HMM... SO YOU ARE BETTER THAN AKIRA...
VWSH
SO WHAT? HE'S JUST A KID IN THE 6TH GRADE, JUST LIKE ME.
OF COURSE YOU'RE BETTER THAN HIM.
What was that, Hikaru?
Did you say Akira is "just a kid"?

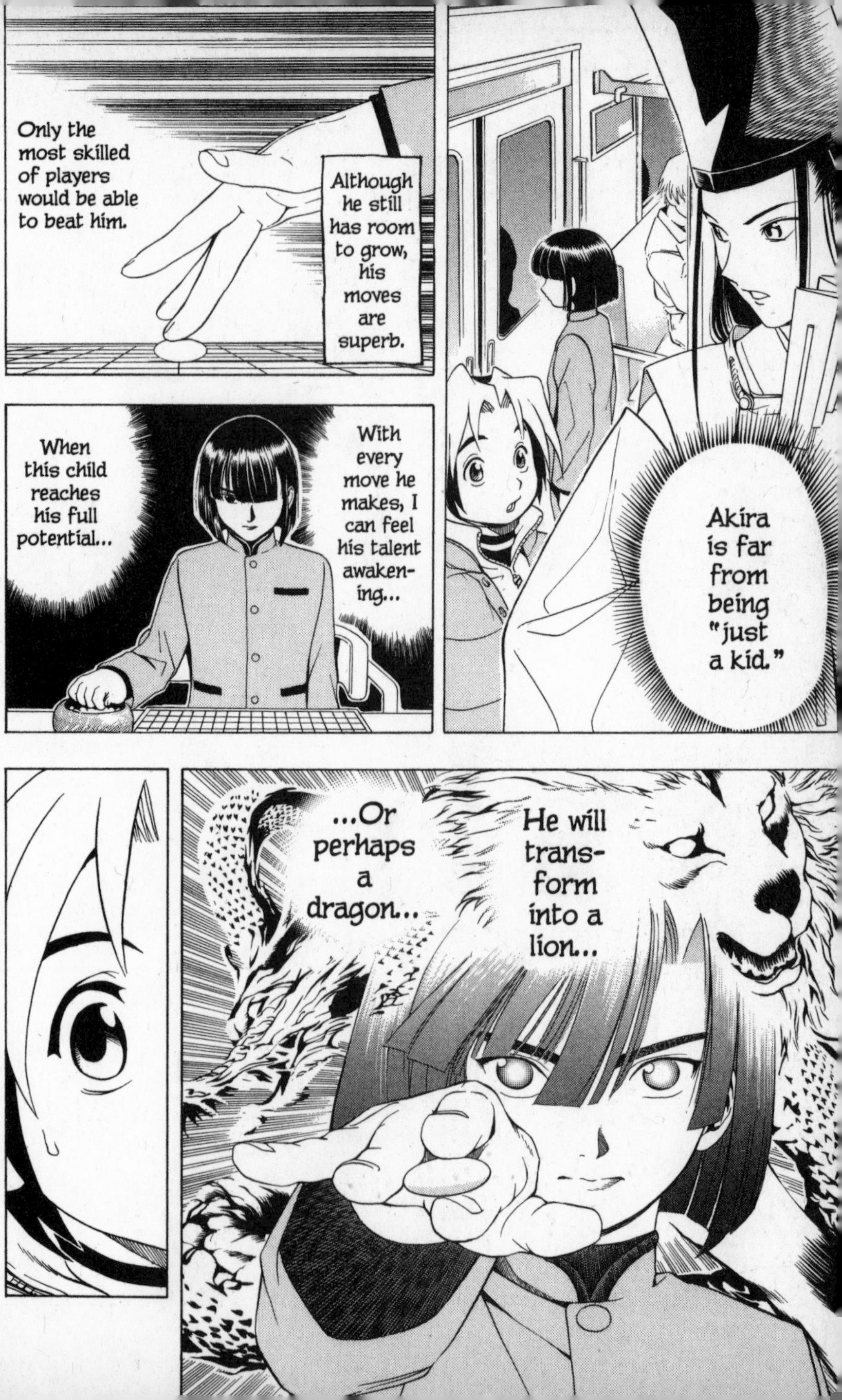
Akira is far from being "just a kid."
Although he still has room to grow, his moves are superb.
Only the most skilled of players would be able to beat him.
With every move he makes, I can feel his talent awakening...
When this child reaches his full potential...
He will transform into a lion...
...Or perhaps a dragon...

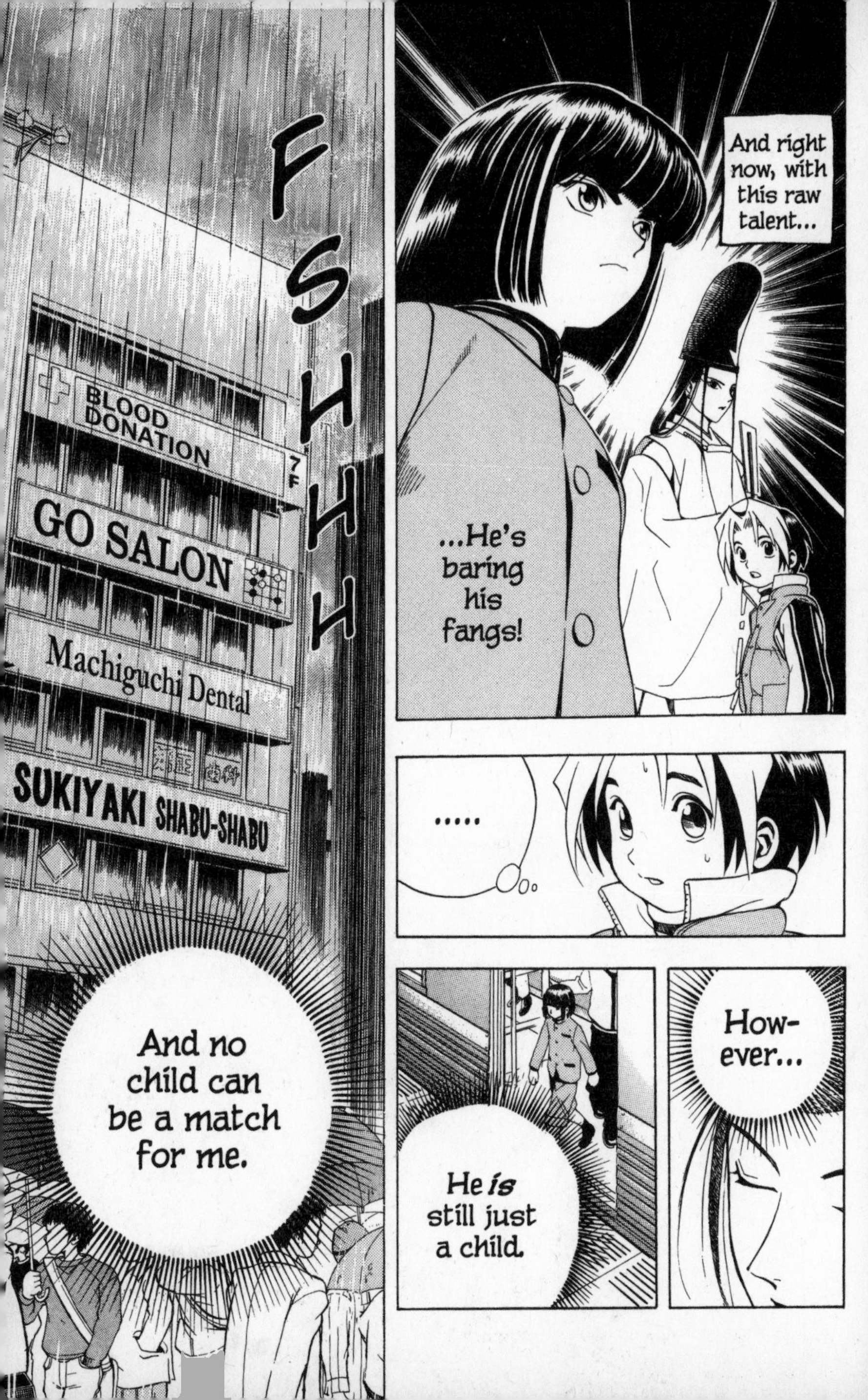
And right now, with this raw talent...
...He's baring his fangs!
.....
How-ever...
He *is* still just a child.
BLOOD DONATION
7F
GO SALON
Machiguchi Dental
SUKIYAKI SHABU-SHABU
FSHHH
And no child can be a match for me.

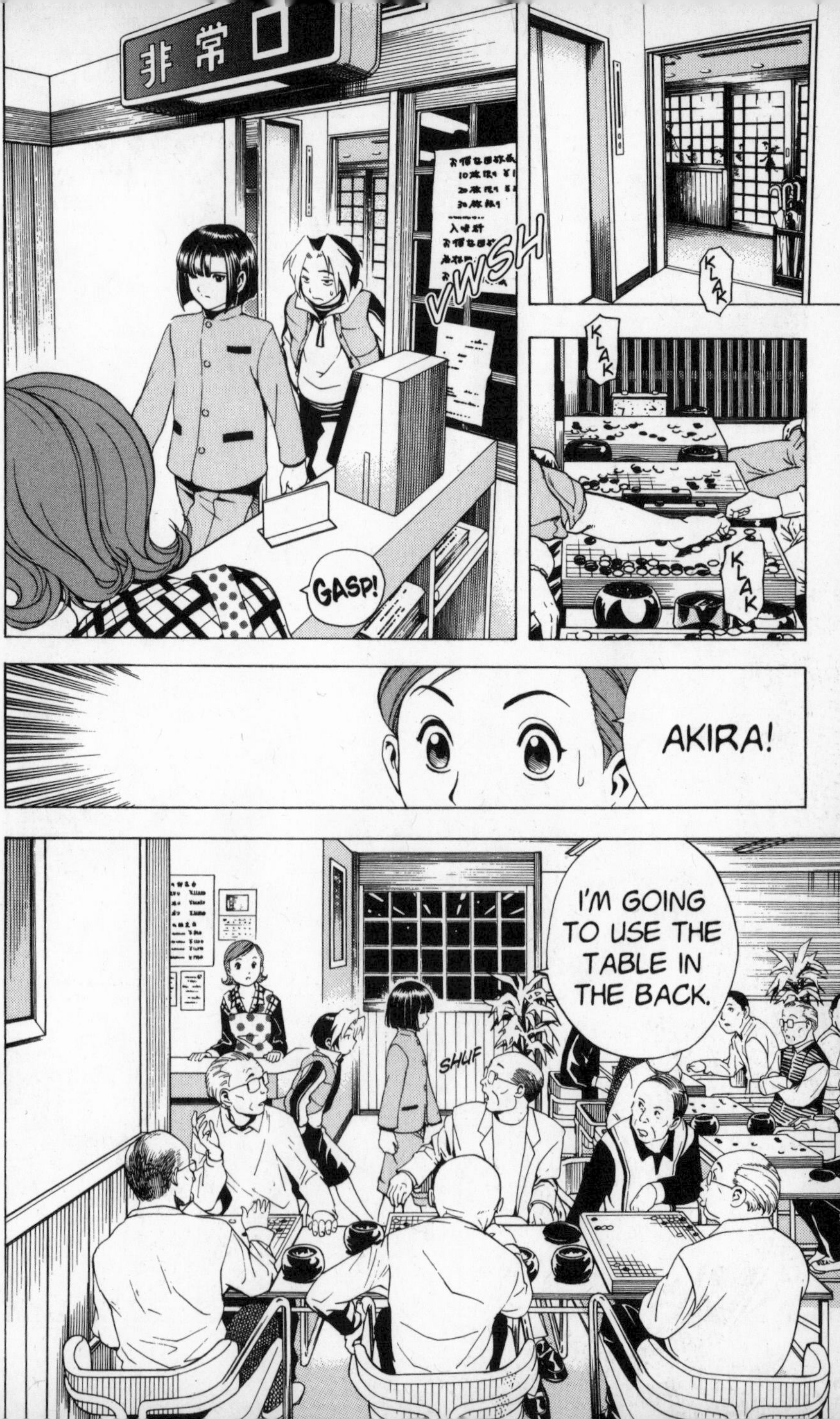
KLAK
KLAK
KLAK
非常口
VWSH
GASP!
AKIRA!
I'M GOING TO USE THE TABLE IN THE BACK.
SHUF

READ THIS WAY

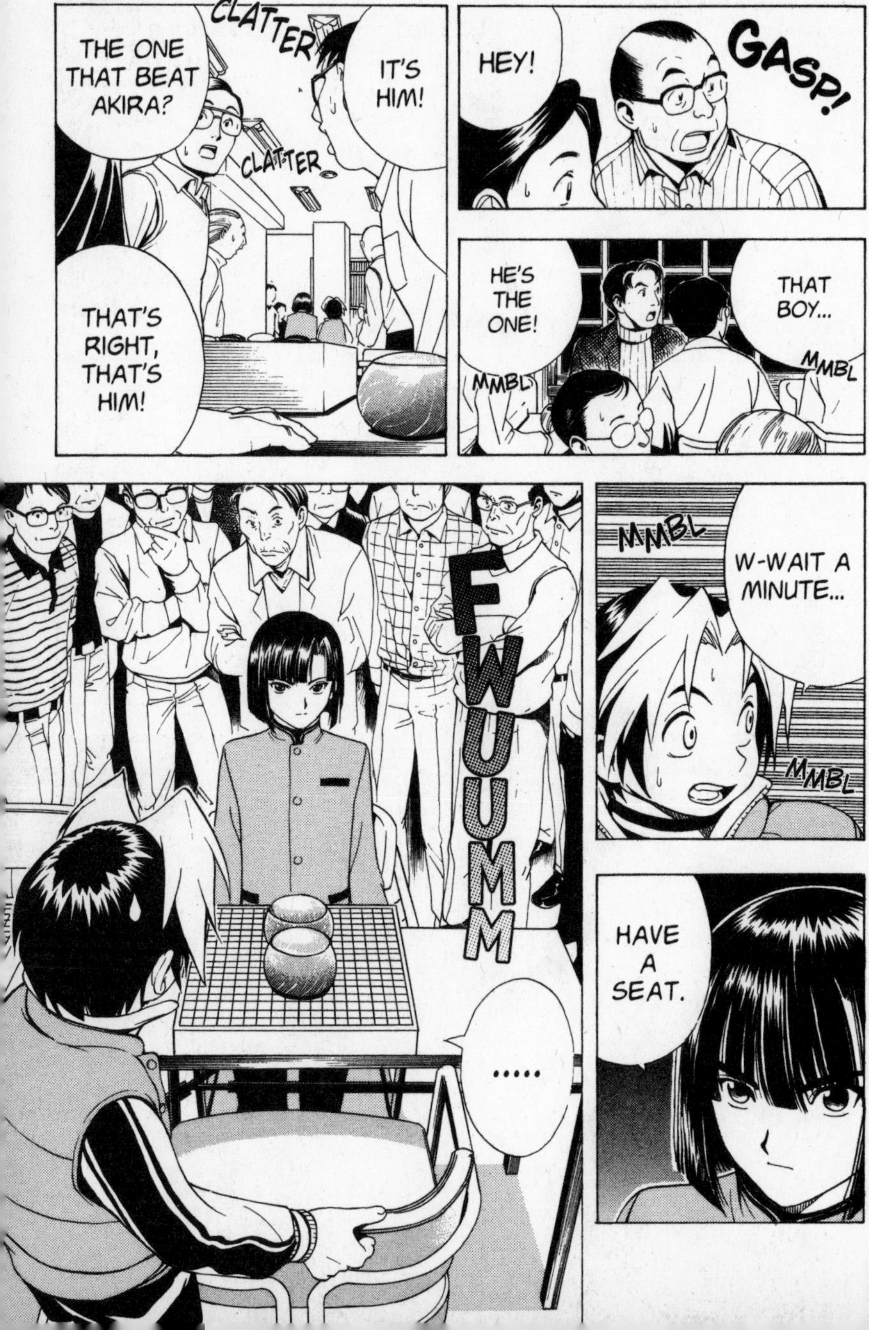
GASP!
HEY!
THAT BOY...
MMBL
HE'S THE ONE!
MMBL
CLATTER
IT'S HIM!
THE ONE THAT BEAT AKIRA?
CLATTER
THAT'S RIGHT, THAT'S HIM!
MMBL
W-WAIT A MINUTE...
MMBL
HAVE A SEAT.
FWUUMM
.....

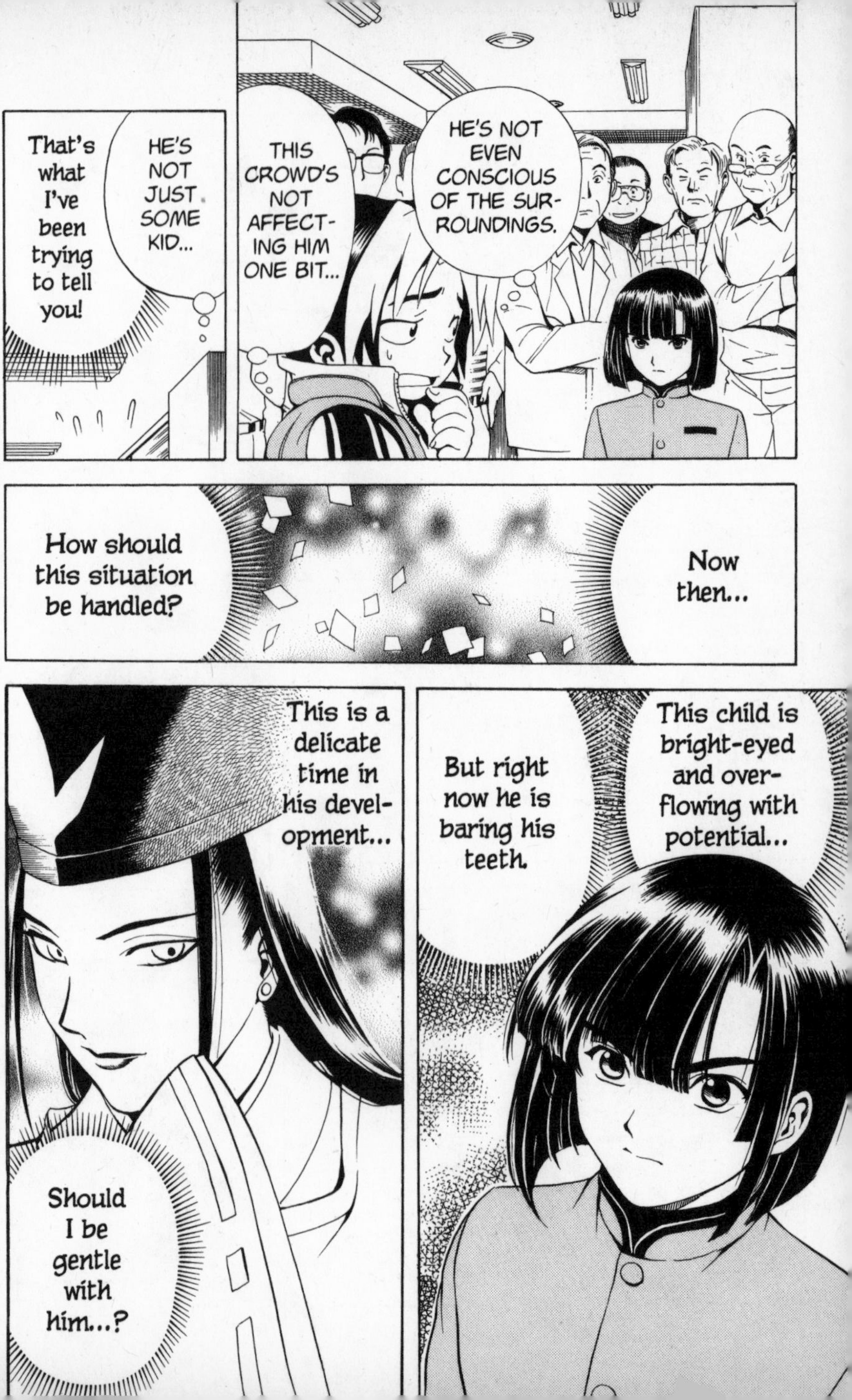
HE'S NOT EVEN CONSCIOUS OF THE SUR-ROUNDINGS.
THIS CROWD'S NOT AFFECT-ING HIM ONE BIT...
HE'S NOT JUST SOME KID...
That's what I've been trying to tell you!
Now then...
How should this situation be handled?
This child is bright-eyed and over-flowing with potential...
But right now he is baring his teeth.
This is a delicate time in his devel-opment...
Should I be gentle with him...?

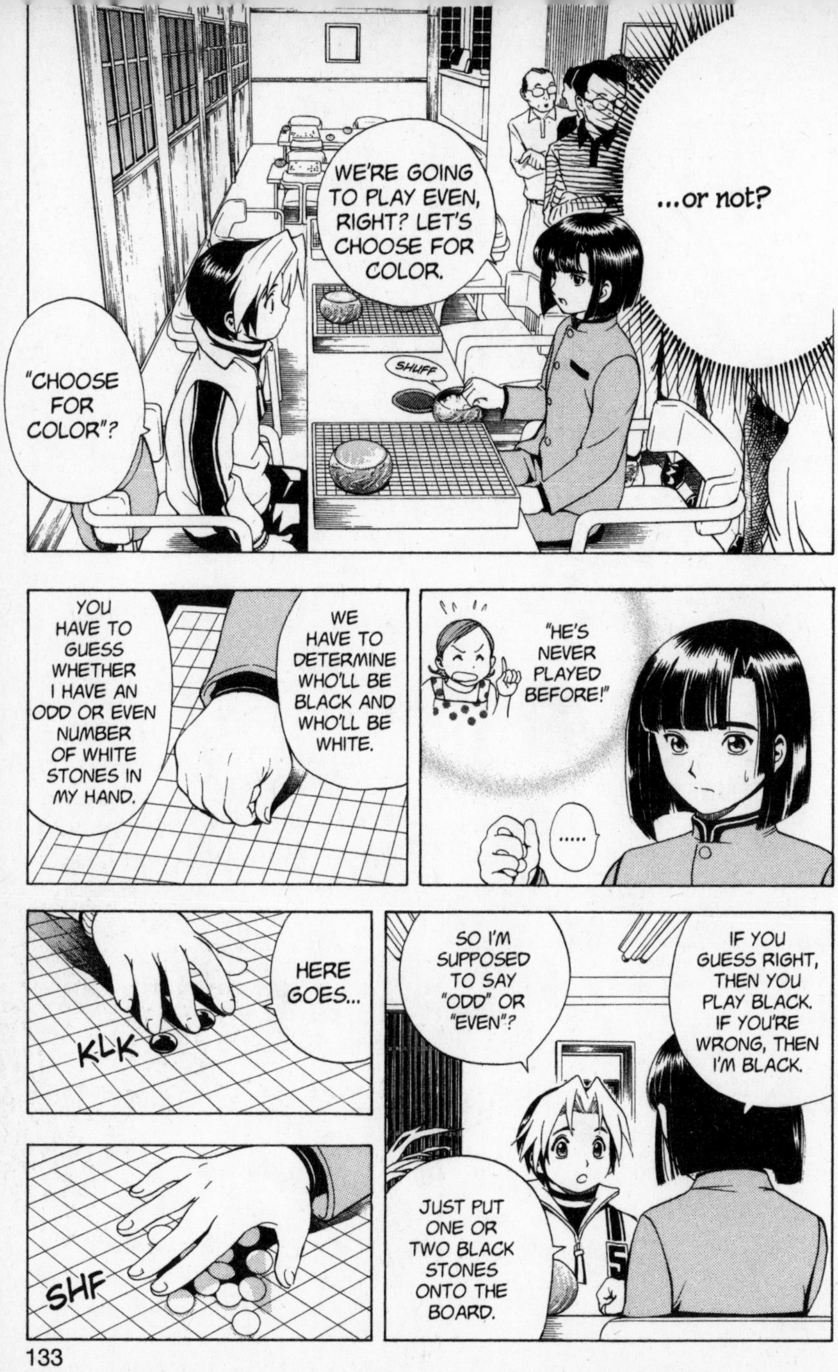
...or not?
WE'RE GOING TO PLAY EVEN, RIGHT? LET'S CHOOSE FOR COLOR.
SHUFF
"CHOOSE FOR COLOR"?
"HE'S NEVER PLAYED BEFORE!"
......
WE HAVE TO DETERMINE WHO'LL BE BLACK AND WHO'LL BE WHITE.
YOU HAVE TO GUESS WHETHER I HAVE AN ODD OR EVEN NUMBER OF WHITE STONES IN MY HAND.
IF YOU GUESS RIGHT, THEN YOU PLAY BLACK. IF YOU'RE WRONG, THEN I'M BLACK.
SO I'M SUPPOSED TO SAY "ODD" OR "EVEN"?
JUST PUT ONE OR TWO BLACK STONES ONTO THE BOARD.
HERE GOES...
KLK
SHF

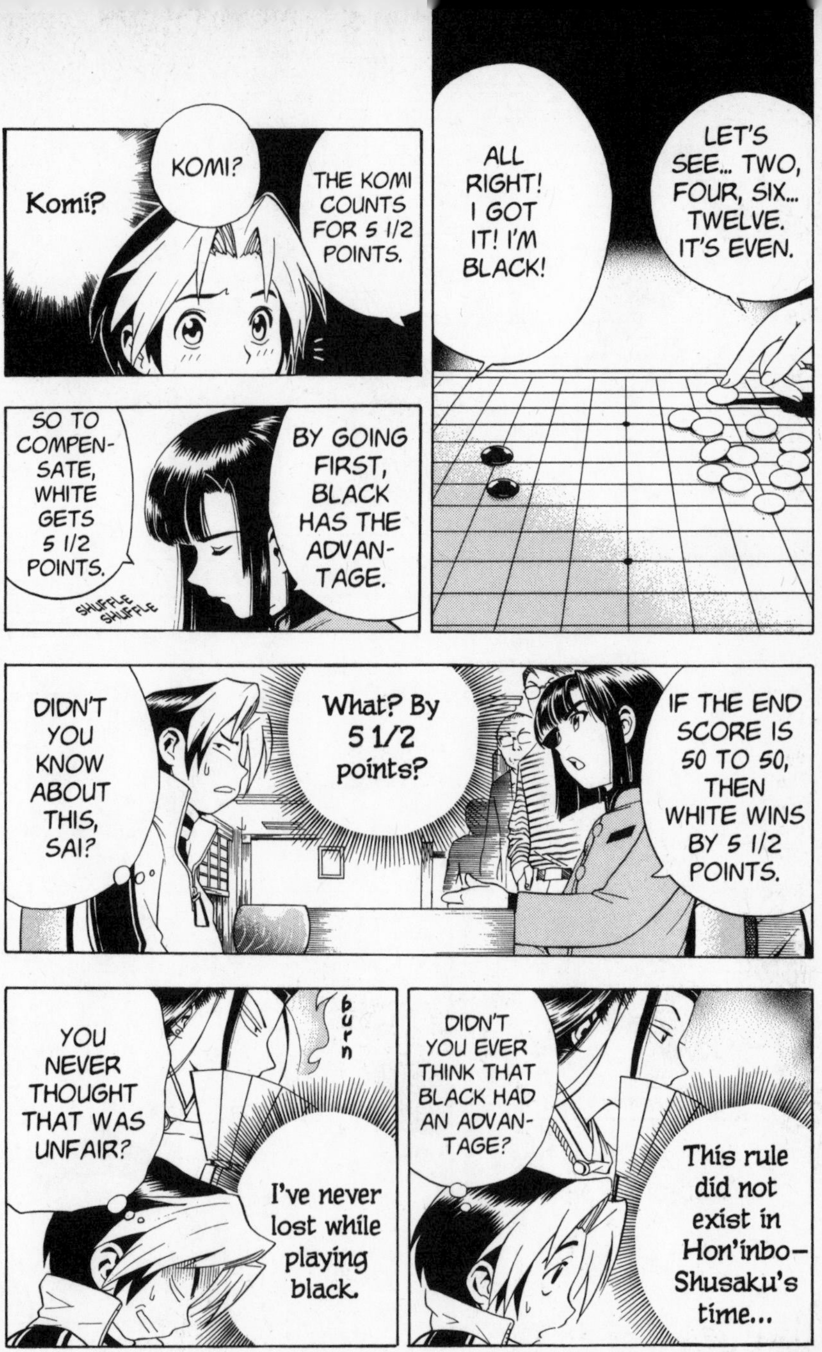
LET'S SEE... TWO, FOUR, SIX... TWELVE. IT'S EVEN.
ALL RIGHT! I GOT IT! I'M BLACK!
THE KOMI COUNTS FOR 5 1/2 POINTS.
KOMI?
Komi?
BY GOING FIRST, BLACK HAS THE ADVANTAGE.
SO TO COMPENSATE, WHITE GETS 5 1/2 POINTS.
SHUFFLE SHUFFLE
IF THE END SCORE IS 50 TO 50, THEN WHITE WINS BY 5 1/2 POINTS.
What? By 5 1/2 points?
DIDN'T YOU KNOW ABOUT THIS, SAI?
DIDN'T YOU EVER THINK THAT BLACK HAD AN ADVANTAGE?
This rule did not exist in Hon'inbo-Shusaku's time...
burn
YOU NEVER THOUGHT THAT WAS UNFAIR?
I've never lost while playing black.

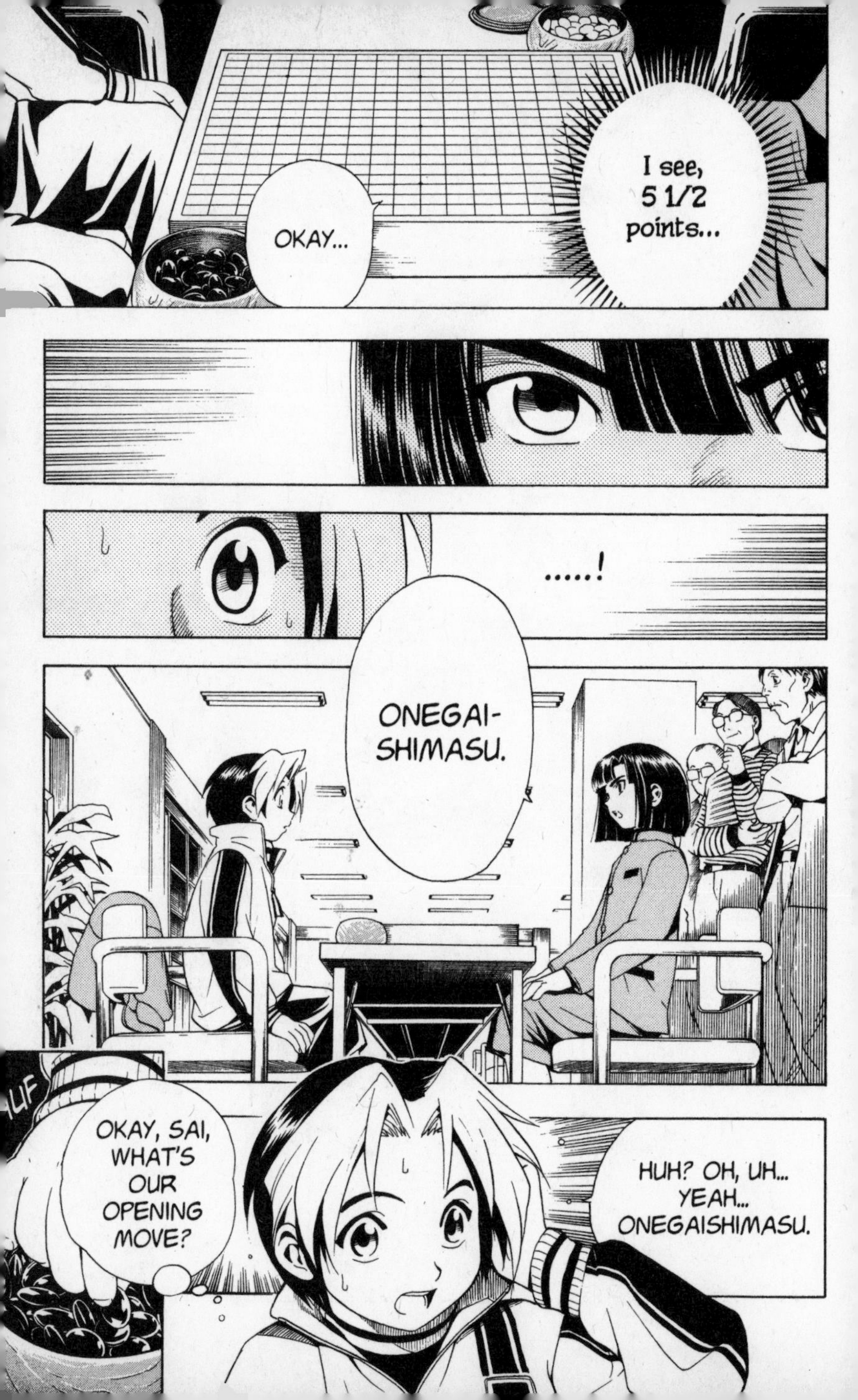
I see, 5 1/2 points...
OKAY...
.....!
ONEGAI-SHIMASU.
HUH? OH, UH... YEAH... ONEGAISHIMASU.
OKAY, SAI, WHAT'S OUR OPENING MOVE?

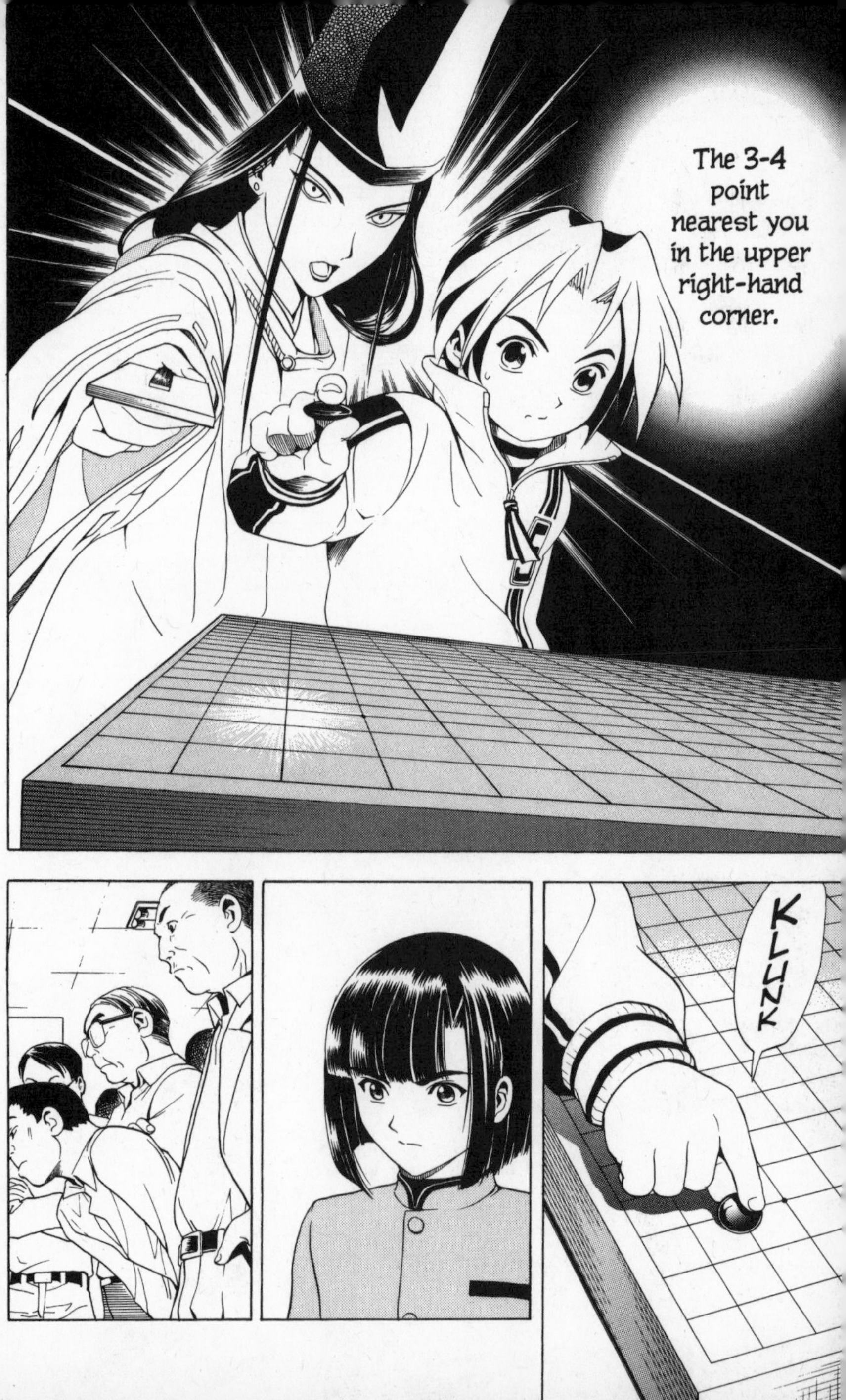
The 3-4 point nearest you in the upper right-hand corner.
KLUNK

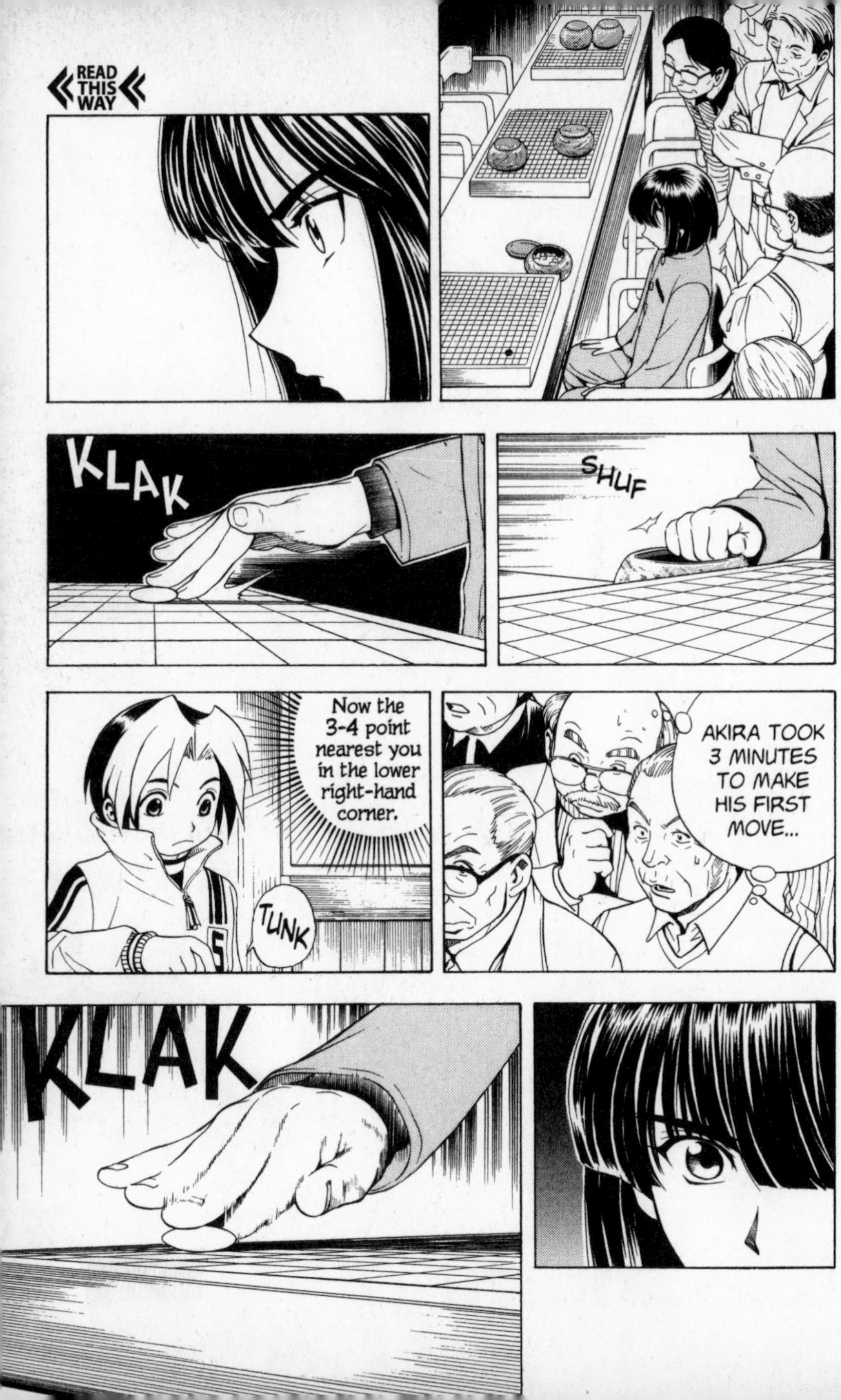
READ THIS WAY
SHUF
KLAK
AKIRA TOOK 3 MINUTES TO MAKE HIS FIRST MOVE...
Now the 3-4 point nearest you in the lower right-hand corner.
TUNK
KLAK

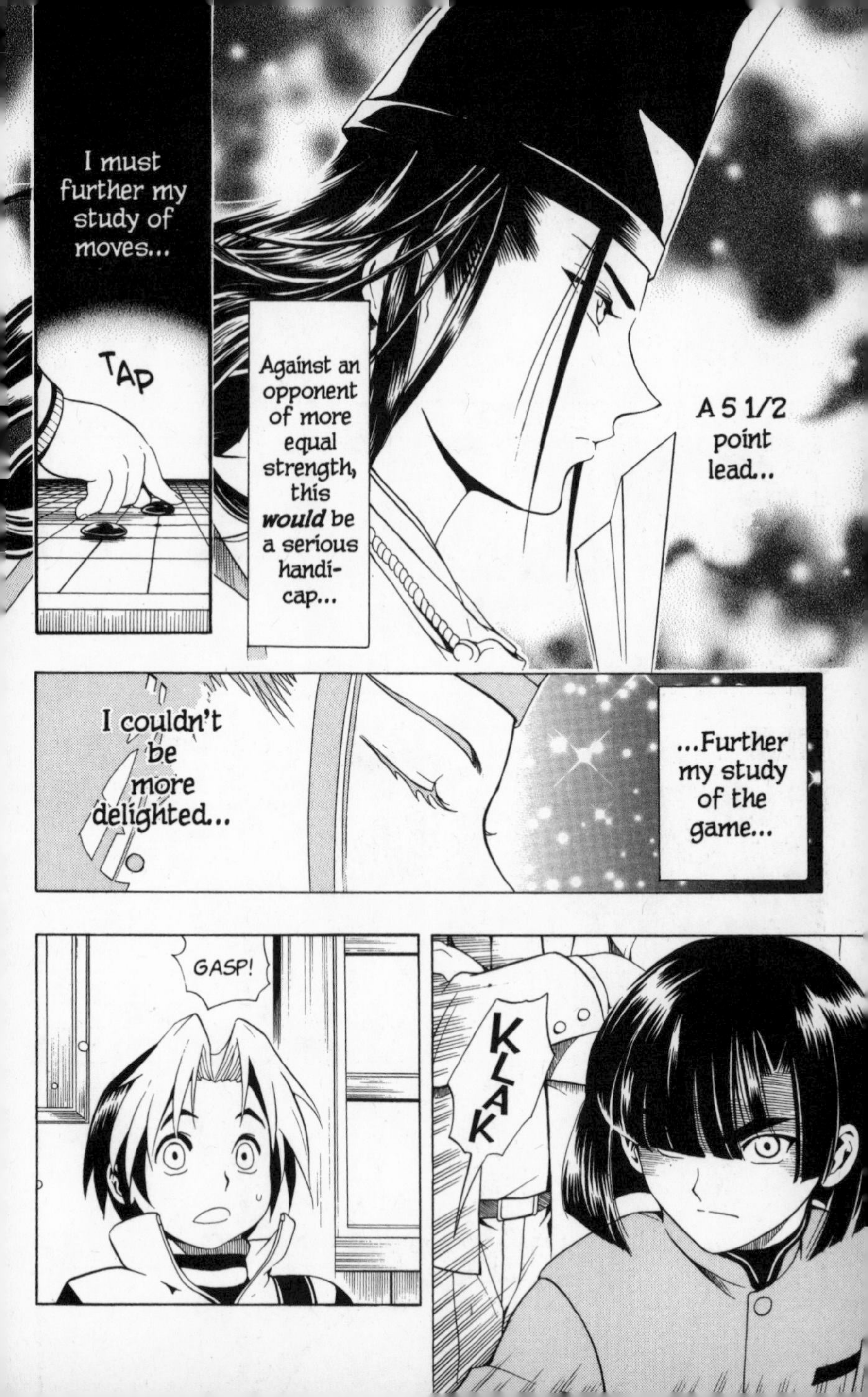
A 5 1/2 point lead...
Against an opponent of more equal strength, this *would* be a serious handi-cap...
I must further my study of moves...
TAP
...Further my study of the game...
I couldn't be more delighted...
KLAK
GASP!

READ THIS WAY

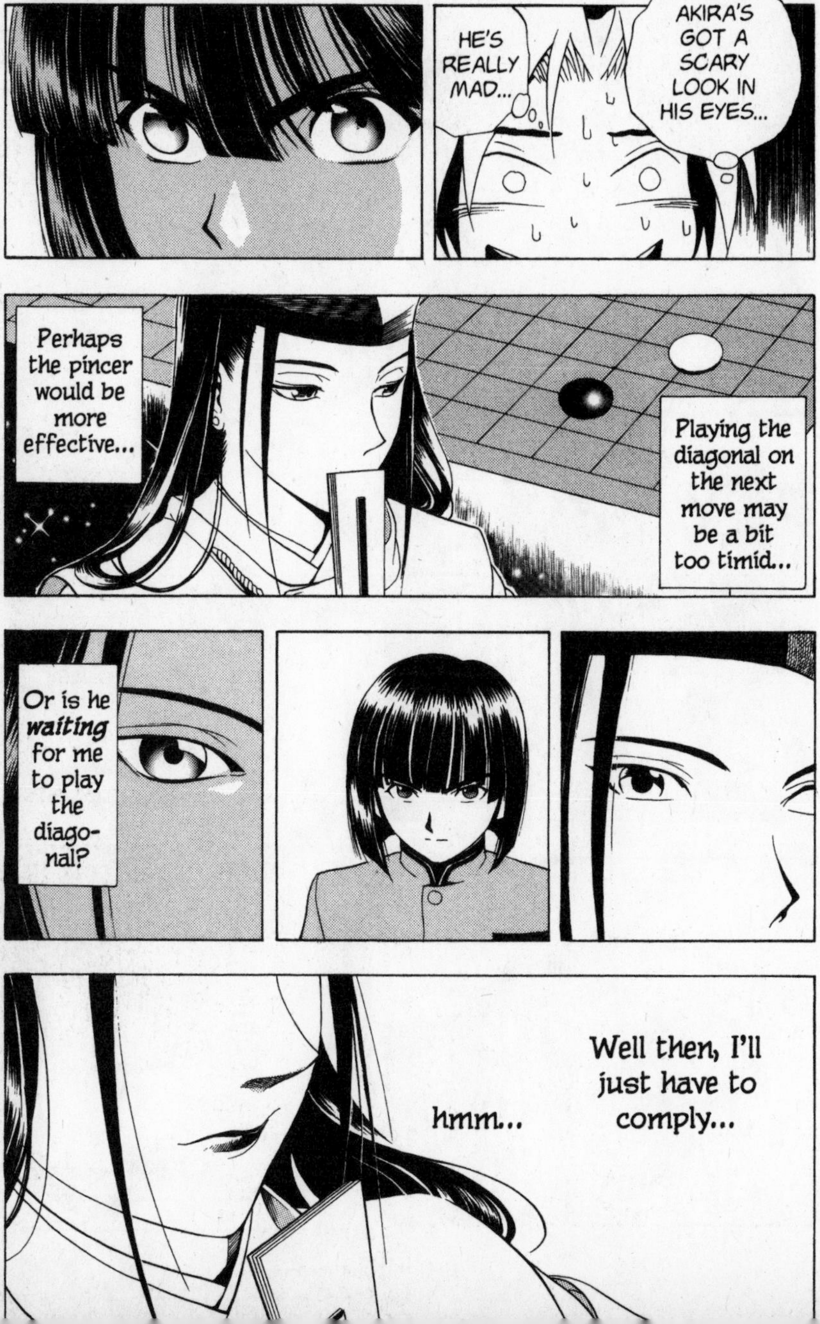

AKIRA'S GOT A SCARY LOOK IN HIS EYES...
HE'S REALLY MAD...
Playing the diagonal on the next move may be a bit too timid...
Perhaps the pincer would be more effective...
Or is he *waiting* for me to play the diago-nal?
Well then, I'll just have to comply...
hmm...

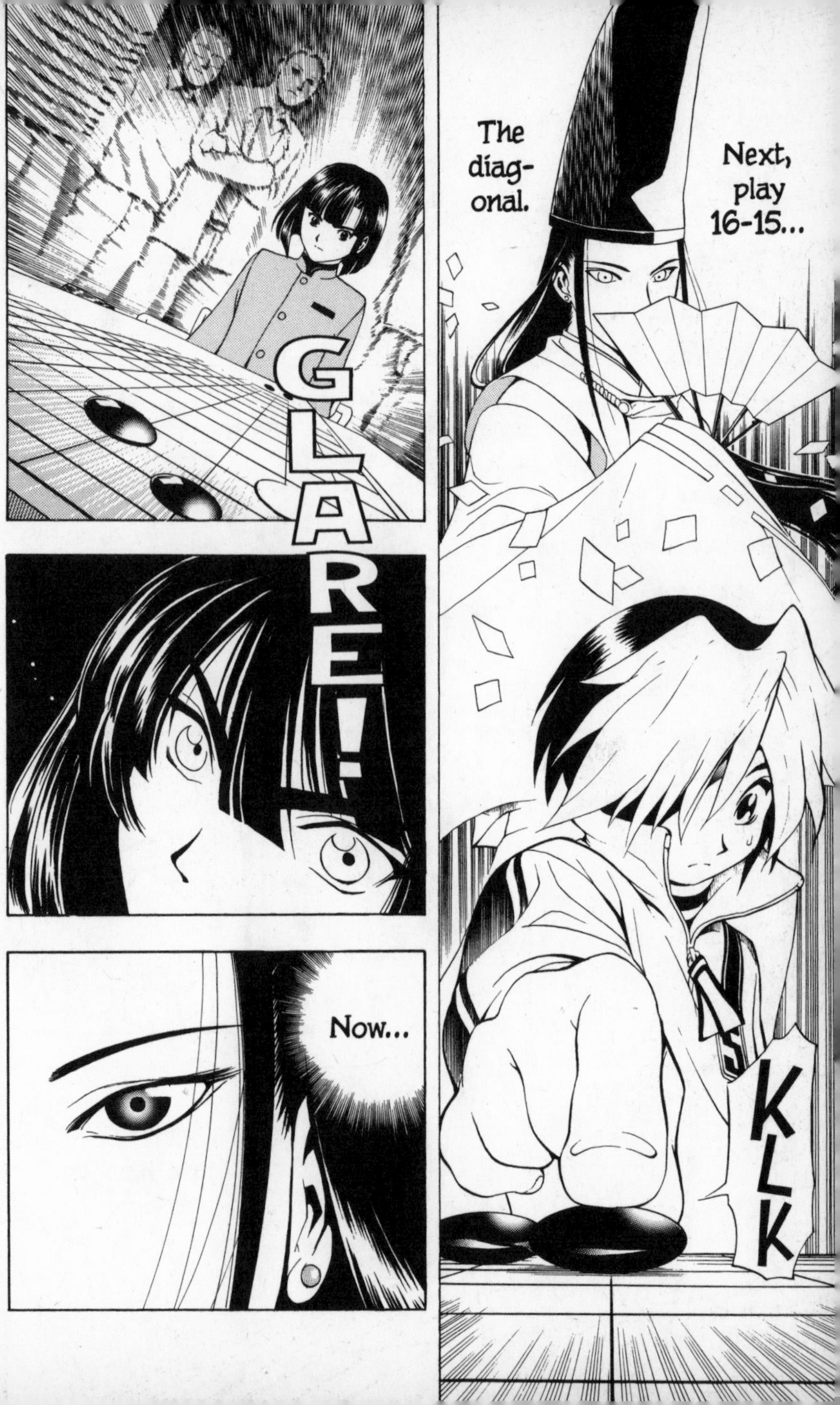
Next, play 16-15...
The diag-onal.
KLK
GLARE!
Now...

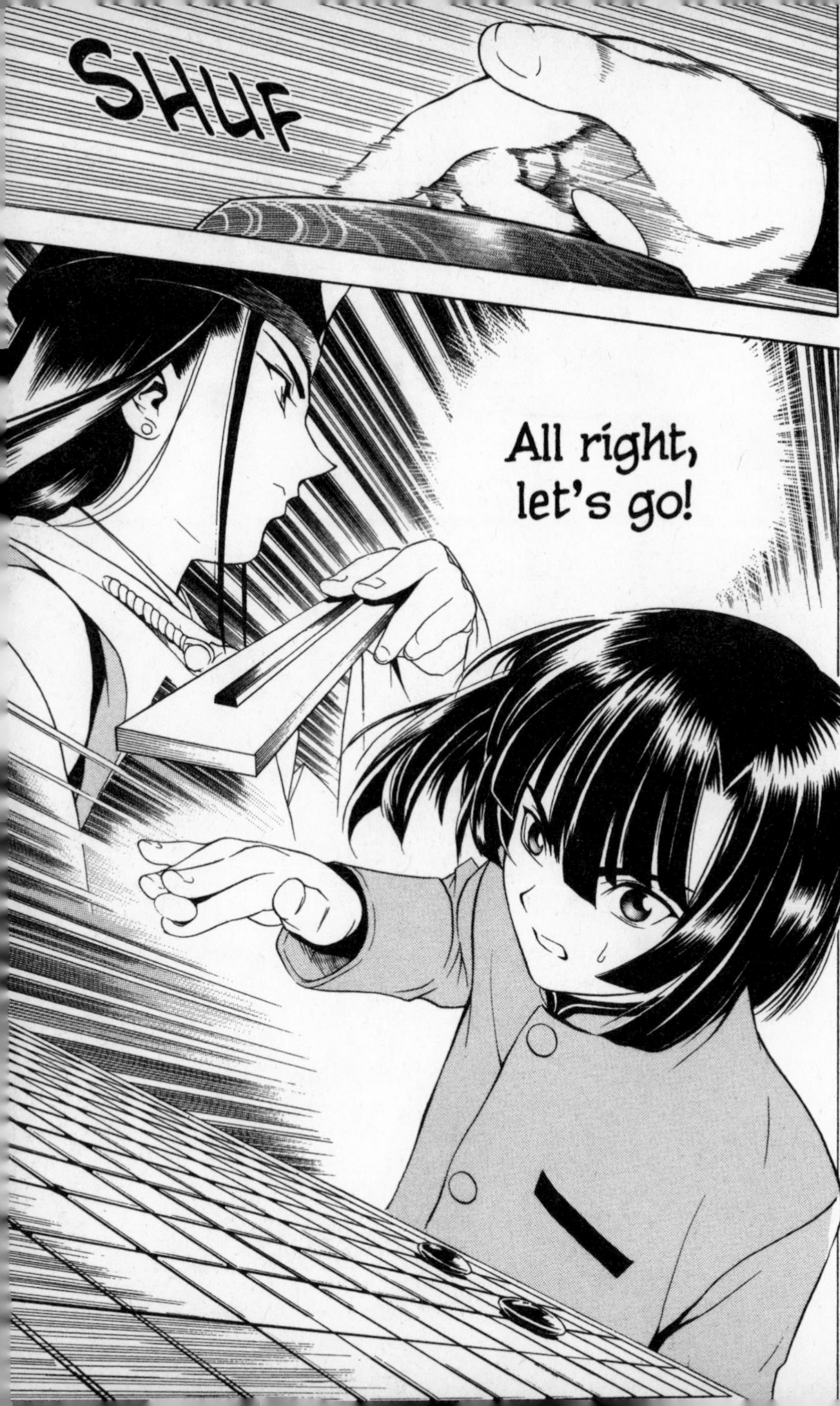
SHUF
All right, let's go!

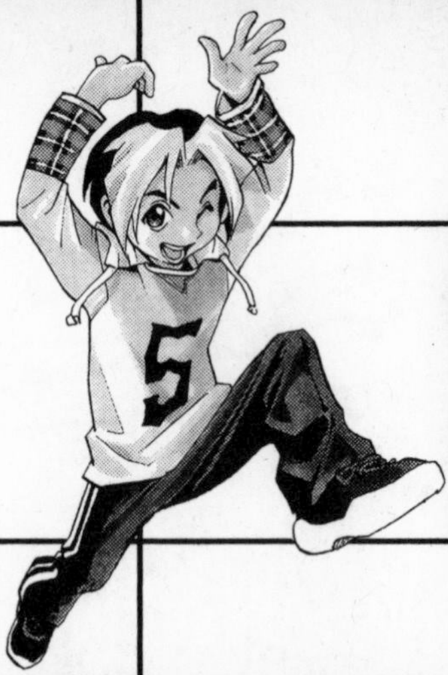

HIKARU NO GO EXTRAS

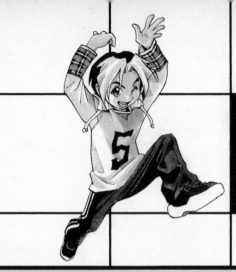

Hikaru no Go Q&A

Q 1 Is it true that there are smaller Go boards?

A A standard Go board, such as the one shown to the right, has 19 by 19 points. This may be too large an area and may cause confusion for beginners. So instead, a 9 by 9 board can be used.

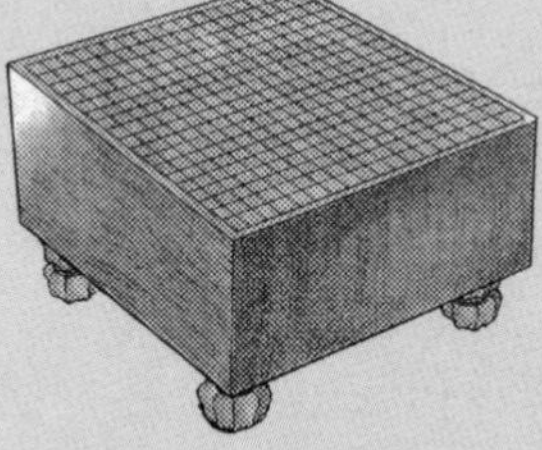

A 19 by 19 Go board with legs typically used by the pros.

Q 2 What kind of person was Hon'inbo-Shusaku?

A Shusaku was a genius Go player born in 1829 in Innoshima. He had such great skill that some called him the greatest player of all time. He learned the game at age 5 and by the time he was 10, he was playing Go in Edo, the capital city. It is said that his master, Jowa, called Shusaku a great player the likes of which had not been seen in 150 years. Shusaku eventually developed into such an outstanding player, he came to be known as a "Go Saint."

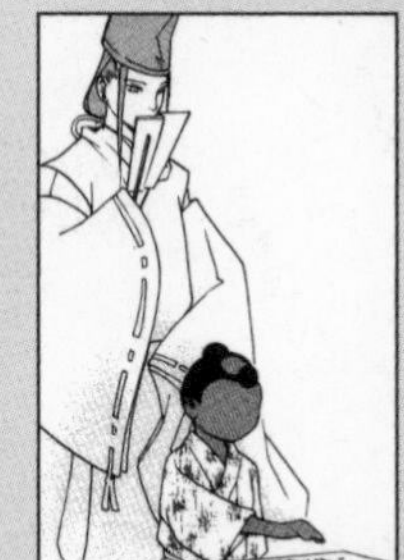

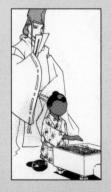

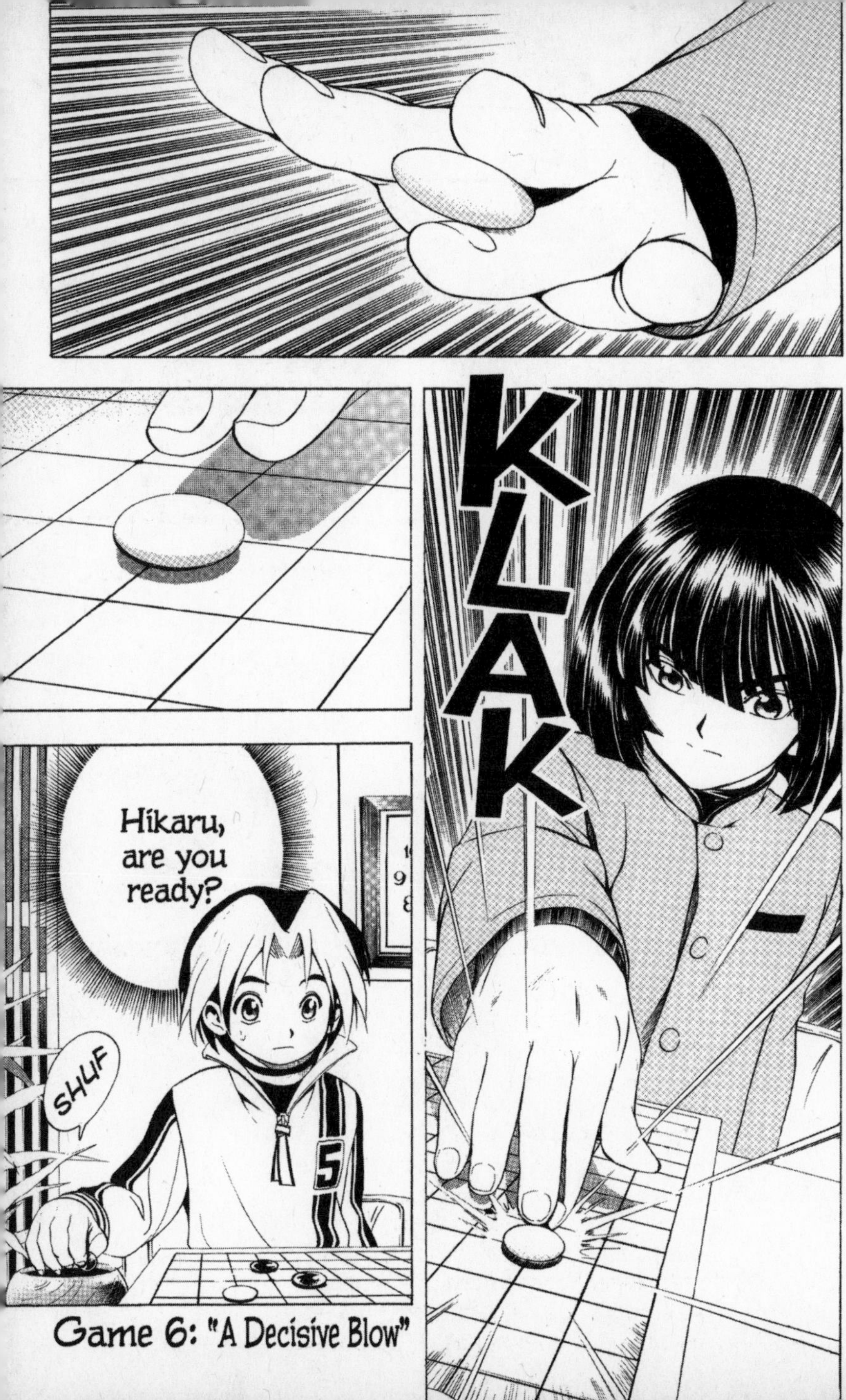
KLAK
Hikaru, are you ready?
SHUF

Game 6: "A Decisive Blow"

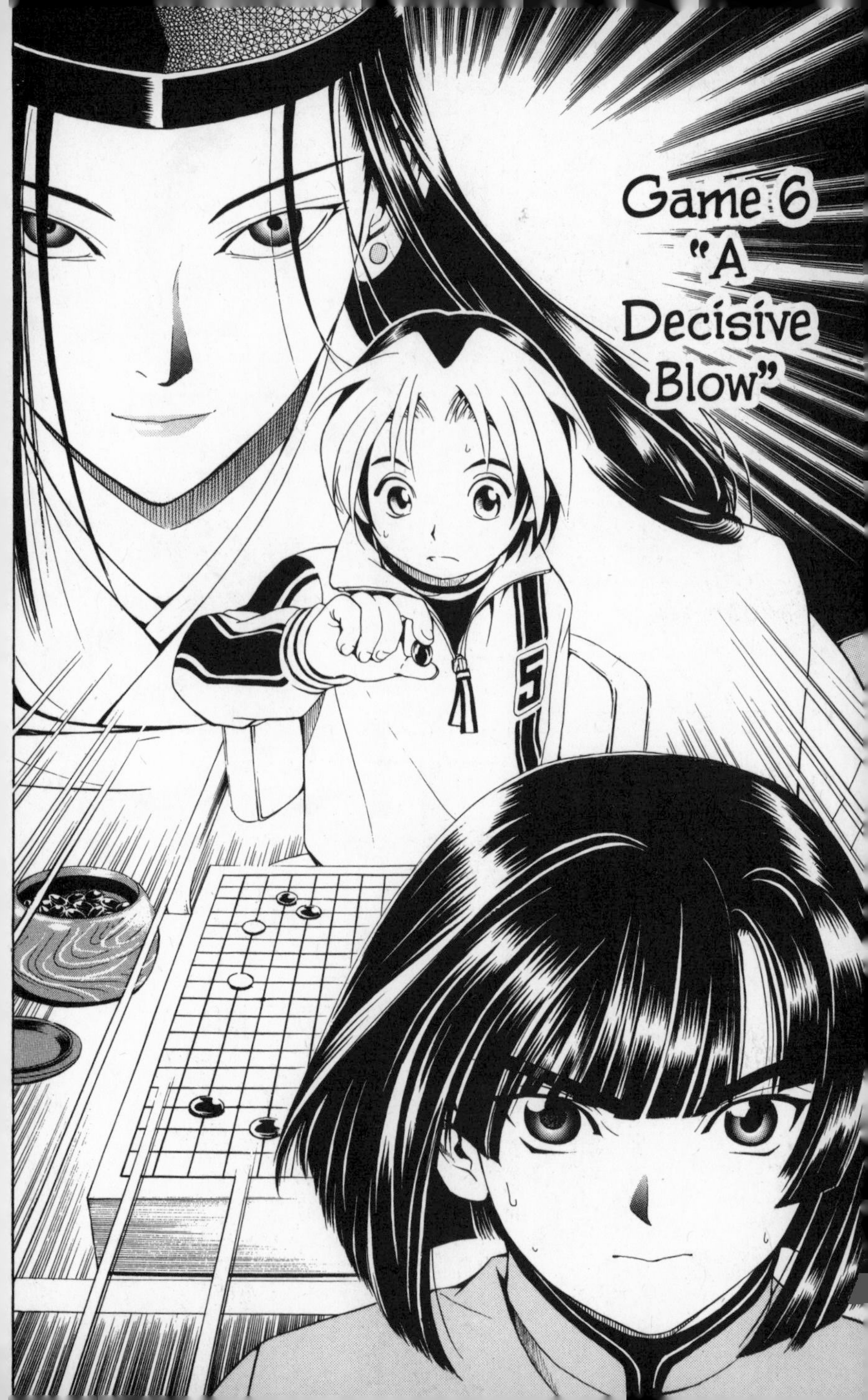
Game 6
"A Decisive Blow"

READ THIS WAY

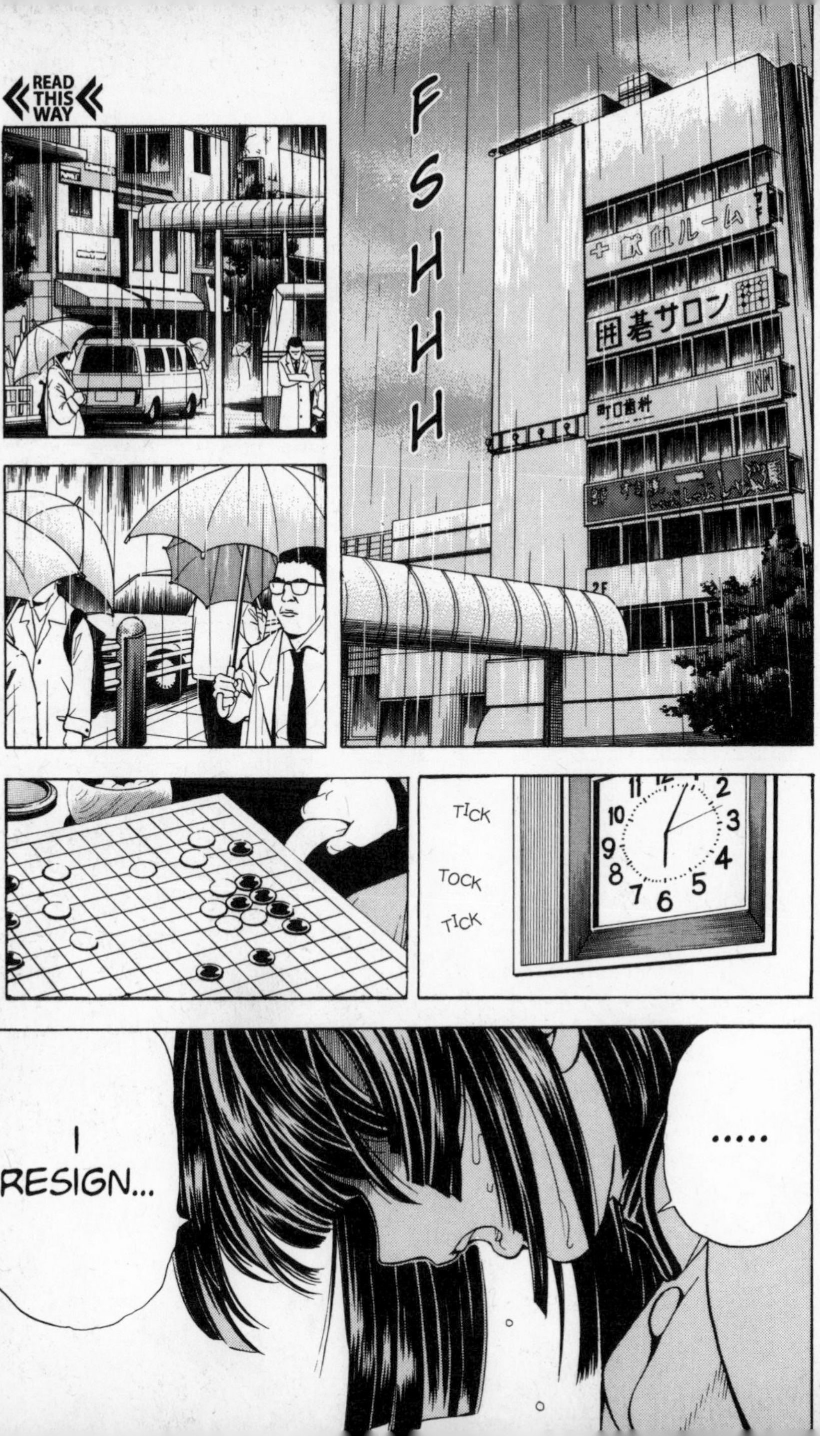
FSHHH
囲碁サロン
TICK
TOCK
TICK
.....
I RESIGN...

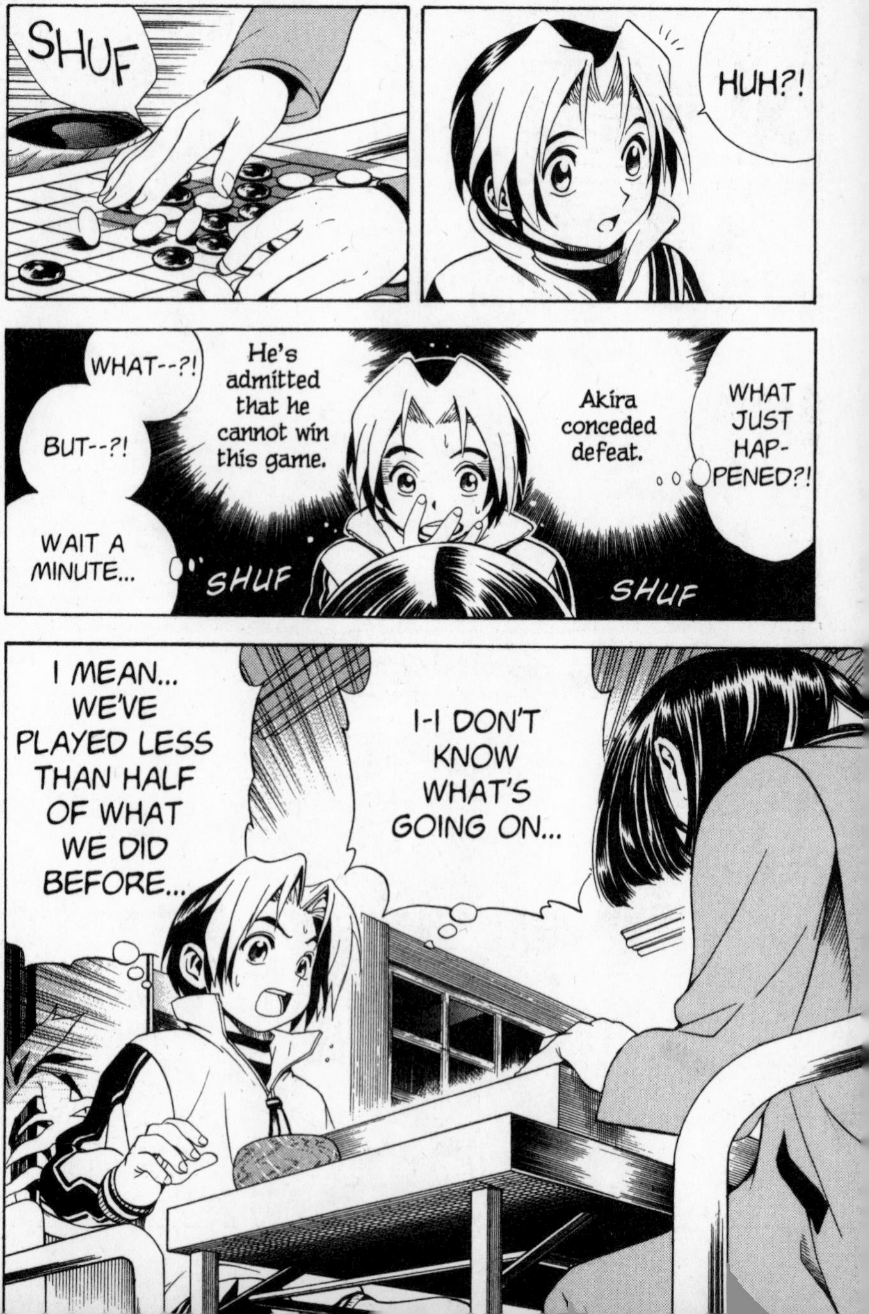
HUH?!
SHUF
WHAT JUST HAPPENED?!
Akira conceded defeat.
SHUF
He's admitted that he cannot win this game.
WHAT--?!
BUT--?!
WAIT A MINUTE...
SHUF
I-I DON'T KNOW WHAT'S GOING ON...
I MEAN... WE'VE PLAYED LESS THAN HALF OF WHAT WE DID BEFORE...

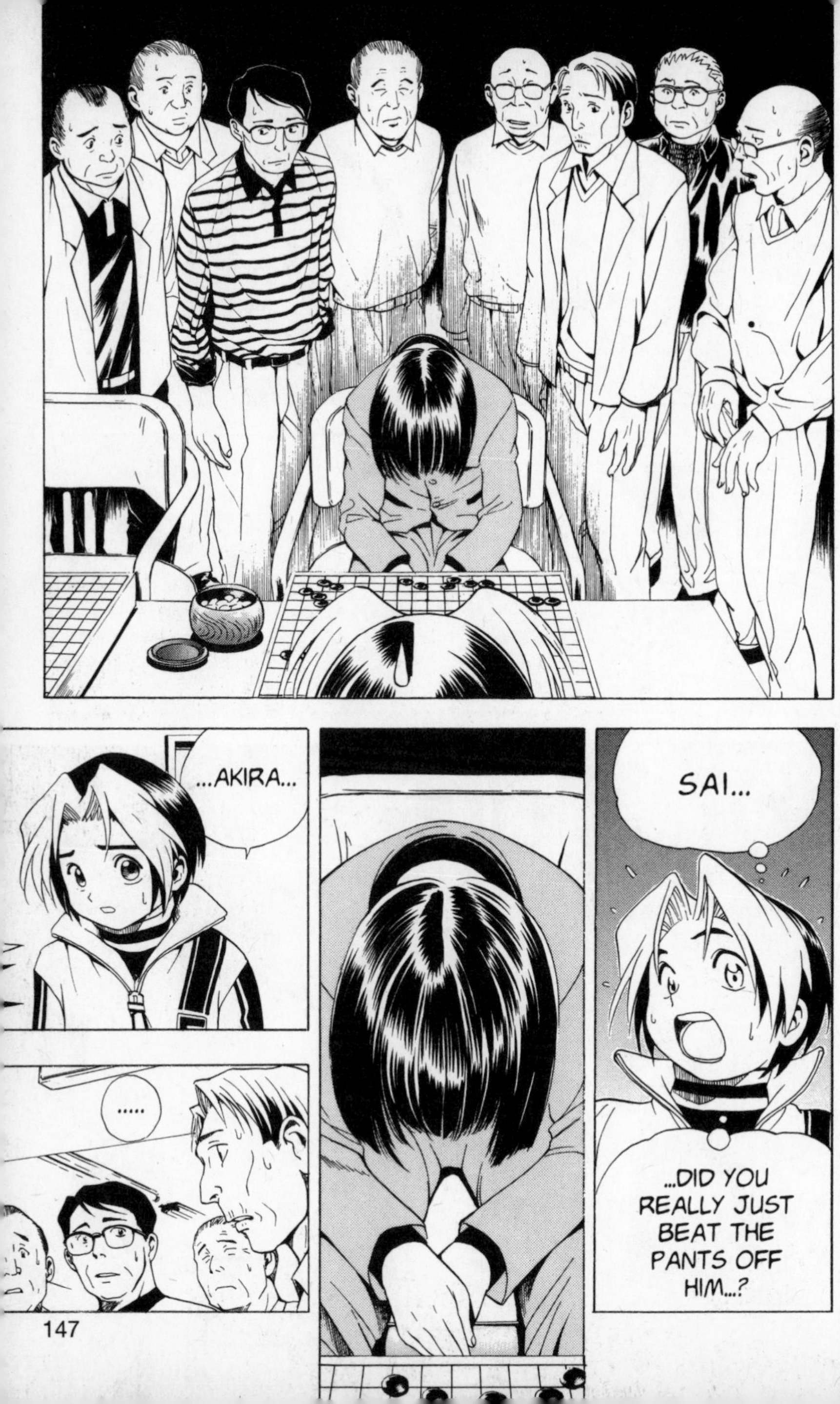
SAI...
...DID YOU REALLY JUST BEAT THE PANTS OFF HIM...?
...AKIRA...
.....

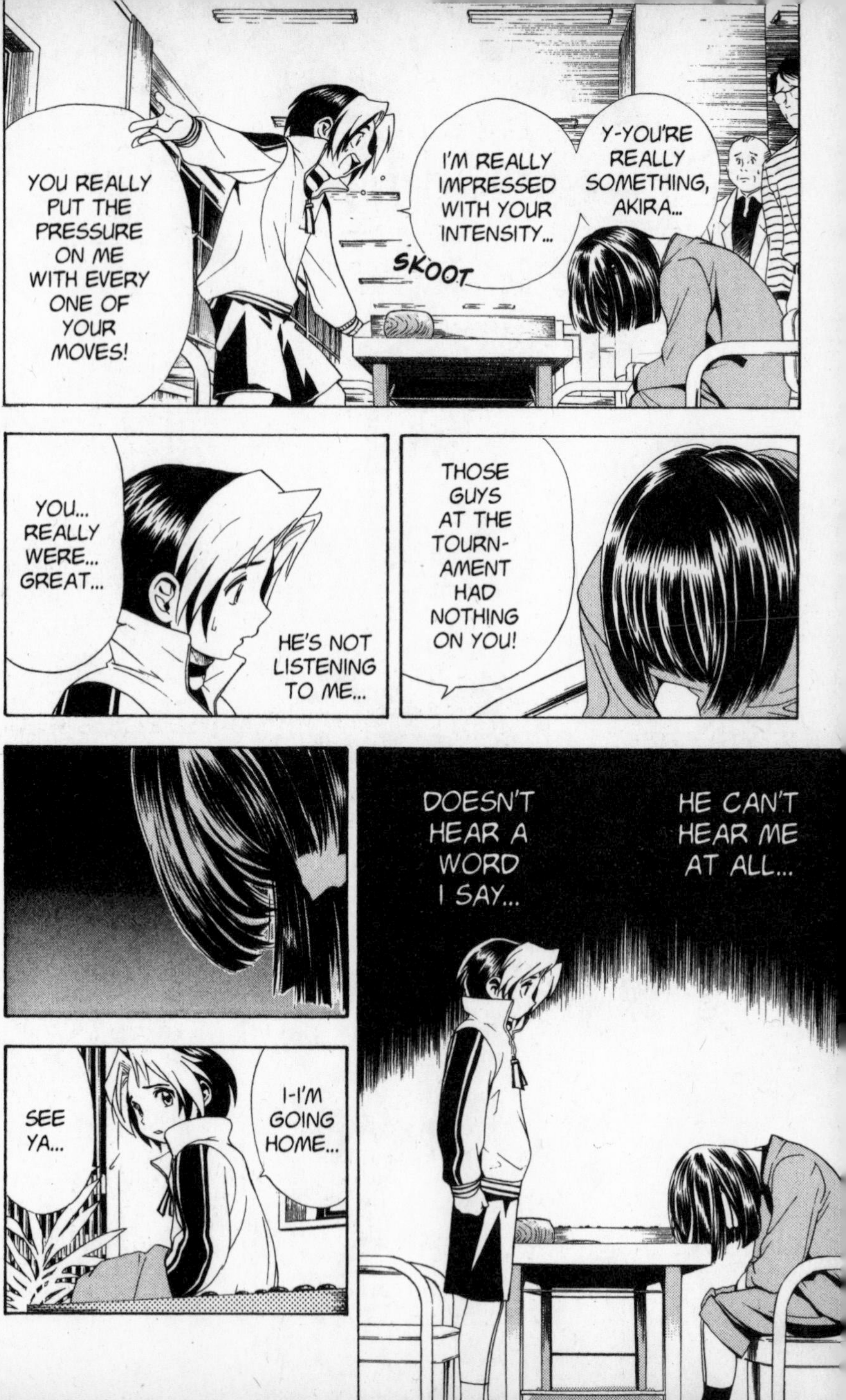
Y-YOU'RE REALLY SOMETHING, AKIRA...
I'M REALLY IMPRESSED WITH YOUR INTENSITY...
SKOOT
YOU REALLY PUT THE PRESSURE ON ME WITH EVERY ONE OF YOUR MOVES!
THOSE GUYS AT THE TOURN-AMENT HAD NOTHING ON YOU!
YOU... REALLY WERE... GREAT...
HE'S NOT LISTENING TO ME...
HE CAN'T HEAR ME AT ALL...
DOESN'T HEAR A WORD I SAY...
I-I'M GOING HOME...
SEE YA...

READ THIS WAY

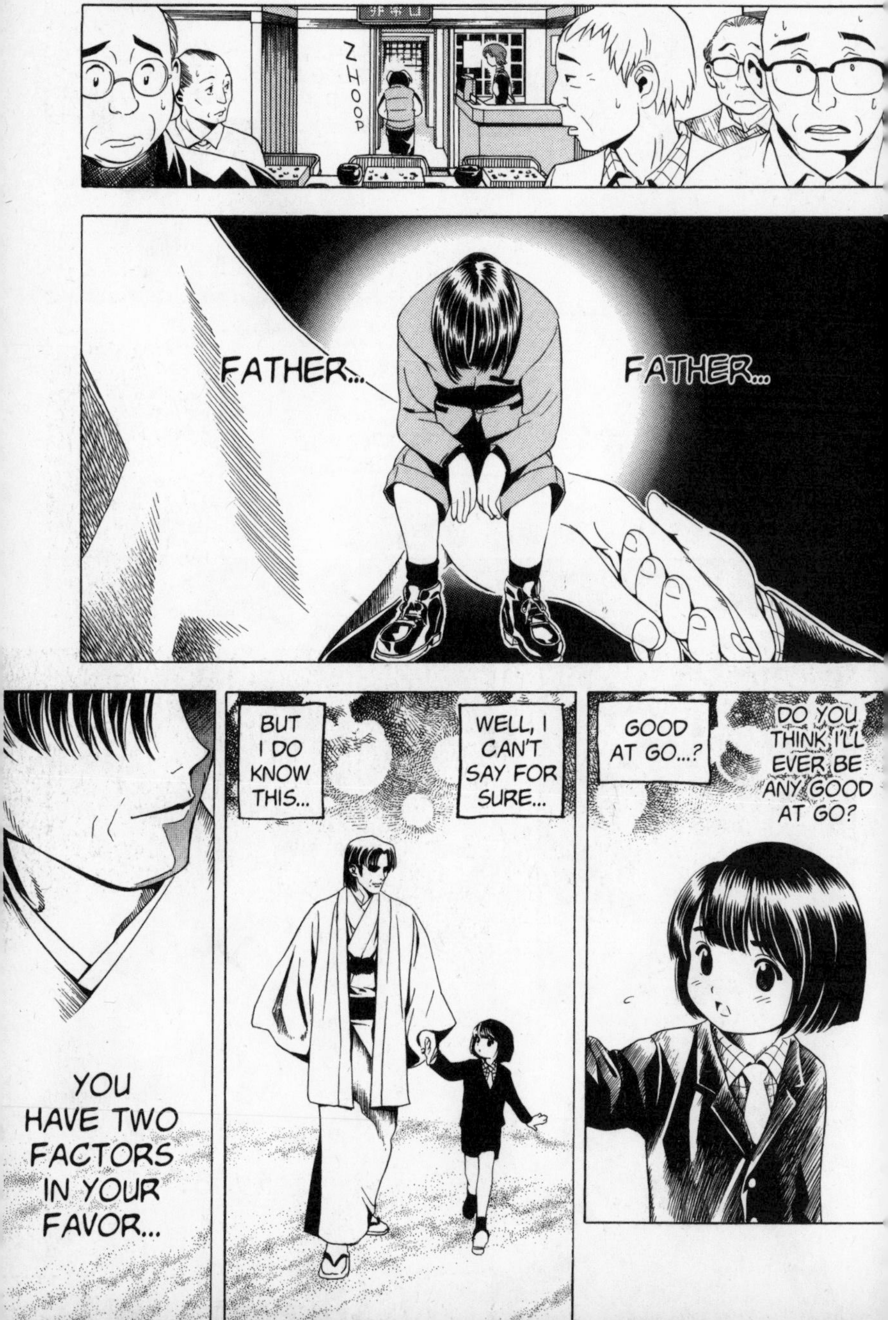
ZHOOP
FATHER...
FATHER...
DO YOU THINK I'LL EVER BE ANY GOOD AT GO?
GOOD AT GO...?
WELL, I CAN'T SAY FOR SURE...
BUT I DO KNOW THIS...
YOU HAVE TWO FACTORS IN YOUR FAVOR...

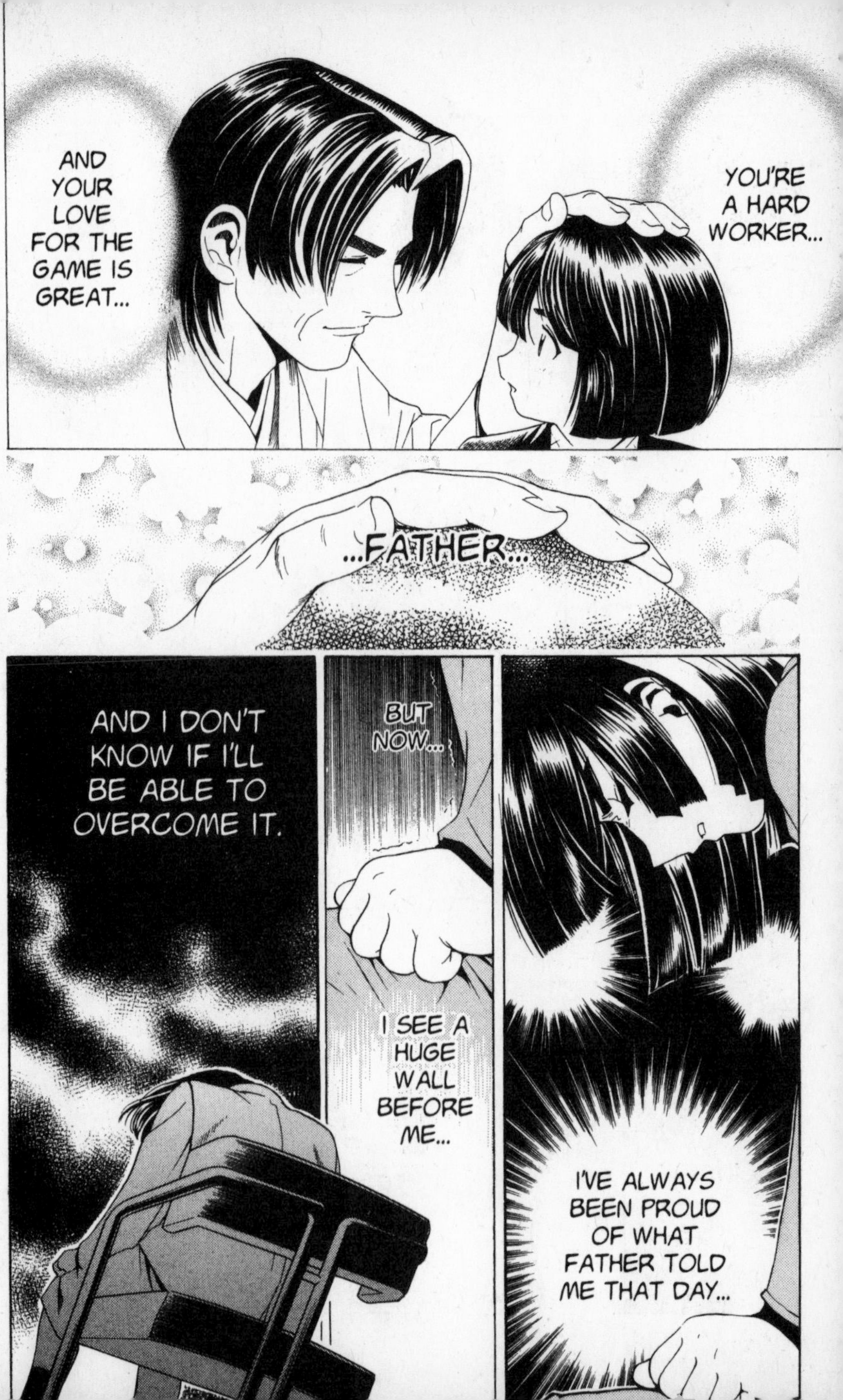
YOU'RE A HARD WORKER...
AND YOUR LOVE FOR THE GAME IS GREAT...
...FATHER...
I'VE ALWAYS BEEN PROUD OF WHAT FATHER TOLD ME THAT DAY...
BUT NOW...
I SEE A HUGE WALL BEFORE ME...
AND I DON'T KNOW IF I'LL BE ABLE TO OVERCOME IT.

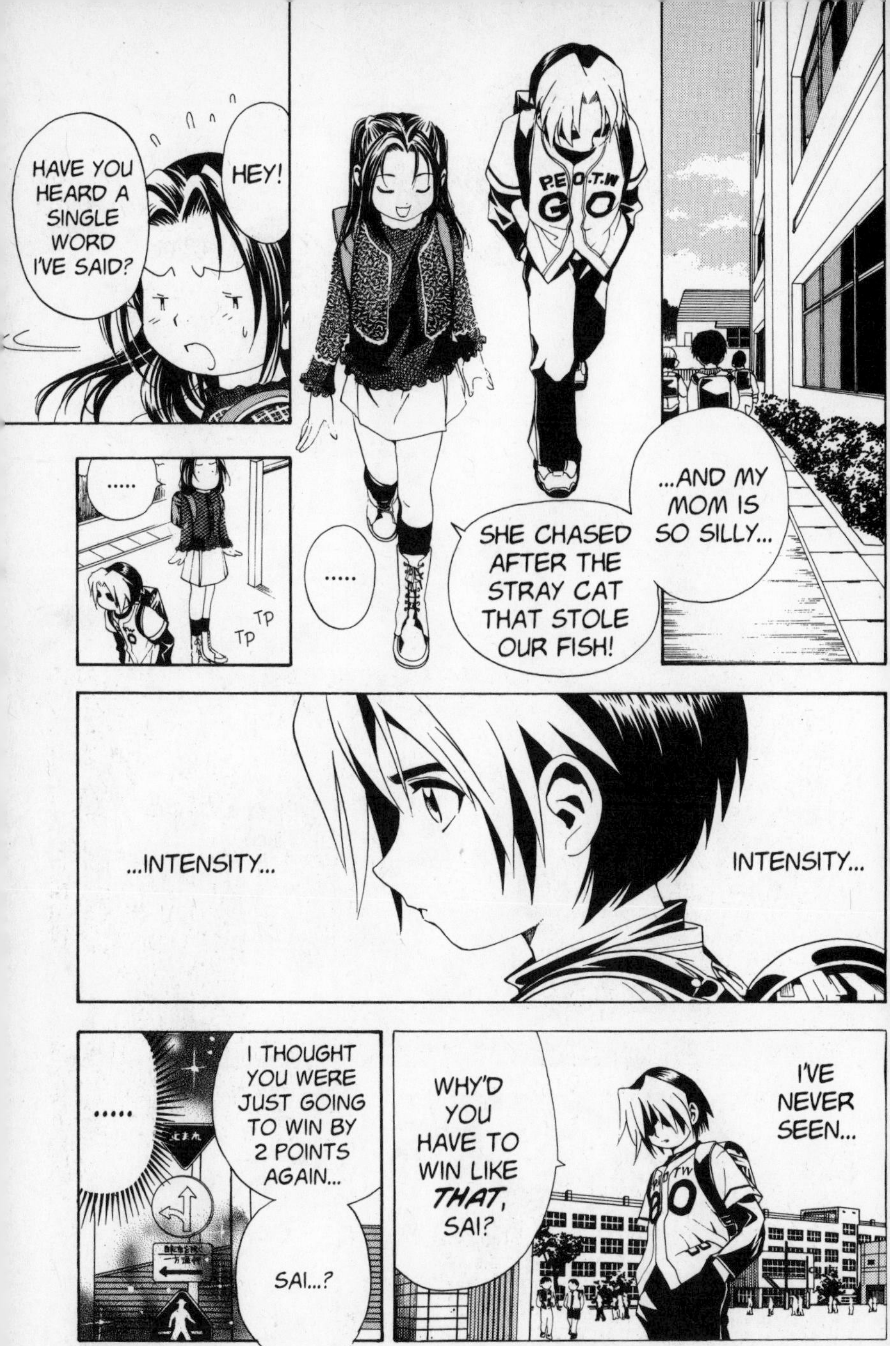
...AND MY MOM IS SO SILLY...
SHE CHASED AFTER THE STRAY CAT THAT STOLE OUR FISH!
.....
HEY!
HAVE YOU HEARD A SINGLE WORD I'VE SAID?
.....
Tp Tp
INTENSITY...
...INTENSITY...
I'VE NEVER SEEN...
WHY'D YOU HAVE TO WIN LIKE *THAT*, SAI?
I THOUGHT YOU WERE JUST GOING TO WIN BY 2 POINTS AGAIN...
SAI...?
.....

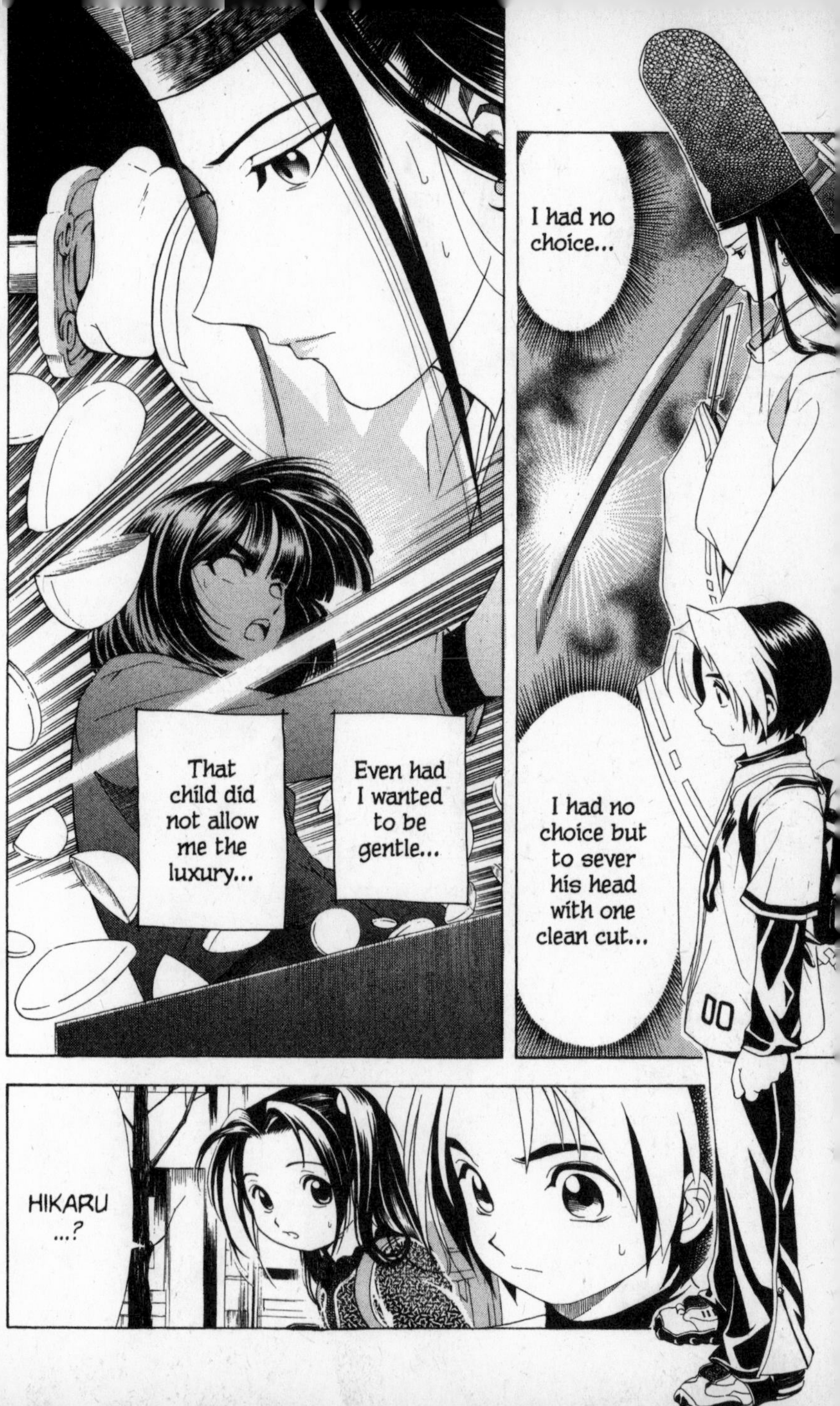
I had no choice...
I had no choice but to sever his head with one clean cut...
Even had I wanted to be gentle...
That child did not allow me the luxury...
HIKARU ...?

READ THIS WAY

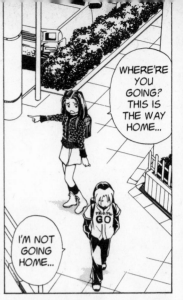

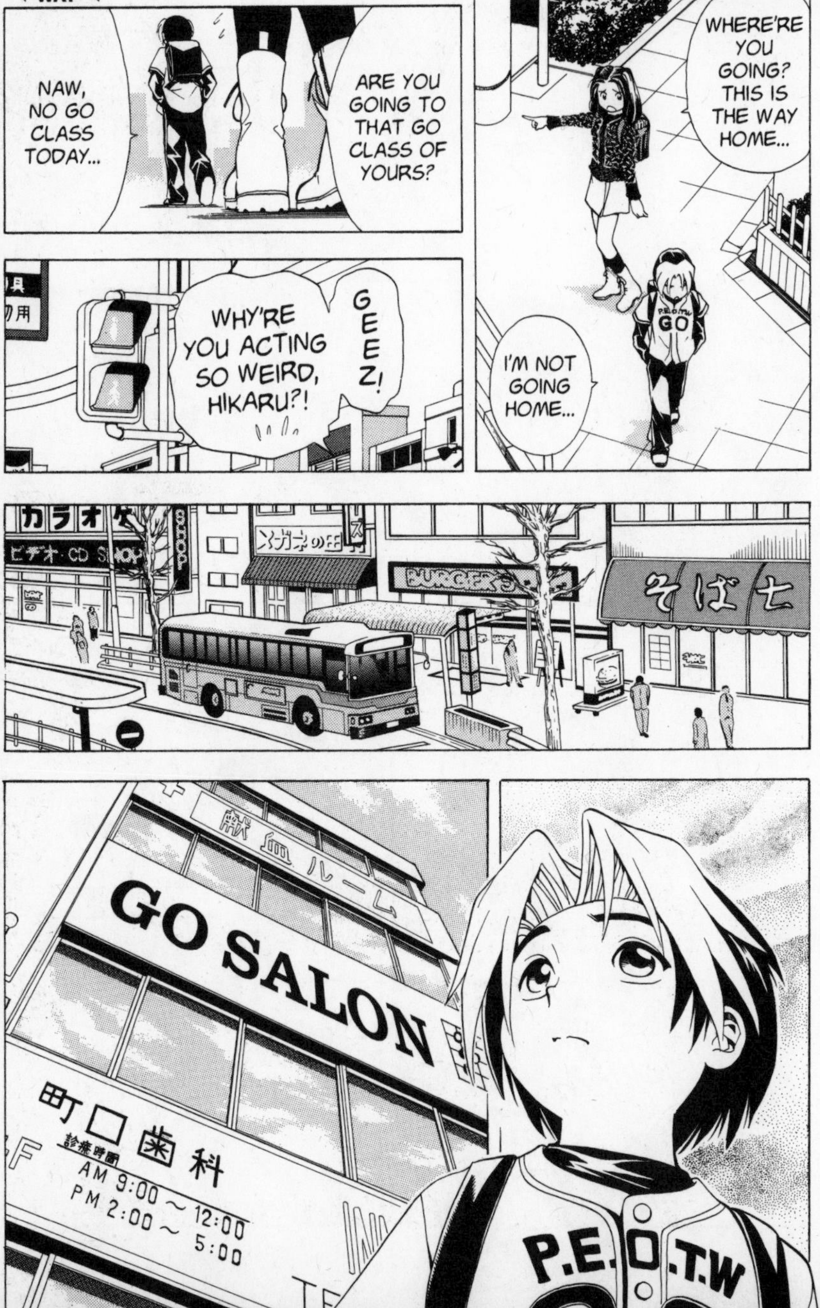
WHERE'RE YOU GOING? THIS IS THE WAY HOME...
P.E.O.T.W GO
I'M NOT GOING HOME...
ARE YOU GOING TO THAT GO CLASS OF YOURS?
NAW, NO GO CLASS TODAY...
GEEZ!
WHY'RE YOU ACTING SO WEIRD, HIKARU?!
カラオケ
ビデオ·CD SHOP
SHOP
P.E.O.T.W
GO SALON
献血ルーム
町口歯科
診療時間
AM 9:00～12:00
PM 2:00～5:00

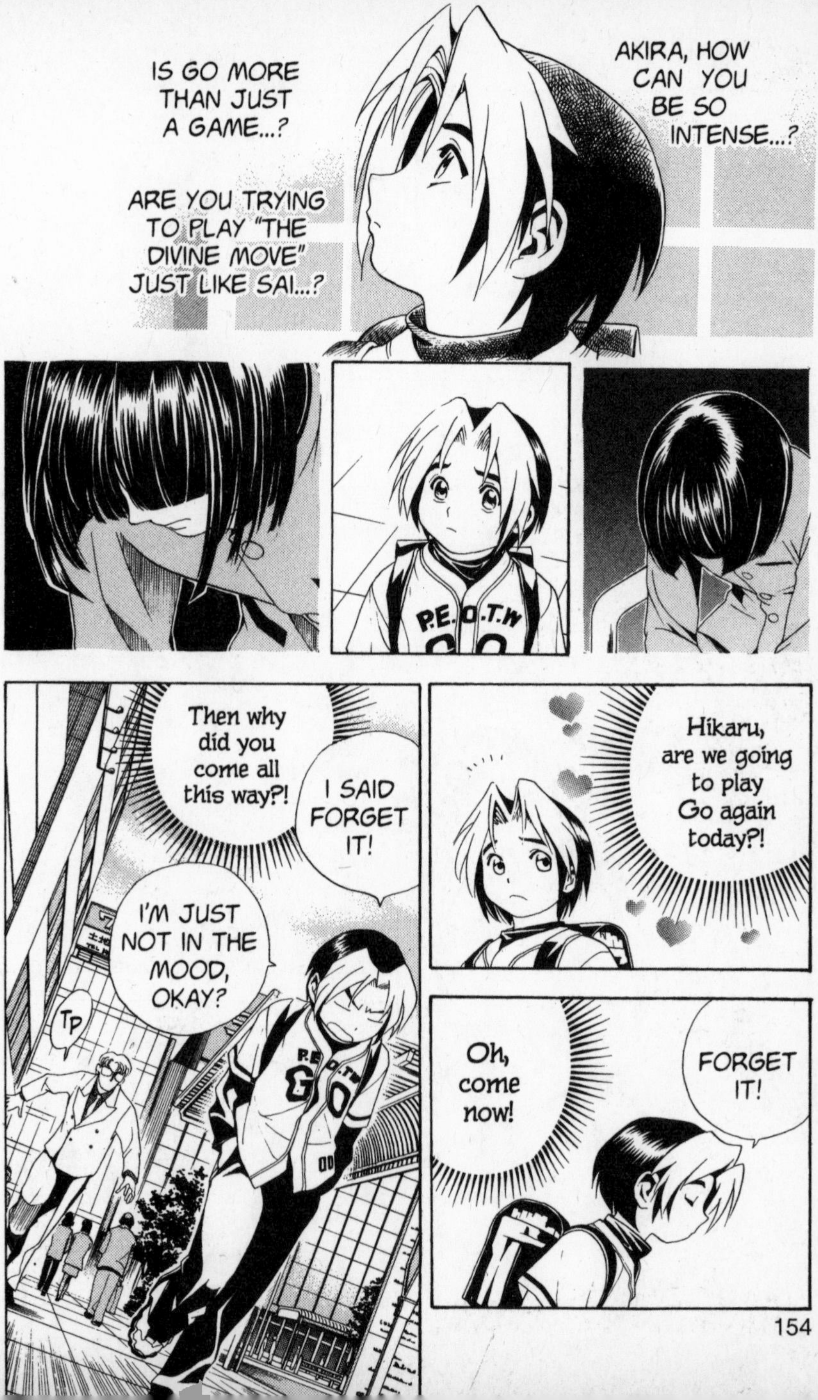
AKIRA, HOW CAN YOU BE SO INTENSE...?
IS GO MORE THAN JUST A GAME...?
ARE YOU TRYING TO PLAY "THE DIVINE MOVE" JUST LIKE SAI...?
P.E.O.T.W
Hikaru, are we going to play Go again today?!
FORGET IT!
Oh, come now!
Then why did you come all this way?!
I SAID FORGET IT!
I'M JUST NOT IN THE MOOD, OKAY?
Tp

READ THIS WAY

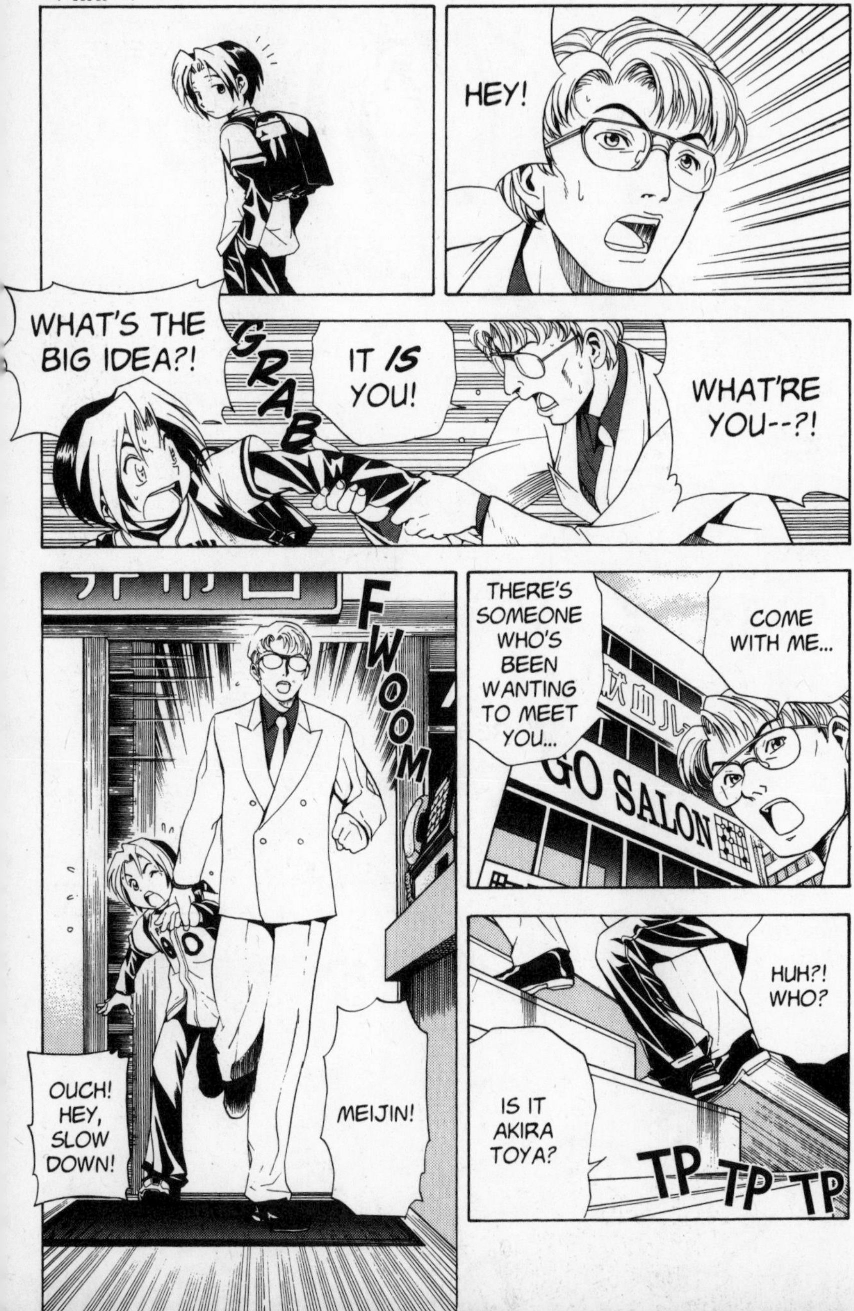
HEY!
WHAT'RE YOU--?!
IT *IS* YOU!
GRAB
WHAT'S THE BIG IDEA?!
COME WITH ME...
THERE'S SOMEONE WHO'S BEEN WANTING TO MEET YOU...
GO SALON
HUH?! WHO?
IS IT AKIRA TOYA?
TP TP TP
FWOOM
MEIJIN!
OUCH! HEY, SLOW DOWN!

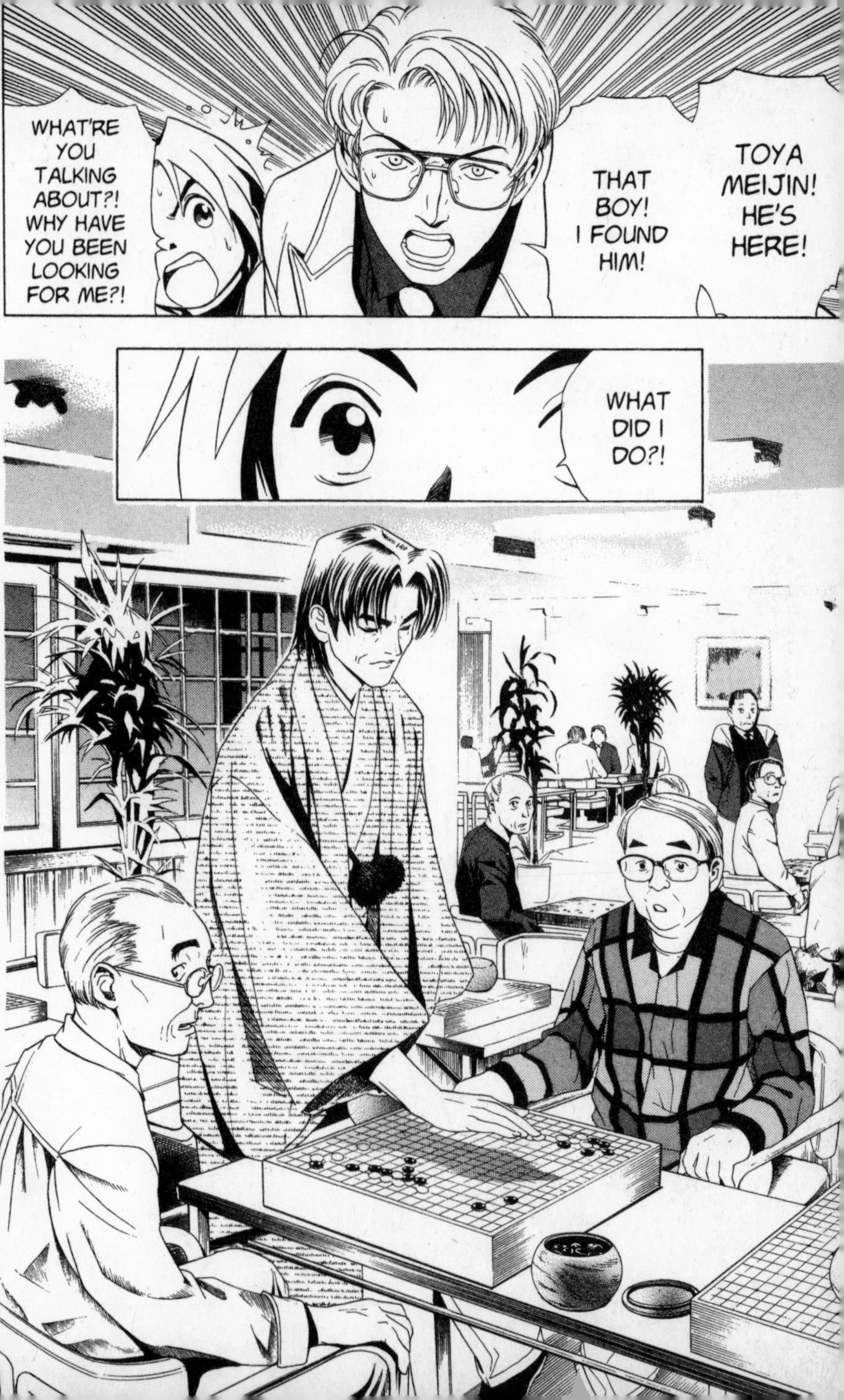
TOYA MEIJIN! HE'S HERE!
THAT BOY! I FOUND HIM!
WHAT'RE YOU TALKING ABOUT?! WHY HAVE YOU BEEN LOOKING FOR ME?!
WHAT DID I DO?!

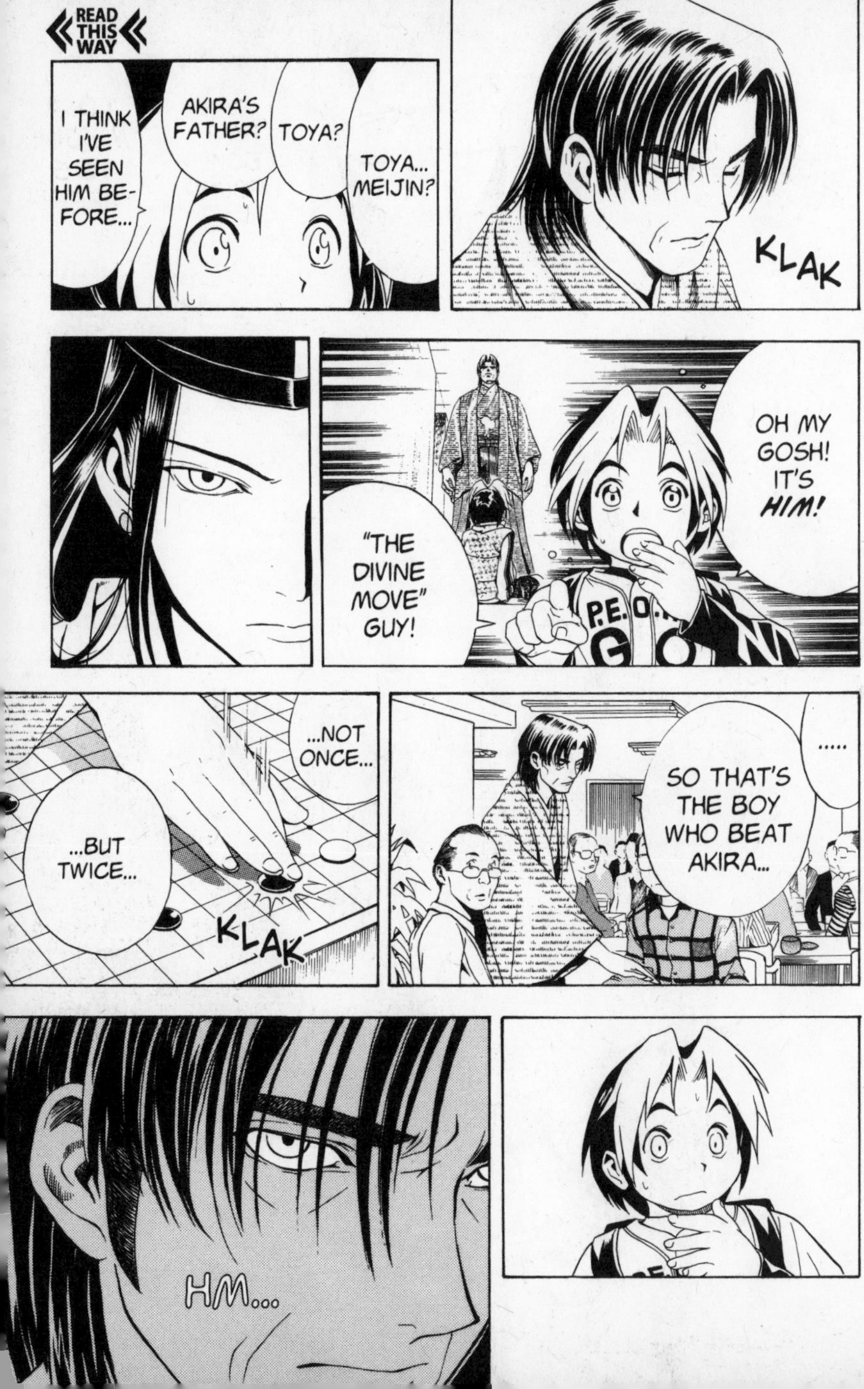
READ THIS WAY
KLAK
TOYA... MEIJIN?
TOYA?
AKIRA'S FATHER?
I THINK I'VE SEEN HIM BE-FORE...
OH MY GOSH! IT'S *HIM!*
"THE DIVINE MOVE" GUY!
.....
SO THAT'S THE BOY WHO BEAT AKIRA...
...NOT ONCE...
...BUT TWICE...
KLAK
HM...

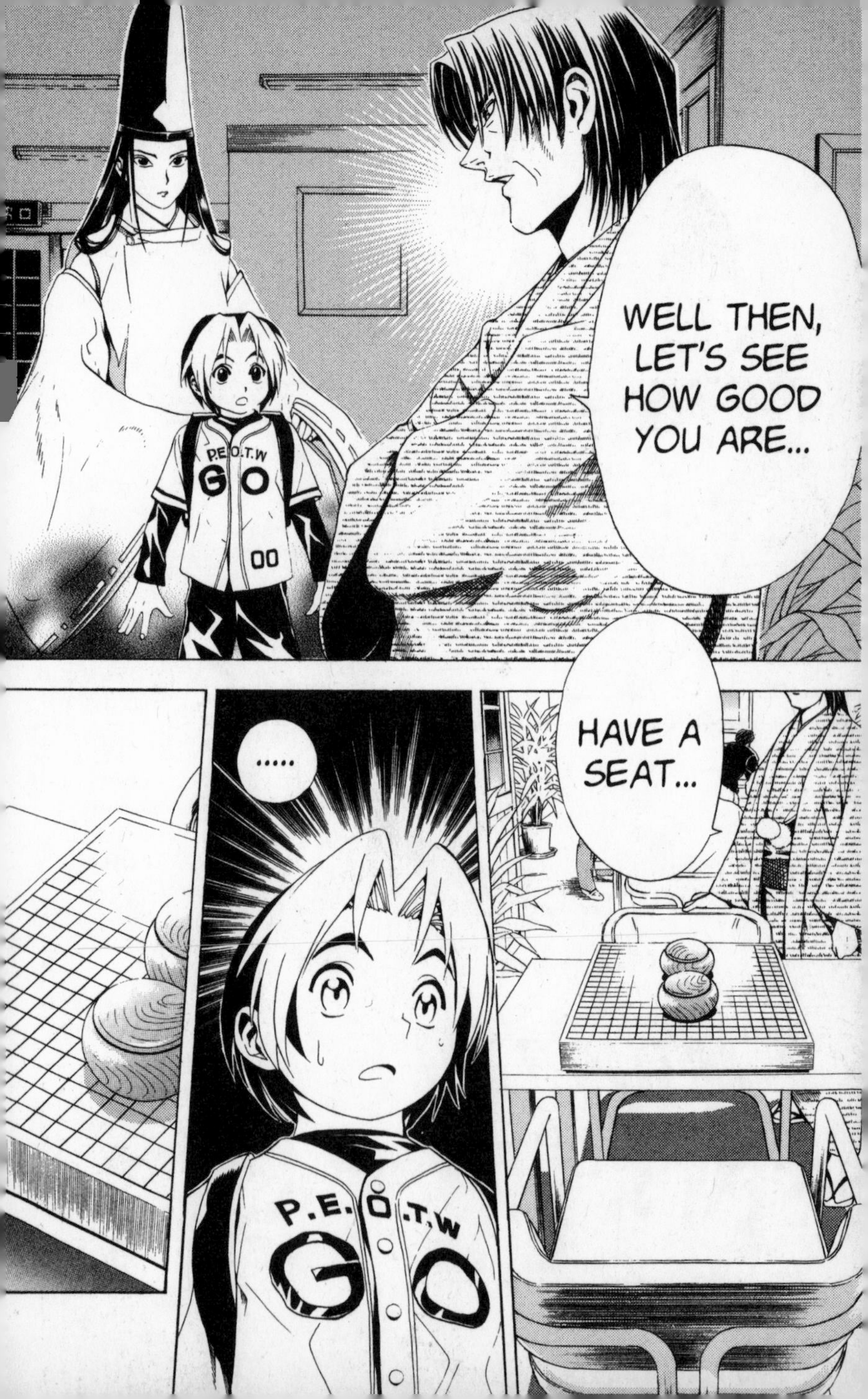
WELL THEN, LET'S SEE HOW GOOD YOU ARE...
P.E.O.T.W
GO
00
HAVE A SEAT...
.....
P.E.O.T.W
GO

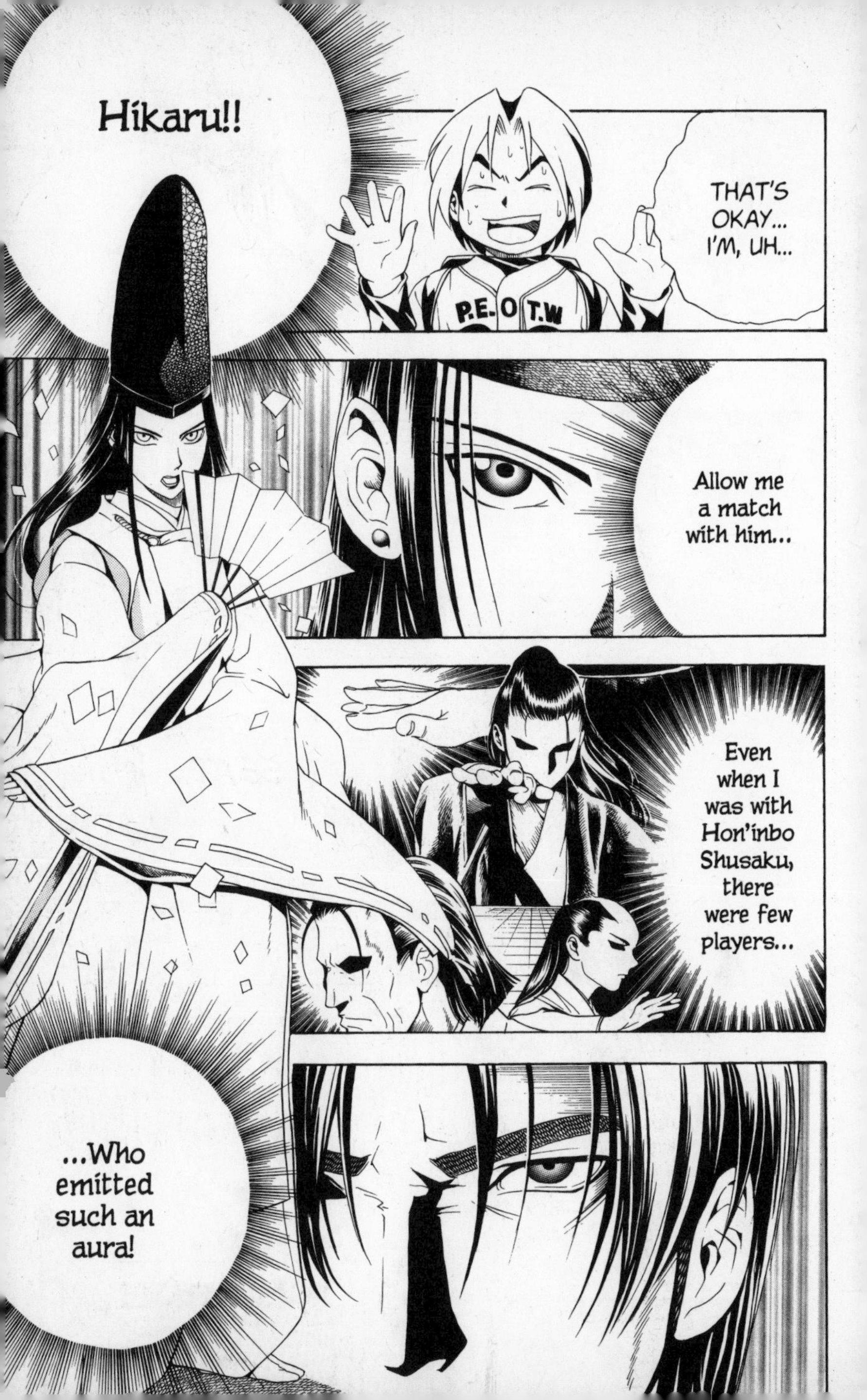
THAT'S OKAY... I'M, UH...
Hikaru!!
Allow me a match with him...
Even when I was with Hon'inbo Shusaku, there were few players...
...Who emitted such an aura!

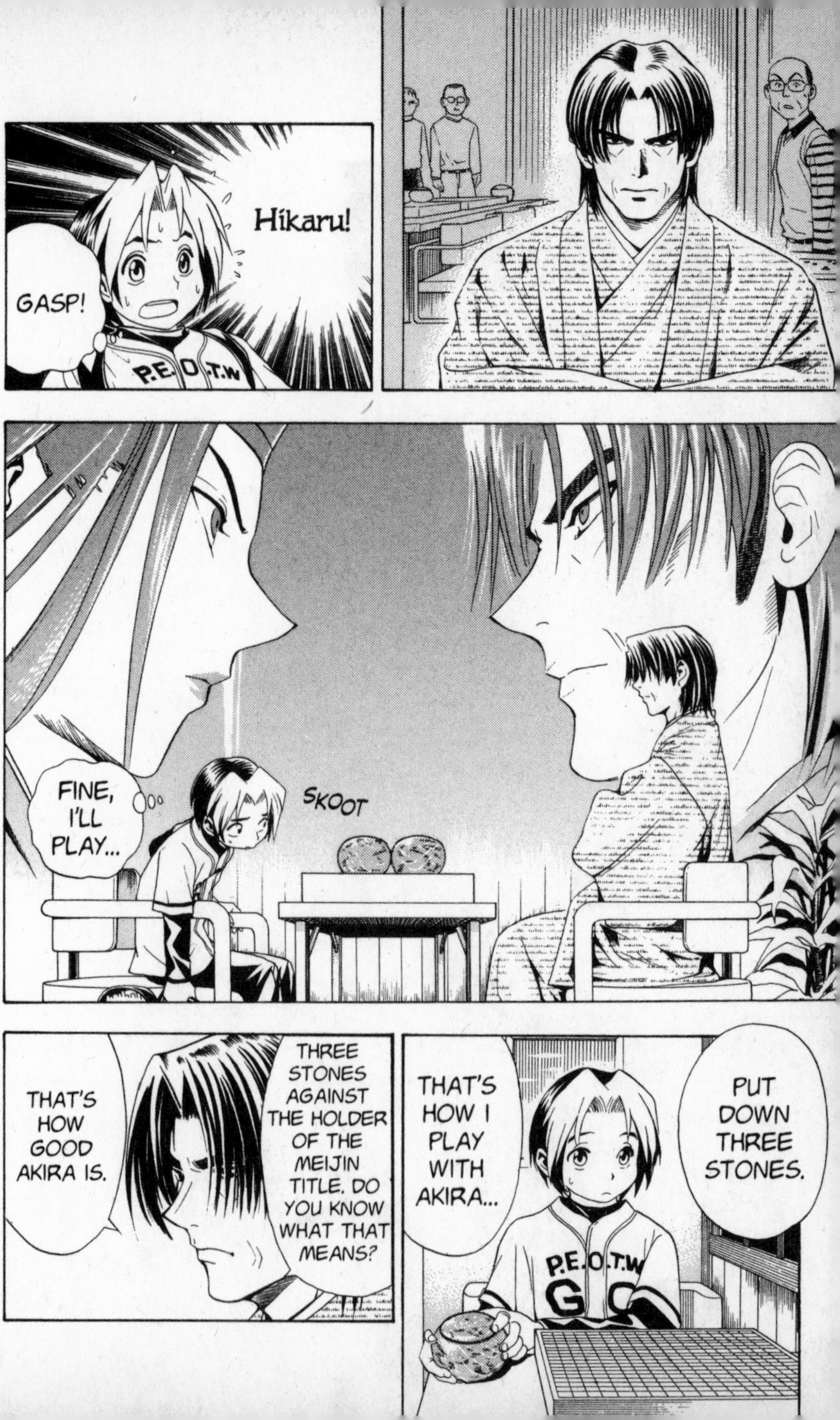
Hikaru!
GASP!
SKOOT
FINE, I'LL PLAY...
PUT DOWN THREE STONES.
THAT'S HOW I PLAY WITH AKIRA...
THREE STONES AGAINST THE HOLDER OF THE MEIJIN TITLE. DO YOU KNOW WHAT THAT MEANS?
THAT'S HOW GOOD AKIRA IS.

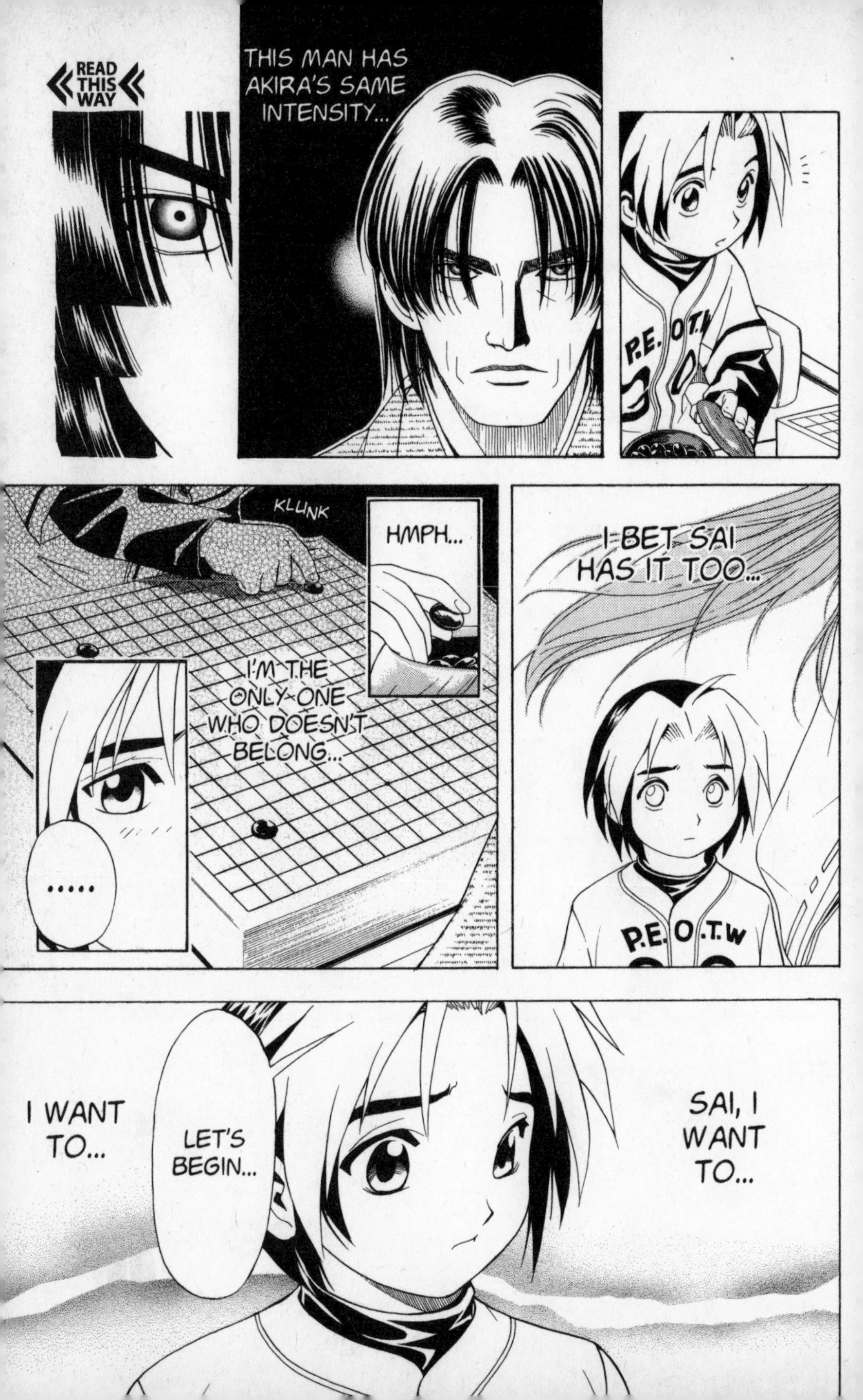
READ THIS WAY
THIS MAN HAS AKIRA'S SAME INTENSITY...
I BET SAI HAS IT TOO...
HMPH...
KLUNK
I'M THE ONLY ONE WHO DOESN'T BELONG...
.....
SAI, I WANT TO...
LET'S BEGIN...
I WANT TO...

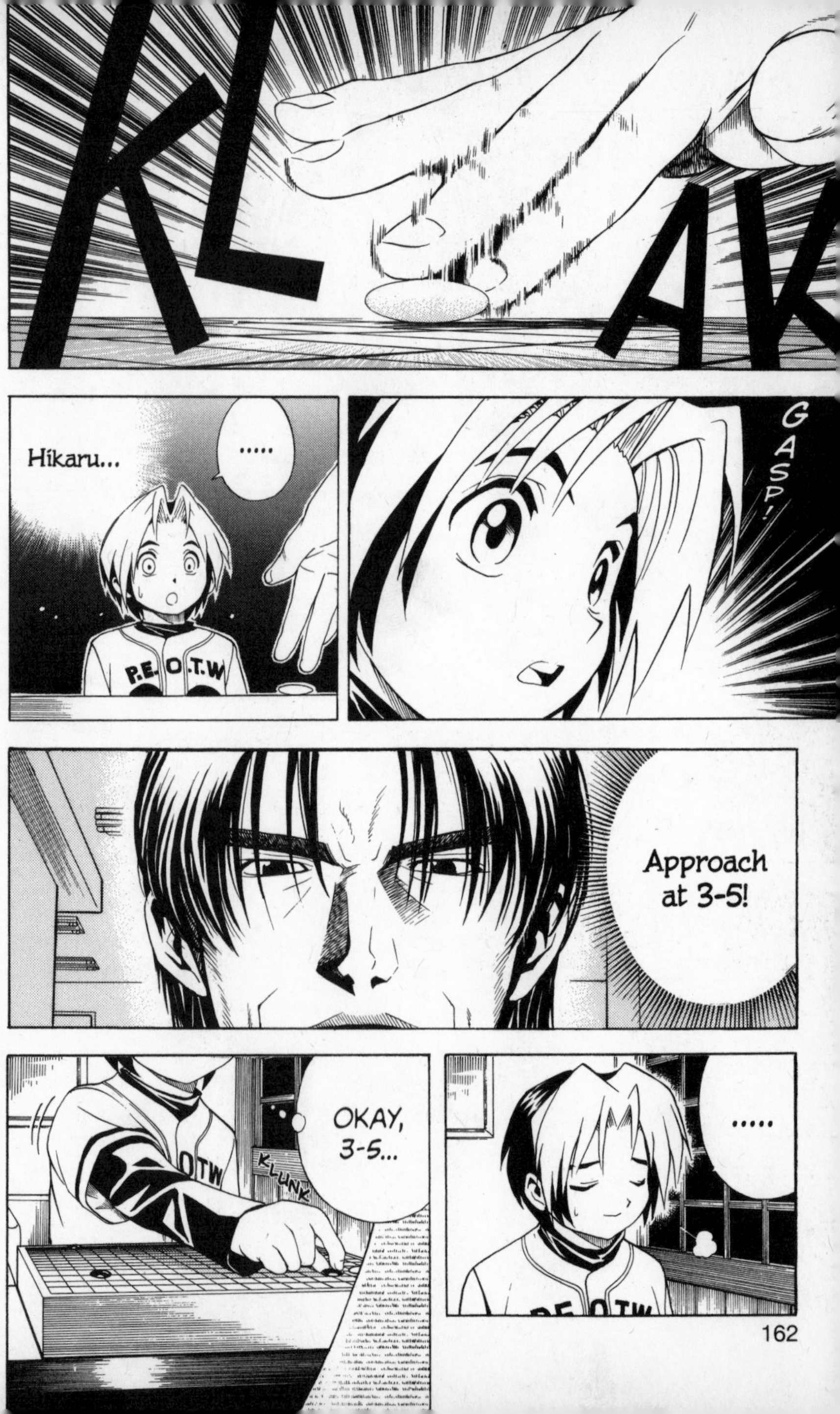
KLAK
GASP!
.....
Hikaru...
Approach at 3-5!
.....
OKAY, 3-5...
KLUNK

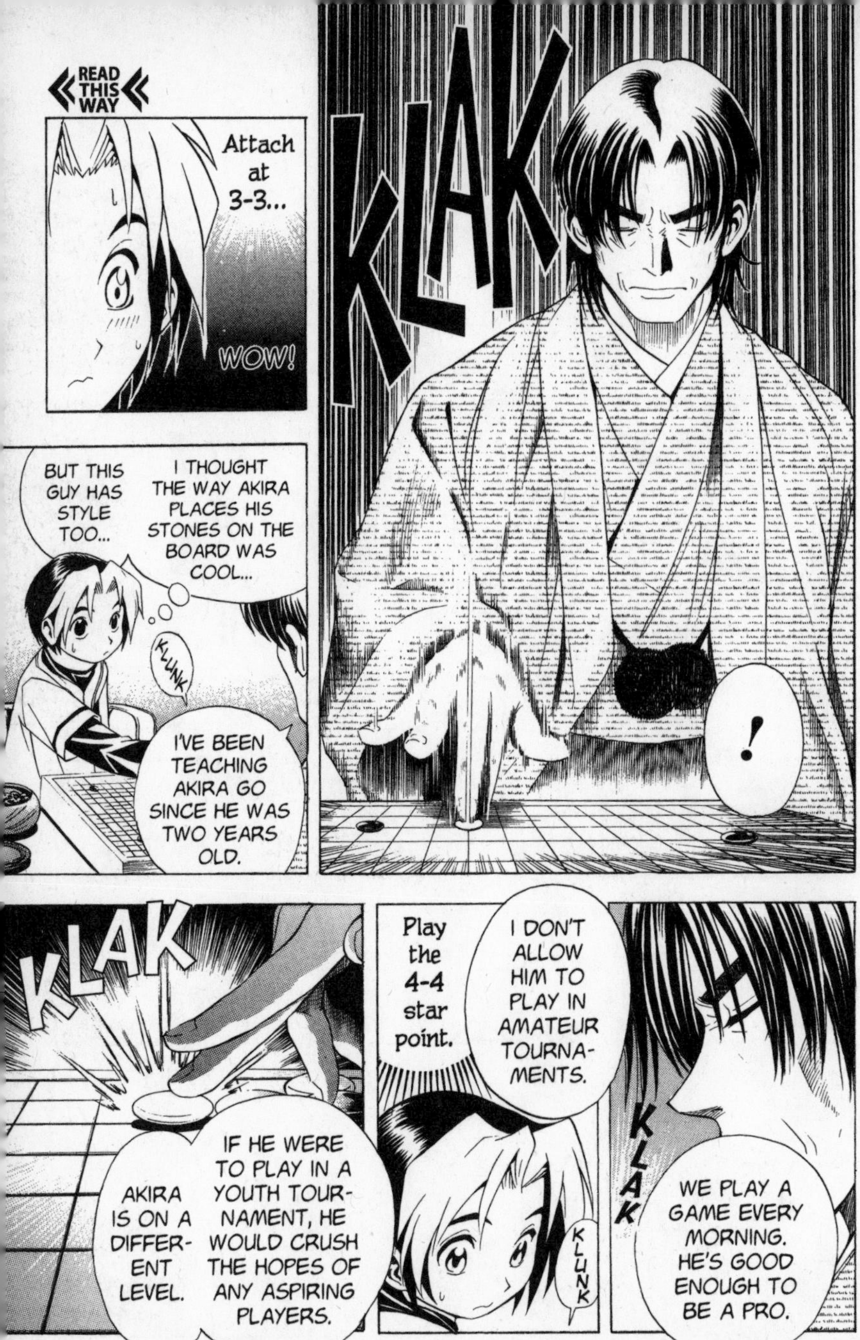
READ THIS WAY
KLAK
!
Attach at 3-3...
WOW!
I THOUGHT THE WAY AKIRA PLACES HIS STONES ON THE BOARD WAS COOL...
BUT THIS GUY HAS STYLE TOO...
KLUNK
I'VE BEEN TEACHING AKIRA GO SINCE HE WAS TWO YEARS OLD.
KLAK
WE PLAY A GAME EVERY MORNING. HE'S GOOD ENOUGH TO BE A PRO.
I DON'T ALLOW HIM TO PLAY IN AMATEUR TOURNAMENTS.
Play the 4-4 star point.
KLUNK
KLAK
IF HE WERE TO PLAY IN A YOUTH TOURNAMENT, HE WOULD CRUSH THE HOPES OF ANY ASPIRING PLAYERS.
AKIRA IS ON A DIFFERENT LEVEL.

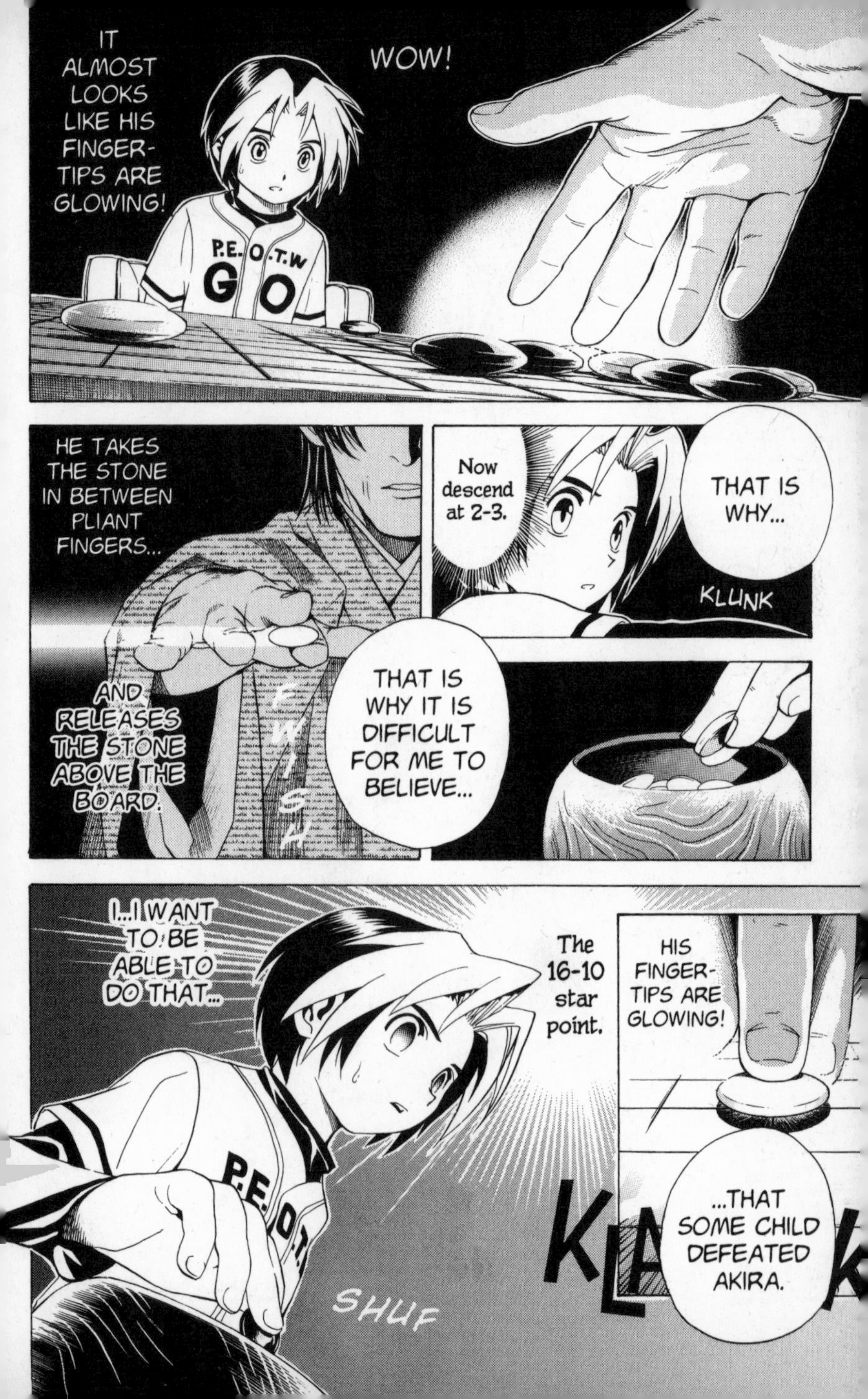
WOW!
IT ALMOST LOOKS LIKE HIS FINGER-TIPS ARE GLOWING!
THAT IS WHY...
Now descend at 2-3.
KLUNK
THAT IS WHY IT IS DIFFICULT FOR ME TO BELIEVE...
HE TAKES THE STONE IN BETWEEN PLIANT FINGERS...
AND RELEASES THE STONE ABOVE THE BOARD.
FWISH
HIS FINGER-TIPS ARE GLOWING!
...THAT SOME CHILD DEFEATED AKIRA.
The 16-10 star point.
I...I WANT TO BE ABLE TO DO THAT...
SHUF

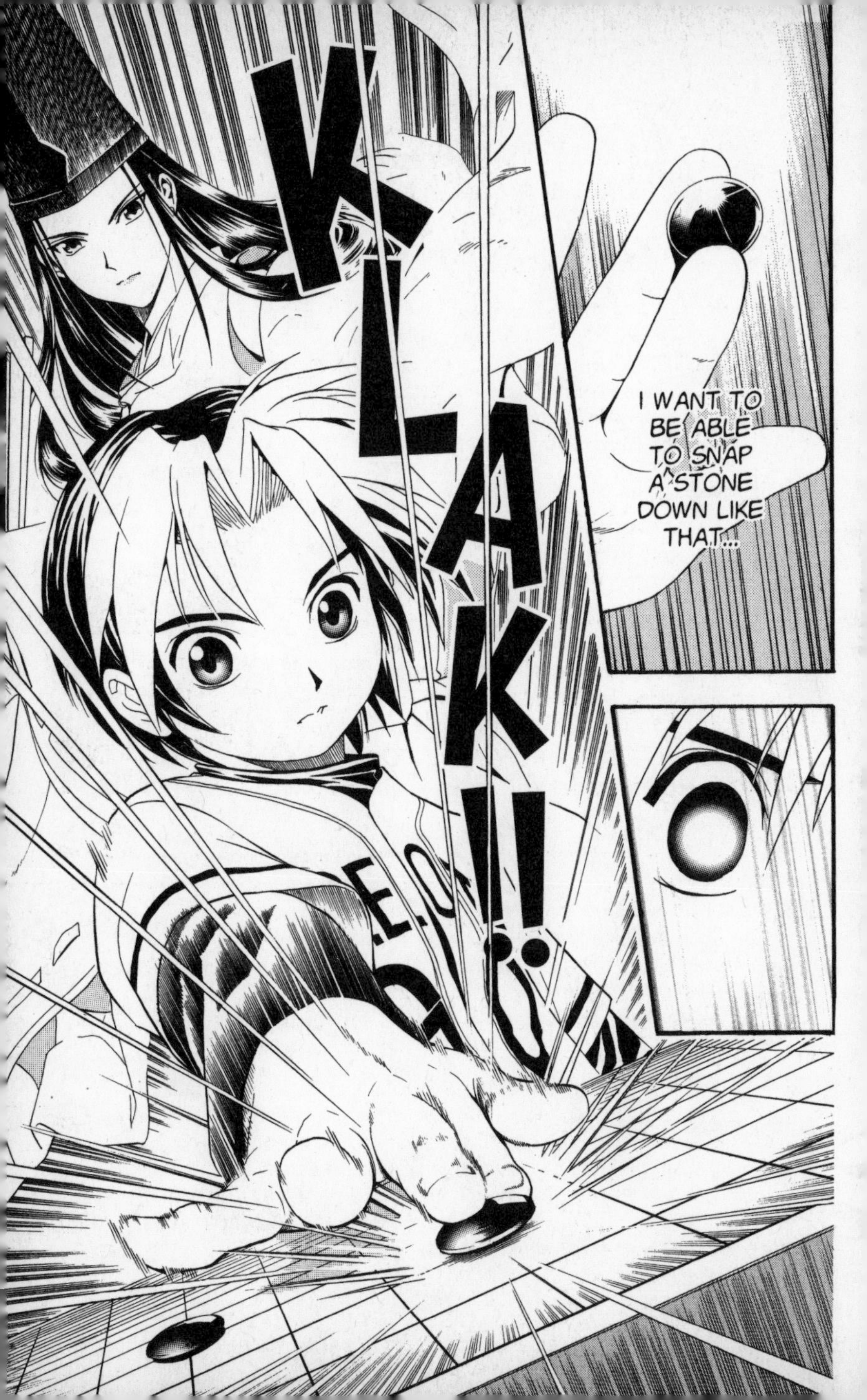
KLAKK!!
I WANT TO BE ABLE TO SNAP A STONE DOWN LIKE THAT...

Hikaru no Go Q&A

Q 3 You win Shogi (Japanese Chess) by capturing the king. How do you win Go?

A The winner of Go is the side, White or Black, that has more territory. In the figure shown, Black's territory is on the right, White's territory is on the left. Which side is the winner?

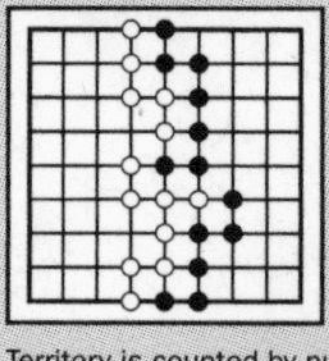

Territory is counted by number of points. In this diagram, Black has 26 points and White has 29 points. White wins by 3 points.

Q 4 Can anyone go to a Go Salon?

A Yes, go ahead and go to one if you see one in town. The people there are sure to welcome children, women, and anyone new to Go.

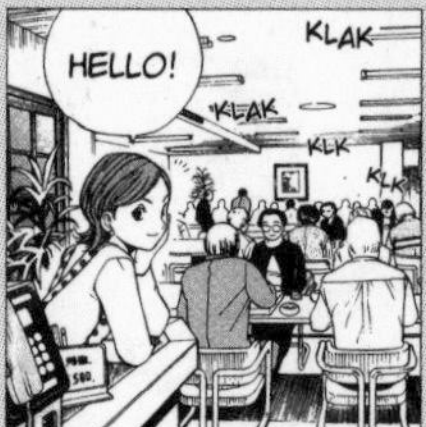
KLAK
HELLO!
KLAK
KLK
KLK

Q 5 How old do you have to be to become a pro?

A Go is strictly a world of ability. Anyone can become a pro as long as they pass the test to qualify, even a small child. Of course, it's not easy. Cho Chi-hoon (known in Japan as Cho Chikun) became a pro at the young age of 11.

Q 6 My school doesn't have a Go club. How can I start playing?

A One way is to learn from Go on TV and from books, but maybe someone you know plays Go – your father, an uncle, or maybe one of your teachers at school. If you can't think of anyone, try going to a Go salon. There's also plenty of Go classes for kids at community centers. You can get more details by contacting the American Go Association at www.usgo.org.

Game 7: "Three Problems of Life and Death"

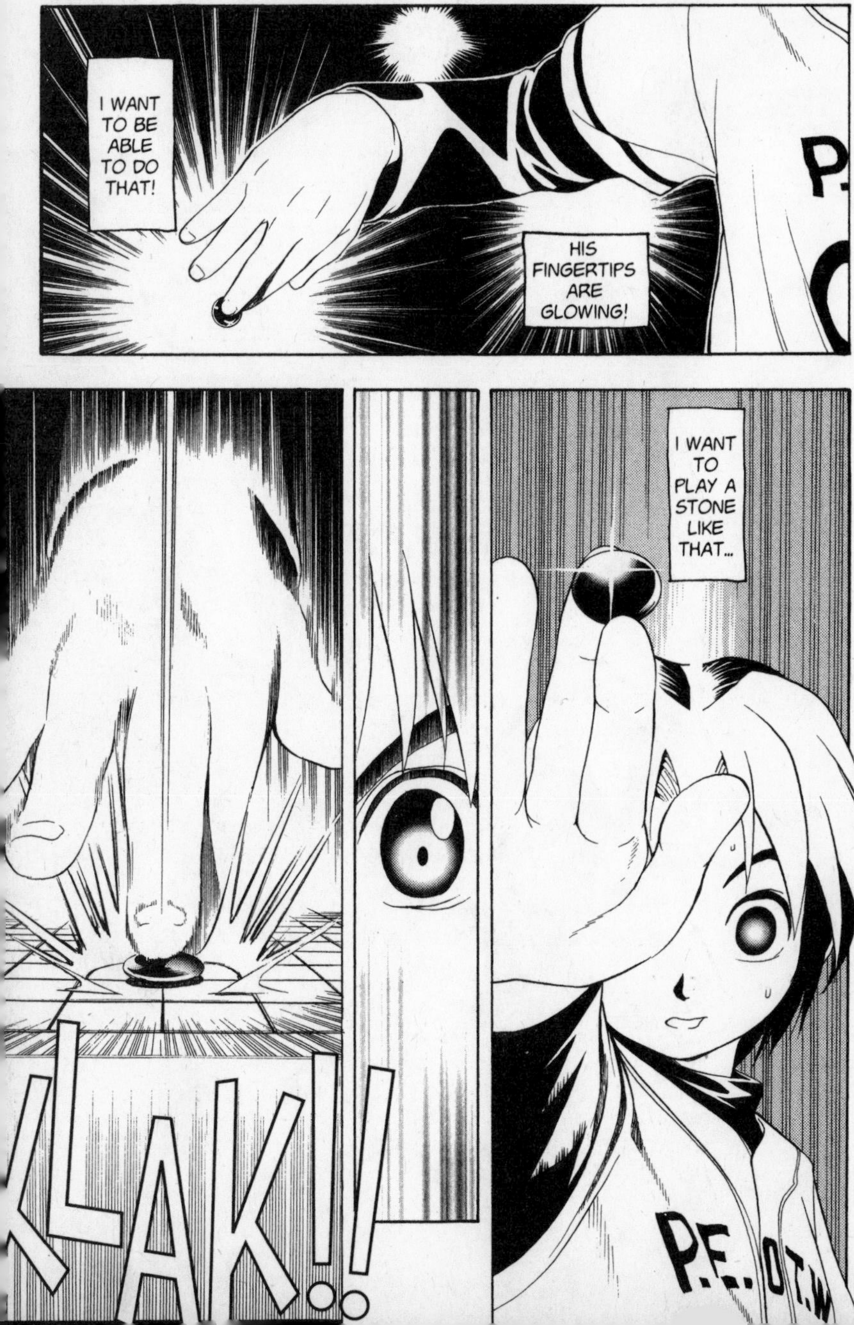

HIS FINGERTIPS ARE GLOWING!
I WANT TO BE ABLE TO DO THAT!
I WANT TO PLAY A STONE LIKE THAT...
KLAK!!

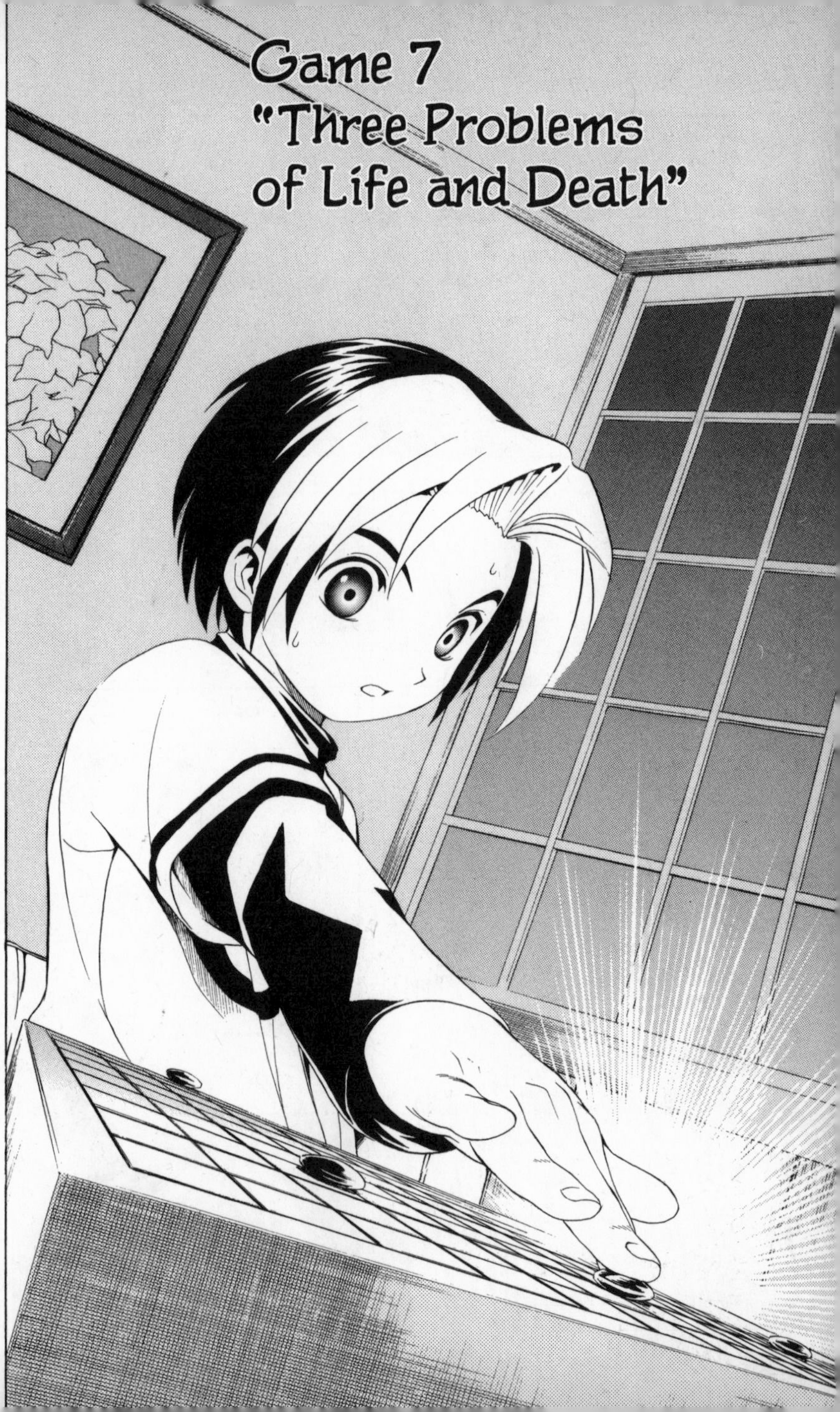
Game 7
"Three Problems of Life and Death"

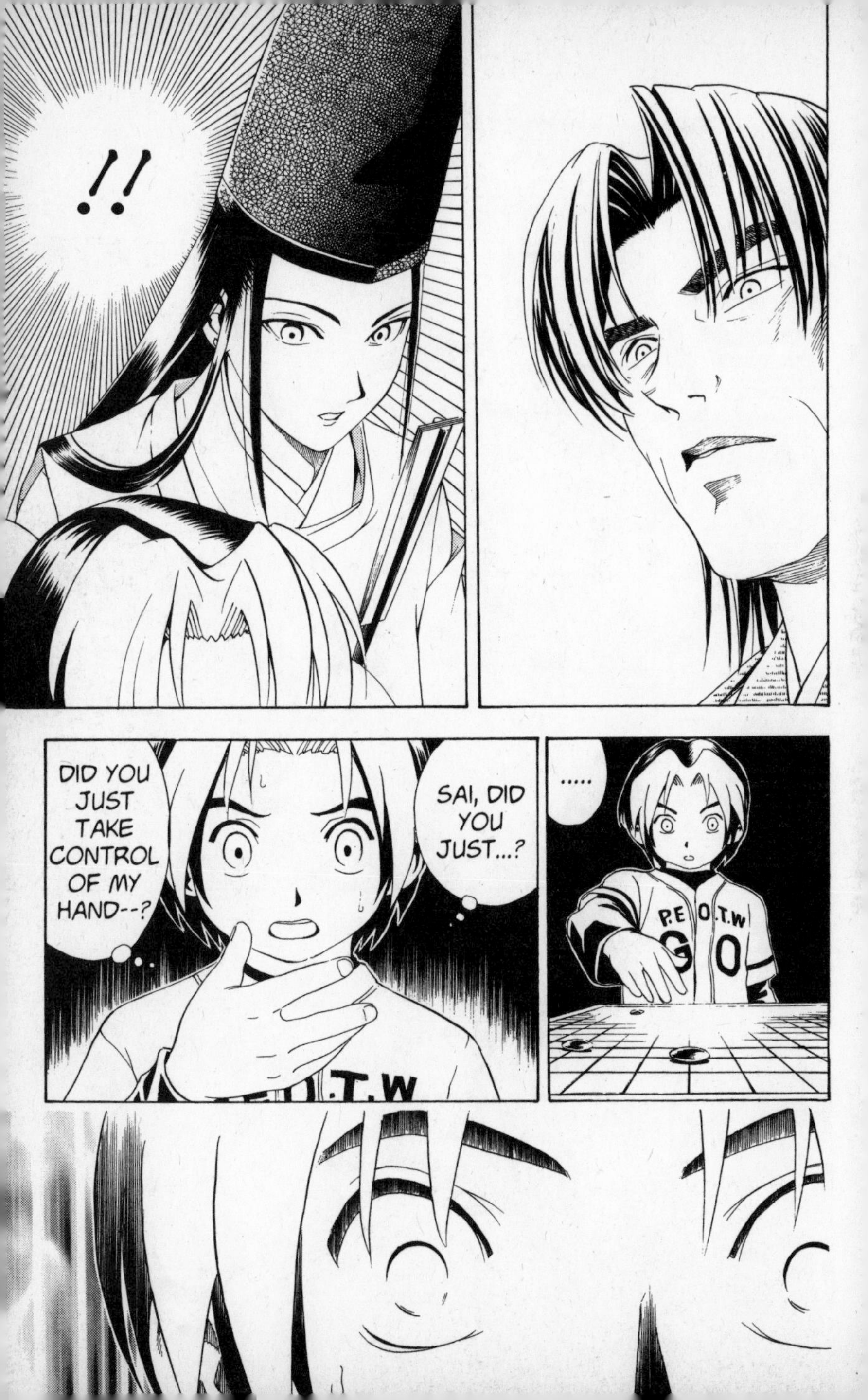
!!
.....
P.E O.T.W
GO
SAI, DID YOU JUST...?
DID YOU JUST TAKE CONTROL OF MY HAND--?
P.E O.T.W

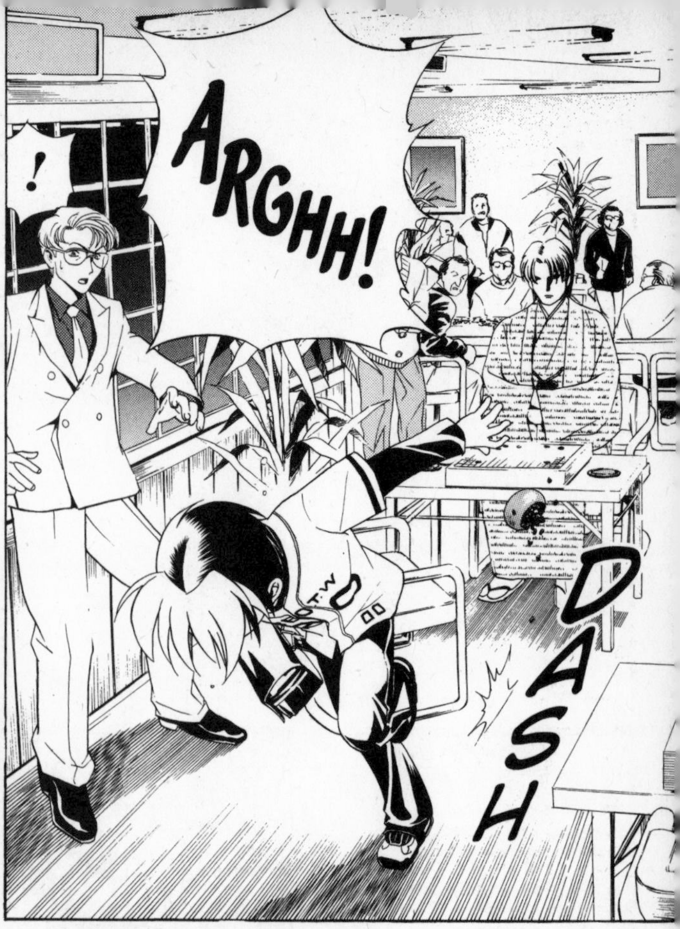
ARGHH!
!
DASH
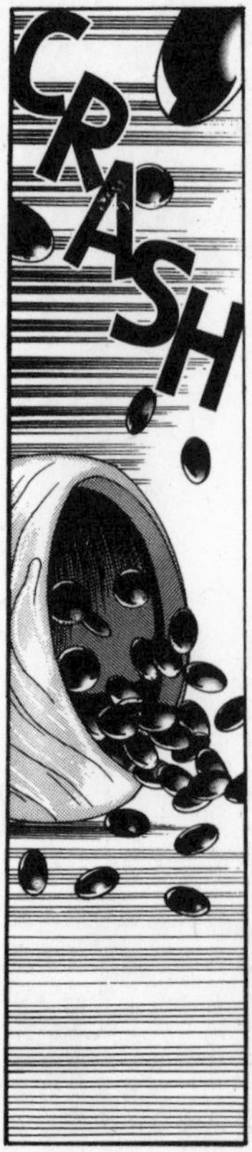
CRASH!
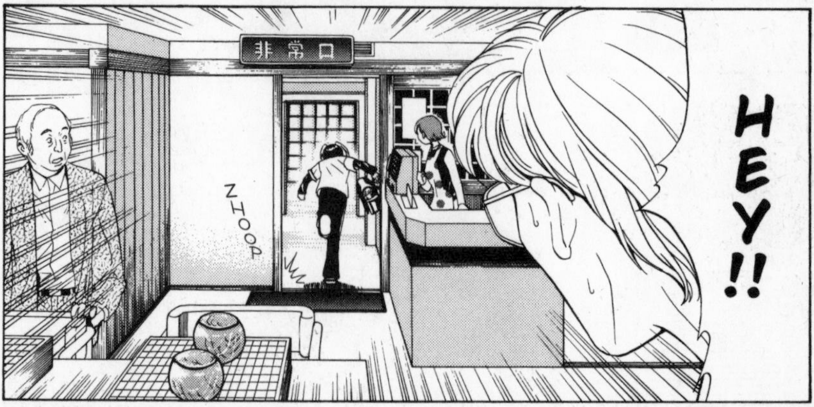
HEY!!
非常口
ZHOOP

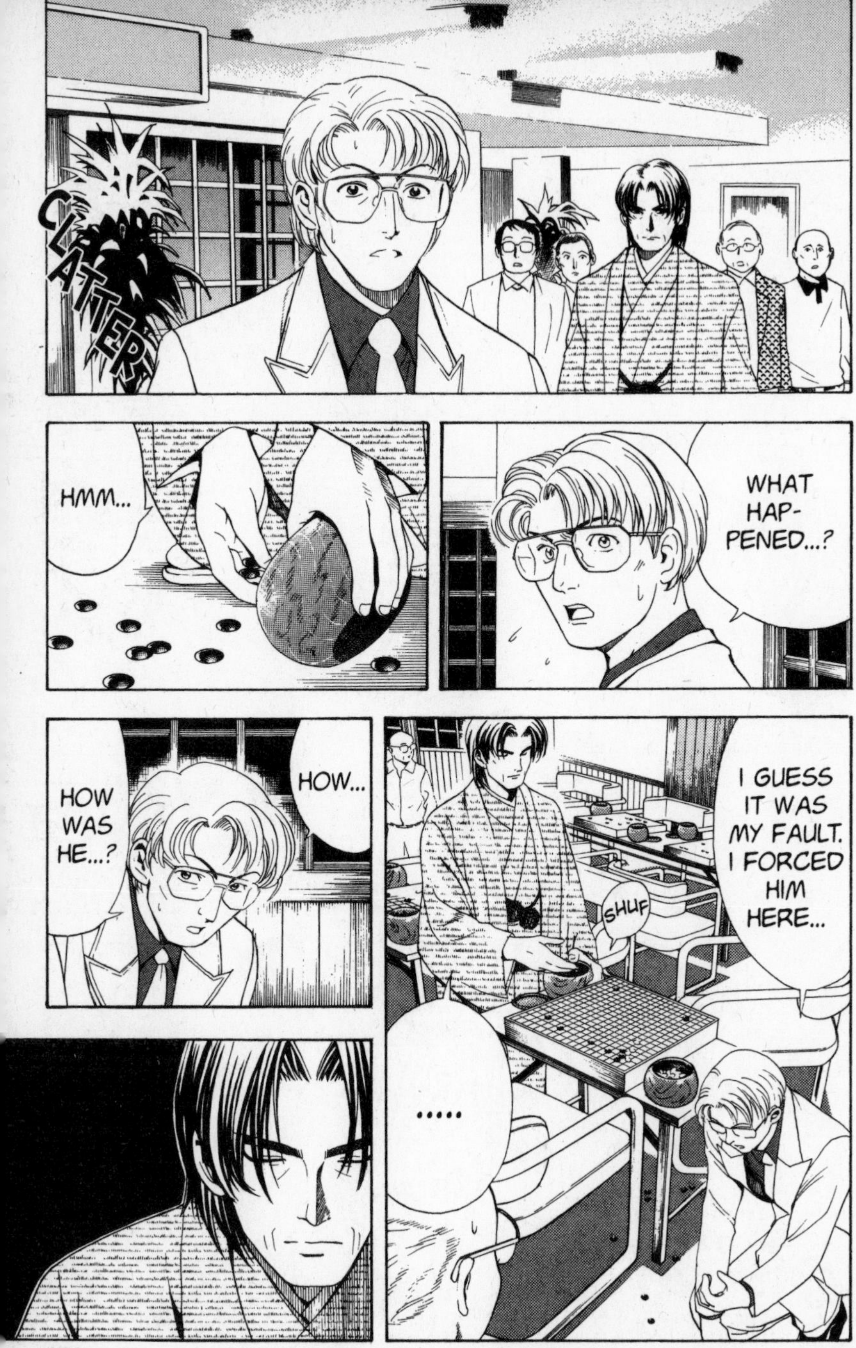
CLATTER
WHAT HAP-PENED...?
HMM...
I GUESS IT WAS MY FAULT. I FORCED HIM HERE...
SHUF
.....
HOW...
HOW WAS HE...?

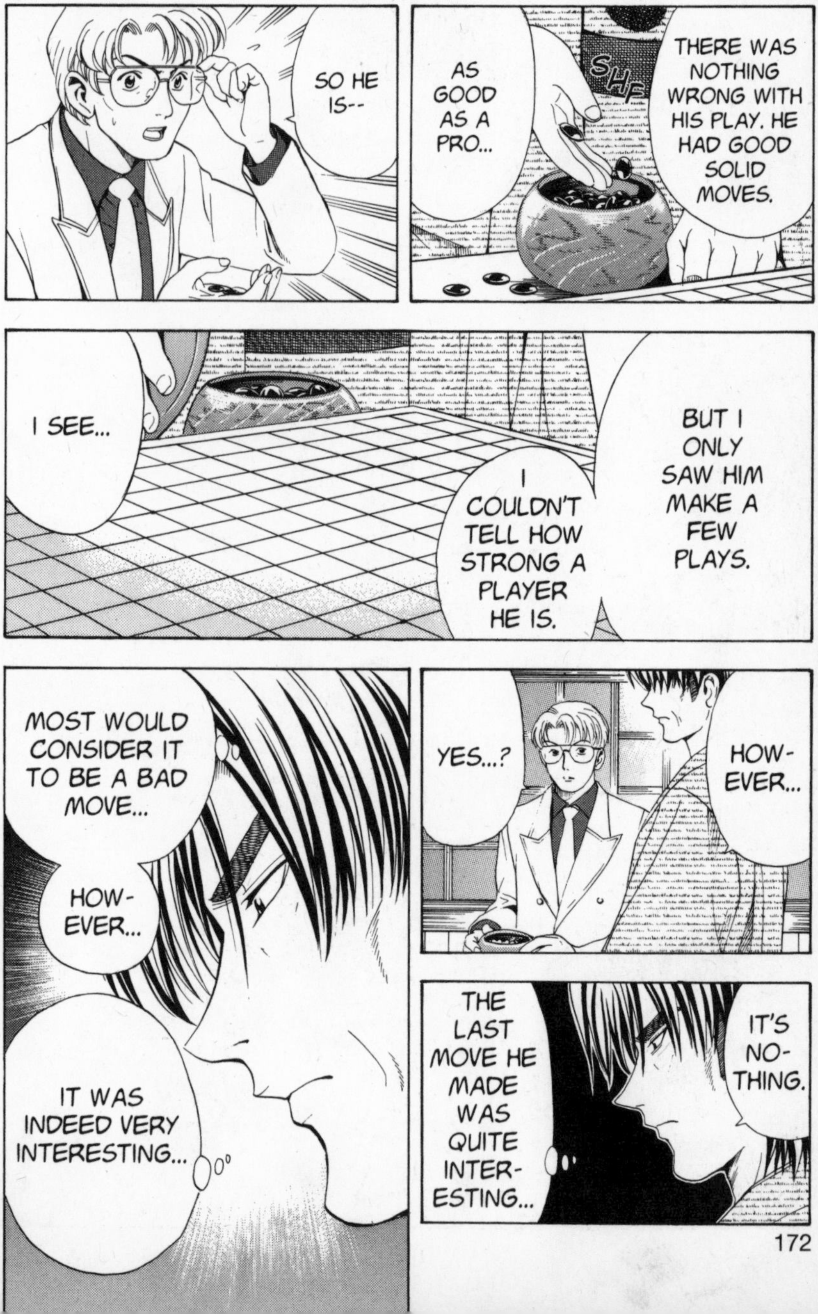
THERE WAS NOTHING WRONG WITH HIS PLAY. HE HAD GOOD SOLID MOVES.
SHF
AS GOOD AS A PRO...
SO HE IS--
BUT I ONLY SAW HIM MAKE A FEW PLAYS.
I COULDN'T TELL HOW STRONG A PLAYER HE IS.
I SEE...
HOW-EVER...
YES...?
IT'S NO-THING.
THE LAST MOVE HE MADE WAS QUITE INTER-ESTING...
MOST WOULD CONSIDER IT TO BE A BAD MOVE...
HOW-EVER...
IT WAS INDEED VERY INTERESTING...

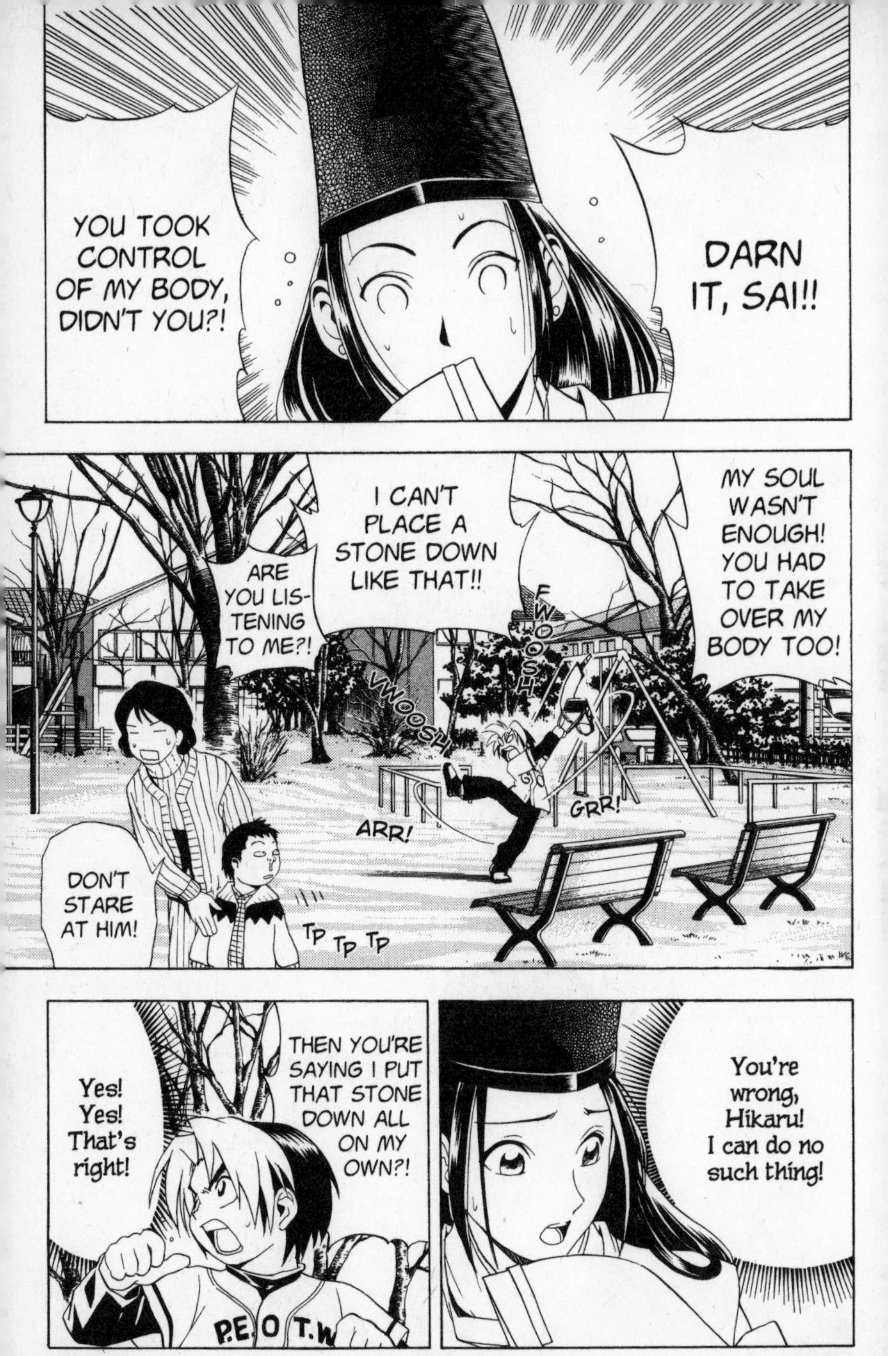
DARN IT, SAI!!
YOU TOOK CONTROL OF MY BODY, DIDN'T YOU?!
MY SOUL WASN'T ENOUGH! YOU HAD TO TAKE OVER MY BODY TOO!
FWOOSH
I CAN'T PLACE A STONE DOWN LIKE THAT!!
ARE YOU LIS-TENING TO ME?!
VWOOSH
GRR!
ARR!
DON'T STARE AT HIM!
TP TP TP
You're wrong, Hikaru! I can do no such thing!
THEN YOU'RE SAYING I PUT THAT STONE DOWN ALL ON MY OWN?!
Yes! Yes! That's right!
P.E. O T.W

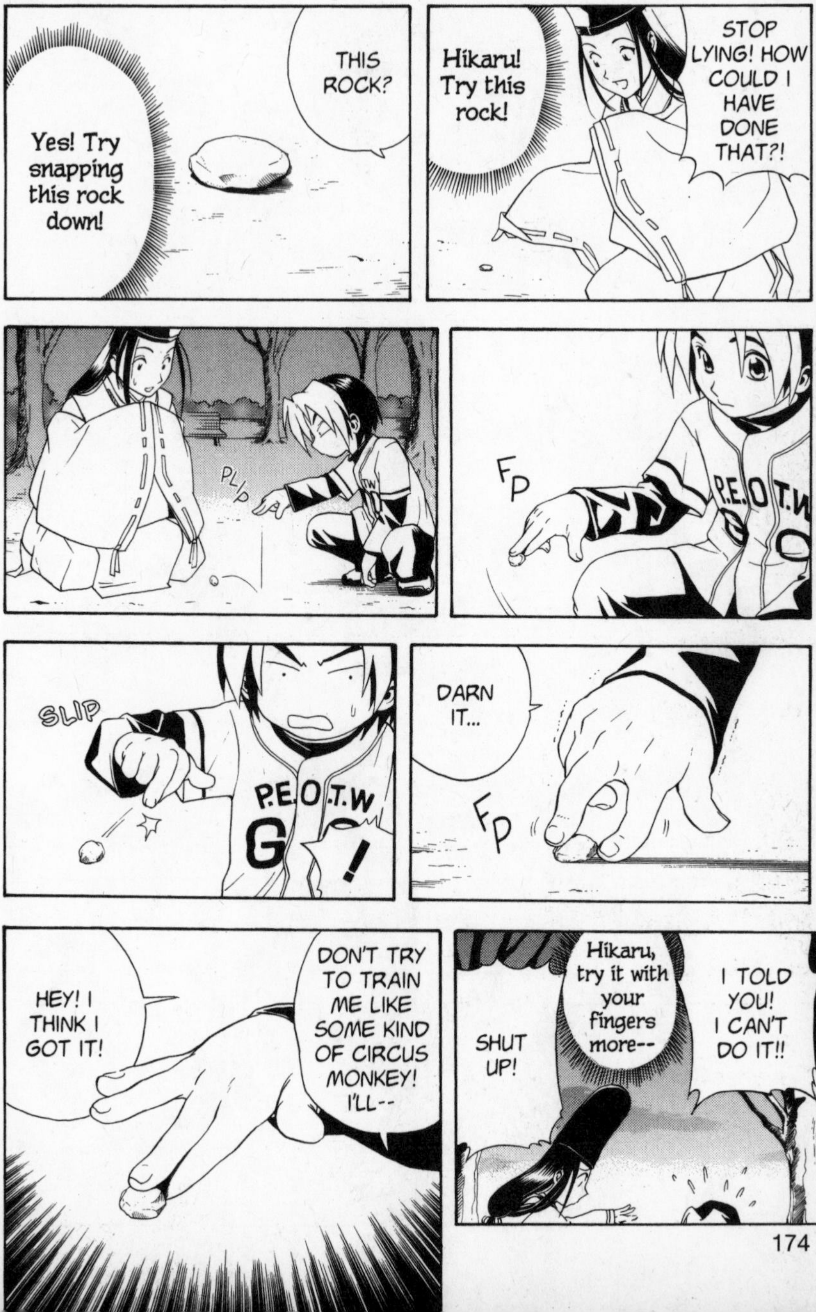
STOP LYING! HOW COULD I HAVE DONE THAT?!
Hikaru! Try this rock!
THIS ROCK?
Yes! Try snapping this rock down!
FP
PLIP
DARN IT...
FP
SLIP
!
I TOLD YOU! I CAN'T DO IT!!
Hikaru, try it with your fingers more--
SHUT UP!
DON'T TRY TO TRAIN ME LIKE SOME KIND OF CIRCUS MONKEY! I'LL--
HEY! I THINK I GOT IT!

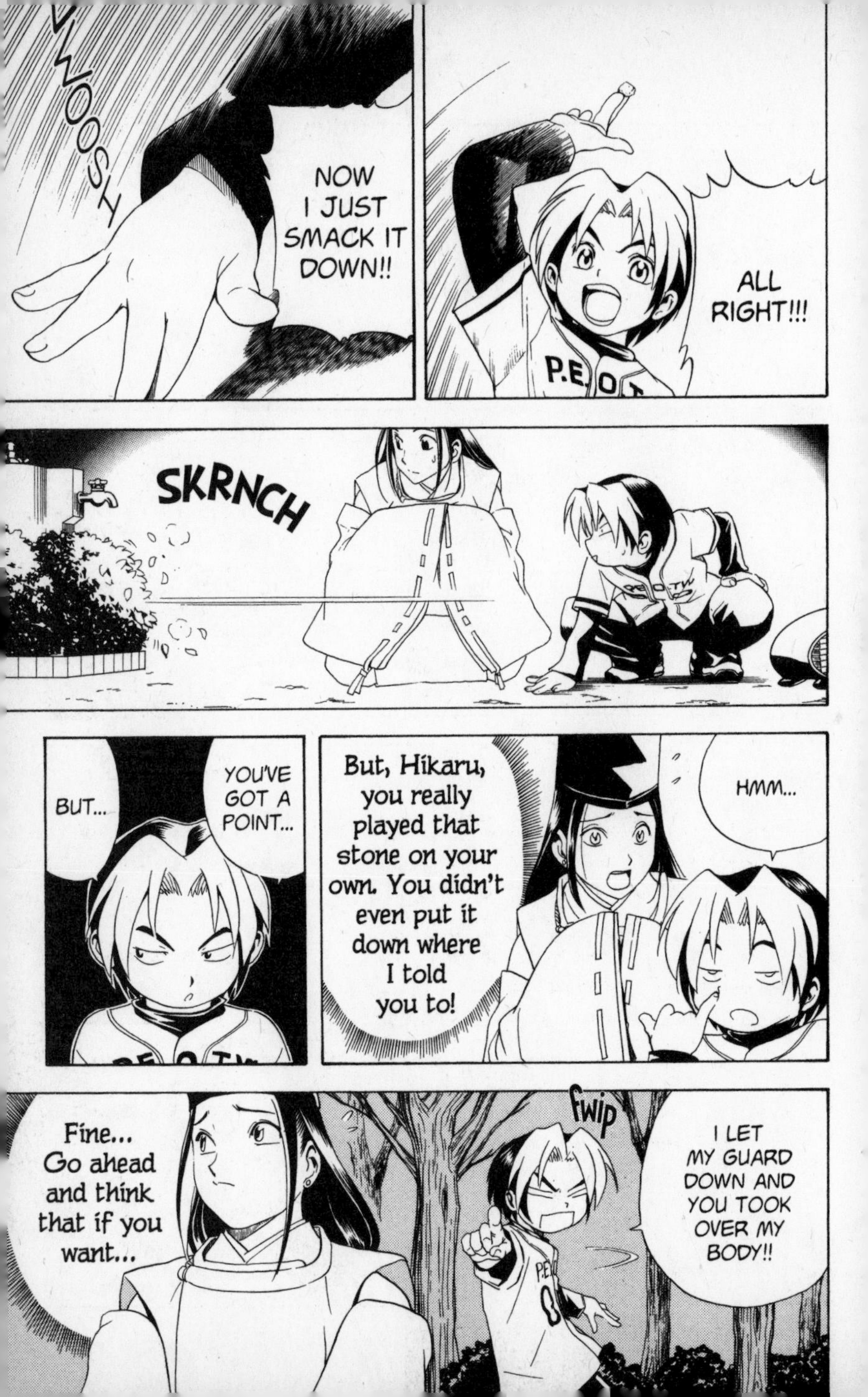
ALL RIGHT!!!
WOOSH
NOW I JUST SMACK IT DOWN!!
SKRNCH
HMM...
But, Hikaru, you really played that stone on your own. You didn't even put it down where I told you to!
YOU'VE GOT A POINT...
BUT...
fwip
I LET MY GUARD DOWN AND YOU TOOK OVER MY BODY!!
Fine... Go ahead and think that if you want...

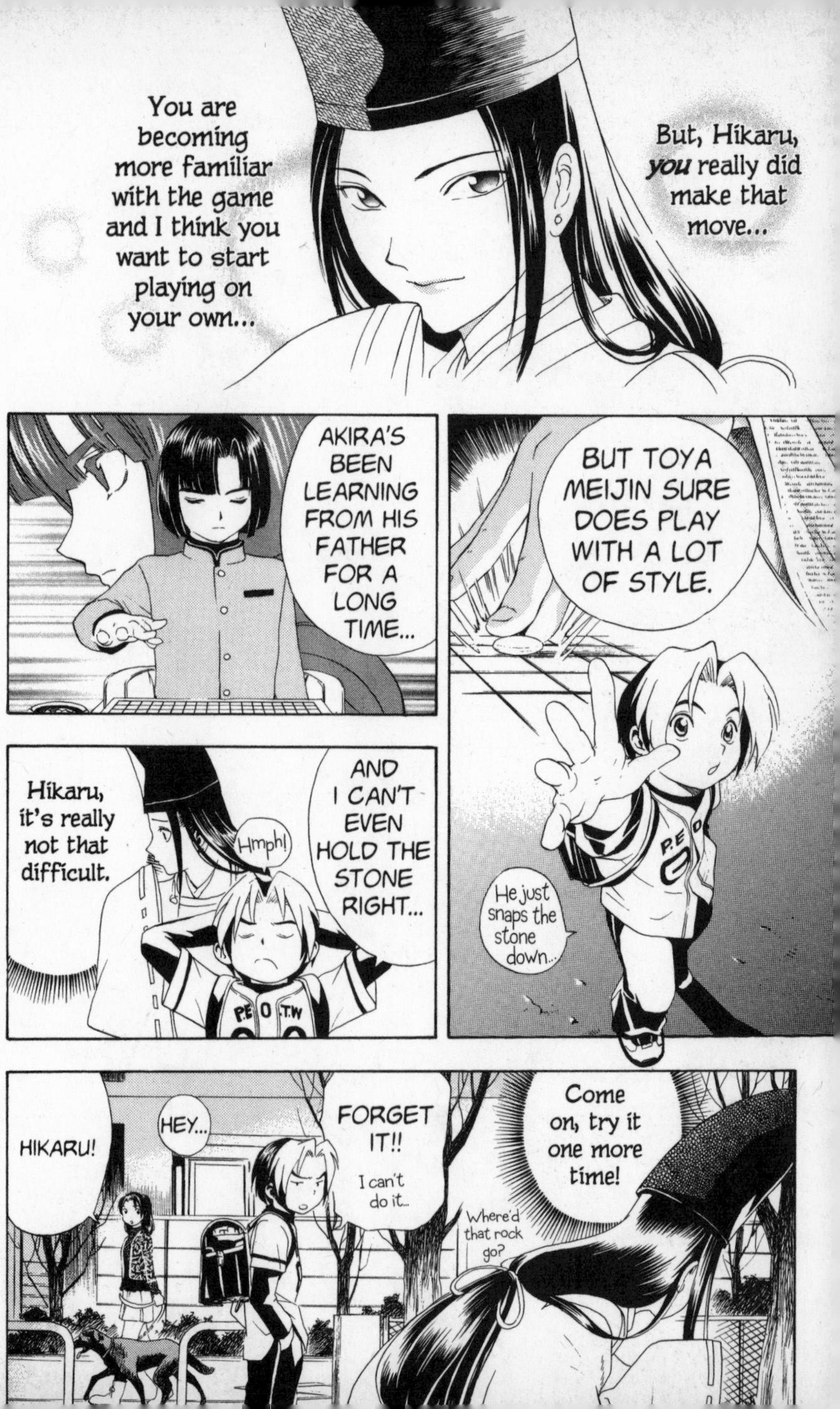
But, Hikaru, *you* really did make that move...
You are becoming more familiar with the game and I think you want to start playing on your own...
BUT TOYA MEIJIN SURE DOES PLAY WITH A LOT OF STYLE.
He just snaps the stone down...
AKIRA'S BEEN LEARNING FROM HIS FATHER FOR A LONG TIME...
AND I CAN'T EVEN HOLD THE STONE RIGHT...
Hmph!
Hikaru, it's really not that difficult.
Come on, try it one more time!
Where'd that rock go?
FORGET IT!!
I can't do it...
HEY...
HIKARU!

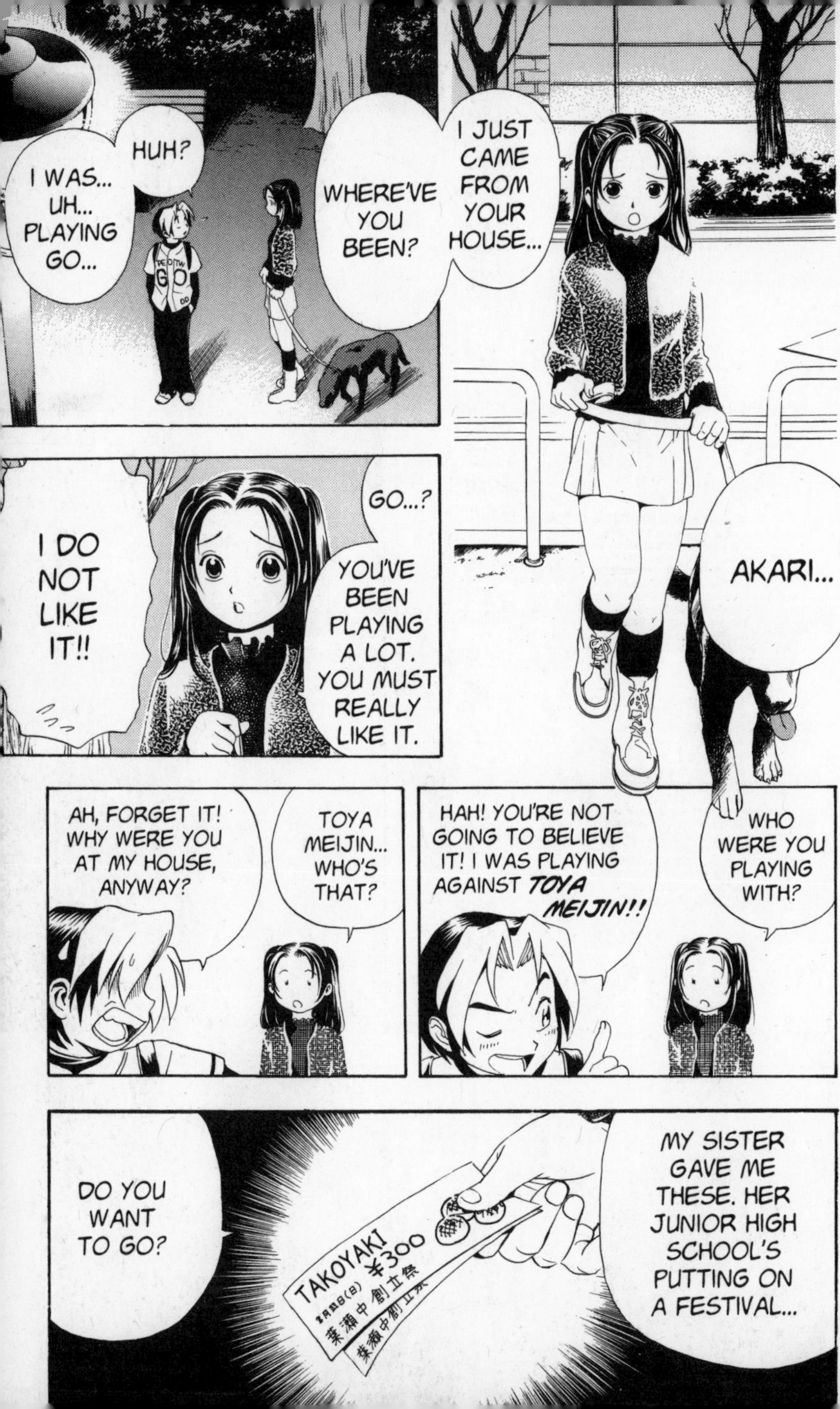
AKARI...
I JUST CAME FROM YOUR HOUSE...
WHERE'VE YOU BEEN?
HUH?
I WAS... UH... PLAYING GO...
GO...?
YOU'VE BEEN PLAYING A LOT. YOU MUST REALLY LIKE IT.
I DO NOT LIKE IT!!
WHO WERE YOU PLAYING WITH?
HAH! YOU'RE NOT GOING TO BELIEVE IT! I WAS PLAYING AGAINST *TOYA MEIJIN!!*
TOYA MEIJIN... WHO'S THAT?
AH, FORGET IT! WHY WERE YOU AT MY HOUSE, ANYWAY?
MY SISTER GAVE ME THESE. HER JUNIOR HIGH SCHOOL'S PUTTING ON A FESTIVAL...
TAKOYAKI ¥300
葉瀬中創立祭
DO YOU WANT TO GO?

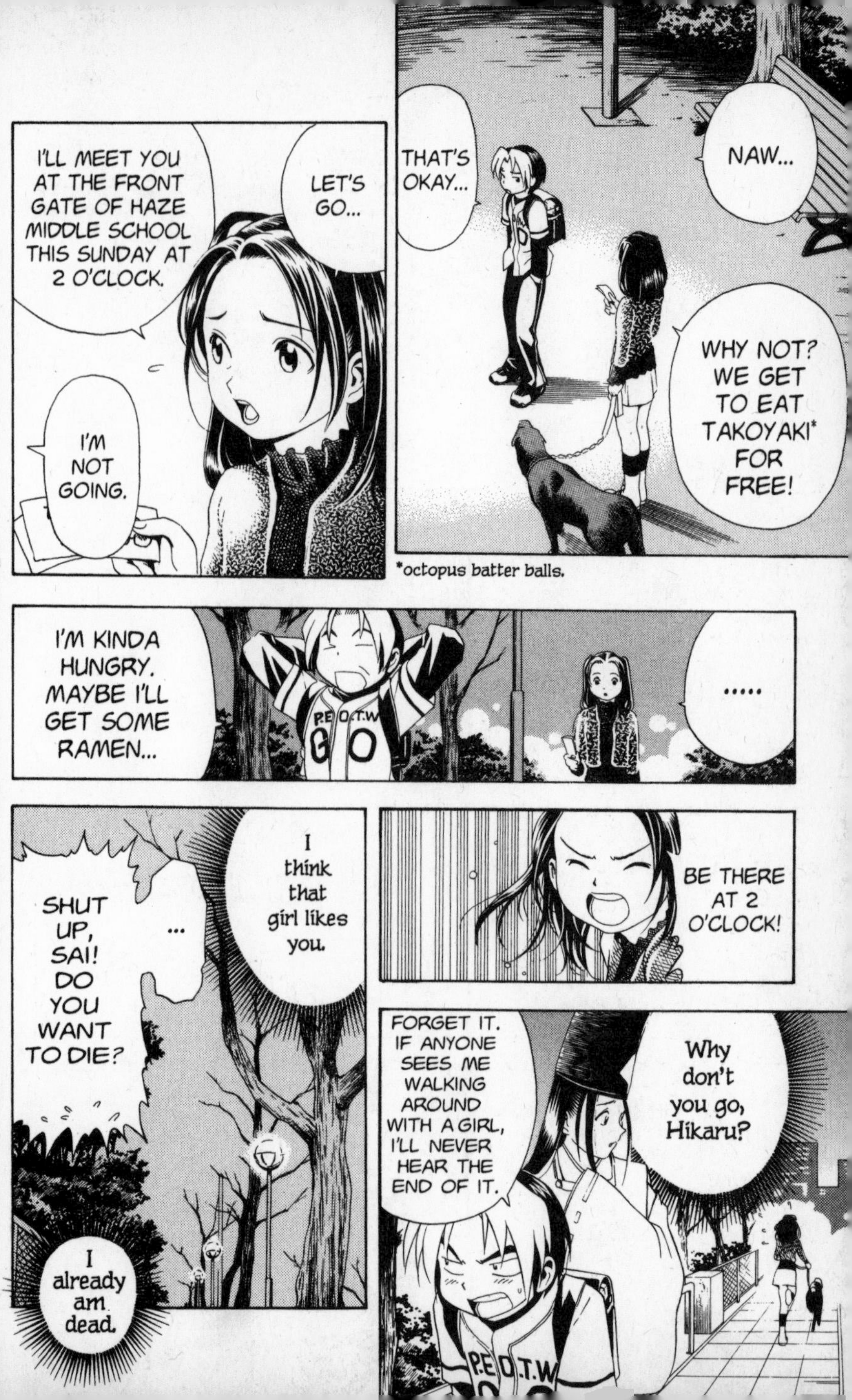
NAW...
THAT'S OKAY...
WHY NOT? WE GET TO EAT TAKOYAKI* FOR FREE!
LET'S GO...
I'LL MEET YOU AT THE FRONT GATE OF HAZE MIDDLE SCHOOL THIS SUNDAY AT 2 O'CLOCK.
I'M NOT GOING.
.....
I'M KINDA HUNGRY. MAYBE I'LL GET SOME RAMEN...
BE THERE AT 2 O'CLOCK!
Why don't you go, Hikaru?
FORGET IT. IF ANYONE SEES ME WALKING AROUND WITH A GIRL, I'LL NEVER HEAR THE END OF IT.
I think that girl likes you.
...
SHUT UP, SAI! DO YOU WANT TO DIE?
I already am dead.

*octopus batter balls.

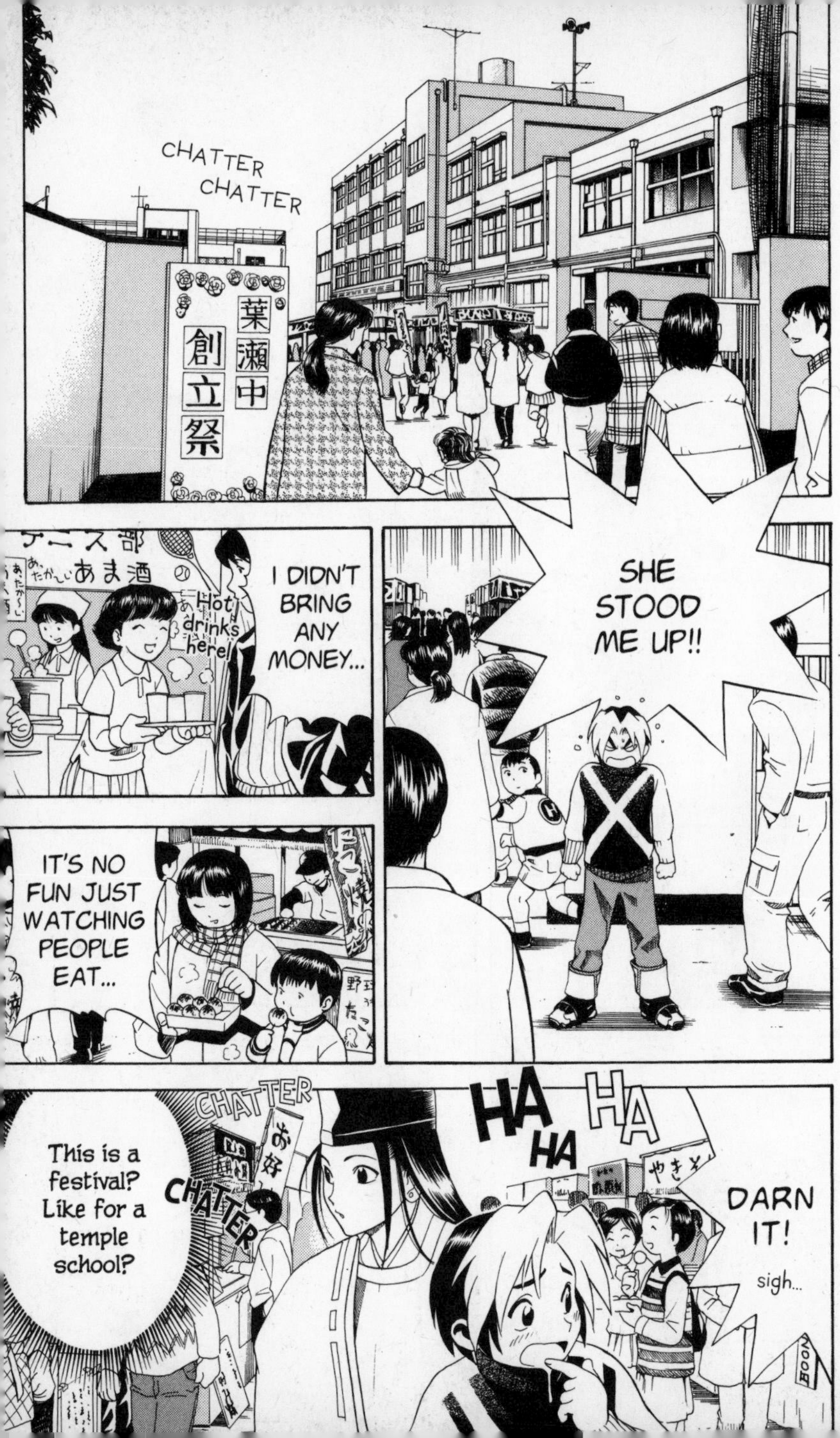
CHATTER
CHATTER
葉瀬中
創立祭
SHE STOOD ME UP!!
テニス部
あま酒
Hot drinks here!
I DIDN'T BRING ANY MONEY...
IT'S NO FUN JUST WATCHING PEOPLE EAT...
DARN IT!
sigh...
やきそ
HA HA HA
お好
CHATTER
CHATTER
This is a festival? Like for a temple school?

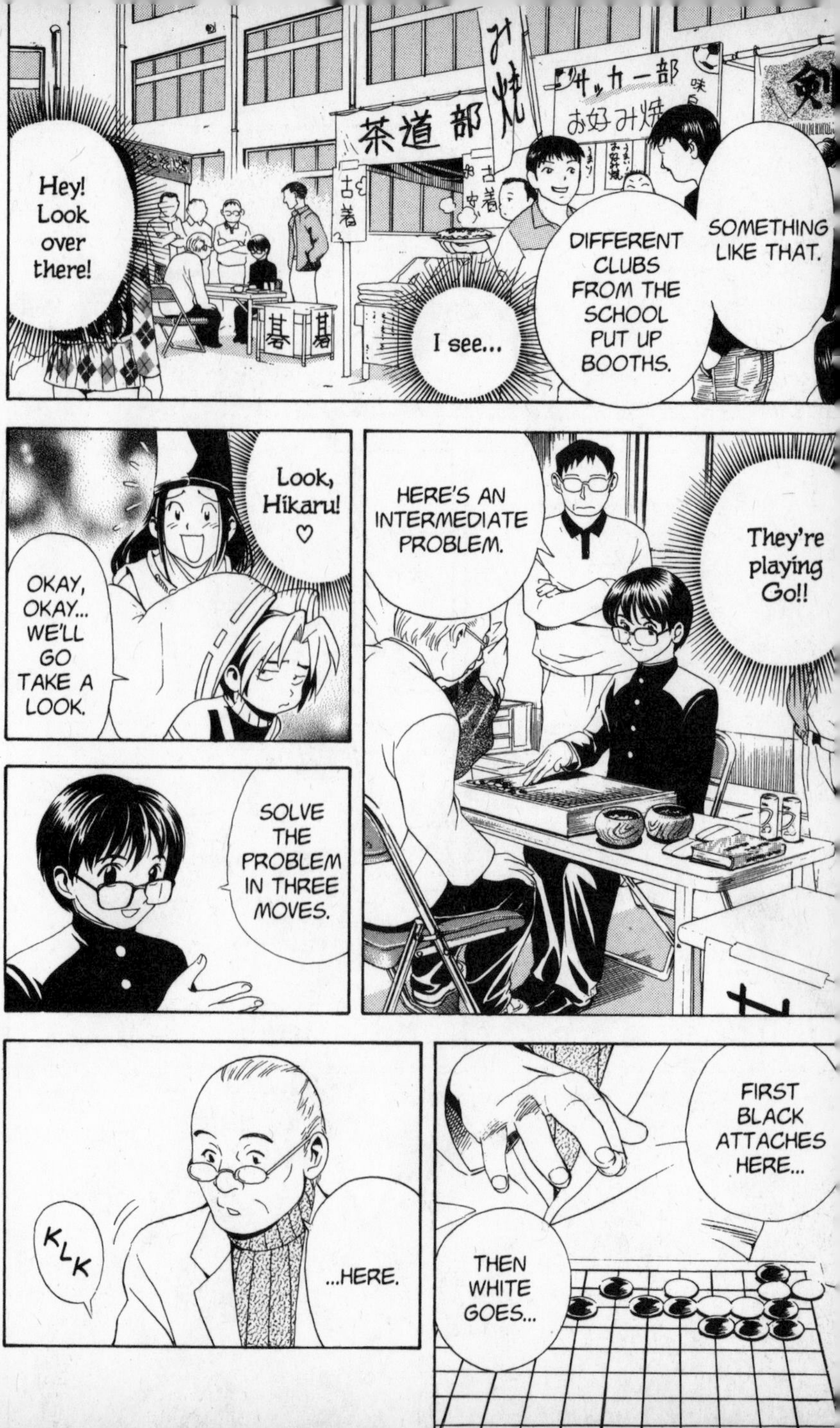
茶道部
サッカー部
お好み焼
古着
碁
DIFFERENT CLUBS FROM THE SCHOOL PUT UP BOOTHS.
SOMETHING LIKE THAT.
I see...
Hey! Look over there!
They're playing Go!!
HERE'S AN INTERMEDIATE PROBLEM.
Look, Hikaru! ♡
OKAY, OKAY... WE'LL GO TAKE A LOOK.
SOLVE THE PROBLEM IN THREE MOVES.
FIRST BLACK ATTACHES HERE...
THEN WHITE GOES...
...HERE.
KLK

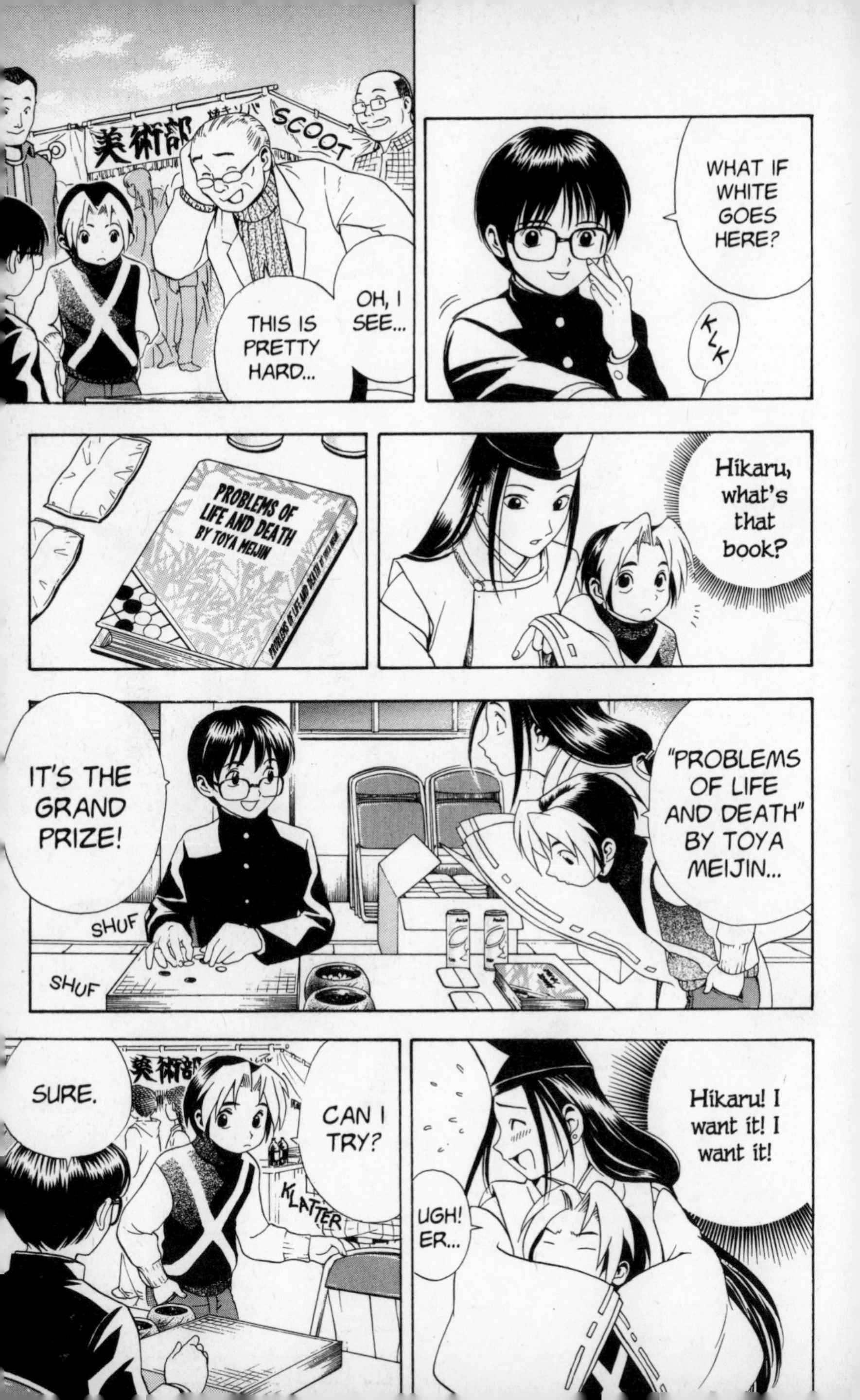
WHAT IF WHITE GOES HERE?
KLK
SCOOT
焼キソバ
美術部
OH, I SEE...
THIS IS PRETTY HARD...
Hikaru, what's that book?
PROBLEMS OF LIFE AND DEATH BY TOYA MEIJIN
"PROBLEMS OF LIFE AND DEATH" BY TOYA MEIJIN...
IT'S THE GRAND PRIZE!
SHUF
SHUF
Hikaru! I want it! I want it!
UGH! ER...
CAN I TRY?
KLATTER
SURE.

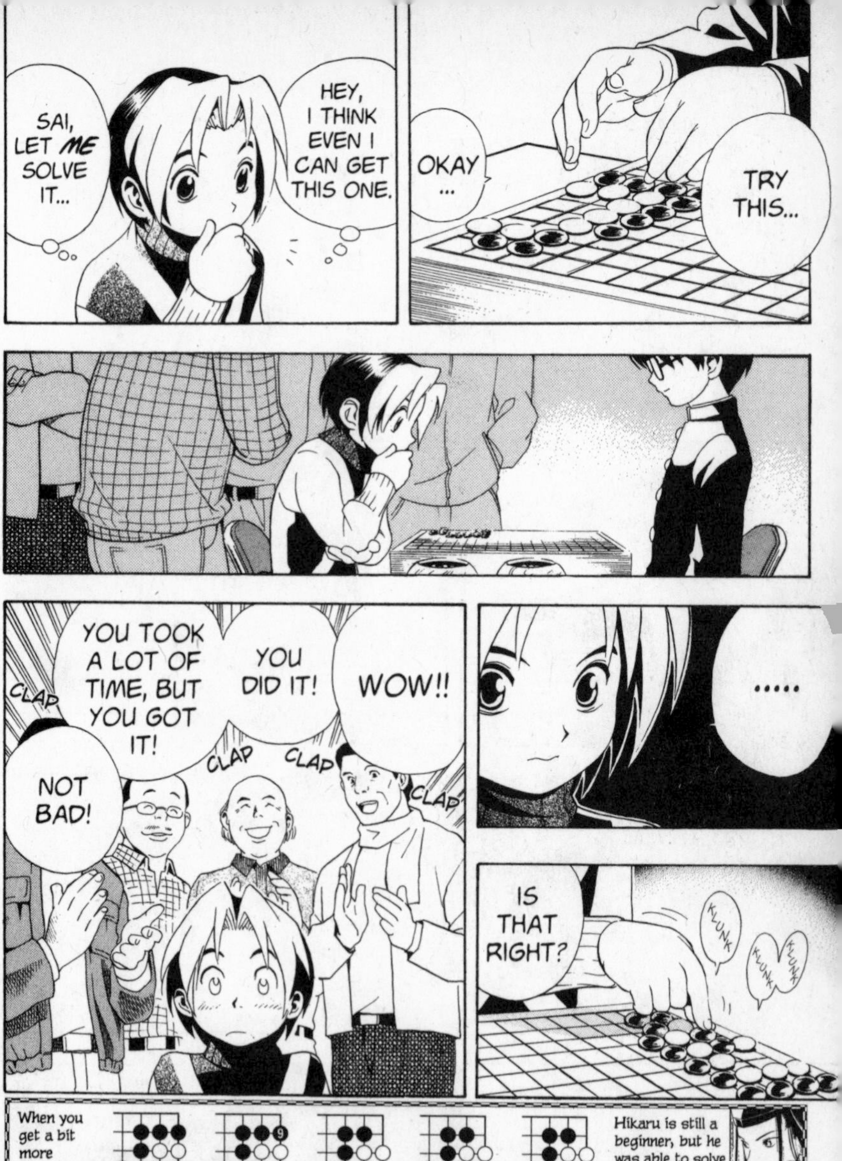
TRY THIS...
OKAY ...
HEY, I THINK EVEN I CAN GET THIS ONE.
SAI, LET *ME* SOLVE IT...
.....
IS THAT RIGHT?
KLUNK
KLUNK
KLUNK
WOW!!
YOU DID IT!
YOU TOOK A LOT OF TIME, BUT YOU GOT IT!
CLAP
CLAP
CLAP
NOT BAD!
CLAP

Sai's Commentary

Hikaru is still a beginner, but he was able to solve this problem because he is learning the fundamentals in his Go class. Here's an explanation of the problem Hikaru solved. (The numbers indicate the order of play.)

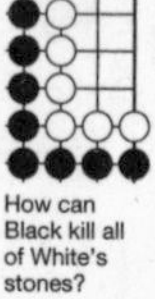

How can Black kill all of White's stones?

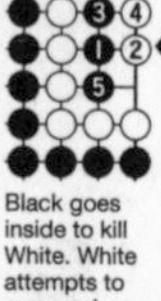
1
2
3
4
5

Black goes inside to kill White. White attempts to surround Black's invading stones.

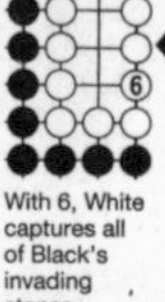
6

With 6, White captures all of Black's invading stones.

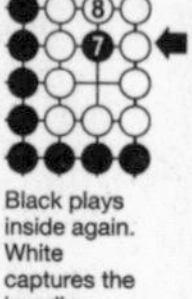
7
8
9

Black plays inside again. White captures the invading stone.

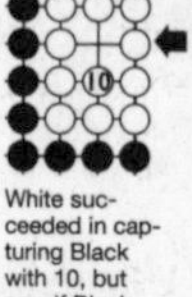
10

White succeeded in capturing Black with 10, but now if Black plays the center point, he will capture all of White's stones.

When you get a bit more familiar with Go like Hikaru, you, too, will be able to see that White was dead after the third move.

READ THIS WAY

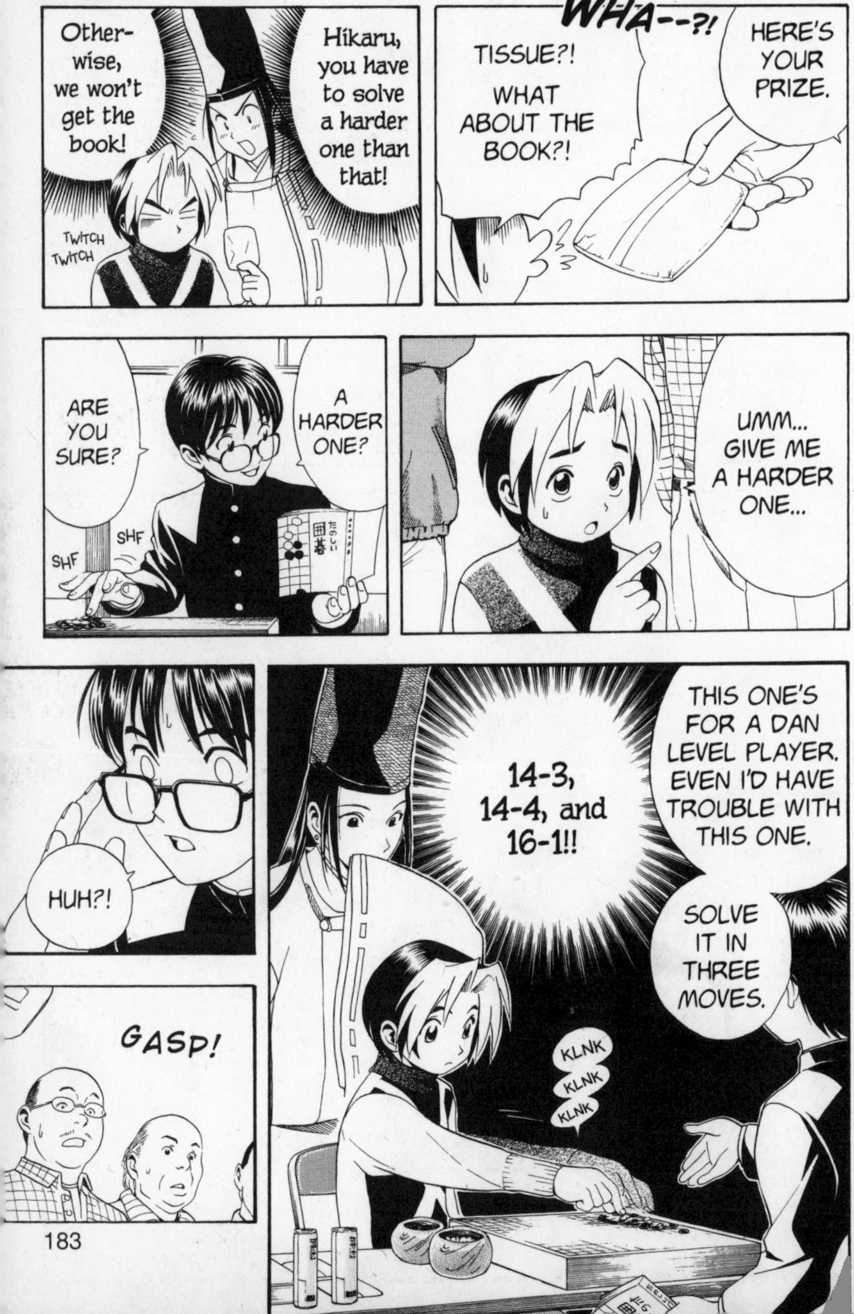

HERE'S YOUR PRIZE.
WHA--?!
TISSUE?! WHAT ABOUT THE BOOK?!
Hikaru, you have to solve a harder one than that!
Other-wise, we won't get the book!
TWITCH TWITCH
UMM... GIVE ME A HARDER ONE...
A HARDER ONE?
ARE YOU SURE?
SHF
SHF
THIS ONE'S FOR A DAN LEVEL PLAYER. EVEN I'D HAVE TROUBLE WITH THIS ONE.
SOLVE IT IN THREE MOVES.
14-3, 14-4, and 16-1!!
KLNK KLNK KLNK
HUH?!
GASP!

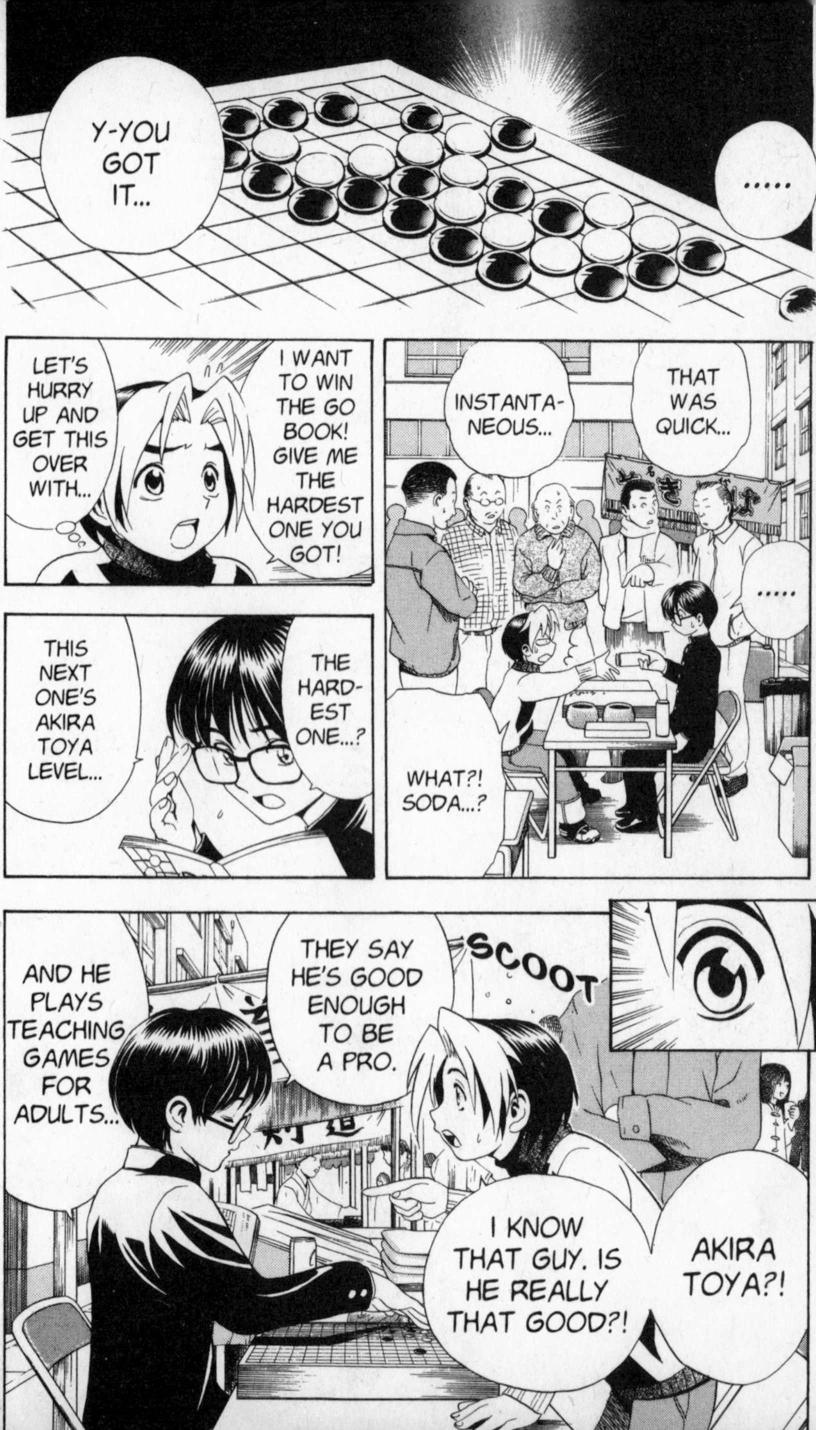
.....
Y-YOU GOT IT...
THAT WAS QUICK...
INSTANTA-NEOUS...
.....
WHAT?! SODA...?
I WANT TO WIN THE GO BOOK! GIVE ME THE HARDEST ONE YOU GOT!
LET'S HURRY UP AND GET THIS OVER WITH...
THE HARD-EST ONE...?
THIS NEXT ONE'S AKIRA TOYA LEVEL...
SCOOT
THEY SAY HE'S GOOD ENOUGH TO BE A PRO.
AND HE PLAYS TEACHING GAMES FOR ADULTS...
AKIRA TOYA?!
I KNOW THAT GUY. IS HE REALLY THAT GOOD?!

READ THIS WAY

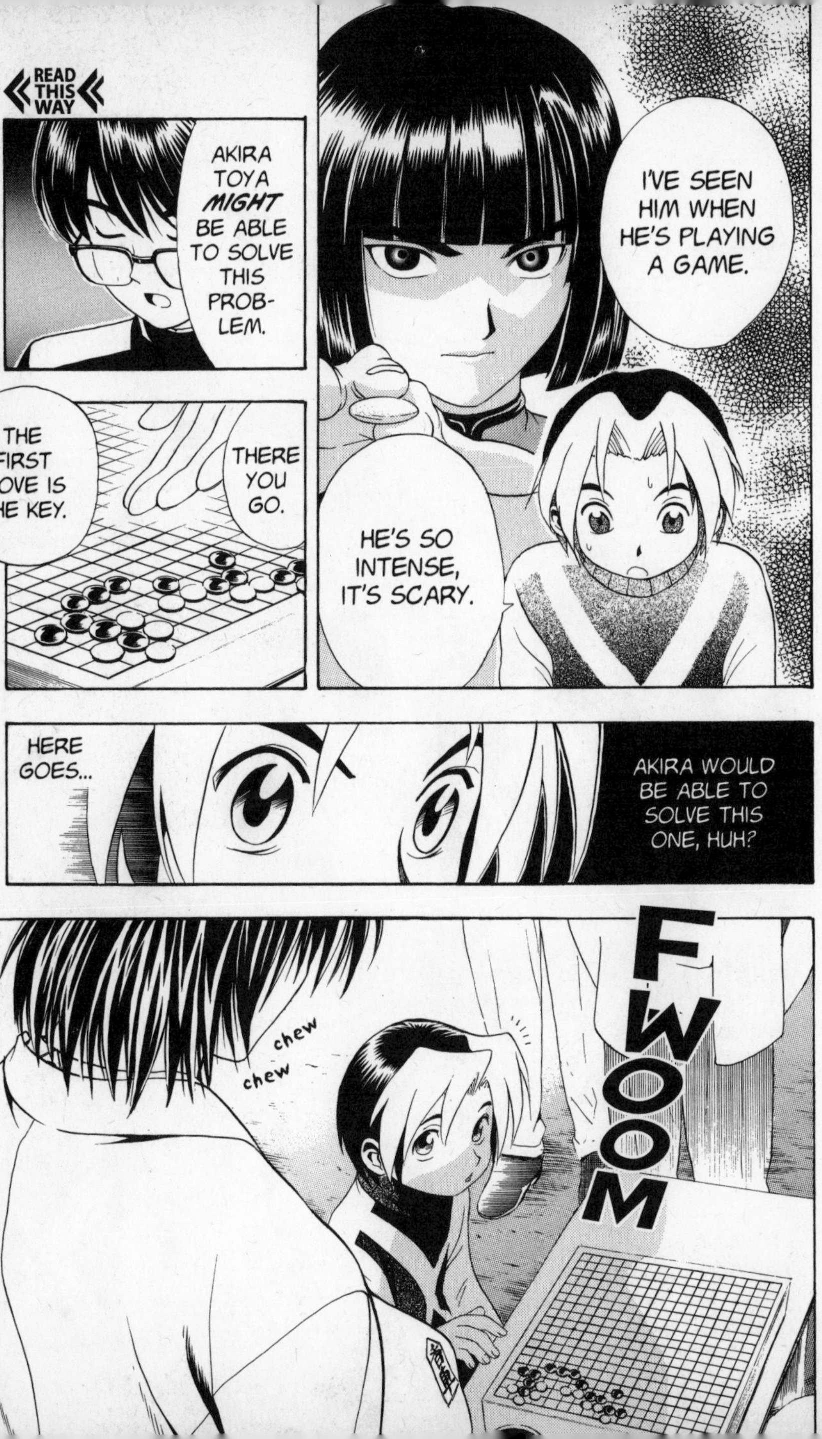
I'VE SEEN HIM WHEN HE'S PLAYING A GAME.
HE'S SO INTENSE, IT'S SCARY.
AKIRA TOYA *MIGHT* BE ABLE TO SOLVE THIS PROB-LEM.
THERE YOU GO.
THE FIRST MOVE IS THE KEY.
AKIRA WOULD BE ABLE TO SOLVE THIS ONE, HUH?
HERE GOES...
FWOOM
chew chew

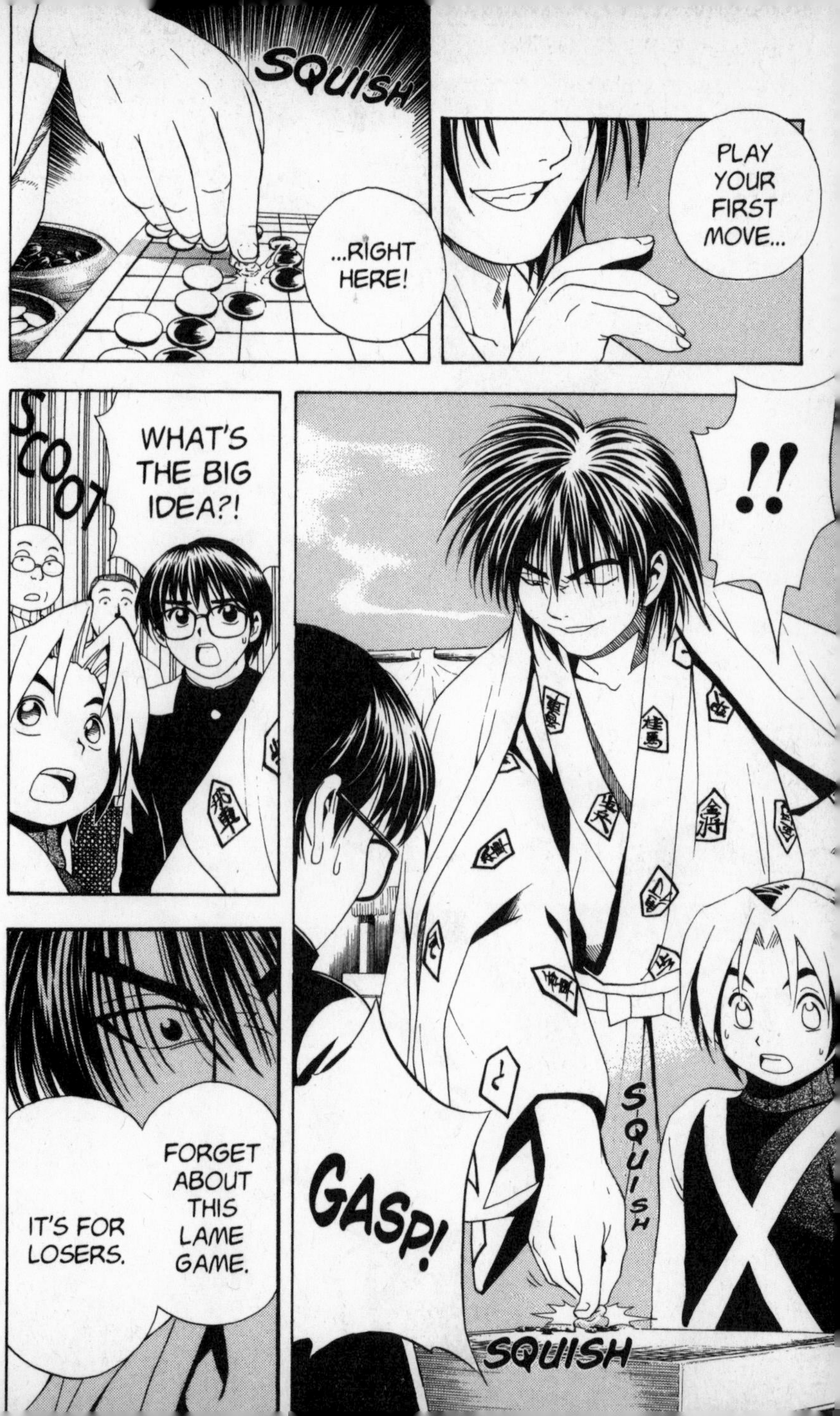
PLAY YOUR FIRST MOVE...
SQUISH
...RIGHT HERE!
!!
SQUISH
GASP!
SQUISH
WHAT'S THE BIG IDEA?!
SCOOT
FORGET ABOUT THIS LAME GAME.
IT'S FOR LOSERS.

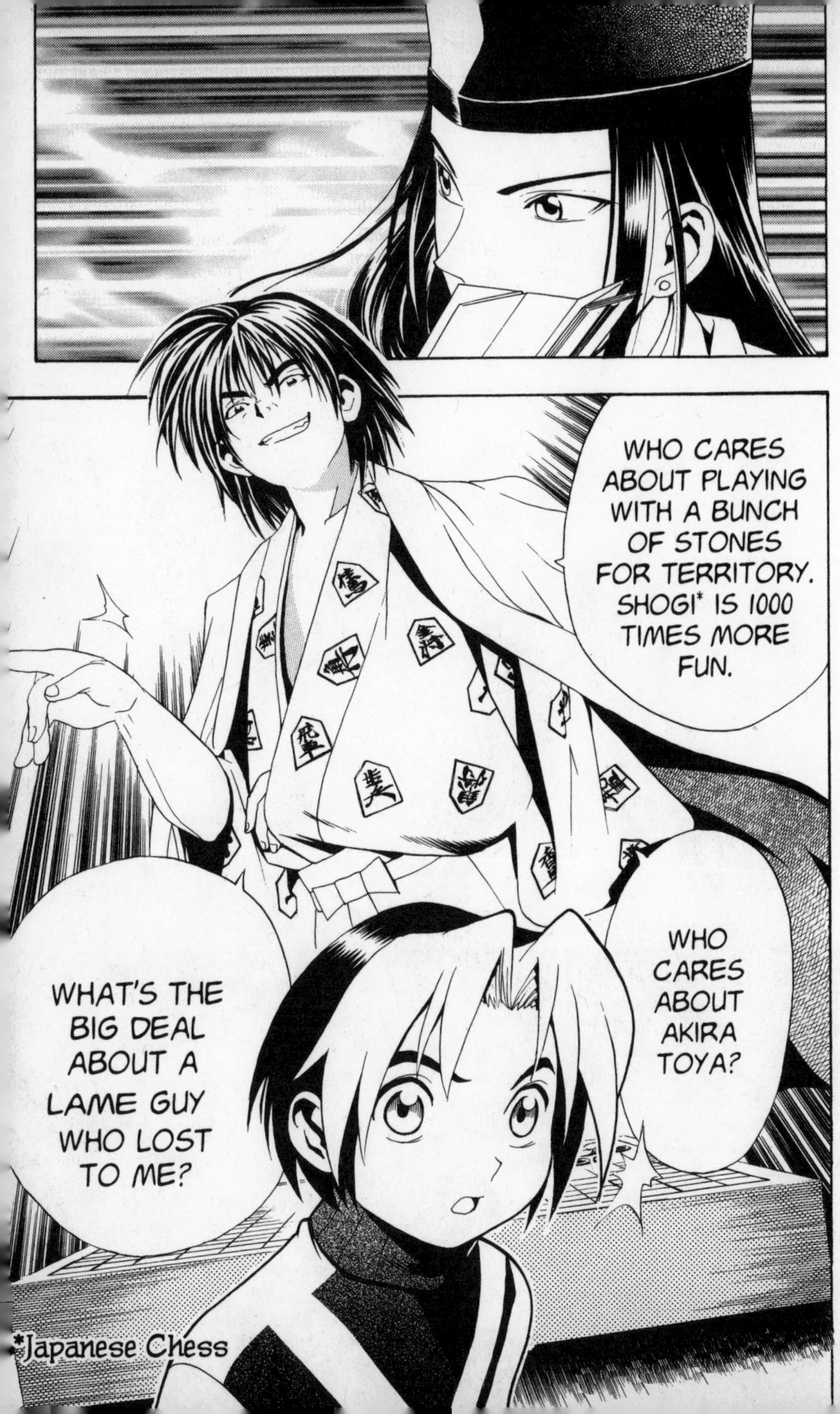
WHO CARES ABOUT PLAYING WITH A BUNCH OF STONES FOR TERRITORY. SHOGI* IS 1000 TIMES MORE FUN.
WHO CARES ABOUT AKIRA TOYA?
WHAT'S THE BIG DEAL ABOUT A LAME GUY WHO LOST TO ME?

*Japanese Chess

Next Volume Preview

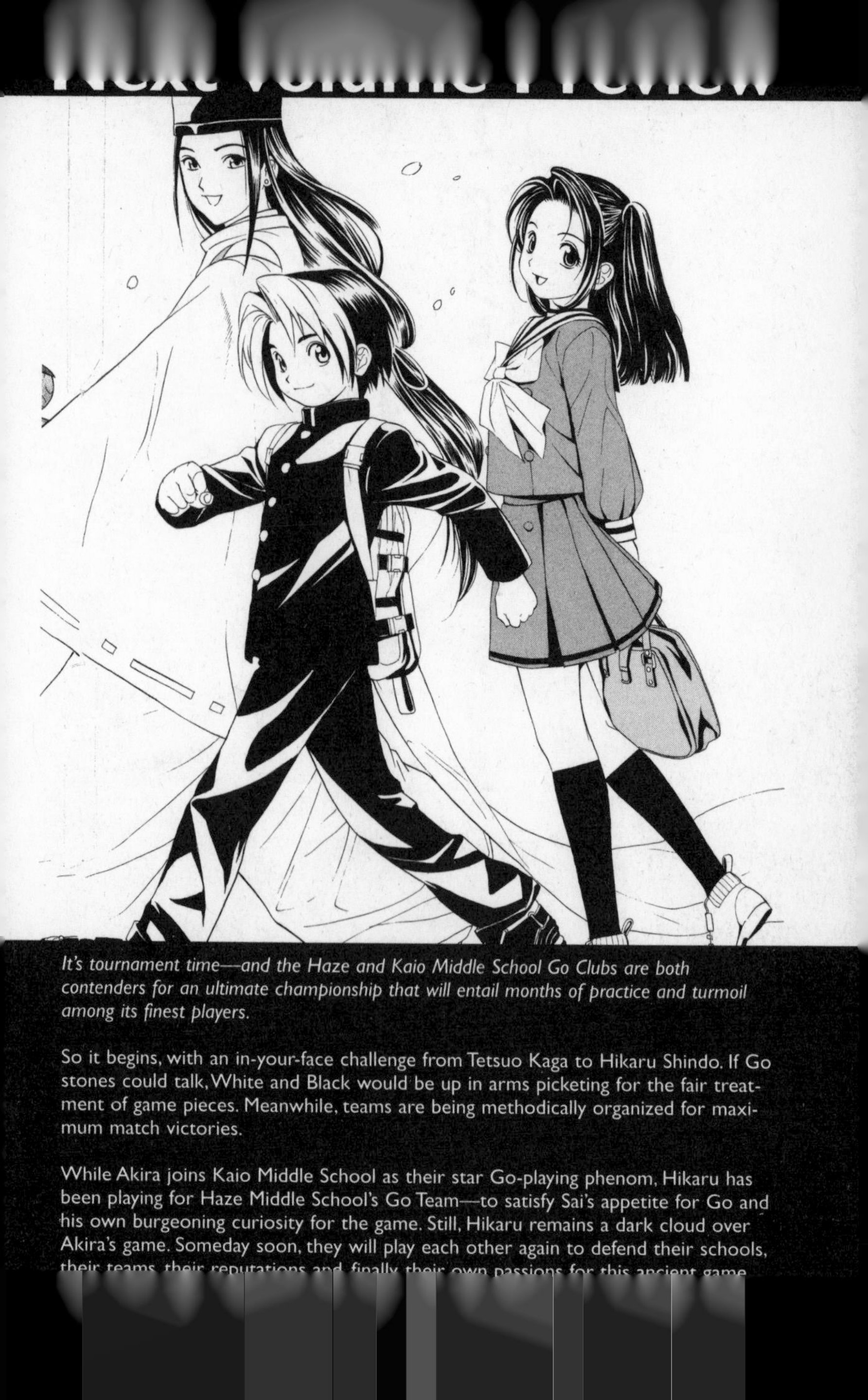

It's tournament time—and the Haze and Kaio Middle School Go Clubs are both contenders for an ultimate championship that will entail months of practice and turmoil among its finest players.

So it begins, with an in-your-face challenge from Tetsuo Kaga to Hikaru Shindo. If Go stones could talk, White and Black would be up in arms picketing for the fair treatment of game pieces. Meanwhile, teams are being methodically organized for maximum match victories.

While Akira joins Kaio Middle School as their star Go-playing phenom, Hikaru has been playing for Haze Middle School's Go Team—to satisfy Sai's appetite for Go and his own burgeoning curiosity for the game. Still, Hikaru remains a dark cloud over Akira's game. Someday soon, they will play each other again to defend their schools, [redacted]

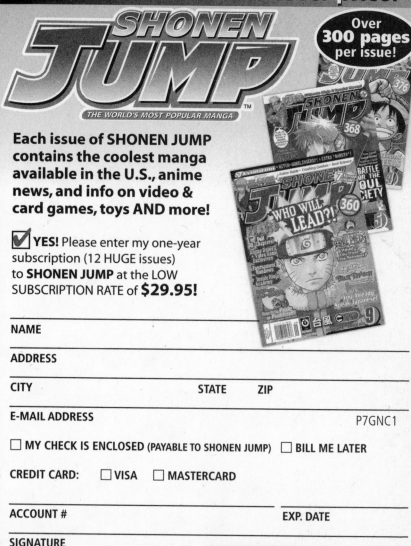